284 ending

self

ele

*Nixon off the Record*

# NIXON IN WINTER

# NIXON
# IN WINTER

## MONICA
## CROWLEY

RANDOM HOUSE

NEW YORK

Library of Congress Cataloging-in-Publication Data
Crowley, Monica.
Nixon in winter / Monica Crowley.
p.   cm.
Continues: Nixon off the record.
Includes index.
ISBN 0-679-45695-3 (acid-free paper)
1. Nixon, Richard M. (Richard Milhous), 1913–1994—Political
and social views.   2. United States—Politics and government—1989–1993.
3. Watergate Affair, 1972–1974.
I. Crowley, Monica, 1968–   Nixon off the record.   II. Title.
E856.C75   1998   973.924'092—dc21   97-38413

Random House website address: www.randomhouse.com
Printed in the United States of America on acid-free paper
2 4 6 8 9 7 5 3
First Edition

*Book design by J. K. Lambert*

FOR MY FAMILY

# AUTHOR'S NOTE

"This is a memoir—a book of memories." So wrote Richard Nixon in the opening lines of his 1978 autobiography, *RN: The Memoirs of Richard Nixon*. This book is also a book of memories, though the memories belong both to the former president and to me. It is a memoir of President Nixon's final years out of the arena and my four extraordinary years working with him.

The first volume of this work, *Nixon off the Record*, published in 1996, is strictly a political volume: it deals with Nixon's views on leadership and his thoughts and activities on the American political scene from 1990 to his death in 1994.

This second volume chronicles his evolving thoughts on foreign policy, his final views of Watergate and subsequent scandals, and his never-ending quest to redeem himself, both politically and personally.

During the course of his political career, Nixon was noted for constantly transforming himself into a more effective and formidable political force, a "new Nixon," clambering back to great heights after falling great distances, driven by that famous unceasing ambition. This is a portrait of the "last Nixon," still driven but tempered a bit by age and experience. It is an epic ending to an epic story, one that I was privileged to witness and, now, to retell in these volumes.

That would not have been possible, however, if he had not allowed me to know both the last Nixon and the real Nixon. I will always be grateful to him for letting me see him as he was, in good times and in bad, and for sharing his wisdom, regrets, triumphs, mistakes, generosity, humor, and friendship. Because of his openness, I was not just an observer of his life but also became a participant in it.

—

Throughout this project, I benefited from the support and encouragement of many people. I extend my deep gratitude to Harold Evans, president of the Random House Trade Group, whose faith in this work never faltered, and to Bob Loomis, whose first-rate editorial skill helped a draft become a manuscript. It was my great fortune to work with them.

I must also thank William Safire, who believed in me when few others did; Frank Gaffney, Roger Robinson, and Rinelda Bliss, for urging me to tackle this project in the first place; my agent, Carl Brandt, who was always ready with advice and good cheer; and my friend Paul Palumbo of Network Integration Consulting, Inc., who offered computer support and reassuring words when I needed to hear them most.

I am particularly grateful to my remarkable family: my mother, Patricia; my sister Jocelyn; my grandparents, Stanley and Florence Baron; and my uncle and aunt, Donald and Nancy Blanchette. They give boundless love and support without asking for anything in return.

Above all, I thank God for granting me such a blessed life.

M.C.
*Warren, New Jersey*
*November 1997*

# CONTENTS

# INTRODUCTION

The invitation arrived in a slim envelope on a hazy, hot day in late August 1989. Handwritten in dark-blue ink, the words were slanted toward the right side of the page, ending in a graceful flourish in the lower right-hand corner. The author of the note wrote how much he appreciated my original letter to him of a month before and offered to meet with me to discuss American foreign policy at a mutually convenient time. It was signed "Sincerely, Richard Nixon."

I put the letter down, then read it again. The words were simple but their meaning profound: the thirty-seventh president of the United States wanted to discuss the state of the world with me, someone whom he had never met, who was born the year he was elected president, and whose first memory of him was an image on television, telling the American people that he had decided to resign the presidency. Just as I watched him then, when I was five years old, speaking words that I could not comprehend, I now held a letter to me from him, unable to foresee the significance of it, for his life and mine.

Three months before I received the letter, I had prepared to leave the campus of Colgate University for the summer prior to my senior year. At the suggestion of Professor Robert Kaufman, I read Nixon's book *1999: Victory Without War*, and it had such a tremendous impact on my thinking about so many crucial foreign policy issues that I wrote Nixon a lengthy letter in which I agreed with many of his positions, disagreed with others, and expressed gratitude to him for writing a book that showed me how "the real world worked." I mailed it and did not expect a reply. Several weeks later, I walked to my mailbox and retrieved that extraordinary invitation.

On October 2, 1989, we met for the first time and had a two-hour discussion about world politics as we sat in his office in northern New Jersey, surrounded by things he had collected on his journey to the heights of power and through the corridors of political recovery: a worn but regal desk that had stood in the Oval Office, a painting of a serene farm scene by Eisenhower, busts of Lincoln and Churchill, bound volumes of his presidential papers. He spoke forcefully, in calm, measured tones perfected over years of persuading and influencing, and he listened intently, absorbing what was being said and comparing it with what he already believed. That initial meeting led to a permanent position as his foreign policy assistant, a job that would take me around the world, across America, and into the mind of one of the most commanding figures of our time.

From July 1990 to his death in April 1994, I was privileged to have hours of daily conversation with the former president, working with him on his last two books, *Seize the Moment: America's Challenge in a One-Superpower World* and *Beyond Peace,* traveling with him abroad and at home, preparing research materials, discussing his ideas, plans, hopes, and frustrations, and sometimes simply lending a sympathetic ear. I became a professional confidante, a member of his inner circle, and one of the few whom he allowed into the shelter he had built around himself.

After *Nixon off the Record,* the first volume of this work, was published in the late summer of 1996, I was asked frequently why Nixon trusted me immediately, particularly since he had been betrayed so often by people whom he trusted. I believe that there are two principal reasons.

First, I was a young supporter, and I did not come to him with an ulterior motive or an agenda. When Nixon spoke with me, it was in the context not of an interview but of an unconstrained conversation during which he had to be neither diplomatic nor defensive. He could simply be himself.

Second, I believe he trusted me because he saw me as a liaison between himself and future generations, someone to whom he could tell his story one last time and upon whom he could rely to relate that story to others. It was a final cathartic act, an expression both of confidence in that story and of contentment that he had at last accepted all of its epic chapters.

In his final years, I was called upon to be a student of his experience, a witness to his last years, to record as much as to be taught. With the end of life coming ever closer, he felt an inescapable need to have his final say before a new generation, to cement the comeback, to allow one last glimpse into the part of himself that he kept so carefully locked away.

That I was chosen to take that last look was remarkable, and I kept a daily diary of my experiences working with him, beginning in 1990. I made notes as we spoke, then transcribed them twice, once immediately after the conversation and again later that same day, in order to maintain the integrity of the dialogue. Nixon's personal and professional disclosures were made in confidence but with the implicit understanding that they would eventually be recounted. Through our conversations, Nixon was ensuring that his message, experience, and vision would carry on long after he had passed from the scene. This book tries to place his activities and judgments in context and to show how they contributed to who Nixon was in the winter of his life.

Many of our discussions involved the careful remarks designed for public consumption, but most involved the completely spontaneous and honest reflections of private conversation. The remarks and experiences described herein are presented exactly as they were said and exactly as they happened. I have done my best to capture the Nixon I knew, with all of his dynamic contradictions and in all of his vivid complexity.

—

To understand Richard Nixon is to understand the dynamics of our political culture, where policy and personality converge and where progress and traditionalism are in constant tension. His arrival at the threshold of power in 1946 coincided with the emergence of the United States as a global superpower, with all of the attendant responsibilities and prone to both grand accomplishment and tragic mistakes. It was in Richard Nixon that we saw ourselves: our potential for greatness and baseness, sin and redemption, scandal and glory. At his first major Washington press conference as the vice presidential nominee in 1952, he was forced to disclaim higher ambitions and dismiss rumors that he might be removed from the ticket in 1956. "I have no further ambition," he said, "except doing the best possible job I can." The ambition, of course, was always there, compelling him to reach for ever loftier goals, even when he was in the darkest dungeons of political exile.

It was this remarkable resilience that set him apart when he sought and held power and that sustained his viability long after he had fallen from grace. Despite having suffered devastating defeats, Nixon remained a hopeful realist, and he believed that when enough time had passed between his presidency and the ultimate history that would be written, once his presidency had been compared with those that came before and after, and once his mistakes had been put in context with his accomplishments, he would be judged as a good, if not great, president. It is my hope that this book, and the earlier volume, *Nixon off the Record,* will advance a historical understanding of him by putting the reader in the room with him as I was, listening to his opinions, watching him react, observing his rituals.

I thought that the best way for Nixon to influence history was for him to speak for himself. If the words on his tapes and his actions from 1969 to 1974 are adequate measures by which to judge his presidency, then the words and actions of his post-presidential years are crucial to evaluating his activities after leaving office. If history is to be fair, then it must judge Nixon based on his complete life and career, from his first day on earth to his last.

This is a memoir of the extraordinary opportunity he gave to me, at the age of twenty-one, to work with and observe him. But it is also his last memoir. It is his story. It is his last testament. It is Richard Nixon in his own voice, telling us who the thirty-seventh president of the United States really was and why he continues to embody the American experience more than any other figure of the twentieth century.

# PART I

---

# JANUARY 16, 1994

Sunday, January 16, 1994, dawned cold and clear in the Northeast. It was one of those rare days that winter when it did not snow, and the sun, usually hidden by low, thick gray storm clouds, seemed particularly brilliant. The temperatures, well below freezing, kept most people inside, sheltered from the brutal cold and the white veil of winter that waited just outside their doors.

The thirty-seventh president of the United States woke at five-thirty in the morning, stepped outside, and, assaulted by the numbing cold, hurried back into the house. Reluctant to allow the elements to deprive him of his daily three-mile walk, he ventured out again, only to turn back once more. He called me at ten o'clock, seized with cabin fever, and requested that I visit in the afternoon so we could continue editing portions of his last book, *Beyond Peace*.

"Monica," he said over the telephone, "I can't get out for my usual walk. I tried to get out twice, but it's just too damn cold. I can't even get out to the paper because the front walk is covered with ice, and I'm afraid I might fall and break a hip or something, and then I'm really out of commission. So I'm just sitting here looking out the window. It's like house arrest." He paused. "Well! I'm sure that my enemies would love to hear *that!*" he said, laughing. "Listen. Would you please come up around four o'clock so we can get going on the last section of the book?"

"I will be there," I replied. "And please, stay inside. Wait for me to bring the paper up for you."

"What if *you* break your hip coming up the walk? Oh, my God! But you won't break anything. You're young. And besides, you'd heal very fast," he said. "In any event, be careful."

I arrived at the residence at the appointed hour, and as I cautiously made my way up the walk, I heard Nixon tapping on the third-floor window. When I looked up, I saw him waving and gesturing to me to take hold of the railing. I did, and he flashed a thumbs-up sign.

The front door was open, and the house was eerily quiet. After Mrs. Nixon's death, seven months earlier, the house had grown still, hushed by the loss of one of the residents charged with bringing it to life. Since the former president spent most of his time in his study, the other rooms became increasingly remote to him, and as he walked past them, he often stopped to peer inside, as if he expected to see something new in them, something to draw him in and make him stay. Finding nothing, he would turn around and make his way back to his study, the familiar room meant for him alone.

"Monica!" he exclaimed as I cleared the top of the stairs to the third-floor study. "I'm glad you took the railing; otherwise, you would have slipped and broken something. And if that happened, my God! Who else would edit this damn book?" he said, smiling. "Take a seat in your usual chair."

He straightened his tie. "Well! I'm glad you could come. I know this editing business is tedious, but we have to slug through it. This will probably be my last book . . ."

I reminded him that he had used that line repeatedly since the publication of his first book, *Six Crises,* in 1962. "You have no credibility left on the issue," I said.

"I know it," he said. "But this time I *really* mean it."

We laughed together.

"Well, I suppose you're right. What the hell. No, I really think that this is it. I'm not sure I have another one in me." He paused. "Maybe I do, if I live to be one hundred."

He lifted draft copies of the manuscript from the ottoman in front of us and put on his eyeglasses. "I really hate these glasses," he said. "I think they make me *look* one hundred!"

He held up his hand before I could speak. "I know you're going to give me your usual line about my not being old. I appreciate it even though it's not true."

He handed a copy of some text to me. "The only way to do this is line by line. We have to be one step ahead of our critics. If you see even the slightest thing that bothers you, we'll take it out. It's hard, hard work, but it's worth it if we turn out something decent, something that people will pay attention to, something that will have an effect."

For almost two hours, we read the text of the two-hundred-page section of *Beyond Peace* entitled "America Beyond Peace," for content and consistency. Nixon often read sentences out loud to determine if they carried the right message and the appropriate tone, wielding his pen mercilessly against ineffective phrases or redundant passages.

When the editing was complete, Nixon tossed the manuscript to the floor, removed his eyeglasses, and propped his feet up on the ottoman. "I'll be damned. We did that in record time! Now we only have to do it about ten more times before we submit it to the publisher." He was visibly tired. "It's important to submit it in top-flight condition so the publisher doesn't have to do anything to it. They appreciate that so much, and frankly so do I. I'd hate to have to look at this stuff again. You know," he said, "I hope this book does well. It should, because it's damn good, but you never know what people are thinking. Every book is a gamble. It may not be as well received if Clinton's popularity goes up. If everyone is going gangbusters for him when this comes out, that may dilute its impact. Well, all we can do is put out the best damn book we can and hope people pay attention. Maybe even Clinton will pay attention."

I told him that although Clinton would not agree with many of his positions on domestic policy, he might be more receptive to hearing Nixon's foreign policy advice, particularly since he had heeded his advice in the past.

"That's a good point," he said. "Even though he believes in the wrong things, Clinton is a fast learner, and he's not afraid to defer to someone else's expertise. My only concern is that if his numbers are up, he may get cocky and not be as willing to listen to me."

He shifted in his chair and turned his attention to a more immediate problem: the impending twentieth anniversary of his resignation from the presidency and the relentless media coverage it would bring. Even after two decades of defending and explaining himself, each new onslaught sent him scrambling to avoid the press. And although he was prepared for their inevitable resurrection, he still dreaded the Watergate-related stories for the impact they had in helping to reverse what he had accomplished since leaving office.

"Maybe we *should* be concerned about the timing of the book," he said. "Maybe we should be concerned about its coming out at the same time as the August Water—" He stopped before finishing the word. "The anniversary." He took a long look out the window, hardening his expression. "If the bastards won't agree to let it go, then I won't give any interviews. And if they ask, I will say, 'Twenty years of Watergate is enough.' And it is! This whole anniversary thing is a bunch of bull. Who cares about Watergate anymore? It belongs on maybe one of the history channels, but not on the major networks. It's purely our enemies, you know. I just don't think there's a lot of interest in the old Watergate story." He paused. "Well . . . maybe there is."

I encouraged him to avoid the stories and focus instead on his new book.

"No, I know, you're right," he replied, smiling weakly. "These people are going to go after me regardless. Every time I write a new piece or book or give an interview, they come out with something negative to offset it. I think they just love to wallow in this Watergate crap until they almost drown. Well, I refuse to do that," he said, raising his voice and his right fist. "They won't get any kind of notice from me. I'll put out *Beyond Peace* and forget about it." Laughing, he tapped me on the head and rose from his chair.

"Well, I think it's about time to gear up for dinner," he said. "What do you say?"

As he completed the book, Nixon invited me to a working dinner almost every Sunday evening. The ritual served two purposes: it extended his work week, and it brought him company on an afternoon that he would have otherwise spent alone.

Nixon strode across the room and into the bar area. "I know that you don't particularly like to drink," he called to me, "so I will make you a gimlet without the booze." I heard him take two glasses from the cabinet and place some bottles on the counter. "They call this the Asian martini. I first had one in Singapore and later in Pakistan. It's a wonderfully refreshing drink. Come in here; I'll show you how to make it."

I walked into the small room off the study and found him wiping up some ice he had dropped on the floor.

"Let me get that for you," I offered.

"No, no. I've got it all cleaned up," he said, standing back up. "Now, if you ever make this for yourself, be sure to use Rose's lime juice and crushed ice. I had it one time—maybe in Thailand—and they didn't use Rose's, and I almost threw up. Anyway, you must shake it and then . . ." He lifted the glass. "It's done. Try it. You know, it's better with the booze, but since I can't drink anymore and you'd rather have it this way—why, we're just no fun, really."

"Tell me honestly," I said, "how *are* those state dinners?"

He winced and waved a hand in the air, dismissing the question. "Mrs. Nixon did all that—the menus and everything. I never knew what they were serving and didn't really care."

"How did you find the small talk at those formal events?"

"It's pretty bad, and I mean excruciatingly bad," he replied, wincing again. "You have to sit with the spouses, and men and women are interested in different things, as you know. That's not to say that I didn't have any interesting conversations with these people; I did. But when, as president, you are hosting a head of state, you have your mind on more important things. Do you think I was really paying attention to what Mrs. Brezhnev was saying? I mean, of course I was listening, but I had to concentrate on whether or not her husband was going to go for limiting nuclear weapons. She was a charming woman, but you know what I mean . . ."

He sipped his tonic water with lemon and glanced at his watch. It was almost seven o'clock. "Let's go. You can watch me make dinner," he said, turning toward the door. "You know, if you weren't here, I'd be doing this alone."

"Well, I *am* here," I replied, and with a gentle nod in the direction of the stairs, I followed him to the first floor.

He walked to the stereo system and put on a tape recording of traditional Christmas songs, then moved into the kitchen, where he peered into the cabinet, removed two cans of chili, and shuffled over to the can opener. With the chili warming on the stove, he tossed a salad and served it on two plates.

"I hope you don't mind chili, but it's the only thing I can make. Oh, and hot dogs, but I don't think you'd go for those," he said, casting a watchful eye on the chili pot. "Fortunately, Heidi [Retter, the housekeeper] left us some salad, and we have these," he said, lifting an unopened package of sesame-seed breadsticks from the counter. Before I could offer to open the package, he began to struggle with the cellophane wrapper, grimacing when it was clear that the wrapper would not yield. With one final jerk, he ripped into the package, sending dozens of sesame seeds to the floor.

"Well, at least I got it open," he said, his face flushed with embarrassment. "Maybe I should stick to the cooking. What the hell! I never thought I'd say that!"

I swept up the stray seeds and moved into the dining room, where he had set the table with fine china.

"It's the good china," he said, emerging from the kitchen with the breadsticks and salad. "I think everyone should always use their good stuff. What are you going to do? Die and never have used it? Please." He nodded to the glasses of chilled grapefruit juice. "I hope you like grapefruit. I find that it cuts the taste of the chili. Here, take this," he said, handing the plates to me and turning back into the kitchen. I picked up my camera and followed him.

"Would you mind if I took a picture of this?" I asked. "Because no one will ever believe that you cooked for me."

Instead of answering, he struck a pose over the stove and smiled. "Give me the camera," he said and snapped a photograph of me. "For posterity— oh, and don't forget, for historical purposes, as we always say." He laughed and escorted me back into the dining room.

Few words were exchanged. During the meal, he made a few stray remarks about some first ladies ("Nancy Reagan is very shrewd; she controlled almost everything. Barbara [Bush] is the same, a tough cookie, but not as controlling. Speaking of controlling, I'm sad to say that Hillary [Rodham Clinton] is becoming an icon") and of the New York Giants' loss the day before ("No Super Bowl this year! And if they had made it, I probably would have gone to the game"), but beyond that he spoke little. As we finished dessert, he looked out across the empty deck to the barren trees swaying in the yard.

"Would you believe, Monica, that this is the twenty-fifth anniversary of my inauguration as president? Twenty-five years ago . . ."

"Does it seem like it's been that long?" I asked.

He nodded his head. "Sometimes. Other times it seems like it was yesterday."

He cleared his throat, blinked hard, and looked straight at me. "Don't worry about the dishes. I'll take care of them." He stood, pulled my chair out for me, and walked with me to the front door. When I turned around to thank him, he preempted me.

"Thank you for working with me on a Sunday. Everybody always thinks that well-known people are surrounded by people all the time. Not true. Fame, notoriety—whatever you want to call it—can be a very lonely thing. A lot of people know you, but not a lot of people *know* you, if you know what I mean. And the more public you are, the smaller your circle gets because you find that you trust only very few."

It was not just Nixon's ambiguities that made him fascinating, but the way the epic moments of his life alternated with moments of pure common sense, humor, tenderness, and vulnerability. Behind the political genius was something disarmingly common, a humanity that was not part of the public image. On those quiet Sunday afternoons, I saw what few others were allowed to see: that Nixon was real.

On that day and on others like it, Nixon was at his strongest and his most vulnerable. Simultaneously defiant and uncertain, complex in his thinking and simple in his tastes, known by millions and utterly alone, Nixon was both a leader of men and one of them, a public man with an intensely private life, larger than life, but vulnerable to all that life brings.

In an endless search for meaning in his own life and in the forces driving the country and the world, he rose to the highest levels of power, fell from grace, and through sheer force of will made his way back. The last Nixon was not a "new" Nixon, not the next self-made political manifestation, but the real Nixon, a man of substance and humor, accomplishment and regret, happiness and sorrow. In the end, he was just a man in the winter of his life, left with a past that had been unafraid of controversy and tragedy, that had delivered exhilarating triumphs and devastating defeats, and that had forced him to negotiate his way between his great strengths and obvious, inevitable weaknesses. It was a completely human process undertaken by an ordinary man who left a citrus grove in southern California to make an indelible mark on the second half of the twentieth century.

# PART II

## NIXON AND THE WORLD

# CHAPTER 1

# THE END OF THE
# COLD WAR

R ichard Nixon feared that the United States might lose the cold war.
The man who began his political career in 1946, at the beginning of
the cold war, led the United States through crucial periods of it, and lived to
see the end of it had worried that we might lose it.

In 1980, he wrote *The Real War,* in which he stated unequivocally, "Unless we act fast, the period of the mid-1980s will be one of maximum peril
for the United States and the west. In a nutshell: The Soviet Union will be
number one; the United States will be number two." Written at a time when
the United States was in grave danger of losing world leadership and national purpose, *The Real War* was meant to renew the courage of America's
convictions, motivate it at home, and strengthen it abroad. The book addressed the crisis and helped revive the willingness of America to play a responsible role in the international arena.

Nixon was concerned that if the United States did not act to turn back Soviet adventurism around the world and increase our own military capabilities in order to provide a credible deterrent, we would not only lose the
titanic ideological struggle with communism but condemn ourselves to
decades of domination and humiliation by the Soviet Union. By the late
1980s, however, when it became clear that the United States might win the
cold war, a new fear seized him: the victory might be squandered.

Nixon had a personal investment in a successful conclusion to the cold
war. He had entered the Congress after World War II and helped Harry Truman build the foundations for our winning strategy. He exposed Alger Hiss
as a spy for the Soviet Union in a sensational case that gave rise to his na-

tional reputation as a vehement anti-Communist. He ran for the Senate in California in 1950, claiming that his opponent, Helen Gahagan Douglas, was a possible Communist sympathizer. He won.

As vice president, he engaged Soviet premier Nikita Khrushchev in the kitchen debate, about the merits of the opposing systems. In 1960, John F. Kennedy and he competed to lead an aggressive challenge to the Soviet Union. He inherited a war-weary electorate and a resource-drained economy when he won the presidency in 1968 and improvised containment by replacing confrontation with cooperation. And he warned against the dangerous consequences of losing the cold war during his post-presidential years.

He was more closely associated with the cold war than perhaps any other living American politician, and he would not allow defeat to be snatched from the jaws of victory during its definitive endgame.

Nixon was awestruck at the collapse of communism across Eastern Europe and in its pioneering state, the Soviet Union. No one had predicted it. No one expected its effects to be determined so quickly. And no one thought it would occur so peacefully.

Nixon spent little time congratulating himself or the United States. Instead, he focused on the short- and long-term challenges facing us and our allies and moved to influence policy. From 1990 to 1994, Nixon wrote two major foreign policy books, traveled the world as a private citizen on fact-finding missions, delivered countless speeches to policy makers and opinion makers, and lobbied American presidents publicly and privately. If his greatest fear was that the United States would throw away victory in the cold war, his second greatest fear was that it would be because those in power did not listen to him.

His approach to foreign policy was realistic and conservative. It was a philosophy grounded in a respect for history, experience, and the stubborn, unpredictable variability of human beings. He brought to policy an irreducible respect for individual freedom, a healthy suspicion of government, and an unwavering commitment to citizenship. He understood that the immutable tensions between individualism and collective identity, and between realism and idealism, generate both conflict and progress.

Because he did not expect a revolution in human nature, he did not expect the future to be very different from the past. He was skeptical of schemes that promised the end of war and the global embrace of democracy. He rejected utopianism and accepted the human capacity for evil as well as good, for indifference as well as empathy, and for selfishness as well as generosity. He took into account complexity and conflict without trying to deny them and recognized that there were real costs and burdens of global leadership.

He despised war but admired some of the virtues that war brings forth, such as solidarity and courage. But he also knew that since the human and economic costs of war are so high and the benefits of peace so great, most American leaders in this century have sought the elimination of war and the achievement of a secure peace. Unlike many of his contemporaries, however, Nixon knew that those goals could never be fully attained. An improved international condition did not mean a perfect international condition.

Equipped with this realist philosophy, Nixon set out to go beyond the superficial reporting of the end of the cold war to determine the deeper trends and meanings for the United States and the world. He often reflected on Alexis de Tocqueville's admonition from 1848: "A new science of politics is needed for a new world." By shattering the bipolar balance and alliance system with the collapse of a once almighty ideology, the end of the cold war brought uncertainty that could have led to a reversal of the outcome. Nixon spent the last years of his life working to ensure that that did not happen.

As the world exulted over a "new world order" premised on the collapse of communism, Nixon knew that any new order must emerge at America's direction and be pursued in the cool light of national self-interest. Complacency, he believed, suffocated national purpose.

Nixon's mission was to guarantee that his successors did not succumb to the kind of comfortable indifference to foreign affairs that would make victory in the cold war short-lived. He rejected the ideas that the United States and the Soviet Union were equivalent declining superpowers and that the United States could be just one of many great powers.

Nixon, therefore, set out to define a new and positive mission for the United States. Since 1945, America's defining goal had been to defeat communism. With that accomplished, Nixon worked to ensure what he called "the victory of freedom." This task was an equally demanding but more fragile and subtle undertaking. With its success, however, rested the hopes of real freedom, real democratic and free-market reform, and real, if not perfect, peace.

—

On April 12, 1990, two and a half months before I began working for Nixon, he delivered a speech to the Boston World Affairs Council that laid out his philosophy on the end of the cold war. His argument was straightforward: editorial writers, columnists, and other observers claimed that with the advent of glasnost and perestroika in the Soviet Union and the leveling of the Berlin Wall, the cold war was over, the West had won it, the Soviet Union no longer posed a significant threat to our interests, and we could now concentrate on issues, such as global warming, that unite rather than divide us.

All of these assumptions, Nixon stated unequivocally, were wrong. The defeat of communism did not mean the victory of freedom. The Soviet loss did not mean an American win. A recessive Soviet threat did not mean the elimination of threats from other sources. The rejection of Communist leaders in Poland, Hungary, Romania, Bulgaria, Czechoslovakia, and East Germany did not mean that democracy would succeed.

Our challenge, according to Nixon, was to assist the countries that had broken away from the clutches of Soviet-installed communism. We should not, he said, assume blithely that if we just talked about "exporting democracy," these countries would find an answer to their desperate need for economic progress. They needed our help in dealing with the infinite complexities of free-market economic systems. This was the beginning of the argument that Nixon would make until his death: that the United States must aid the forces for real democratic and free-market reform in Eastern Europe and in the former Soviet Union. Failure to do so would result in having to fight a new and potentially more dangerous cold war.

Soviet president Mikhail Gorbachev, whom Nixon identified as "the most remarkable statesman of our time," had earned respect for initiating political reform and a greater freedom of the press within the Soviet Union, for not using the Red Army to keep his Eastern European clients in power, and for withdrawing that army from Afghanistan. But Nixon also recognized that Gorbachev simply had no alternative.

All of the Soviet Union's third world conquests were draining it economically by fifteen billion dollars annually. Dissent and outright rebellion were boiling beneath the surface in the captive nations of Eastern Europe. Most ominously, the Soviet economy was crippled by the symptoms of the inefficiencies and internal contradictions of communism: shortages, crime, and corruption.

Gorbachev saw that his major potential adversary, the United States, had recovered from the malaise of the late 1970s and the recession of the early 1980s, had a growing economy, a stronger military, and the Strategic Defense Initiative, which would cost him billions of dollars to match. He had no choice but to reform at home and retrench abroad.

By shattering the illusion that Gorbachev was a committed democrat, Nixon hoped to inject some realism into the debate over whether the United States should provide aid to the Soviet government. Helping Gorbachev did not, Nixon argued, serve his interests or ours if his reforms did not go far enough to work. And even if they did go far enough, it did not serve our interests to help Gorbachev if, as a result, we faced an economically stronger Soviet Union with the same aggressive foreign policy. Even without Eastern Europe, the Baltics, and its third world outposts, the Soviet Union would not be an "international pussycat." Nixon reminded his audience that the USSR still had thirty thousand nuclear warheads, the world's largest conventional army, a modern, blue-water navy, and a long tradition of expansionism. We should not be in the position, Nixon argued, to aid Gorbachev as long as he and the system he headed remained Communist.

The United States was the only power that could lead in a post–cold war world. America, he told his audience, could not be at peace in a world at war and could not be prosperous in a world of weak economies. He urged his listeners to meet the challenges of peace as his generation had met the challenges of the cold war. If they did, their legacy would be that they helped to make the world "safe for freedom."

"Monica, I want you to read this speech I gave a few months ago and let me know what you think," Nixon said to me on July 11, 1990. "I know you just started, and you can't expect to decide the fate of the earth overnight, but I would like you to read it. You weren't there, of course, so you didn't hear it delivered, and it's always better delivered than it is on the page. But you'll get the general idea. We can talk about it tomorrow, OK?"

I had only been working for him for a week. He had hired me to do research for him and to offer opinions and arguments that would improve his own thinking on the issues and perhaps even inspire new ideas.

I took a copy of the speech home that night and made notes as I read it through. The next morning, I entered his office fully prepared to talk about the speech. Nixon, however, wanted to pose a question.

"What does Gorbachev *really* want?" he asked.

I responded that after Boris Yeltsin quit the Communist Party, taking the radical reformers with him, Gorbachev had to focus first on mending the fissures in the party in order to maintain a platform of support for his reforms. The reforms, however, would repair communism, not eliminate it. Nixon agreed.

"I know that you have always said that states' internal structures are secondary to how they behave internationally," I continued. "So what do you say to the argument that until a state stops waging war on its own citizens, it won't stop waging war internationally?"

Nixon narrowed his eyes. "I know the argument: that democracies are more benign or that they don't initiate war, at least not against each other. Sometimes it's necessary to choose the lesser of the two evils and work with them. I used to be a Wilsonian to a certain extent. But that view of the world is largely ineffective."

He sipped some tonic water and pointed the glass at me. "Tell me, Monica, if you were Gorbachev, what would you do?"

"If I were Gorbachev," I said, "I would come down on the side of Yeltsin, admit that the party has no future, and state an intention to move *with* the historical forces, not against them. Eventually, he has to make a decision. He can't keep up this balancing act between the Communists and the reformers."

"No, he can't," he replied. "He runs the risk of losing both sides if he continues on this way. You know, this idea of salvaging the Soviet economy with a fifteen-billion-dollar Western aid package is complete nonsense. There's no way in hell something like that—which is a nutty idea anyway—is going to ensure Gorbachev's survival. The train has left the station as far as the collapse of communism is concerned."

"The administration seems to think that it's in our interest to keep Gorbachev in power. Doesn't that assume that a Gorbachev successor would be worse? What about one that would be better?" I asked.

"Bingo. But Bush is too soft on Gorbachev. He places too much emphasis on the personal relationship and thinks that since they like each other personally, their systems will work together without a problem. Wrong! But telling Bush that is like telling the wall.

"I think it's nauseating that the media have proclaimed Bush a newly strong leader who can and should cut billions out of the defense budget now that Gorbachev's Soviet Union no longer poses a threat. This is wrong, wrong, wrong.

"This reaction is a symptom of what is occurring in the United States as well as in Europe and, particularly, Germany—an incredibly naïve passion for peace which will make it almost impossible for even hard-line leaders to raise doubts about Gorbachev. What this amounts to is that I cannot publicly be skeptical—not yet anyway. I think that Bush has an intense desire to be popular . . . and I do think he *needs* to be liked, don't you?"

He stopped me before I could answer. "I think that need will override caution and skepticism about Gorbachev. Unfortunately, we have a major political problem on this score because the right will not raise any warning flags because they have to stand by Reagan, who, based on his performance during his last months in office, would go even further than Bush toward making a deal with Gorbachev. When the media goes gaga over Gorbachev, I can understand it; they are so susceptible to that type of charm. But when the right goes gaga—well, we know there is a serious problem.

"Now you see why I can't say anything strongly against him right now? I don't want to be the skunk at the garden party. But when the time is right— when some observers come back to their senses—I will make my point that we cannot be in the position of aiding Gorbachev or cutting our defense budget."

"About defense . . ." I said.

"I know you're a defense bug. Everyone is going hog-wild to cut defense because they think the threat is gone. Not true. This country will suffer a hangover of immense proportions if it cuts defense and then finds itself weakened and having to face a stronger and leaner enemy."

When I asked him how we could maintain current levels of defense spending when the enemy no longer posed an immediate threat, he replied, "That's the problem. But the American people—who are generally idealists—must hear some realism. I've found that when you go to the people with the cold, hard truth about foreign affairs, they'll support you."

"What do we do about Eastern Europe?" I asked.

"Dealing with them is of course far easier than dealing with the Soviet Union. They should be welcomed back into the European community economically and politically," he said, marking his points with his finger in the air. "Our goal must be to have nations with market-oriented economies that are friendly to the West but not unfriendly to the Soviet Union, because we can't have a hostile situation there. It could kill the early stages of reform."

He paused. "Economics is not really my bag. But I do know this: rather than a Marshall Plan, what is needed is a Bush Plan, under which the nations of Western Europe and the United States would develop a coordinated program for credits, debt relief, technological assistance, and even aid to compensate for the years lost during the period they have been under Soviet domination."

He smiled. "You're Polish. Poland and Hungary are the first candidates. These poor countries have been through hell this century. And if the incentives are solid enough and big enough, the Czechs will follow suit. The Romanians, East Germans, and Bulgarians, of course, will be resisting for different reasons."

"The obvious omission is the Soviet Union," I said.

"And it should be omitted, for now anyway. We should offer them the benefits of these kinds of policies on the same terms, but only if Soviet foreign and defense policy is clearly defensive and not aggressive. That's the measuring stick."

I encouraged him to begin a public campaign with this message.

He looked at me and smiled again. "You may be right. The time has come for Gorbachev to respond to our initiatives rather than for us to respond to his. He wants to negotiate about the weapons of war, and we should insist that we negotiate about the causes of war." He stopped. "How do you like that line? I'm road testing it on you before I put it in a speech or article. I think it sums up the differences between Gorbachev's priorities and what ours *should* be."

"I have one other question for you," I said.

"Shoot," he replied.

"Can communism survive in the Soviet Union when it's collapsing every-where else except China?"

He paused. "No. It cannot survive unless Gorbachev is prepared to use force. And even then, I don't think it can survive because the fear that kept it in place for so many years is gone. And without fear, communism is kaput."

That early conversation contained many elements of Nixon's post–cold war philosophy. He advocated only very modest defense cuts. He urged a re-structuring of the North Atlantic Treaty Organization to make it more re-sponsive to the needs of the new era. He supported opening the economic and military sectors of the European Community to the newly free nations of Eastern Europe when they showed an irreversible commitment to de-mocracy and free markets. And above all, he warned that the United States must be prepared to aid the democratic forces in these regions or face re-newed confrontation.

Nixon argued these points in one form or another, publicly and privately, until his death. He felt so strongly that victory in the cold war might be lost by misguided policy that he spent his final years arguing for more aggressive American action in behalf of those who rejected communism and em-braced democratic and free-market reform. Many issues concerned him, but the one that consumed him was the need for the United States to aid *signifi-cantly* the forces for real and lasting reform, particularly in Russia.

"If the democratic experiment in Russia fails, we can kiss the peace divi-dend and every other domestic issue good-bye," he said.

On September 14, 1990, Nixon wrote a three-page letter to General Brent Scowcroft, George Bush's national security adviser and a veteran of the Nixon White House's national security team. The main subject of the letter was the need for the United States to maintain a positive relationship with China, but Nixon also addressed the role Gorbachev had played in Asia. He warned that although the cold war had ended in Europe, Gor-bachev was still practicing "skillful diplomacy" in Asia. Nixon predicted er-roneously that in an effort to draw the two countries closer together, Gorbachev would return to Japan the Northern Territories, the four small is-lands off northern Japan that were seized by the Soviet Union in the closing days of the Second World War. He also warned Scowcroft that Gorbachev was reaching out his "tender loving hands" to China. And the Japanese, he added, had restored full economic relations with China.

From a long-range, strategic standpoint, the United States had no choice but to strengthen its relationship with China while watching carefully the actions of the Soviet Union in Asia. Nixon sought to remind Scowcroft—and through him, Bush—that although Gorbachev had taken some bold actions toward reform, many of the traditional Soviet impulses toward expansion remained.

"You know what today is, don't you?" Nixon asked me over the phone on September 23, 1990.

"Yes, sir," I said quickly. "It's the anniversary of the Fund speech."

"That's right. Thirty-eight years ago today I went straight to the American people with my case and won because I had the truth on my side. I learned then and there that you cannot rely on the press to carry your message. You have got to go over their heads and right to the people. And this is exactly what we must do when talking about the challenges of dealing with the Soviet Union in this so-called new era."

I asked how he intended to get people focused on foreign policy.

"You've got to hit it hard day in and day out. I've always said that the mark of a great leader is to take the unpopular and make it popular, to lead the polls, not to be led by them."

"Is Bush up to the job?"

He paused, considering the question and the most diplomatic answer. "He can do it if he wants to. The problem is that I'm not sure he wants to. He has been so seduced by Gorbachev and has earned such praise in the press for waltzing with Gorbachev that he may not want to endanger that by talking about the fact that Gorbachev is still a Communist, the Soviet Union is still Communist, and that it's still spending like hell on the military."

"So the job falls to you?" I asked.

"Well, I guess so. What the hell. I've taken on harder tasks before! Whether or not Bush talks about it, you can bet your life I'll be talking about it!" He cleared his throat. "And I want you to continue writing those hardline opinion pieces for me. They inspire me because," he said sarcastically, "you are so soft on Gorbachev."

In my first letter to Nixon, dated July 19, 1989, I wrote:

> My most plaguing concern is the reckless trust exhibited by American leaders in embracing Mr. Gorbachev and his proposals. I believe Gorbachev could be using his new openness as a tactical stall to consolidate his own power and restructure the Soviet system to make communism work. The U.S., for its own security, must plan on the basis of this view of Gorbachev. . . . America must keep the pressure on the Soviets by continuing a strong defense for extended deterrence and as leverage for negotiation.

This hard line resonated with Nixon's own thinking, and at his request I wrote almost daily essays for him on the evolving state of reform in the Soviet Union. One piece, entitled "The United States Cannot Save the Soviet Union from Itself," argued that once the internal contradictions of communism made it as untenable in the Soviet Union as in Eastern Europe, the United States would have very little influence in determining its replacement. Aid to a dying system would be an irrelevant waste. Aid to democratic forces still trapped in the dying system might be stolen or squandered. We had to allow communism to die a natural death in the Soviet Union without entangling ourselves in the process with premature pronouncements and financial assistance.

For Nixon, these arguments allowed him to adjust his own thinking on the issues. He commissioned my pieces to reinforce his belief that we were serving a great cause, the "victory of freedom," as he continued to make his case against pouring aid into a collapsing system.

America was the sole superpower with a recognized monopoly of force. Democratic in politics, capitalist in economics, and liberal in trade, the United States could lead a new wave of such ideologies abroad. Nixon believed that this was the best way to define a post–cold war world reeling from its recent totalitarian past and vulnerable to a protectionist future.

"As you know, I am going to use you on this new book," he said on October 4, referring to *Seize the Moment.* "You're so tough on the Soviets and I want that to come through. You know, I can write op-eds until I'm blue in the face, but putting it in a book gets the job done. It's far more permanent. Besides, with Bush and Baker in there, I just don't see how American policy will be on the right track."

Nixon's opinions of Bush and Secretary of State James A. Baker III had evolved little since they assumed office in 1989. Bush was "a good man, but not a strong man politically," who, despite his formidable experience in foreign affairs, failed to respond to the end of the cold war with vision and creativity. His foreign policy seemed to reflect dominant public opinion rather than a firmly articulated agenda. He reacted to events rather than developing strong policies to affect them. He was not, according to Nixon, a leader of ideas.

Baker, Nixon said, did not "know anything about foreign policy, and what he does know is wrong." Nixon speculated that the former campaign strategist received the prime job of secretary of state primarily because of his close personal association with Bush. Both may have been equipped to manage the nation's foreign policy during a time of great stability and certainty, but for Nixon they were ill suited to manage it during the end of the cold war. They were too close to events and too sensitive to world opinion to recognize the dangers they were creating for future security policy.

"There is no vision there with Bush and certainly not with Baker," he said on November 12, 1990. "Baker was overrated as a strategist, and now he's in totally over his head with foreign policy. He just looks like an amateur out there with [Soviet foreign minister Eduard] Shevardnadze, holding his hand and sounding like he has no backbone. And Bush isn't much better. There is no grand thinking going on over there, no vision. They call it crisis management; I call it lack of leadership."

Nixon's frustration with Bush's weak leadership stemmed from his idea that the president must lead not only the nation but the free world with a dynamic foreign policy that deals effectively with existing situations and anticipates future ones. Although Nixon conceded that Bush faced a difficult challenge in making policy in a new and unsettled era, he faulted him for failing to take some risks in behalf of the democratic revolution in Europe.

"The guy has got to be wondering what to do. What does the United States do when the entire international system it has known for forty-five years collapses without anything to replace it? It's a tough nut to crack. I'm not saying it's easy. It's just that Bush has shown absolutely no command of this situation, and Baker—forget it. [Henry] Kissinger kept the State Department in line by intimidating the hell out of them. Baker doesn't have that ability. But both of them have overinvested so much in Gorbachev that they are blind to the fact that he is a Communist who is not going to quit the party. What I find most unbelievable is that they seem willing to try to save him at any cost, even at the cost of sacrificing the better democratic alternatives. It's beyond me."

Confronted with separatist movements in some of the republics within the Soviet Union, Gorbachev tried desperately to save his empire. Having allowed greater political openness and some market-oriented economic reform, he loosened the ties that bound the nation. No longer held hostage by a totalitarian Communist system, the people of Russia and the other Soviet republics demanded independence from central control.

Reconciling resurgent nationalism with order, liberty, and security was problematic for American policy. The Bush administration's ambivalence toward the first of these drives for independence—in Lithuania—stemmed largely from the fear of instigating a violent, spasmodic, and uncontrollable breakup of the Soviet empire.

Bush's deference to Gorbachev on the issue may have also been aimed at preserving a constructive Soviet-American relationship. But Bush's decision to ignore Lithuanian demands for independence from Moscow created an unfortunate precedent for the other separatist movements and the prospect of reform. Bush failed to find a principled way to distinguish demands for national independence in the Soviet Union from far less legitimate demands elsewhere.

As the unfolding drama in the Soviet Union revealed, new arrangements would not survive unless they provided reasonable protection for those seek-

ing independence. Anti-Soviet nationalism deserved American support because the Soviet empire denied its people the right to choose their own leaders, systems, and country. In the long term, Nixon recognized that the Soviet
Union united remained a more powerful and dangerous adversary than a
confederated or even fractured successor state.

Bush's logic was that if Lithuania were not granted its independence,
there might be greater stability and a better chance of successful reform
there and elsewhere in the Soviet Union. But for Nixon, the United States
also had to allow the Soviet Union to evolve by neither encouraging nor dis-
couraging a breakup. A successor state might have been worse, or it might
have been better. If, by adhering to moral, democratic principles and recognizing Lithuania, the United States accelerated the Soviet collapse, at least
we would have been on the right side.

The former president, aghast at Bush's failure to recognize Lithuania as a
nation independent of Moscow, summoned me to his office on November 6,
1990.

"Monica. Has Bush lost his mind?" he asked as I walked in. He threw his
pen on his desk and moved to his corner chair. "Has he been asleep throughout the entire cold war? Look at this: he isn't moving an inch on Lithuania.
He just keeps letting his friend Gorbachev roll over the poor place. We've
been talking about captive nations for forty-five years. Forty-five years! Were
we just gassing around, or what? Captive nations means captive to the Soviet Union—and held against their will. And now they finally have the guts
and the power to leave, and we don't do anything to support them? Please."

He shot me a disgusted look. "Look, I have been fighting this goddamned
battle against the Soviets my entire life. If Bush blows it at the end, I will—
well, I don't know what I'll do. But it won't be quiet, it won't be private, but
it will have an impact. I guarantee that."

"Why don't you consider saying something now?" I asked.

"I know it. I can't really go to Bush because he'll resent it—too close to
Gorbachev to be objective. And I cannot and will not go to Baker. So what can
we do? I can speak out, but I'm not sure it's worth it. What do you think?"

I urged him to make public his disagreement with Bush's silence on
Lithuanian independence. The stakes were too high, the end of the cold war
too immediate, and the principles too important for Nixon to simply acqui-
esce to the administration's policies. How the United States resolved trade-
offs between nationalism and "stability" was a question that concerned
Nixon because the Bush administration seemed willing to forgo principle in
the name of saving Gorbachev.

Nixon understood, however, that there were limits to what we could do.
We could not decide Gorbachev's fate, and we could not impose our system

on the states striving for their independence. To avoid the worst and encourage the best outcome, the United States needed to support the independence drives and encourage those states to introduce democratic institutions slowly and in ways consistent with their national characters. By bolstering the emerging institutions in the republics, the United States could cultivate real democracy where it was impatient to grow.

Nixon believed that the United States should pursue principled policy that served our long-term interests. This meant reaching out to the republics trying to escape Moscow's grip while easing the departure of the Communists, and it meant acting on a moral, political, social, and ideological responsibility to help the forces of democratic reform.

Democracy, however, would not come to the Soviet Union overnight. The only taste of democracy that the Soviets had had during the reform days of Gorbachev brought them chaos, disarray, civil discord, and economic catastrophe. They would be tempted to abandon it when the transition became intensely difficult. Order and freedom needed to be reconciled if the democratic experiment were to succeed.

Nixon, meanwhile, had decided that the best way for him to have an impact was by writing another book. During the fall of 1990, he asked me to begin to assemble background material for the book that would become *Seize the Moment.*

On November 12, I found a memorandum on my desk, instructing me to find particular facts, such as the number of international wars since 1945, the number killed in those wars, the average per capita income of those living in the third world, and information to support his contention that prosperity does not necessarily accompany democracy. He concluded with a thought about the deterioration of the social and economic situation in the Soviet Union.

One of the favorite jokes in Austria and Hungary, he wrote, had one Hungarian asking another if he could imagine any situation worse than the one in Hungary. The reply: "Yes! Look at the Soviet Union!" Nixon noted that the Russian soldiers stationed in Germany did not want to return to their homeland since the conditions at home were "infinitely worse."

"I'm writing this book not because I need to do it for myself but because the country needs to hear this kind of realism from me," he said on November 17. "They aren't hearing it from Bush, so it has to be me. You agree?"

I agreed, and he continued. "I want my positions on the record. After all, if the Soviet Union goes down and we don't do anything to encourage reform there, we will be just as guilty as the Communists for screwing up the place. Only I don't want to be included in that group. That's why this book is so important. It could have as much effect now, at the end of the cold war, that *The Real War* had in 1980: different time, different issues, same need to get the message out."

He turned his attention to Gorbachev's increasingly desperate moves toward saving his presidency and his empire. "Just look at him running around in the Kremlin, trying to hold on to whatever power he can—screwing around with the rubles, removing people who disagree with him, moving to crack down in Lithuania and Latvia. Mark my words: he *will* use force to preserve the empire. And all of this is geared toward strengthening central power, which of course will fail because all of the movement now is away from the center. Leaders can change history, but usually they have to be moving in the direction history is going. Very rarely can they buck those forces, but this is what Gorbachev is trying to do. I don't know if he realizes it yet, but he's doomed to fail."

He paused and looked out the window. "Some of our more naïve friends in the press and the so-called experts are saying that in this new world order—or whatever the hell they call it—we can cut our military, disband NATO, redistribute our economic assistance to places like Upper Volta, and rely on economic competition."

He waved his hand in the air in dismissal. "None of this is true. In fact, the cold war just made our challenges easier to define. It's so much harder now because we just don't know what lies around the corner."

When I said that it could be democratic progress or chaos and disaster, he pointed at me. "Most people don't realize that although Gorbachev has done some very progressive things at home and abroad, he's trying to restructure the system so that it's more efficient. It cannot be done, but he doesn't realize that yet because he's a Communist. Russia historically has had central control. Even without Gorbachev, you're going to have a situation there that will be authoritarian. Even democratic reform will not be the type of democracy we are used to seeing in the West.

"And as far as the military pullback is concerned, even without Gorbachev there will still be thirty thousand nuclear warheads pointed at us. Either Gorbachev survives, or he doesn't. We have to plan for any outcome."

He flashed a faint smile. "I've been around a long time. I've seen a lot. I've seen dictators come and go. I've seen ideologies come and go. But this—" He stopped. "This collapse of communism has got to be one of the most breathtaking things I have ever seen. Look at us," he said, pointing to the two of us. "A generation apart. I started my career at the beginning of the cold war; you are starting yours at its end. My God." He leveled his gaze at me and lowered his voice. "To be young at such a time! How lucky!"

His generation had to meet the challenges of the cold war; mine would have to meet those of the post–cold war era. For places that had known only tyranny for much of the century, we could now define policies that would steer the course for greater political and economic liberalization. Believing that they were on the right side of history, his generation fought an ideological struggle that had its manifestations in arms races and domino theories. Having succeeded in their mission, they passed the responsibility for securing the peace to the next generations. The new challenge, as Nixon said enviously, was based on the far more positive premise of waging peace.

On December 11, I entered his office and found him pacing. "Monica, if Baker doesn't stop drooling over Shevardnadze, I am going to gag."

Baker had forged a close and constructive relationship with Eduard Shevardnadze, the Soviet foreign minister who advised and supported Gorbachev's decision not to use force in Eastern Europe. Nixon believed that Baker was making the dangerous mistake of replacing the detached approach needed for high diplomacy with the interpersonal warmth of his relationships with the world's leaders. Although personal relationships can enhance already positive relations and improve negative ones, they cannot substitute for real negotiation conducted in full view of self-interest. The Soviets were acting in behalf of their national interests. If the United States did not do the same, it would find itself at a political, economic, and military disadvantage.

"It's OK to laugh and enjoy their company," Nixon continued. "But all of that 'ha, ha, ha, how've you been?' crap only goes so far. I was never one for small talk. But the shrewdest leaders I've met used it well, in limited quantities. If you happen to strike up friendships with these people, fine. But you mustn't let it cloud your judgment about the way your country or theirs is acting. I can't tell you how many times I've heard well-meaning diplomats argue against aggressive action because they've struck up a friendship with one of their counterparts." He smirked. " 'But he's so sincere, so nice.' Nice? What are we talking about? Bush has said, 'Gorbachev has a firm handshake.' What in hell is that supposed to mean? I guess he felt that since Gorbachev looked him straight in the eye—which is something that [Romanian president Nicolae] Ceaucescu could never do—and delivered a firm handshake, well, then, gosh, he must be a good guy, on our side." He pointed a finger dramatically in the air. "Wrong! Smart leaders act on behalf of their national interest, personal relationship be damned."

Nixon's point was illustrated when Shevardnadze resigned his post on December 20 over Gorbachev's acquisition of special powers and his halting and erratic execution of reform. The government was increasingly paralyzed, and potentially bloody anarchy loomed. A collapse of central authority, despite Gorbachev's efforts to preserve it, was a real possibility. Shevardnadze saw encroaching dictatorship: rule by force by Gorbachev and the reactionaries with whom he aligned himself. A martyr of the transition, he resigned.

This caught Baker by surprise and sent the administration on a mad dash to reassure its critics that its foreign policy was based not on personalities but on actions.

"It could be a charade," Nixon said, referring to Shevardnadze's resignation. "But I doubt it. I really think he disagreed with Gorbachev on using force in the Baltics and on not committing himself to reform." He shook his head. "Boy, Baker must be climbing the walls. He lost his pal. And I heard that Shevardnadze gave him no notice, that he heard when everyone else did. Ho, ho! That friendship came back and bit him in the ass!"

"I think that since Shevardnadze was the only real heavyweight who had Gorbachev's ear and was also a moderate, Gorbachev might try to persuade him to stay," I said. "He needs him for political reasons."

"He does, but I don't know. It will be an interesting twenty-four to forty-eight hours. By the way," he said, changing the subject, "I cannot believe that Bush said 'We'll kick Saddam Hussein's ass.' Can you picture Gorbachev saying 'We'll kick ass in the republics'?"

We shared a big laugh, despite the fact that Nixon's frustration with the Bush administration's handling of the nation's foreign policy consumed him. Rather than advancing the cause of democratization in the Soviet Union by supporting the independence movements and encouraging the democratic reformers, such as the former Communist Boris Yeltsin, the administration propped up the Gorbachev régime. Nixon, the unabashed cold warrior, was appalled.

On the snowy morning of December 28, he called me at seven-fifteen. "Some snow we have here," he said.

I shook myself awake. "I hope you didn't try to take your walk this morning."

"Oh, God no. Wouldn't want to slip, you know. Did I wake you?"

I tried to convince him that he had not. "When you get to my age," he said, "fifty years from now, you'll be up at five A.M. too! Not much time left. Got to make the most of every minute—can't waste it sleeping!" He laughed. "What do we have on the foreign policy agenda today? Look, I think that Gorbachev is going to try to rule with an iron fist as well as he can, but the republics are going to have a hell of a time going it alone. They may work out some kind of deal with Russia. You agree?"

"That's a possibility," I replied, "but I think their need to break away is too strong for them to stay chained to Moscow in any way. Communism may be discredited, but there is nothing yet to replace it. What are these people going to turn to?"

Nixon paused. "I don't know."

For insight into the unfolding drama in the Soviet Union, Nixon often turned to Dimitri Simes, a senior associate at the Carnegie Endowment for International Peace and later the director of the Nixon Center for Peace and Freedom. A Russian émigré who had come to the United States during Nixon's presidency, Simes cultivated high-level contacts in both countries and wrote well-informed and eloquent pieces on the state of the Soviet Union and Soviet-American relations. Nixon trusted Simes to guard confidences, to provide honest and objective appraisals of Soviet politics, and to accompany him on his trips to Russia throughout the 1990s.

On January 7, 1991, he spoke by phone with Simes and told him that he did not believe that the breakup of the Soviet Union was imminent.

"I told him," Nixon said to me after their conversation, "that I thought the republics knew that there was no way for them to survive economically without the center. Gorbachev, of course, is a transitional figure, but now it seems he's moving to the right while giving almost no thought to how that affects his reforms. Look at the way he is shoring up the KGB and the army and threatening the Baltics. He doesn't look like much of a reformer these days.

"Simes is right, though, when he says that nothing short of a brutal crackdown could keep the country together. I think the republics will stay close to the center even if they get their independence, but it will be for economic reasons, not because Gorbachev rolled the tanks in."

I posed a theory to him. "Have you considered that what Gorbachev has done is a sort of a reverse détente?"

He raised an eyebrow. "What do you mean?"

I told him that the détente with the Soviet Union that he initiated as president was a direct result of the domestic situation, particularly the constraints he faced in trying to end the Vietnam War. "There was no way that the United States would have supported an aggressive approach to the Soviet Union at the time," I said, "with the military increases and rhetoric that would have been necessary."

"No way," he confirmed.

"You needed to devise a strategy that was politically sustainable at home and effective abroad," I said.

"Right," he agreed.

"Consider what you did and what Gorbachev has done. He has tried to serve his interest abroad through accommodation and cooperation until he could get his domestic situation under control or until he could get the domestic support he needed to take a more traditional approach to the West. Of course, his whole ideology and system are collapsing, but both of you redesigned foreign policy to take into account your domestic situation. Both of you were trying to stall."

He looked at me and smiled. "Of course, I'm a democrat—small *d*," he said, "and Gorbachev is a Communist. But foreign policies are almost always related to how things are going at home. And sometimes," he said, "they are used as diversions."

As he discovered in his attempt to pursue a policy of détente based on restrictive conceptions of the national interest, realpolitik alone does not suffice to win the domestic support necessary to sustain an effective foreign policy. Americans must also believe that their foreign policy is right and legitimate as well as in their self-interest. But just as morality cannot be fully divorced from foreign policy, foreign policy cannot be separated from domestic politics.

"You don't have to be in a democracy to see this," Nixon said. "It happens everywhere. Leaders use foreign policy to serve domestic ends—sometimes. Not always, but sometimes."

I paused. "Some say that the reason you went to Egypt in 1974 was to deflect attention from what was happening at home."

He blinked. "I know what they say. Look, that trip had been on the schedule. We were making enormous headway in the Middle East, thanks to Henry and me. We deserved to take that trip. Besides, it didn't help us at home one iota. And I didn't expect it to. But the reception we got in Egypt was overwhelming. And that gave me personally a great lift. But it didn't give the Watergate Committee a lift, and I didn't expect it to. That wasn't the purpose of the trip—far from it."

On January 11, Nixon turned his attention to the violent crackdown the Soviet government had unleashed in Lithuania. Armed forces stormed into the capital, terrorizing and killing several of those who were campaigning for their independence.

Nixon called me into his office in the morning and glared straight ahead. "Hypocrites!" he said. "All of these people who condemned the Chinese for firing on their own people in Tiananmen Square allow Gorbachev to literally get away with murder in Lithuania. All because Gorbachev has wrapped them around his finger with charm and 'new thinking.' What crap. And here is another example of Gorbachev using foreign policy to turn attention away from the chaos at home. We're so busy with the Persian Gulf that we aren't paying attention to what Gorbachev is doing. And he knew it. Gorbachev may lack the ruthlessness of some of his predecessors, but he still has some. Look at what he's done here! And we aren't standing up for the goddamned captive nations. What's wrong with Bush?"

Nixon believed that Bush's investment in Gorbachev was leading the American president to pursue unprincipled policies. Not only had Bush abandoned fifty years of U.S. support for the independence of the Baltic states, but he was propping up a Communist gasping for the last breaths of ideology and empire.

The president issued a mild rebuke of Gorbachev's violent actions on January 13, leading Nixon to speculate that Bush and Gorbachev had reached an understanding that the United States would not object if Gorbachev used whatever means necessary to hold his country together.

"Enormous mistake," Nixon said. "Not only is it wrong, but it sends a bad signal to dictators around the world. How can we condemn and punish the Chinese while we're stroking Gorbachev? This is just the beginning of the violence in the Soviet Union, and I'm afraid that we have let them know that it's OK."

Nixon was outraged. "Did you hear Bush's remarks about the crackdown? Pro forma. Could he spare it?"

On January 14, Nixon was even more distressed to see that *The New York Times* indicated that the crackdown had been initiated by unnamed Soviet "loyalists" without mentioning the sanction it had to have received from Gorbachev. Nixon called me at home at seven-thirty in the morning to vent his frustration.

"I've just finished the paper, and I can't believe it," he said. "The *Times* refused to acknowledge that Gorbachev was behind this whole thing. If he didn't order it, he certainly gave his OK, and for Gorbachev to deny ordering it is crazy. I mean, really now. What are we talking about? And for [White House Chief of Staff John] Sununu to say 'Gorbachev is our best hope' is so bad and so outrageous that I can't even believe it. These people should know better. I think they have all lost their minds."

"And on top of everything else," he said the next day, "because the administration has taken a soft line on Gorbachev, the Democrats have taken a hard line." Nixon glared at me. "You *know* the administration is wrong when people like Ted Kennedy are stronger on this than Bush is. Ted, for crying out loud! The next thing you know, Gorbachev will be going after the other republics."

Nixon was correct. On Sunday, January 20, tanks rolled into Latvia and killed four people.

The next morning, I found an intriguing three-page memorandum from him on my desk. It began by asking me to locate some research material for the early drafts of *Seize the Moment*. He wanted to demonstrate that after World Wars I and II and the cold war, we had been subjected to euphoric talk about a new world order, only to have those hopes dashed. His realist view of the world would underpin everything else in the book, and he wanted the facts to support his arguments.

He wrote that he had seen a quote from Cordell Hull in 1945 in which the former secretary of state had said that with the war ending and the United Nations in development, there would be no further need for alliances and weapons of war. Nixon wanted the exact quote and asked me to find one similar to it by [Franklin] Roosevelt. Their naïveté would seem quaint and idealistic in view of the events of the rest of the century, and Nixon wanted to use the quotes to highlight his own argument that the world remained a dangerous and unpredictable place.

He also wanted to attack the "reporters who gushed over Gorbachev." He wrote incredulously that one columnist reported that *The Washington Post's* David Broder likened Gorbachev to Mahatma Gandhi and a prominent American businessman "compared him to Jesus Christ!" He asked me to compile the most "outrageous" quotes, particularly from media "pundits" and "left-wing politicians" who had praised effusively Gorbachev's efforts.

He indicated in the memorandum that he realized that these items seemed petty and "even boring" compared with the bigger issues that he intended to discuss in the book, but he had found in writing his previous books that a few hard numbers were more effective than general statements.

"Monica, I realize that these little assignments may seem like a bore to you," he said during our morning conversation. "But they are absolutely indispensable. Not only do numbers and quotes make the point, but nobody can run away from them."

"Particularly when we make the point that Gorbachev is really a moderate conservative, not a reformer anymore," I said.

"Well, that's right. And he can no longer be characterized as a victim of the hard-liners since he has become one. I hear that Bush is still seriously considering going to this summit in Moscow next month. If he does, he's lost me."

"Even Gorbachev has determined that his reforms are expendable," I said.

Nixon waved his fist in the air. "When the *reformer* ditches the reforms— well, then you *know* it's all gone to hell."

Nixon was convinced that the empire Ronald Reagan appropriately called "evil" was in its death throes. The Communists were utterly defeated politically, but privatization was the only way to ensure the irreversibility of the nascent democratic reforms. Gorbachev and his early change-oriented comrades were now reformers terrified of reforms, afraid of losing power and yielding property to private hands. The situation over which Gorbachev presided in early 1991 combined the vices of command planning with an absence of any economic responsibility. The result was economic chaos.

Nixon knew that if reforms were to continue and be built upon, a rapid and decisive transition to a market economy was needed, including private property, free enterprise, currency convertibility, and free prices. The United States could assist in helping Russia create an attractive climate for foreign business and investment without issuing loans to the dying central government. Nixon advocated linking this assistance to strict political and economic conditions, such as the elimination of central planning, the security of private property, and the guarantees of access to the Soviet economy by foreign investors. Unless the government gave appropriate guarantees and took real steps toward privatization and free enterprise, no loans or most-favored-nation trading status would be granted. If Gorbachev continued to placate the reactionaries and temporize on reform, the Soviet Union would dissolve into dictatorship and disorder, and talk of reform would be irrelevant.

"I'm not sure if Gorbachev can contain the momentum of change by force," he said on January 22. We had been discussing the difficulties involved in writing a book that would have to be changed daily as warranted by circumstances in the Soviet Union. Anxious about having to rewrite manuscripts, Nixon tried to predict the outcome of the current upheaval.

"I suppose he could crush the spirit of reform if he just rolls over everyone who previously supported him. But I don't think he has it in him. Even his crackdown in the Baltics was sort of halfhearted. Nobody really fears him or the system anymore. Communism is dead; there's no doubt about that. But the problem is that there is nothing to replace it. The opposition isn't organized and doesn't have a leader. The only alternative is the Communists. But eventually Gorbachev—or somebody else—will have to deal with this mess."

When I reminded him that the Baltics were ahead of their time because they had spent fewer years under communism, he replied, "Nineteen forty-five versus 1917. Those poor, poor people . . ."

"Gorbachev's priorities have changed," I said, "but ours haven't."

"Bingo!" he said, tossing his pen inadvertently in the air. "We are so far behind the tide of history right now, and it's all Bush's and Baker's fault. They can't see beyond Gorbachev. But they aren't going to listen to me, not when they're riding high on eighty-five percent approval. They're just not open to suggestions."

As he fished for the pen that had fallen to the floor, he said, "They should hear from me *because* they don't want to hear from me."

Two days later, on January 24, Nixon expressed concern that the book might be rendered irrelevant by the time it got to press and that policy makers and opinion makers might not be interested in hearing his views.

He was sitting in his corner chair, biting the end of his eyeglasses, when I walked into his office. The bright winter sun was streaming across his desk, bouncing off items that had also graced his desk in the Oval Office.

He cleared his throat and flashed a smile. "I thought I'd ask you the hard question today," he said. "Why should I write this book?"

I gave him my usual reassurances that the country and the world needed to hear from him, that they had been seduced for too long by those arguing that the cold war was over and that the West had won it, and that they needed a dose of realism and a lesson in how the real world works.

He looked at me and smiled again. "So that's the justification?"

"I think that's a pretty good justification."

"But will anyone listen?" he said, leaning toward me. "Will they listen to *me* anymore?"

It was an earnest question. Nixon believed that with every passing year his power to influence weakened and the danger of becoming a marginalized historical figure increased.

I reassured him again, and he listened without saying anything else on the matter, apparently convinced that writing the book was necessary but still unconvinced as to the impact it would have.

Meanwhile, Aleksandr Bessmertnykh, the new Soviet foreign minister, shocked Baker by criticizing U.S. operations during the Persian Gulf War.

"This first criticism by the new Soviet foreign minister of our tactics in the Gulf was exactly what I predicted," he said on January 28, "and which Bush dismissed by saying that he had personal assurances that Gorbachev would totally support our actions. While mobilizing an alliance, including the UN Security Council, was useful in helping build support in the Congress and in the country for military action, the cost is that our 'allies' may now in effect try to exercise a veto over our conduct in the war and will insist on building a peace after the war is won. The Soviet foreign minister's statement is just the first shot across the bow of what I anticipate will be a very hairy situation, which will develop as the war reaches its end and we start to debate what our position should be after the war is won."

Bush was scheduled to deliver his State of the Union address that night, and Nixon feared that he would try to accommodate Gorbachev and dismiss his tactics in the Baltics. He professed his unwillingness to watch "the damn thing," but when I called him after the speech, it was clear that he had seen it.

"Mr. President? I thought you'd—" I began to say.

"Bush was too soft on the Soviet Union," he barked.

"If we don't punish the Soviet Union now for what it's done in the Baltics, we never will," I added.

"God's sakes! When Bush slapped them on the hand, he looked like he was in pain! Whether or not Gorbachev is a victim of the conservatives is no longer the point. The point now is that he's comfortable with them. And for

Bush to flail around in his State of the Union, which is sort of a loser speech for a president anyway, and talk about supporting Gorbachev, essentially at any cost—well, that's just too much."

Nixon was equally aghast the next day, when he heard that Baker had negotiated with Bessmertnykh a joint U.S.-Soviet communiqué calling for a cease-fire in Iraq.

"I heard from a confidential source that Bush is really angry, and some are talking about an imperial State Department. Imagine! Baker goes skipping over to the Soviet guy and leaves with this outrageous damn thing? Can you even *imagine* Henry doing something like this? My God! Baker was out of line, and Bush must be spinning."

He paused. "He should fire him for this, but he won't."

"The White House scrambled to clarify Baker's statement, like they were unprepared for it."

"Of course they were unprepared for it," Nixon shot back. "Baker took it upon himself to do this. God, he's just *dying* to be president."

Nixon's visceral contempt for Baker and his apparently unlimited appetite for power was obvious. "Baker is bad, bad news. He doesn't even realize that the linkage he created between the United States and Soviet Union on handling the end of the war might completely alienate the Israelis. The Soviets are full of empty promises, and we bit." He shot me his best look of disgust. "The Soviets are floating peace plans with an eye to their postwar position. And here we are with Baker running around saying everything is hunky-dory. Kissinger would *never* have been so irresponsible. Never."

Nixon's rage at Baker's freelancing activities with the Soviets continued on February 5, when he remarked to me that Baker was "out of control" and that his agreement with Bessmertnykh was "a major screw-up." Despite the war in the Persian Gulf, Nixon remained fixated on developments in the Soviet Union and the U.S. policy that he considered so weak.

He threw up his hands as I walked through the door to his office the next day. "Have a seat. I am absolutely at the end of my rope," he sighed. "If they don't take a harder line on Gorbachev now, I will have to seriously consider my options."

The Soviet president had sent armed patrols into the streets, not to rein in petty crime but to create an atmosphere of intimidation and perhaps even to instigate a disturbance.

"I think you would agree that Gorbachev is not a victim of this shift to the right but a leader of it, even if it were unintentional," I said.

"Things have changed," he replied, "but not to the extent everyone thinks. And all of these clowns in the media—and Bush and Baker themselves—write off Gorbachev's reactionary shift as temporary and necessary to keeping the country together. What country? It's a jumble of states that have been held against their will. You don't salute a kidnapper because he has come to depend on those he's kidnapped."

"Even the Russians think we have been misled," I said, telling him that on a recent edition of *60 Minutes* some Russians were quoted as saying that they did not consider Gorbachev a hero but that the Americans had made him one.

Nixon clapped his hands together. "Aha! Isn't that great? It's true. We have built up this guy so much that it's almost impossible to break away from him."

On February 14, Nixon called me into his office and sat me down. He stood, looking at me with a grave expression. "Monica," he intoned. "After Gorbachev emerges as a peacemaking hero by offering all of these postwar peace plans, he'll cause even more swooning." He sat down.

"The Soviets are trying to delay the ground war with all of these peace proposals they're floating out there. They're trying to show that they're still global players. They're also trying to maintain their relationship with Iraq and cooperate with the third world. The thing we have to watch out for is their relationship with the Iranians. The Iranians are the really dangerous ones, even though Iraq is currently getting all of the play."

Nixon's concern was that the Soviets were using the situation in the Gulf as a stalling tactic. Their overtures to the United States, Iraq, and, implicitly, Iran were designed, Nixon believed, to develop a reservoir of trust. If the Soviets could deflect enough attention from their internal crisis, they might be able to recover some political and economic control. With Western attention focused on the Persian Gulf, the Soviets could use force within their own borders without incurring the full brunt of Western outrage.

"What Bush doesn't see, I'm afraid, is that Gorbachev is serving his own interests, which he is entitled to do," Nixon said on February 18. We sat together in his office, reviewing the Soviets' latest peace proposal in the Middle East. "The problem is that we assumed he'd be looking after our interests too. Bush has to choose between saving Gorbachev and defeating Saddam Hussein. Right now, he's in a hell of a position because he wants to do both. He can't. But I think he's more inclined to defeat Hussein, because he has committed such an enormous amount of resources to it. Gorbachev will have to wait."

I told him that I thought that Bush seemed to resent the Soviet peace plans because Moscow tried to usurp the leading role played by the United States and buy time to correct the Soviet Union's internal problems.

"I know," he said. "It's brilliant and it's also very basic. Every leader does this at some point. Things at home not going well? Why, make some noise in another part of the world. Cynical? Maybe. Wrong? Depends on what it is. Starting a war someplace or otherwise putting troops into danger is bad. But creating a little diplomatic stir somewhere gives a lot of bang for the buck. Gorbachev is guilty of this. So was Reagan. Most leaders have to do it at some point."

"And face some criticism doing it," I said.

"Well, that's part of the game," he said. "But I think if he's going to do it, he has already figured out that the positives outweigh the negatives."

Nixon watched Gorbachev balance hard-liners in his government with the reformers who had abandoned him, which put him in a precarious and ultimately untenable position. He maintained his verbal commitment to reform but aligned himself with those opposed to it. He pledged support of the American actions in the Persian Gulf yet sought to retain his political and military relationship with Saddam Hussein. Nixon admired his ability to hold on for as long as he had, but he knew Gorbachev would not survive the tumult sweeping the Soviet Union. Bush's challenge was to capitalize on the change in the most peaceful and advantageous way. Nixon, however, doubted that Bush could do it.

On February 19, the president had decided not to accept the latest Soviet peace proposal. Nixon was relieved that Bush had stood up to the Soviets, even at the risk of alienating Gorbachev and splitting the coalition aligned against Iraq. For Bush, defeating Saddam Hussein was a more immediate concern than placating Gorbachev. Once the war was brought to a successful end, however, Nixon feared that Bush would once again devote his energies to improving Gorbachev's fortunes.

By the end of February, both the hard-liners and the reformers were calling upon Gorbachev to resign. Having himself been asked to resign, Nixon took full measure of the situation. Political and economic chaos gripped the nation. Violence rocked the periphery. The president was unable to govern the country. He was increasingly marginalized by forces he had set into motion. Obstructing those forces and becoming irrelevant in the process made his resignation seem inevitable. If he continued to stall Gorbachev's departure, Bush himself would be left behind.

At ten o'clock on the evening of February 21, Nixon left a message on my answering machine: "To give you a nightmare, I think Bush will back the Soviet peace plan."

I returned the call and asked why he thought that Bush was going to change his mind.

"I have no confidence in him to continue to stand up to Gorbachev. He showed some spine when he turned down the proposal, but now I think he's feeling bad about it."

I disagreed, arguing that the allies to whom the plans would be unacceptable—such as the Israelis—would apply the brakes.

"But my concern is that this has started a *process*—you know what I mean," he said.

The Gorbachev "apologists," as Nixon called them, appeared desperate. They continued to applaud the Soviet president's efforts at home and abroad, but because his weakness was real, their praise was "nauseating." How thinking people could support a man now of the past who represented a failed and destructive system and who now blocked the way for more progressive democratic and free-market reforms bewildered Nixon, and he intended to use his new book to express his outrage and put his views on the historical record.

I traveled to the Nixon residence for a meeting with him on February 27 at eleven in the morning. Upon entering the house, I found the former president standing in the foyer, waiting for me. The family dog, Brownie, a shorthaired mixed breed that Nixon had adopted after finding him wandering on his property, bounded toward me. Nixon's affection for the ill-mannered dog baffled everyone around him, including Mrs. Nixon, who resented the mess the dog created around the house.

As we sat down in his study, a brilliant fire blazed in the fireplace, and Brownie curled up at his feet. "I'm writing the new book with this in mind: I want to bash the hell out of anyone who has supported Gorbachev this far into time. I'm going to paint Gorbachev as a tragic figure."

I agreed, and as I warned that he should be cast as tragic not in a sympathetic way but in terms of the failure of his brand of reform, the dog suddenly jumped up and headed toward me.

"I don't want any misunderstanding on that score," he said. "But I want to make the point that Gorbachev is tragic in the sense that he was the right leader for the Soviet Union at the right time, but events have overtaken him, and instead of getting out of the way, he has held on. Reform in the Soviet Union . . . Nobody thought it was possible. Gorbachev made it so, and for that he'll always hold a place in the history books, but the tragedy comes in when the reforms he began cause him to lose his power. The reforms he started to save his system ended up destroying it."

I almost missed these points because the dog was standing directly in front of me, emitting a low growl. I tried to wave him away with my pen, but undaunted, he took a step toward me and bit at the pen, taking off the plastic cap. Afraid that I might soon be responsible for killing the former president's dog, I tried to coax him into returning the cap. He stared at me with mocking insolence and swallowed it. Nixon, oblivious to the entire scene, made his point, which I jotted down after quickly locating another pen, and he called the dog back to his side.

"This book will be very important," Nixon said, "in terms of making people understand the reality around Moscow right now. Gorbachev has destroyed his country. That's good news for us but bad news for him. Revolutionaries seldom make effective leaders. You see that throughout history. Gorbachev led a quiet but quick and total revolution. Now he has been thrown out by it."

He lowered his voice and put his hand on the dog's head. "When I went to the Soviet Union in '86, [Soviet ambassador to the United States Anatoly] Dobrynin sent over some vodka. I, of course, didn't touch the stuff. But that was the visit when I met with Gorbachev at the Kremlin for an hour and forty-five minutes. He's a very forceful personality; frankly, he mows over Bush and [British prime minister John] Major and Baker and even Reagan. But I remember that we discussed mainly arms control. There was no talk— and I mean *no talk*—about political and economic reform. He did it only when circumstances forced him into it. And the results were beyond anything he ever intended or wanted."

He lowered his voice again. "I spoke with Dimitri, and he told me that Gorbachev and Shevardnadze had a screaming match—that Shevardnadze misled Gorbachev about the end effect of reform in Eastern Europe. Gorbachev, of course, didn't even see it coming. And at this point, he doesn't know what the hell he is, although he does still believe that communism can be saved. He can't see that the train has left the station on that score."

His face brightened. "I have something in mind, but I want to think it through before I tell you," he said.

Nixon informed me several days later of his decision to travel to Russia before the end of March. He believed that he could get a full understanding of events there only by "going to the goddamned place." He would meet with Gorbachev, Yeltsin, Shevardnadze, Bessmertnykh, and other leaders in and out of the government. "You must always meet with the opposition when you go abroad," he said, "particularly in Russia, because opposition today could be leadership tomorrow." Nixon believed that the situation in the Soviet Union had deteriorated to the point where he should evaluate it firsthand and report his findings to the president and the American people.

His only concern was that Baker, who was scheduled to leave Moscow on March 16, would try to intervene with Bush and stop Nixon's trip. Baker wanted to portray U.S.-Soviet relations in the best light possible, and Nixon would undoubtedly offer a far more realistic view of the danger associated with the current U.S. policy of propping up Gorbachev. In order to prevent Nixon from contradicting them, Bush and Baker might ask him to postpone his trip or, worse, request that the Russian leaders not meet with him.

"In that case," Nixon said, clearly annoyed by this possibility, "I will tell Bush that I'll have to tell the media why I'm not going. Then they would be in a dicey situation and have to explain themselves." It was a clear and explicit lesson in behind-the-scenes politics: if Bush and Baker revoked Nixon's right to travel abroad as a private citizen, then Nixon would revoke their right to lie to the press about it.

In mid-March 1991, the Soviet Union was a study in catastrophic contradictions. Gorbachev wanted to turn the impoverished Soviet economy into an efficient mixed economy and keep the union together. He accomplished neither. Reform could not continue without breaking up the empire, so Gorbachev chose to abort reform. Neither law nor order, neither war nor peace, prevailed. Reform was impossible in an atmosphere of disorder, and it was impossible under hard-line order. By attempting to lead everyone, Gorbachev was leading no one: the right had taken over, and the left was gone from power. Was it possible, Nixon wanted to know, for Gorbachev to resume the process of reform?

Shevardnadze said in early March that Gorbachev was still worth helping because he would be able to resurrect reform once the country regained stability. This, however, assumed that Gorbachev was a temporary captive of the hard-liners and would be able to break away from their influence. His interests now were bound up with the KGB, the interior police, the army, and the Communist Party. All represented the central government, and Gorbachev was best positioned to protect their interests.

Since Gorbachev did not intend to dismantle communism, he set out on a quixotic quest for a brand of democratic reform that would be compatible with it. And since many of the genuine reformers did not trust him, they dissociated themselves from him and began to create their own platforms for credible democratic reform. The movement had already begun under Yeltsin.

The reformers, however, were neither in a position to effect genuine change nor in a position to succeed Gorbachev. They enjoyed wide popular support but lacked organization. They lost positions in the government when Gorbachev moved to the right. And they were unable to deliver their soaring promises for democracy and free markets. The Communists had power without legitimacy. The reformers had legitimacy without power.

The hard-liners, meanwhile, argued that strict central rule offered security and familiarity in chaotic times, which is what they claimed the people wanted. They argued that when given the choice between bread without democracy and no bread with it, the people overwhelmingly would choose to have bread without freedom. The hard-liners pointed to Eastern Europe, with its 200 percent inflation and 35 percent unemployment, and offered to rescue the Soviet people from the same fate.

Since this played on the public's fear of change, Nixon argued that the West had to work to remove that fear. When the hard-liners asked the peo-

ple, "Bread or freedom?" the West should have told them, "We will help supply the bread if you do the hard work of reform." Then, Nixon argued, they
could have both.

Nixon often compared the situation in Russia with the French Revolution. The radical attempt to extinguish all institutions, customs, and traditions of the old régime resulted in unlimited tyranny under the guise of new
freedom: mob rule, the Reign of Terror, and authoritarian conquest. If the
French Revolution yielded any lesson, it was that radical political, economic, and social upheavals often invite authoritarian responses. If genuine
democratic reform were to succeed in the Soviet Union, all institutions and
customs created by seventy years of Communist rule had to be eliminated
without provoking massive violence.

Nixon was skeptical that it could be done. By this time, 91 percent of
Lithuanians, 78 percent of Latvians, and 77 percent of Estonians wanted
independence from Moscow and had already sacrificed blood and treasure
for it. They wanted self-government. The Kremlin said that self-government
was provided by the Communist Party. The clash intensified.

The Baltics represented the weakest link in the Soviet chain. The crackdowns were intended to halt the independence movements, reinstate fear,
and intimidate other republics. Instead, they brought hundreds of thousands of people into the streets, rallying in support of independence and in
defiance of the Kremlin. The principles of self-determination and sover-
eignty that had permitted the liquidation of communism in Eastern Europe
were not allowed to be applied within the Soviet Union. Gorbachev therefore
sought to preserve what was left of his empire by any means necessary.
When the weakest link dropped from the chain, even force could not hold it
together.

This was the state of the Soviet Union as Nixon prepared for his visit in
March 1991. Americans needed a sense of Gorbachev's relative weakness
and loss of control, the frustrations and direction of the reformers, the pervasive influence of the hard-liners, the republics' desire for greater autonomy, and most important, the Soviet people's desire for greater liberty. Nixon
prepared to gather the information he needed to make his case.

He asked me to assemble Gorbachev's "most striking contradictory statements" about subjects such as one-party and multiparty government and
state and private ownership. He wanted examples of Gorbachev's ideological schizophrenia and his tenuous grasp of the political center. By telling different audiences what they wanted to hear, Gorbachev prolonged his
political survival but courted disaster with each contradiction.

Of the many statements I uncovered, the following summed up Gorbachev's vacillation: "I consider myself a democrat" (September 25, 1990)
and "I am a communist, a convinced communist" (June 8, 1990).

On Saturday morning, March 16, the day before his departure, I drove to the Nixon residence to give the former president the materials I had gathered. I arrived at the house at eleven o'clock and rang the doorbell. No one answered. I moved to another door, which led into the kitchen. Hearing voices, I knocked, then opened the door. Suitcases lined the outer hallway, and Tricia Nixon Cox and Mrs. Nixon stood laughing in the kitchen. Brownie, having survived the pen ordeal, came barreling around the corner. The former president spun around when I closed the door behind me.

"Monica, dear, please come in," Mrs. Nixon said. "We must not have heard the bell. Dick? Oh, here you are!"

Nixon shook my hand and looked at all of us. "Why, the gang's all here."

Mrs. Nixon slowly made her way to the kitchen table and picked up an enormous birthday card, signed and framed by members of the Bush administration.

"They said they wanted to wish me a proper happy birthday," she said, smiling. "Imagine the size of the thing! But they have written some very lovely things. Oh, and Monica, why don't you take home one of these bouquets? We have far too many flowers in here, and I'd like for you to have some." She picked up a stunning orchid arrangement and gave it to me.

I thanked her and added, "I hope the president has a lovely celebration planned for you when he returns!"

Mrs. Nixon laughed, and the former president winked at the three of us. "Her gift is that I'm leaving for a few weeks!"

Nixon called me into the study so I could turn over the researched material. He put on his eyeglasses, sat down, propped up his legs on the ottoman, and looked over the material quickly.

Suddenly, he ripped the glasses from his face and pointed them at me. "You know what really burns me up? The fact that Baker is there now. Of course, he has to meet with Yeltsin, but he's only meeting with all of these people because he knows I will."

"I think," I said, sitting down, "that you shouldn't be too concerned about Baker's trip. It was meant to fortify Gorbachev, but the Soviet people resent Gorbachev's globe-trotting, so it may not help him."

"OK," he replied, "but Baker went over there just to see Gorbachev, and now he's seeing the Lithuanians and Yeltsin and God knows who else. It's spite is what it is."

He put the glasses back on. "This stuff looks fine. Dimitri, of course, will be with me, and he wants me to give a speech in Moscow. I'm considering it. But if I do it, I will be sure to use this. Nobody seems to realize the degree to which Gorbachev has swung back and forth on reform. Reminding the Russians may have the effect of also reminding the Americans."

He smiled. "I'm on my way to the evil empire."

"I think that the American media will cover the trip, perhaps more extensively than you think," I said.

"No," he said. "They hate to cover me anyway, but I'm not sure there is enough controversy built into this trip to generate a lot of attention. I would have to liberate Lithuania myself for the media to pay attention!" He laughed. "We'll see. The Soviet media won't cover it either, of course. They're more irresponsible than the American media. Oh, boy! What a group!"

He stood and walked me through the kitchen, where I bid farewell to him, Mrs. Nixon, and Mrs. Cox. The former president stood in the doorway and waved as I walked to my car. It was the last I would see of him for two weeks.

His trip to Russia was a success, even by his own standards. During this seventh trip to the Soviet Union since his celebrated 1959 kitchen debate with Khrushchev, he kept an exhausting schedule of substantive meetings with Gorbachev, Yeltsin, Bessmertnykh, Shevardnadze, Dobrynin, and numerous other leaders in and out of the government. He traveled to Lithuania and Ukraine to evaluate their drives for independence and the relative strength of their leaders. He attracted some media attention when he took his usual stroll through the streets of Moscow, talking to common Russians about their plight, fears, and expectations. He gave a speech on March 22 to the Institute of World Economic and International Relations in Moscow, in which he warned his Russian audience that if, after accepting relatively free elections, the liberation of Eastern Europe, the unification of Germany, some free speech, and the beginning of disengagement from the third world, they turned back to the dark days of reaction, they would find themselves "on the sidelines of history." In the life of a nation, he said, moments like this came "once in ten generations." Their moment of truth had arrived, bringing the possibility of democracy and free markets to a land that had only known tyranny and oppression.

The speech was well received and accomplished part of Nixon's mission: to get his views across to the Russians. Upon his return to the United States on April 4, he would try to get his views across to his fellow Americans.

At ten o'clock in the morning, shortly after he landed and returned home, my phone rang.

"Monica!" he bellowed.

"Mr. President!" I said, not expecting to hear from him so soon after his return. "Welcome home."

"Well, I'm glad to be back. It was a miserable place this time around. They're in a hell of a mess. Did you know, by the way, that my meetings with Gorbachev and Yeltsin were the only ones that any major leader has had with both on the same day? I thought you would find that interesting.

"Well, the Soviet media covered the trip, even with its censors, far more than the American media did. And speaking of the media, I'd like to do some of these shows, so I'll need an update from you on the Gulf and any questions they might ask about anything. I know I can count on you to prepare those briefing books." He paused. "How is your spirit? Still up to fighting the fight?"

"As always," I said.

"Good," he replied. "Now, I will see you tomorrow, and I'll give you a full rundown of the trip. Prepare for a long meeting. Do you think you can stand me for that long?"

When I approached him for our conversation the next morning, he was dictating his thoughts into his handheld microphone and wanted to postpone the meeting until later that afternoon. I drove to the house at three o'clock and noticed that the front door was open. I walked through it and saw Nixon standing in the foyer with his back to me, reading a piece of mail.

"Sir?" I said.

He turned around, startled. "Oh, hi," he said. "I just opened the door for you, but I wanted to get some air. It's so stuffy in here."

He took my coat, and we moved into the study.

"I'm about to give you a lesson in high diplomacy and geopolitics. This trip was one of the most interesting—and depressing—I have ever made to the Soviet Union. First of all, it's just a miserable place. Lines, long lines wherever you look—for all kinds of scarce things. It's just sad . . ."

He sat up in the chair. "Gorbachev is firmly in control of himself; he's not on the verge of a nervous breakdown, as some have suggested, but he is troubled. I know that some have enjoyed themselves over the years by asking, 'Is it a new Nixon or the old Nixon?' The point is here, Is this the old Gorbachev or a new one? Gorbachev, of course, claims he's the same one.

"There is no alternative to Gorbachev at the present time. No one is in his league—yet. He's not going to leave the scene—at least not anytime soon. He's a brilliant politician, a competitor, and he likes power. Most leaders do, but he intends to keep it. He is," Nixon said, drawing a parallel to himself, "a fighter."

Nixon punched his right fist in the air. "The confidence I saw when I met him in 1986 and 1988 was not as evident this time around. He's sharp but politically exhausted. I think it's this exhaustion that has allowed him to be vulnerable to the pressures from the right. But he's unpredictable. This guy can change on a dime according to what the political circumstances are. He might be able to get out from underneath reactionary control, but I doubt it. The pressure on him is just too great. He's with the reactionaries now."

"Is he leading them or being led?" I asked.

"Both."

I asked if it were possible for him to continue reform, and he shook his head. "Possibly, but I doubt it. How can any reform undertaken by Gorbachev and the Communists be credible? It can't. We must not forget that he is at heart a Communist and a great Russian nationalist. He's not about to allow the breakup of his country or private property. No way. The statements you put together for me before I left show that. He just about told me that in our meeting. The guy is not a democrat the way we think of democrats."

His face brightened. "You know, there was one surprise of the trip."

"What was that?" I asked.

He pointed a finger in the air. "One word. Yeltsin."

Several long moments went by before he continued. "Goddamn the press! If you listen to them, you'd think Yeltsin was an incompetent, disloyal boob. The only reason the press have treated him as badly as they have is because he has some rough edges. He doesn't have the grace and ivory-tower polish of Gorbachev." Nixon shuddered with self-recognition. "He moves and inspires the people despite what the Western press says about him."

Yeltsin's defiance fed into his own. "The guy has enormous political appeal. He has the potential to be a great revolutionary leader, charging up the people, his own Silent Majority," he said, making the parallel explicit. "He is very direct. He looks you straight in the eye. He has core convictions that no longer involve communism. He is infinitely better for the United States than Gorbachev. But I don't think he wants Gorbachev's job."

"Do you mean that he doesn't want to lead the *Soviet Union*, but he may want to lead an independent Russia?" I asked.

"Right, because he knows that there's no future for the Soviet Union. None. Even Gorbachev's crackdowns have been half-assed. I just don't see how the country can stay together, even though Gorbachev will not let it break apart. No way he wants that stain on his historical record. By the way, I told the hard-liners, with regard to the Baltics, that it was far better to have nonthreatening neighbors on your border than angry, bitter people within it."

He smiled. "But the difference between Gorbachev and Yeltsin is that Yeltsin stands for democratic principles. And he doesn't have the material resources to launch a dictatorship. If Russia has any future, Yeltsin is it."

He lowered his eyes. "You know, it's interesting. In 1959, I went to the same market I went to this time. The people, of course, were poor, but they were confident and warm. That spirit is almost totally gone. The people today are richer in the material sense, but they are poorer in spirit. That's a line I want to use in the future because it just sums up their condition.

"They believed back then that their system might pass ours by. Today, they know that it has just come to its end. The people are in despair. There is a deep malaise. The difference is among the people. There is an absence of fear and an absence of hope."

I told him that I had collected some newspaper clippings on the trip, and he smiled again. "Good. I haven't seen a newspaper in two weeks, and you know, it wasn't so bad! But I don't want to see the articles; just tell me how they covered it."

I told him that most major newspapers carried a photograph of him with Gorbachev but not one of him with Yeltsin.

"Bastards!" Nixon exclaimed, shooting his fist back in the air. "Although I don't know why I expected anything different.

"By the way," he continued, lowering his voice, "Baker tried to sabotage my meetings with Gorbachev and Yeltsin. He doesn't want to hear the truth. And he *hates* the fact that I'm the one out there telling it."

Nixon, of course, read some of the newspaper clippings about his trip. He was reassured by the coverage *The New York Times* gave him and saddened though not surprised by the coverage by *The Washington Post*.

"I just happened to see the pieces by the *Times* and the *Post* because Mrs. Nixon was reading them," he said, using his familiar tactic of blaming the former first lady for his own curiosity. "The *Times* was great. They covered the trip fairly and well. I will never hesitate to give [Serge] Schmemann another interview. *The Post* always has to get some needles in. They said the children in Moscow shied away from me. Well of course they did! I was being followed directly behind by the KGB! They just hate to admit that I'm still around and having an effect."

Nixon continued to have an effect by drafting an essay for *Time* magazine. He wrote a memorandum to Simes, in which he strung together some random thoughts, which gave rise to the arguments he ultimately made in the piece.

Living under communism, he wrote in the memorandum to Simes, is unnatural. It is natural for nations, individuals, markets, and ideas to be free. He pointed out that Gorbachev was criticized around the world for being ruthless when the Red Army massacred and injured hundreds of innocent demonstrators in Tbilisi, Georgia, in 1989 and when the notorious Black Berets of the Interior Ministry killed over twenty peaceful demonstrators in Lithuania and Latvia in January 1991. The irony, Nixon wrote, was that the same man who was charged with responsibility for those bloody actions was now being criticized for not being ruthless enough to preserve his country.

Nixon made the point that during all of his previous visits to the Soviet Union he had met only with "the man at the top." This trip was remarkable since he met not only with Gorbachev but with leaders of the opposition. There was some freedom of speech, some free elections, and an absence of fear. But, Nixon warned, Gorbachev was now fully aligned with the reactionaries, and the people were suffering from "massive malaise," a total loss of confidence in themselves, in their government, and in the ideology that once sustained them.

Unless the reformers prevailed, the Soviet Union would evolve into an "irrelevant empire," a nuclear superpower with a third-world economy. The United States needed to adopt policies that recognized the legitimacy of the reformers and supported them accordingly. Gorbachev was not our best hope for economic reform and a benign foreign policy. He would not break with communism as Yeltsin had done. He remained a great Russian nationalist who refused to allow the independence of the Baltics and to let go of "losers" like Cuba, Afghanistan, and Angola. Unless we strengthened the hands of the reformers, Gorbachev would continue to cast his lot with the reactionaries. Finally, he wrote to Simes, "we might want to take a shot at the intellectual elite" in the media and the foreign service who still supported Gorbachev.

Much of what Nixon wrote to Simes survived in the final draft for *Time* that appeared the week of April 14. Nixon made the case against Gorbachev as the best hope for reform and proclaimed Yeltsin a genuine reformer who would best serve Russia's and our interests. He did take that shot at the American media, whom he said "put style over substance" and sacrificed progressive democratic reform for the stagnant and destructive status quo. And, he wrote, we had to strengthen ties with the reformers without interfering in Soviet internal affairs.

"Supporting reform is morally right," he concluded.

William Safire, for his part, wrote a column about Nixon's trip for *The New York Times*, in which he emphasized Nixon's position that we should support Yeltsin since "economic reality makes Yeltsin ascendant" and, consequently, Gorbachev irrelevant.

With these arguments made, Nixon began a series of interviews to discuss what he had found in Russia. On Sunday evening, April 14, he appeared on *60 Minutes* to press the need for the United States to shift its focus from Gorbachev to Yeltsin.

I called him after the broadcast, and he spoke quickly. "What did you think? I didn't watch it of course, but Mrs. Nixon and Julie said it was very good."

I agreed and noted that his emphasis on Yeltsin was the key to the interview.

"Good!" he replied. "That's exactly what I wanted to get across. Got to wake people up out there. So it was worth doing?"

I assured him that it was. "OK, then. Last night I stayed up much of the night and wrote a lot of notes about realism and idealism in American foreign policy. I'll let you see them tomorrow. You'll see how I work, and I know you will appreciate their historical value."

I had just sat down at my desk the next morning, April 15, when Nixon called to me over the intercom. He was preparing to go into New York to do a live interview with CNN's Bernard Shaw, but he wanted to give me a copy of his handwritten notes before he left.

Nixon pointed at them with his pen. "That copy is yours to keep. You will notice the date and time written on top," he said.

He had scribbled "Saturday, 4-13-91" and "1:50—A.M." Underneath that he had written "American Mission" and underlined it. What followed was an extensive treatise on the delicate balance between the need to infuse foreign policy with idealism and the realistic means required to achieve that goal.

"I have concluded," he wrote, "that idealism . . . must become part of the policy." In other words, he argued, idealism was inextricably linked to our interests. It was no longer sufficient for the United States to be concerned only with what a nation does outside its borders; we also have to address what nations do within their own borders and to their own people because, he said, "murder within a home is just as much a crime as murder outside a home." This was a clear reference to Gorbachev's actions in the Baltics.

He acknowledged that this line of reasoning leads us into ambiguous areas. From a moral standpoint, however, it was hypocritical to say that the "Vietnam invasion of Cambodia justified an intervention because of its ties to the Soviet Union and that Pol Pot's murder of two million does not concern us because it took place in his country."

He argued that aggression within a border is just as egregious as aggression across a border and that we must first act to protect our interests. And then, in a startling rebuff to realism, he argued that we should expand our interests to include "crimes against humanity" even when our interests in the narrow sense are not involved.

He concluded with a personal note. It moved him to be cheered by people in Georgia, Lithuania, and Ukraine strictly because they knew he represented America, which was to them "not just a Santa" for their material needs but a symbol of ideas. There was, he said, a picture of America far bigger and more profound than the one of "Cokes, Pepsis, Pizza Huts, and rock stars." Our system of government, though not perfect, unleashed and encouraged people to live not only a rich material life but also a "decent, humanitarian, moral life."

His final thought was poignant: they cheered him abroad not because of what he had done or could do for them but because they knew that as an

American he wanted them to live a better and freer life while keeping the rich culture of their own history.

His middle-of-the-night scribblings were an attempt to relate the recent events in the Soviet Union to a broader philosophy for a new American policy. Nixon believed that realism needed an overhaul. Interests continued to reign supreme, but they now had to be viewed along with less tangible concerns, such as basic human rights. The traditional balance between idealism and realism in American foreign policy had to be realigned in favor of *slightly* greater idealism if the United States were to remain an example worth following. The notes were Nixon's earliest effort to establish a new philosophical foundation for American foreign policy and a new justification for a vigilant international role.

Nixon then set to work on translating some of these disjointed ideas into concrete advice for Bush. He began work on an "eyes only" memorandum for the president that assessed the Soviet situation and recommended some policy options. Although immensely frustrated that neither Bush nor Scowcroft had called him upon his return, Nixon made sure that that disappointment did not creep into the memorandum.

"I really don't think, based on the way they have ignored me since my return, that I should send this goddamned thing for another two weeks," he said on April 16, referring to his draft. "And I cannot believe my ears, but I heard that Bush may have a summit with Gorbachev, even without an arms treaty," referring to the Strategic Arms Reduction Treaty II, which was under consideration.

Nixon was flabbergasted. Not only was it a signal to Gorbachev and his hard-line associates that the United States supported them, but it was a blatant rejection of Yeltsin and the progressive democratic reform he represented. International outlaws and thugs everywhere would be emboldened, and Nixon was concerned about the message it relayed to the conservative leaders in Beijing.

"What in hell is Bush thinking? Forget about the poor Baltics for a minute. If he goes over there now and holds Gorbachev's hand, Yeltsin will remember it when he inevitably assumes power. And the Chinese—well, that's *all* they need to see. Mow down your own people? Fine by us. In fact, we'll even have a summit to chat about it."

Nixon was furious. He took some comfort from the fact that Safire's April 18 column condemned the idea of a summit until the Soviets halted their circumvention of the Conventional Forces in Europe Treaty. Nixon agreed but doubted that the administration even considered such vital security issues in its quest to rescue Gorbachev.

"Safire is right," he said to me, throwing his newspaper in the trash, "but it doesn't mean a tinker's damn to the Bushies. I'm going to send Bush this memo tomorrow, when it's done, but I hate like hell to do him any favors when he hasn't even called."

Fortunately, Bush called. Later that morning when the phone rang as I sat in his office with Nixon, I answered it, and the White House operator spoke. "The president of the United States is calling for President Nixon." I put her through to Nixon, whose eyes widened with surprise.

They spoke for fifteen minutes, after which we talked. "Well, Monica, you will be pleased to know that I had an interesting conversation with Bush. I didn't think he'd call. Scowcroft probably put him up to it. In any event, he invited me to the White House for lunch on Monday. I told him you'd come to the White House tomorrow with the memo, and even though he said he'd be at Camp David, you could leave it with Scowcroft. At least he'll have read the damn thing before I get down there."

He smiled, content with the latest gesture from the White House. "I'm going to finish editing what I'm doing on it now and then do a final go-through in the morning when I'm fresh."

He revised the memorandum throughout the morning of April 19, until he was satisfied with its style and content. He signed and dated it in front of me, then sealed it in an envelope. "I will give you a copy after I confer with Bush on Monday," he said, handing the package to me.

"You know," he said, focusing on Gorbachev's recent trip to Japan, "it was a flop. Two years ago, he may have had the leverage at home to return maybe two of the Northern Territories to Japan. Now he's a captive of the hard-liners. He couldn't give the Japanese a rock back, never mind any islands."

I agreed, and Nixon added, "The big news was that Raisa [Gorbachev] went to a market and bought an octopus. Big deal. Mrs. Nixon has been doing that for forty-five years! But a summit should not center around that!"

I told him that the most powerful point he could make to Bush was that Russia reforms only under pressure.

He smiled. "I hit that very hard in the memo. But you'll see."

I flew to Washington and deposited the memorandum at the White House. Nixon met with Bush at midday on Monday, April 22, and the network news that night indicated that the administration would seek stronger ties to the republics and rely less on Gorbachev.

The former president returned the next day in a horribly bad mood that had no apparent cause. He answered questions abruptly, barked orders, and slammed doors. After storming out of the office at eleven o'clock, he returned at three o'clock, still annoyed.

After placing calls to former secretary of state Alexander Haig and Simes, he asked for me. I opened the door to his office and closed it quietly behind me. Nixon, wearing his glasses, was glaring at a newspaper from behind his desk. I sat down, and he looked at me.

"Well, I'm sure you know about the McGovern thing," he said. "It was a crazy damn thing. On the shuttle home, I was reading before we took off, and I heard somebody say to Jerry [Rosalia, his security escort for that day], 'I know that guy!' Well, it turned out to be [George] McGovern. So after we took off, I had Jerry see if he had an empty seat next to him, and we had a nice talk. He was thinking about running in '92, damn fool! But he was always a very decent guy. He at least had the guts to stand up for what he believed in, not like the current bunch of clowns."

He got up and sat down across from me, propping his legs up on the ottoman. He recounted some of the discussion at the White House, and then with a frown he said, "Their whole outlook on Soviet policy is wrong. They don't understand the potential or the energy of the reformers. I tried to imply that a summit will not help Gorbachev. The Russian people, who have to stand in line two hours for bread, don't care if Gorbachev is tipping vodka glasses with Bush!"

He was distressed to hear that nine of the fifteen Soviet republics had signed an agreement with Gorbachev that day to turn the Soviet Union into a voluntary union of sovereign republics, with a legitimately elected government and a market-based economy. Nixon dismissed it as a cynical ruse to buy time and make Gorbachev look more inclined to reform. And Nixon believed that the administration would naïvely make policy based upon it.

He shot me another disgusted look. "I got the feeling that Bush wants the summit even if the conventional treaty and the START treaty aren't ready to sign. It's really a pathetic thing."

"You may not want to hear this," I said, "but Baker announced that he's going to Moscow tomorrow on a side trip from the Middle East."

"What?" he barked. "Well, that just goes to show what an opportunist he is! He just couldn't stand that I went and brought back the kind of message I did to Bush. And you *know* that he's going to squeeze a summit out of it!"

To distract himself from his own frustration, Nixon decided to take a brief vacation. He left for the Bahamas on April 25 but called me from a holding room in the Fort Lauderdale airport, concerned that the latest "condominium" between Gorbachev and Yeltsin would marginalize Yeltsin.

"What do you make of this agreement between them? I hope to God Yeltsin understands that Gorbachev is trying to co-opt him," he said.

I said that Yeltsin might be using the agreement to stall until he can consolidate his own support.

"Did you see where Gorbachev offered to resign as general secretary? I think both sides are trying to regain their footing, don't you? I mean, both of them agree that they have to stop the chaos, but that's where their agreement ends. It doesn't matter if Gorbachev quits as head of the Communist Party because the Communists have only eight percent approval."

"And it wouldn't be credible anyway," I said.

"Well, it's time for me to get on the plane. But I'm thinking that we need to do this book [*Seize the Moment*] more than ever, because this administration makes foreign policy ad hoc. Bush involves himself personally and would rather compromise, and Baker bases everything on expediency, on what's right for Baker." He paused. "When I get back, we're going to talk about this book. I'll see you in a few days."

Nixon's vacations never lasted very long. His impatience with his successors drove him back to work long before he was supposed to return. Four days into a scheduled week-long trip, Nixon was back.

"It's the end of April," he said as I gave him some newspaper articles I thought he might have missed. "I'm glad I spent the last few days away. I needed a little break. Now we focus on the book, full steam ahead. OK?"

The next day, as we met in the morning at the residence, he posed a familiar question but did not wait for an answer. "What is our mission in writing this book? OK, so where do we want to discuss the defense issues? I think we want to put them in the Soviet chapter. That's where they belong. Did you know," he said, "that if total military expenditures were cut by five percent, we could feed the world?"

He paused. "On SDI [the Strategic Defense Initiative], we have to have a feasible plan. A total protective umbrella is ludicrous. A partial counterforce shield may be possible, not to guard against a Soviet missile attack but for regional threats."

Nixon then got up, walked to the bar area, and poured two glasses of mineral water. He tossed in two wedges of lime and carried the glasses back to our seats.

"To the book!" he said, raising his glass. "Today is April 30, 1991. Let's see," he said, glancing at the ceiling. "On this day in 1973, I had to let [chief of staff H. R.] Haldeman and [John] Ehrlichman go."

He paused before changing the subject. "OK. Monica, I want you to develop some thoughts on the Pacific chapter. You did all of the background on the Soviet Union," he said, "and if you can cover that, with eleven time zones, I think you can handle Asia, with five."

He smiled. "When we cover the Japanese, I want to include a passage in there on how their women are a vital resource and how they should get rid of their chauvinism. We can find a way of saying this diplomatically. Although," he said with a wink, "I think that a woman's place is in the home, without any of this career stuff. What do you say to that?"

"You know what I say to that."

Nixon laughed, then turned serious. "If we are moving to a new world order, American leadership is indispensable. That said, we must use that role effectively, constructively, and creatively. We've bungled the first test in the Middle East because whether or not there were new circumstances, we went in without a plan.

"But we really have to watch the Soviets. The real reformers in there are so impressive. They've got enthusiasm and intelligence. No one in the Congress or administration now could hold a candle to these guys. One of them said to me, 'I've been reading *The Federalist Papers*, and we don't want the Jeffersonian model; we want the Hamiltonian model.' Hell, most Americans don't know the difference! All they know is that Hamilton was killed in a duel!"

Two days later, he turned his attention to a potentially serious development: the agreement reached between Gorbachev and Yeltsin to work together to advance reform. "I hope Yeltsin hasn't done himself a disservice by trying to stabilize the situation. He shouldn't try to alleviate the crisis that has brought them this far. The Communists lie, pure and simple.

"But what the administration has to realize is that the only way to reform the Soviet Union is to dissolve it. Bush and Baker are too personally involved. They don't want to admit that they're wrong in backing Gorbachev. Well, sometimes a president has to eat crow. I did.

"The United States should have backed ties to the republics back in September [1990], when Gorbachev rejected the Five-Hundred-Day Plan [the proposal to accelerate economic reform, including privatization], and certainly after January 13 in Lithuania. They're reaching out now only out of necessity.

"But look at Shevardnadze. Where do you think he stands on the independence of his own republic [Georgia]?"

"Split," I said.

"Split to the gut," he added. "But he's part of the diplomatic set. And Bush and Baker are more inclined to listen to his view of helping Gorbachev than the Baltics' leaders, who say, 'Don't help Gorbachev.' I heard that [Jack] Matlock [the U.S. ambassador to the Soviet Union] is retiring. I hope his replacement isn't a foreign service jerk. We don't need a goddamned hack in there."

Matlock would eventually be replaced by Robert Strauss, a Democrat and an effective negotiator. Nixon liked Strauss and thought his selection was wise politically. "It allows Bush to win over the Democrats who are to the right of him on this." Strauss's selection was a signal that Bush considered the American policy toward the Soviet Union nonpartisan—an admirable strategy, Nixon believed, though not particularly effective.

Bush, meanwhile, had not taken Nixon's advice to embrace Yeltsin as the best hope for reform. The president issued a strong statement in support of Gorbachev on May 8, in which he indicated that the United States would continue to reward him for his historic achievements. Nixon reacted angrily.

"He didn't listen to a damn word I said," he fumed. "Listen. I know that they don't want to appear to be taking directions from me. But now I'm going to have to break with them.

"The Baltic leaders look kind of pathetic. I hate like hell to be associated with an administration that has done nothing—*nothing*—on their behalf. I've done too much in my political career for these people, and I'm not about to abandon them just because Bush has.

"And I know why Bush praised Gorbachev the way he did. He's trying to turn attention away from the deteriorating situation in the Middle East, to refocus attention on the Soviet Union, issue A. Politics may have reared its ugly head. I'm going to talk to Kissinger and run this by him." His face fell, and in a mild outburst of despair he said, "But I don't even think Bush read the damn memo. He isn't listening to me on it.

"We've read it, but Bush—well, who knows. I know it wasn't what he wanted to hear, but come *on*."

Nixon's frustration eventually gave way to more detached analysis. On May 13, he ripped George Melloan's column from *The Wall Street Journal*, underlined it heavily, and left it on my desk. Entitled "Gorbachev's Troop Use Should Give Us Pause," it argued that the Soviet Union remained a military state that used force internally to suppress and intimidate anti-Communist groups. When the West ignored this activity, it became a party to its immorality. Nixon scribbled my name on top of the piece and added "Right on!"

"Very few people see this clearly," he said when I brought the article into his office. "He does. No one seems to be listening, though. The hard-liners won't just hand over power, but the transition isn't guaranteed to be peaceful anyway. We could have a situation in which the republics have the reformers handle domestic policy and the center manages foreign policy."

"But there's no way the two sides can survive like that," I said.

"And there is no way that the center can hold," he replied.

Nixon, always ready to uncover political motives for U.S. action abroad, suspected that Bush needed to appear strong in international affairs since the relatively weak domestic economy left him vulnerable to criticism from Democratic candidate Bill Clinton.

"He's had the Sununu flying thing," he said, referring to the chief of staff's overzealous use of government aircraft, "and of course the persistent questions about [Vice President Dan] Quayle's adequacy and the fact that despite the war Saddam Hussein remains in power, which has focused a lot of negative attention on the administration. We know that Gorbachev has his problems. Both of them want a situation where positive press is guaranteed. Voilà!" he said, waving a hand in the air. "A summit."

"And now that Bush has dropped arms control as a precondition for a summit," I said, "they can have a summit for the sake of having a summit."

Nixon pointed at me. "You see? Look, you only give them something when you get something in return. By the way," he said, almost parenthetically, "I thought you'd like to see this."

He handed me a copy of a story by the Associated Press in which Gorbachev was quoted as accusing Nixon and Kissinger of poisoning Soviet-American relations. I looked up at him, and he smiled. "Well, we're having an effect!" he said, leaning toward me. "You know what I think? I think it's time for another book powwow."

On May 16, Nixon flew to Washington to meet with Simes. I traveled to the capital several hours later and met with the former president alone. He began talking immediately about the central message of the book and how he wanted to cover domestic policy only to the extent that it affected the example we presented to the rest of the world.

"I think our book is going to require a heavy dose of idealism to get the message across. Remember when I met Mao for the last time and he said, 'Is peace your only goal?' I answered, 'Peace with justice'—and now, of course, freedom. Materialism is a good objective, but it shouldn't be the only one." 𝐴

When I said that he needed to take realistic goals and set them in idealistic terms, he replied, "You can't get anyone to do anything unless they believe in it. That's one of the most basic keys to leadership." He paused. "I'm really getting down on arms control. I know we were arms controllers, but it seems so useless. I'm not sure we should even discuss it with any kind of seriousness. Then again," he said, correcting himself, "I suppose we have to if it's on the administration's plate."

During the flight back to New Jersey, Nixon sat by the window, Rosalia sat on the aisle, and I sat between them. Nixon opened his briefcase and shuffled some of the papers inside. "Did you have a chance to meet [Senator John] Seymour when he came up to the suite? You know, he's a good enough guy, but he just doesn't have . . ." He slammed the briefcase and made a fist. "You know what I mean."

"Maybe it's because he hasn't faced a statewide election yet," I said.

"Maybe," Nixon replied, "but I'm not sure how effective he'll be on the tube. And in California, that's the only way to win. The Democrats will put up [Dianne] Feinstein, and she's good on TV. I'm afraid it doesn't look good for him. Too bad, because he believes in the right things. Look at Bruce Herschensohn: fantastic on TV but a little too extreme in his views. He wants the UN out of the U.S. He's right, but that was an issue in the 1960s. [Congressman William] Dannemeyer, too. His big issue is AIDS—wants to quarantine AIDS patients. My God!" he exclaimed, rolling his eyes. "Way out! Unpractical and immoral."

Without a cold war to wage, the Republican Party had turned on itself, sacrificing solidarity for polarizing and divisive issues. Lacking an enemy from without, the Republicans had found one within. But because they were consumed with internal battles, they were missing, as Nixon put it, "the larger picture": the developments in the Soviet Union.

"With a guy like Seymour, there's no way that he can understand all of the dimensions of what is happening in Russia and the republics. And [Senator Phil] Gramm—well, Gramm understands it, but he isn't talking about it. He's too worried about running for president."

When he turned toward the window, I asked if he enjoyed flying.

He turned toward me and grimaced. "I've done it so much it's neither here nor there. Planes are now just big buses. Trains are beautiful. People miss the beauty of travel today—always in a rush to get places . . ." he said, pretending to jog in his seat.

When I reminded him that he used to campaign on trains, a gentle smile crossed his face. "Whistle-stops. Twelve in a day. It was a different time then. Very different." We sat in silence for the rest of the flight.

After we landed in Newark, we got into the limousine waiting on the tarmac. During the drive back to the office, Nixon opened his briefcase again and handed me some essays from the Council on Foreign Relations.

"They put out some good stuff, but do you know how they answer the phone? They say, 'The Council.' The council of what? Next time you call, tell them you didn't think you were calling attorneys!" He laughed. "You know, I read an article by [former U.S. ambassador to the United Nations] Jeane Kirkpatrick recently, and she argued for a new type of isolationism." He made a fist. "What the hell has gotten into her? She says we have no interests in the Soviet Union except the military threat. That's a big maybe! Thirty thousand nuclear weapons isn't a small maybe. And what about the democratic reformers? They're an interest to us, or their success is, anyway. So, as you can see, we're fighting an uphill battle when it comes to writing this book."

Nixon, of course, loved the challenge. Part of the gratification came from knowing he was right; the other part came from knowing that, as a voice of dissent, he would attract attention. He welcomed the chance to deny legitimacy to the conventional wisdom and advance his own cause in the process.

In late May, former Soviet foreign minister Eduard Shevardnadze requested a meeting in New York with Nixon. It was scheduled for May 24, and Nixon invited me to attend. They had already begun their conversation when I arrived at Shevardnadze's hotel. As I stood in the doorway of the suite, waiting to be announced, Nixon caught a glimpse of me and waved me in. Both men stood and asked me to sit next to the interpreter. A few things struck me immediately.

First, Nixon spoke in clipped sentences, pausing for the translation and response. He almost always referred to Shevardnadze in the third person: "I am going to say a few things about reform that the foreign minister may not like to hear but are things that are necessary for the foreign minister to hear."

Second, Nixon used liberal doses of flattery. He said, "The foreign minister's brilliant leadership led to freedom for Eastern Europe," to which Shevardnadze replied, "I have always considered you the foremost statesman."

And third, Nixon spoke directly to Shevardnadze but looked to the interpreter as he translated. I, however, studied Shevardnadze's expressions as he heard Nixon's words in Russian. They were revealing. When Nixon suggested, for example, that Gorbachev might bring Shevardnadze back into the Foreign Ministry to prove he was resuming reform, Shevardnadze stared at the floor and did not address the possibility.

Nixon asked Shevardnadze immediately about Gorbachev's plea to the West for one hundred billion dollars. Shevardnadze shook his head and replied that he had "no idea" where Gorbachev got that figure and that he had asked Gorbachev where he expected the West to come up with such a huge sum. Gorbachev, he said, did not have an answer. Nixon deduced that the request had actually undermined Gorbachev's reformist credentials, since it was clear that he had not thought out the process.

On Cuba, Nixon said, "Cuba is a neuralgic issue for most Americans. You could get more aid from us by cutting your subsidies to Cuba."

Shevardnadze replied, "We have treaties and obligations to Cuba that we cannot terminate overnight." It was a standard diplomatic line that promptly ended that phase of the conversation.

On arms control, Shevardnadze indicated that the Soviets realized that their country could not remain a militarized state and survive. He acknowledged that the U.S. arms buildup during the 1980s, which they were forced to match, resulted in economic bankruptcy. "But the United States," he said, "here, you are bankrupt too, because of defense. I know you have a large deficit."

Nixon smiled at the diplomatic turnaround and did not follow it up.

On the republican movements for independence, Nixon raised the claims of the Baltics first, to which Shevardnadze added those of his native Georgia. The former Soviet foreign minister said that Gorbachev's directive to send tanks into the rebellious republics was not only "inhumane" but "politically unrealistic." After the tanks rolled into Lithuania, the other republics were emboldened to fight for the cause.

The conversation quickly turned to the potential of democratic reform. Shevardnadze indicated that the Russian democrats were not as synchronous or monolithic as the reactionaries. If they were to succeed, they needed greater organization. Nixon nodded in agreement.

"We must make the Soviet Union attractive for Western investment," the foreign minister said. "During my trip here, I've encountered many businessmen who are interested in investing."

Aware that this was an exaggeration, considering the disastrous condition of the Soviet economy, Nixon pursued it. "If the Soviet Union embraces full-fledged market reform, there is no question but that American investors will see the huge untapped market and invest in it," he said.

Shevardnadze nodded, then criticized Gorbachev for attacking Nixon and Kissinger. "It was wrong for Gorbachev to try to identify scapegoats," he said, particularly those, like Nixon and Kissinger, who had long been open to constructive relations with the Soviet Union.

When the meeting ended and I prepared to hail a cab, Nixon said, "I'll give you a ride home because I want your immediate impressions."

During the ride back to New Jersey, he said, "Well, how do you like that? Your first meeting with an honest-to-God Communist! Communists generally are ice-cold, like Gorbachev. But Shevardnadze's a Georgian, like Stalin—far more emotional. You could see that as he made his points."

I told Nixon that his most effective point came at the end of the conversation, when he told Shevardnadze that he would make an outstanding candidate for *elected* office in the new Soviet Union. Nixon had said that he had "courage, high intelligence, strength of character, and effectiveness on television. I don't mean to pander to the foreign minister's vanity," he told Shevardnadze, "but I think you'd make an excellent *candidate.*"

I also told Nixon that his emphasis on making the Soviet Union attractive to Western investors was a key point and that Shevardnadze understood that the hesitant, partial free-market reforms were not enough.

"You see," Nixon said, "Shevardnadze is divided on every issue, especially Georgian independence. He's a reformer but a Communist. It's getting harder, if not impossible, to have it both ways."

The central government in Moscow and officials from most of the republics agreed to determine how to divide economic power and how to devolve political power to the republics. It was a promising signal that new cooperation was under way, although the pressure from the hard-liners that led Gorbachev to reject earlier attempts at decentralization remained. Under the threat of civil discord, the task of revamping the highly complex centralized structure would be made more difficult. But the apparently new spirit of reconciliation was driven by a realization on all sides that confrontation had achieved little but chaos and bloodshed and that the catastrophic implosion of the economy had been accelerated by the deadlock involving Moscow and the republics.

The movement that Nixon saw toward compromise had the potential to transform the Soviet Union into a far more democratic state, but now elections and a market-oriented economic plan were needed. To stave off complete collapse, then, the competing political factions had no choice but to try to work together.

Nixon dictated a memorandum to me after the meeting with Shevardnadze, in which he described this situation and added that Gorbachev's apparent return to reform was as tactical as his turn toward the reactionaries had been several months before. The result, however, would have a significant impact on the European community, particularly if Baker and "his foreign service 'be kind to Gorby' clique increased its influence" in the White House.

He concluded that the latest agreement between Gorbachev and the reformers might be able to slow the downward spiral but could not stop it. Although the reformers were derided as too weak to run the country, Nixon knew that they would soon be in control. They had begun to recover from weakness, disorganization, and repression to renew a legitimate bid for power. It was an underdog fight that earned Nixon's respect and support and drove his very public break with the administration.

During the last week in May, he decided to write a piece for *The Washington Post*'s "Outlook" section. He spent two days on it and asked me to work on it with the *Post*'s "Outlook" deputy editor, Jeffrey Frank. Nixon chose to place the op-ed in the *Post* because he knew it would attract attention, if not for its content then for the fact that he was writing for the newspaper that had tirelessly pursued the Watergate scandal.

It ran on Sunday, June 2. Entitled "Gorbachev's Crisis—And America's Opportunity," it argued that the Soviet Union had to decide whether to move toward a democratic and free-market system. The United States, rather than continue to be obsessed with every swing by Gorbachev between reform and reaction, had to base its strategic interest on the dismantling of the Communist Soviet system. American policy should be focused, he wrote, on promoting the best chance for democratic government, free-market economics, and self-determination for all fifteen Soviet republics.

He demolished the myth that Gorbachev was a closet democrat and suggested that rather than prematurely deliver aid that would effectively stall reform by subsidizing the Communists, the United States should set three preconditions for the consideration of aid: geopolitical accommodation, including the termination of assistance to Cuba, and irreversible market and democratic reforms.

Nixon discounted the idea of a summit "for the sole purpose of bolstering [Gorbachev] politically" and argued that Gorbachev's only long-term hope was to "set aside the ideological baggage" of Soviet history and "lead this new revolution." In order to do this, he needed to submit to a nationwide free election. If he did not, he would be overtaken by the very forces he helped to unleash.

The next day, Scowcroft called to praise the article, leading Nixon to speculate that "it had reached Bush." Its impact, however, remained to be seen.

"The split in the administration between responsible advisers like Scowcroft and Baker, who doesn't know a goddamned thing, is deep. Everyone was afraid to take on Bush. I'm really the only one who did it. Even the academic conservatives were sucked in by the Harvard influence and their so-called 'Grand Bargain,' " he said, referring to the assistance plan designed by professors Graham Allison and Jeffrey Sachs.

"We called it a 'grand con job' in the piece because that's what it is," he continued. "It will only prop up the center. Aid to the real democrats in Russia—well, that's a different story. But not until that aid can be targeted to those forces and those forces only—and *not* to Gorbachev and his gang."

When I mentioned that Bush's heart was with Gorbachev, Nixon scowled. "You can't run foreign policy by emotion. I have very little confidence in the team now. Look around. They're all soft on Gorbachev, except for Scowcroft. One hawk? Not good.

"I hope Scowcroft stays firm. I know Bush wants this to be his policy and not President Nixon's. Understandable. But come on, Monica. They are so wrong that it's becoming dangerous."

Russians, meanwhile, went to the polls on June 12 and elected Boris Yeltsin their president in the first free election in Russian history. Nixon saw the full results the following day and called me into his office to discuss them. He was clearly excited.

"Yeltsin won by sixty percent!" he said, clapping his hands together. "But did you see the way the media played it down by projecting low polls for him and the possibility of a runoff? You know, this reminds me of the Ortega-Chamorro election in Nicaragua," he said, referring to the 1990 race between the Communist Daniel Ortega Saavedra and the democrat Violeta Barrios de Chamorro. "Everyone was waiting for Ortega to win. Jimmy Carter was ready to throw his arms around the bastard. Chamorro won, and everybody was thrown for a loop.

"You know this vote and the vote to change the name of Leningrad back to Saint Petersburg were repudiations of communism.

"Sometimes you've just got to say that you've backed the wrong horse. I think I took a risk by pushing Yeltsin during my meeting with Bush, but I was proved right. If Yeltsin comes to New York, I'll call on him. Here," he said, handing me a draft of a Western Union telegram addressed to Yeltsin. It was a short note of congratulations. "I thought he'd like to know that somebody out here is for him.

"My concern is that Gorbachev will co-opt Yeltsin and justify calling for aid to the center. They always say that the money would come from international sources. Bullshit! The U.S. contributes one third to the World Bank and the IMF [International Monetary Fund]."

When I told him that Sununu had praised the agreement between Gorbachev and Yeltsin by saying that "one plus one equals three," Nixon erupted in disbelief. "*Sununu,* for God's sake? Who the hell is he? He's smart, but a chief of staff shouldn't be gassing around about foreign policy. The only one who is responsible down there is Scowcroft, and he doesn't like Yeltsin because he made a horse's ass out of himself the last time he was here," he said, referring to Yeltsin's alcohol-fueled boorishness during his 1990 visit to Washington. "But we have to understand that he is our best hope for reform in Russia."

Nixon, meanwhile, continued to work on the book, focusing primarily on developments in the Soviet Union. He watched closely Yeltsin's visit to Washington on June 20 and how "pained" Bush looked receiving him, even as Yeltsin supported policies and ideas that had long been a part of America's cold war philosophy: the end of communism, democratic and free-market reform, Baltic independence, and an end to Soviet subsidies to Afghanistan and Cuba. Nixon was disappointed with, though not surprised by, Bush's reaction to Yeltsin and totally impressed with the Russian president's conduct and agenda.

"I am going to include a major section in this book on Yeltsin because the way this administration has treated him and what he represents is despicable," he said on June 21 as we spoke in his office.

"Yeltsin is vigorous and energetic—no political small talk, forges real connections with people. I think he left a very good impression. I can't understand Bush," he said with a look of dismay. "When they were talking about the independence movements, Bush said it was the center's decision to make. He should have said, 'Fine. We accept that for now, but we hope that the center will take notice and make way.'

"What they do within their borders is secondary to their foreign policy, but it *is* important. Yeltsin believes that they have to mind their internal business; Gorbachev still believes that they're an international player. They are, but only to the extent that they have nuclear weapons. I'm putting all of this into that chapter. It will raise a lot of eyebrows, but what the hell; it's right!"

On June 26, Nixon happened to see a ten-page article and interview with Bush in *U.S. News & World Report* in which the president reaffirmed his trust in Gorbachev. Nonplussed, Nixon walked into my office and tossed the magazine on my desk.

"Read this. You're not going to believe your eyes. I know that we used to think it was all Baker's influence, but now I know that it's Bush. I am so damned disappointed. He's just got to prove he was right in backing Gorbachev, even when all the signs are pointing the other way."

I asked if he would consider writing to Bush to express privately his displeasure with the policy, and he frowned. "No, I don't want to fly right into him on this and tell him he's wrong. He knows where I stand." Nixon had decided that whatever political capital he had could be used against Bush at a more opportune time.

Meanwhile, the failure of the Communist ideology that had held Yugoslavia together since 1945 prompted a violent dissolution of the state. With the collapse of their unifying philosophy, the republics of Yugoslavia broke away from central control and began to confront one another, armed with historic, religious, and ethnic enmity. The crisis was not a civil war between Serbia and Croatia; it was an international war between two nations that had been forcibly and artificially brought together by communism. Nixon feared that the disintegration of Yugoslavia would set a dangerous precedent for the Soviet Union. And unlike Yugoslavia, the Soviet Union was a nuclear power.

The administration's "stability at any price" approach to the crash of communism involved trying to stifle the upheaval associated with the demand for democratic and free-market reform in order to preserve the certainties of the old order. It was a desperate and ultimately unworkable trade-off. Stability was an admirable goal, but not when the alternative would generate a more democratic order. The tumult in Yugoslavia, however, represented the worst of both worlds: instability and undemocratic reaction. The world could not afford to have a similar situation in the Soviet Union.

The American-designed "grand bargain" became central to the Western push to preserve Communist stability in the Soviet Union. According to Nixon, the major infusion of Western aid it proposed was about three years too late. When Gorbachev's reforms in the late 1980s seemed promising and when he was the best hope for some brand of democratic reform, aid might have been considered reasonable. But once Gorbachev was overtaken by forces more democratic, aid to the center was counterproductive.

On July 11, Nixon met with one of the primary authors of the "grand bargain," Harvard professor Graham Allison. After their discussion, Nixon invited me to meet Allison, who defended his proposal but conceded that aid could not be delivered as long as the center did not represent the best choice for reform.

After Allison's departure, Nixon nodded for me to go into his office. "I think he came because he wanted to cover all VIPs when pushing the plan. The problem with the plan is that, How does the Soviet Union reform its economy when the only functioning part is the military-industrial complex? Demilitarization is impossible without causing major problems. Our money would be poured into a sinkhole.

"He listened to my arguments and said that he wasn't arguing for stability at any price. He did say, which I think you'll find interesting, that the *Post* piece we did had a big impact on what they finally produced in terms of this plan. But the point is that the plan is the wrong thing at the wrong time."

Allison may have wanted only to cover the VIPs, but Nixon was still pleased by the visit. The "grand bargain" made headlines and sparked debate over how best to preserve and advance the gains of reform. Although Nixon disagreed with the premise of the plan, he was certain that his meeting with Allison would have an impact on how the academic community viewed the Soviet transition.

Simes called with some gossip from Washington on July 14. He told Nixon that Baker had tried to block Nixon's meeting with Gorbachev in the Soviet Union and that he had instructed the embassy not to send anyone to escort Nixon to the airport. Nixon declared this behavior "reprehensible" and "petty" but gleaned some satisfaction from the fact that Baker perceived him as a real threat to his hold over the nation's foreign policy.

The annual meeting of the Group of Seven (G-7) industrial countries, meanwhile, was about to convene in London. The heads of state of the United States, Great Britain, Germany, France, Japan, Canada, and Italy attended the gathering, which is typically long on photo opportunities and short on substance. This year, however, Gorbachev was invited to represent the Soviet Union as an observer, a status that allowed him to prevail upon the other participants to help him save his dying system.

The mission was futile. The other nations did not announce a major aid package for the Soviet Union, and despite reaching an agreement with the United States on START, the Soviet Union ended the week of July 14 as it had begun it: without financial support from the rest of the world.

Gorbachev, arriving home empty-handed, began a series of desperate measures to signal to the West that he remained committed to reform. In late July, he proposed that Leninism, the ideological foundation for communism, be removed from the platform of the Communist Party of the Soviet Union. He devised a new "union plan," which would have created a voluntary association between the center and the republics, based ostensibly on self-determination and reform. This was simply the next in a lengthy succession of erratic proposals put forth by Gorbachev.

In 1986, he had proposed a general reform plan to begin streamlining the economy and increasing the emphasis on social priorities in the economy. Its slogan was "Acceleration!"

In 1987, he had proposed a broader plan to encourage competition and individual initiative, saying "A house can be put in order only by a person who feels he is the owner" and introducing "democratization."

In October 1989, he had proposed a plan to restore financial soundness to the economy, create a consumer market, regulate monetary demands by the people, and emphasize forms of "socialist public ownership."

In November 1989, a plan had been put forth to denationalize state property, create a stock exchange, provide social protection for the dislocated, and establish antitrust laws and competitive wages.

In December 1989, another plan had been proposed to continue central planning by means of a mixed economy, reduce the budget deficit, and free some prices.

In September 1990, Gorbachev had endorsed the Five-Hundred-Day Plan to allow the republics to set the pace of privatization, decentralize banking, grant property rights and financial markets, and provide a social safety net—only to reject it later that month.

In October 1990, he had proposed a gradual sell-off of state properties, with the center still retaining control over monetary policy, defense, energy, and national resources.

In April 1991, an "anticrisis" plan was advanced, which called for the privatization of some business, emergency measures for food distribution, and economic sanctions for republics that did not meet their obligations to the center.

In July 1991, at the G-7 summit, Gorbachev offered a plan to make the ruble convertible and privatize "nearly 80 percent of retail outlets, public establishments and services, and a number of enterprises in other sectors" through a massive aid commitment from the West. Within a year, "land reform," to alter agricultural production methods, and the conversion of the military-industrial complex to civilian uses would be under way.

The confusion caused by all of these competing proposals led to increasing chaos and dissent. What Gorbachev failed to realize was that events in the Soviet Union were outpacing his proposals. Communism was already discredited; the union was already collapsing. In trying to keep up with forces beyond his control, Gorbachev inflated his rhetoric and tried unsuccessfully to seem as innovative and groundbreaking as he had just a few years before.

Bush, meanwhile, traveled to Russia in early August and met with Gorbachev and Yeltsin, then flew to Kiev, Ukraine, where he warned the Ukrainians against "suicidal nationalism" and seceding from the Soviet Union. He implied that if they seceded, they would find no political, economic, or moral support for their effort in the United States.

The Kiev speech quickly became an indication of how distorted the administration's policy was toward developments in the Soviet Union. The source of the centrifugal forces pulling the republics away from the center was the collapse of the fearsome ideology that had kept them together. The process was irreversible, yet the administration was clinging to outdated notions of what constituted the Soviet Union. Bush's decision to preserve the status quo despite most Ukrainians' desire for independence flew in the face of the principles that had always informed American policy.

The administration's argument that chaos would prevail if Gorbachev left the scene did not hold. As they faced increasing hardship, the Soviet people did not run hysterically and violently into the streets. Instead, they demonstrated peacefully for change, then elected leaders who promised to take them systematically and methodically toward reform. Until mid-August, in fact, the Soviet transformation had been more orderly than most of the revolutions in Eastern Europe, Gorbachev's policy swings notwithstanding.

Suddenly, that changed. During the early morning hours of August 19, a hard-line contingent of KGB, army, and Interior Ministry personnel overthrew Gorbachev, placed him under house arrest, seized power, and announced a state of emergency. Nixon called me at seven o'clock, panicked that much of what he had written for the book on the Soviet Union was now irrelevant.

When I arrived at the office that morning, his attention had turned to the immediate political situation in Moscow. He had spoken with Kissinger, Haig, Simes, and Ambassador Robert Ellsworth to get their analyses and to give them his own. Nixon summoned me after the conversations.

"Well, Henry admits that he was right!" he laughed. "But you know, he was, and frankly so was I. Gorbachev is under house arrest at his dacha, but there aren't any large demonstrations supporting him because he's so unpopular."

"Which may explain why they didn't apprehend Yeltsin," I said.

"I know. Can Gorbachev come back? Not really," Nixon continued. "If there is a counterrevolution, they won't bring back Gorbachev but someone willing to go further." Nixon rolled a pen between his fingers. "But there is the possibility that he could become a martyred reformer and come back to power. I don't want to sound too conspiratorial, but Gorbachev may even be in on this. Who knows?

"And have you noticed how foolish Bush looks—wrong all along."

The coup d'état was under way. Hard-liners who had had enough democratization and chaos overthrew their weak and irrelevant president and tried to restore some kind of dictatorship. Soldiers swept into the streets of Moscow, tanks surrounded key government buildings, and the Communists promised a return to the darkness of iron rule. Old tactics, however, proved meaningless in the new situation.

The following day, Nixon complained to me that Bush was too available to the press. "Sometimes silence is the most powerful weapon. Then you come out with a statement," he said. When informed of Bush's decision to send Robert Strauss to Moscow on a "fact-finding mission," Nixon cried, "What the hell is that? What more do we need to know? And I'll tell you another thing: I heard Bush say 'I've said over and over again that Yeltsin is supported by the United States.' He said it once!"

He shook his head. "I don't see Gorbachev coming back, and I don't see massive violence. If the hard-liners can hold on for two months—which I don't think is possible—they may be in for a while."

The coup collapsed the next day, August 21, to Nixon's mild surprise. "I didn't think it would be over this soon, but it goes to show that the center cannot hold. There is no power there—and no more fear. Gorbachev will have to submit to an election now, which he cannot win. He's finished."

The coup may have finished Gorbachev, but it led to the rise of Yeltsin. During the height of the coup, when its outcome was uncertain, Yeltsin climbed atop one of the tanks surrounding the seat of the Russian parliament, the White House, and proclaimed defiantly that the hard-liners would fail and democracy would succeed. His courage in the face of reactionary might served him well politically: he emerged from the coup a respected and popular leader, the symbol of positive change in a new Russia.

Nixon was impressed. "Yeltsin is the best hope for the goddamned place; no one can deny it now. Freedom and democracy and free markets—whatever type they have and end up with—are on trial. If they don't work, there could be massive disillusionment and a counterrevolution. No revolution is permanent if it doesn't work. But governing after winning is just hard: that's Yeltsin's challenge. The guy's got guts, but he's going to need our help."

Four days after the coup began, Gorbachev held a press conference and wasted an opportunity to make himself newly relevant. Rather than embrace the inevitable transformation, he quoted Lenin and reiterated his commitment to communism. It was clear that Gorbachev was now the last Communist, not the first democrat.

He did, however, opt to form a coalition government with Yeltsin, and five days after the coup began, he quit as general secretary of the Communist Party.

People poured into the streets, destroying statues of Lenin and Marx and changing the Communist mantra inscribed under their likenesses from WORKERS OF THE WORLD, UNITE! to WORKERS OF THE WORLD, FORGIVE ME. Seven republics immediately announced their independence from Moscow, and the others soon followed. Gorbachev, stripped of power, was a figurehead. Many Western countries, with the obvious exception of the United States, recognized the Baltics' independence. Most remarkably, the Communist Party was outlawed in Russia.

The tumultuous events of the week sent Nixon scrambling to rewrite his chapter on the Soviet Union. The entire premise of the chapter had been that the United States needed to support the gradual move to democratic and free-market reform while the Communists were eased from the scene.  Fortunately for history but unfortunately for Nixon's book, the Soviet people had taken matters into their own hands far more quickly, peacefully, and effectively than anyone had predicted. Nixon's argument had to be recast from the point of view of how the United States should deal with the Soviet Union to that of how it should deal with a disappearing center and fifteen new states.

Gorbachev had claimed in the past that the West should support him because he was the only guarantor of reform and stability and the sole protector against a return to power by the hard-liners. The claim was proved false. The hard-liners who overthrew Gorbachev and assumed power were able to retain power for only sixty hours. In the battle between the old reactionaries and the young democratic forces, tanks were pitted against ideas, and the tanks never had a chance.

Gorbachev returned from house arrest believing that the Communist Party—from which he recruited a cabinet of reactionary betrayers—might still become a vehicle for reform. "I will fight to the end," Gorbachev said at his first post-coup news conference, "for the renewal of the party."

Lacking an electoral mandate and heading a rapidly weakening central government, Gorbachev had only the Communist Party as his constituency, and even the party betrayed him. Now the party was withering away—with the radical reformers on their own track—and Gorbachev was left with a constituency of one: himself.

He was a classic transitional figure. Too closely associated with the tyranny of the past and the chaos of the present, he lacked the credibility to be an effective reformer. He took the crucial first step, but the rest of the steps would have to be made by others.

When the West assumed that Gorbachev was indispensable, it assumed that the alternative to him would be worse. In fact, the alternative turned out to be better: Yeltsin stood atop a tank during the coup and faced down dictatorship.

Franz Kafka once observed, "Every revolution evaporated, leaving behind the slime of bureaucracy." Real reform meant a dismantling of the old institutions and a full uprooting of the system. Like their French revolutionary counterparts of 1789, the Russian revolutionaries might attempt to conduct the revolution to its professed end—freedom—and keep it from descending further into chaos, or they might create a vacuum to be filled by those wanting some variant of communism or democratic socialism.

"This coup had an eight-column head in the *Times* for eight days straight," Nixon said on August 27. "The last time that happened was Watergate."

He was sitting at his desk in the study of his residence, gazing over a pile of material he needed in order to rewrite the chapter. "Look at all of this," he said, tapping the top of the pile. "I've got newspaper clippings, magazines, books—you name it. But I suppose it's better that it happened now rather than right as the book went to press!"

He rose from the desk and moved to his favorite chair. "Sit down, please. Oh, no. You look like you just heard something bad. What is it?"

I explained that I was irritated by Bush's lingering support for Gorbachev and by the failure of the United States to offer diplomatic recognition to the Baltic states.

Nixon smiled. "I know. Even Finland beat us to the punch on that one."

I looked directly at him and asked, "Did you ever think that you'd see the end of the cold war?"

He looked at me for several long moments. "No, never. When Khrushchev said 'Your grandchildren will live under communism' and I said 'Your grandchildren will live in freedom,' I knew he was wrong, but I wasn't sure I was right. Now it turns out that I was."

It was a poignant moment. Nixon had witnessed the beginning of the cold war, led the United States through it, both in and out of office, and lived to see the end of it. It was a tremendously gratifying experience for him. His entire political career, which had been based upon a steadfast and vigilant approach to containing and ultimately defeating Soviet communism, had been vindicated. Witnessing the successful conclusion of the cold war brought him pure, unadulterated satisfaction.

Meanwhile, the waning Soviet presidency forced Gorbachev to threaten to submit his resignation in late August, but because the state itself was collapsing, the threat carried little weight. Nixon reacted on August 29 with biting sarcasm.

"Threatening to resign, huh?" he asked of Gorbachev's professed intention. "Ha! Kissinger threatened it four or five times. Haldeman did almost every day, until I told him to watch it because I might say 'fine.' "

"The threat only means something when there is leverage involved," I said. "Gorbachev doesn't have any, and besides the country may take him up on it."

Nixon smiled weakly, perhaps reflecting on his own situation. "I know. By the way, I can't believe that the *Times* questioned Yeltsin's democratic ideals. They never questioned Gorbachev's! Yeltsin may not mean the same kind of democracy as, say, we do, but he's a far better choice in terms of reform than Gorbachev ever was!"

He shifted in his chair and switched subjects. "People attacked détente, but for all its faults it—like our China initiative—opened up the Soviet Union to the world and probably accelerated the cause of reform.

"By the way," he continued, "I wish Bush wouldn't talk about serious issues looking like he does. They catch him coming off the golf course, no tie, baseball cap—my God! Put on a tie! He should be dressed formally when discussing something as important as this. I always wore a suit—perhaps too much. I know it, but I was comfortable in it, and it was appropriate."

Changing subjects yet again, he demolished the idea that it was now a more propitious time to aid the Soviet Union. "Absolutely not. I wouldn't give them a damn thing. I understand the humanitarian aid—Americans are too damn generous anyway—but if you notice who is pushing for it—[Les] Aspin and [Richard] Gephardt!"

"The farm belt," I said.

"Yes!" he exclaimed. "That's just politics. And I see that Kissinger had a disappointing article in *Newsweek*. He's for aid now, but aid now would be just as wasted as if it had been given a few years ago to Gorbachev."

Aid given at this point in the transition would have been lost in a maze of bureaucratic corruption. Power was being wielded arbitrarily through the lower levels of society. Local Communists still controlled the means of production and prohibited the sale of land. Potential entrepreneurs knew that their property could be seized at any time for any reason. Inflation skyrocketed to 250 percent. Productivity declined by 10 percent in 1991, primarily because of worker frustration with rising prices. The threat of strikes loomed. Food and fuel shortages grew worse. Housing was scarce. Goods shortages intensified because of bottlenecks in distribution. Age-old ethnic conflicts raged.

Before the West committed any substantial aid to the Soviet Union, the Soviets needed to prove that they were helping themselves. They needed to adopt democratic and free-market principles and the institutions to sustain them.

Nixon warned that we should not have expected these structures to take root immediately. In fact, the greatest threat facing Yeltsin in the short term was not tanks but the possible loss of confidence among Russians waiting impatiently for better lives.

Aid for this early stage, then, would be humanitarian, technical, and directed to the reformist republics. Its conditions included the proper identification of the constitutional and economic relationships between the republics and the center so the West could determine who was getting the aid; economic stabilization programs; the beginnings of banking and tax systems; laws to protect private property and contracts; and independent judiciaries. Further, the Soviet Union needed to reduce defense and security spending drastically, speed the return of troops from Eastern Europe, and terminate all aid to clients such as Cuba.

As the union fell apart, various entities inevitably emerged—some independent, some confederated, some more powerful than others. This was an inconvenience to those in the West who were accustomed to hearing the Soviet Union speak with a single voice. To many Western observers, particularly Bush and Baker, the sound of many voices was a cacophonous riot. Regauging our diplomacy would not be easy, but we had to recognize that while democratic unity is a strength, Communist unity was a prison.

"And you know," Nixon said, with a slight hint of resentment, "Bush is in the glow of all this, but he didn't do a goddamned thing."

Even when it was clear that Yeltsin had emerged as the new and legitimate leader of Russia, the American president failed to give him the vote of confidence he needed. Bush stalled in his support and hesitated to deal with him. Nixon suspected that he was counting on the collapse of the new Soviet confederacy. This was not only poor policy but a dangerous waste of time: the United States needed to maximize its influence on Russia while the situation there was still in flux.

"I don't want to get bogged down in 'will the interim government work?' " he said as we edited the final draft of his Soviet chapter on September 9. "As you can see, I focused on the meat-and-potatoes questions: Gorbachev and Yeltsin, reform, what it means for their foreign policy, what it means for the United States—the profound stuff. I think it reads pretty well."

It did read pretty well, considering Nixon had spent the previous weekend rewriting the entire chapter once again.

The Soviet Union, he argued, was on an irreversible path of decentralization. The discrepancy between the center—which still wanted to preserve the command structure—and the republics—which wanted a structure based on democratic and economic self-determination—was enormous. The United States had to adjust its relationships with the central body and the republics as power devolved and interests changed. With real and enduring democratic change, the successor states of the Soviet Union could become constructive partners.

The next day, September 10, Nixon wanted to celebrate the completion of *Seize the Moment*. I went to his residence in the late afternoon and found him holding two glasses of white grape juice.

He smiled. "Have a libation. Nonalcoholic, you know. Doctor's orders. Bebe [Rebozo] always tells me to get a second opinion." He raised his glass and toasted the book.

"We came close to not having a book," he said. "Who would have thought that we could pull off a whole rewrite in just a few days? Now we just have to hope that Gorbachev and Yeltsin live! Now that's something we couldn't fix! But at least it's done, and now," he said, lifting a copy of the final draft, "it's up to the publisher."

Two days later, however, he wrote a memorandum to me expressing alarm over how recent developments might affect his manuscript. He feared that the administration would commit itself to an aid package through the IMF, which in turn would direct the money on a government-to-government basis. "Baker could say, 'Who me?,' glossing over the fact that the U.S. provides approximately twenty percent [of the capital for the IMF]." Nixon was concerned that the administration's actions would overtake his point that aid should be provided only after reforms were in place.

He was not inclined to modify the manuscript because he believed that the book would be in stores prior to any action taken by the administration. He did think, however, that Bush might be tempted to make "a grandstand play" by joining with other industrial countries to help the Soviet Union.

The problem with most of the aid proposals was that they failed to recognize that political and economic control in the Soviet Union could not be divorced. The "grand bargain" detached economics from politics as if economic reform were going to proceed in a vacuum apart from the political and social chaos. Economic reform, however, could take place only when the political situation was relatively stable and could succeed only if the political institutions existed to sustain it.

Bush delivered a speech to the United Nations on September 23, and Nixon watched the broadcast nervously. The president did not announce a major plan to aid the Soviet Union, much to Nixon's relief, and focused on the politically safe big picture.

"I thought the speech was OK for the audience," Nixon told me later. "I've done the UN a few times. Worthless, but the media love that fluff. I heard that there are those still pushing for Gorbachev to be UN secretary general."

"A Communist head of the UN?" I asked incredulously.

"We've come far but not that far," he replied.

"I'm surprised they haven't suggested Castro!" I said.

"They will!" He laughed before changing the subject. "You see, what is happening in Yugoslavia is a devastating thing. The center is much stronger there than it is in the Soviet Union, and they're trying to keep the country together by bombing away their opponents. And the administration has got to take a stand on this. They put down nationalism, but they are in effect supporting Serbia, the center, the Communists, at the expense of democracy. All of these words from State? Meaningless. When Baker faults both sides . . ."

"He's guilty of moral equivalence," I said, finishing the thought.

"I'm writing a note to Scowcroft on Yugoslavia, for the record. I don't want historians to think I went along with what this crowd is doing."

Continued U.S. neutrality sent several dangerous signals. First, it signaled to the Soviets that the United States would look the other way if the center tried to regain control of the empire. Second, it signaled to potential demagogues and despots in Eastern Europe and the Soviet Union that the United States would look the other way if they gained power and used authoritarian methods to "stabilize" their situations. And third, it signaled abandonment to China's democratic movement. A neutral American position appeased the aggressors and left the world's democrats adrift. Yugoslavia was a vital test case of our commitment to these democrats, and so far we were failing the test.

In his letter to Scowcroft, Nixon urged the administration to denounce strongly the actions of Serbia before the situation spun out of control and spilled over the borders. This was a war of conquest by the hard-line, Communist Serbian government and federal army against the democratic, independence-minded Croatia. A "profoundly dangerous precedent"—particularly for the democrats in Eastern Europe and the Soviet Union and those wanting more freedom in China—could be set if the hard-liners succeeded in dismembering or destroying with impunity the democratic government of Croatia. He called the Western response "comically tepid," and urged that the president denounce in the "strongest possible terms the brutal aggression" by the Communist Serbs and lead a response to support the democratic forces in Slovenia and Croatia. In post–cold war Europe, as in the Soviet Union, we had to do whatever was necessary to prevent the reversal of peaceful democratic change.

We did not have to commit troops, Nixon argued. But the conflict had to be contained through diplomatic channels by recognizing the democratically elected leaders of Slovenia and Croatia and by seeking a balance of force on the ground. The Serbian Communists would not negotiate unless they were forced to do so.

The world could not afford a war at the very center of Europe. Scowcroft would deliver Nixon's advice to Bush with no guarantee of action, but at least the former president had made his position known.

Nixon ripped Richard Perle's piece, "What the Soviet Army Fears," out of the September 30 issue of *U.S. News & World Report* and left it on my desk. Perle argued that the once powerful Soviet military-industrial complex feared Yeltsin and the new democrats, who would cut military spending drastically. At the top of the piece, Nixon wrote that those running the State Department should read it.

Arms control, meanwhile, dominated much of the discussion between the United States and the Soviet Union. Both sides proposed deep cuts, and Nixon thought that Bush's reductions were "premature" and "distressing." They sought to eliminate a whole category of weapons—tactical or short-range nuclear weapons stationed on land and in the sea—and to take certain long-range missiles off high alert. Nixon reacted cautiously. The Soviets, he said, would not be willing to give up their only remaining claim to superpower status.

"The freeze on mobile missiles is ridiculous," he said on October 6. "It doesn't matter because the Soviet Union has over three hundred and we have zero. I'm worried that Bush is just doing this to shore up Gorbachev."

I indicated that the State Department said it would agree to a nuclear test ban. Nixon erupted. "What? Outrageous! I hadn't heard that one. Well, I hope to God that Baker gets mired down in the Middle East so that it keeps him out of trouble in Russia. What he and Bush don't understand is that this Soviet revolution isn't over."

On October 17, Nixon was the keynote speaker at a fund-raiser for Christine Todd Whitman, who was running for the U.S. Senate in New Jersey against incumbent Democrat Bill Bradley. Polls showed her running far behind Bradley, but Whitman's strategy was to gain recognition and experience in order to be better positioned to run for governor in 1993. Nixon liked Whitman, thought she had a dynamic future in the Republican Party, and was pleased to have the chance to support her.

"I hope the audience got something out of it," he said to me later that night. "When I give a speech like that, I usually make five to eight drafts and go over it enough times until I know it and can deliver it from memory. But I never memorize it word for word because it would sound too fake. Doing it this way allows for greater flexibility, spontaneity, and extemporaneous humor." He suddenly sounded dejected. "But I can never understand why no one really mentions that I do all of this without notes and get standing ovations. Is it the message or the messenger?" And then he answered his own question. "Both I think. For your own political future," he advised me, "make a note of the fact that the media may just ignore you.

"A speech is conversation—remember that. It's important that you connect with the audience even if they have no idea what you are talking about. It's hard to talk about, say, Soviet reform with people who aren't clued in to it as well as you are. It's hard to bring your arguments down to a level they can understand. It's not that they aren't smart; it's just that foreign policy isn't their bag. And it's hard to simplify it when it's *your* bag. But you've got to do it, or you're going to lose them."

Nixon had cast the revolution and the reform process in terms everyone at the Whitman fund-raiser could understand. His mission was to convince the American people that it was in the interest of the United States to support the forces of reform because if they failed, we would be forced to wage a new cold war. It was a message he would repeat until the day he died.

Charles Krauthammer's October 14 essay in *Time,* "The Man Who Loved Dictators," appeared on my desk on October 30. It criticized harshly the Bush administration's tendency to favor dictators and stability over democrats and independence as "shortsighted" and irresponsible.

"I didn't think you had seen this yet," Nixon said when I brought it with me for our usual morning discussion. "It's damn good. He's right, you know. Bush is still taking the stability line with regard to Gorbachev. The Soviet Union is kaput. It's nauseating."

Nixon anticipated that his own book would generate controversy not just in the policy community but within the administration. His advocacy of Yeltsin and his dismissal of Gorbachev were contrary to the administration's long-standing position, and since neither Bush nor Baker was willing to take Nixon's advice, both clung to their outdated support of Gorbachev. Even as late as November 1991, the State Department's position was that the Soviet Union needed to be re-created politically, which not only was a grave misreading of the situation but showed an utter disregard for the will of the Soviet people. Nixon was dumbfounded, but he knew that *Seize the Moment* would draw public attention to the administration's antiquated and failing policy and bring pressure to change it.

Yeltsin, meanwhile, gathered greater power. He asked for and received new authority to push his plan for radical economic reform in a drive that was tantamount to ending the old Soviet central government. By taking control, however, Yeltsin became vulnerable to accusations of authoritarianism, even by those who conceded that authoritarianism was needed to save the country from total economic collapse. Unable to handle a disintegrating economy, increasing shortages, and a growing threat to public order, reform leaders favored strengthening executive power in order to be able to make quicker economic decisions.

This did not concern Nixon. Yeltsin was far more determined than either Gorbachev or any other political rivals to put Russia on a democratic and market track. Authoritarianism, with its long tradition in Russia, would inform all attempts to change the system.

Nixon said to me on December 4, "Gorbachev is fading fast. As I told Bush in April, he's burned out. His appeals for union are pathetic. People are willing to condemn Yeltsin for exercising authoritarianism, but they still praise Gorbachev for being a Communist and wanting to hold together a state that was put together and held together by force. It's unbelievable. But look, Yeltsin has to do what he has to do to keep the goddamned place from falling apart."

Nixon wanted Yeltsin to prevail, but he grew increasingly worried that Gorbachev would resign before *Seize the Moment* was published, dating the book immediately. "Emotionally," Nixon said reflectively on December 14, "he may resign. How can he still be a president of a country that doesn't really exist anymore? This new agreement to form a commonwealth between Russia, Byelorussia, and Ukraine put the nail in the coffin for the Soviet Union.

"But he seems like he's lost it, talking about the union as if it still exists and irrationally attacking Bush for being disloyal to him!" He lowered his eyes as he sat across from me in his office. "I know that when you are at the center of something like this, it's easy to lose touch with reality. But he's got a greater responsibility here than protecting himself. The right thing for him to do is to resign, even if it's the wrong thing for our book!"

The material in the book would survive the rapidly changing situation in the Soviet Union, but Nixon knew that Gorbachev would not. December 18 brought the announcement that the Soviet flag, which had flown over the Kremlin for over seventy years, would be replaced by the Russian tricolor before the last day of the year. The end of the Soviet Union, one of the most feared, tyrannical, and deadly empires in the world, was at hand. The country that had killed millions of its own citizens, terrorized and repressed those who survived, and extended its domination by force over millions of others now limped to its demise.

Nixon called me into his office early that morning, his voice filled with emotion and satisfaction. "The symbolism is so important," he said. "I have seen that damn flag—the hammer and sickle—seven times in seven trips over there. It will be good to see it come down."

He cleared his throat. "Well! It's a moving thing."

Nixon rarely showed emotion, but when the country that he had devoted his entire life to trying to defeat was finally vanquished, his sense of vindication was overwhelming. When Gorbachev resigned and the Soviet flag was finally lowered from its Kremlin perch on Christmas Day, the anti-communism on which Nixon had so successfully built his career was exonerated.

That Nixon had lived to see that day was a form of justice in itself. He and others—such as Reagan—who had been often derided for calling the Soviet

Union an evil empire could now take comfort in the fact that they had been on the right side of history. Nixon, of course, had known that all along.

Hundreds of copies of *Seize the Moment* arrived during the last week of December, and Nixon signed personalized letters to those receiving a complimentary copy. Policy makers, opinion makers, heads of state, and friends got copies as soon as they could be shipped. Timing was critical: Gorbachev had just resigned, and the newly independent republics were positioning themselves for Western attention and aid. Nixon wanted the book in the hands of those making decisions and those influencing the decisions as quickly as possible.

In almost every interview Nixon gave in support of the book, he emphasized the need for the United States to consider financial support for the democratic forces in the former Soviet Union, particularly in Russia. During the cold war, the United States and its allies had spent trillions of dollars containing Soviet expansionism and influence. For a fraction of that amount, the West could help prevent the former Soviet Union from slipping back into repression.

He stressed the urgency of the Russian situation: the need to maintain social cohesion, purge old thinking and old structures, contain enflamed nationalism, implement lasting political and economic change, and establish new ties with the nations of the world. He argued for a serious reevaluation of our own political, military, and economic relationship with Russia. He emphasized the need to work with leaders whose power flowed from the votes of the people.

Although encouraged by positive reviews of the book, Nixon was disappointed that he had not heard any direct and immediate response from either Bush or Scowcroft.

"I am shocked to hear that Congress has invited Gorbachev to speak," Nixon said when he called me on January 16, 1992. "Haven't any of these clowns been paying attention? Bush and Baker I can understand, but Congress? What the hell is going on?"

I suggested that the invitation may have been issued to offset Yeltsin's visit to the UN and his summit with Bush, and Nixon considered it. "This is why we haven't heard from Bush, Scowcroft, and the rest," he said. "Our message is one of tough pragmatism. It goes against everything they've done so far. We have got to seize the moment, as the book says. And we don't have much time. They have enormous problems over there. Yeltsin should not have to worry about tepid support from us."

Nixon positioned himself to be the West's foremost spokesman and advocate for aid to the new Russia. Just as the United States helped our adversaries in World War II to recover, we needed to help Russia recover from the cold war. An investment in peace and a new democratic partnership, aid could help to ensure the survival and success of the Russian democratic and free-market reform process. Instead of leading a global rescue effort, the United States needed to lead efforts to give targeted and accountable assistance that would help the Russians help themselves. It was, Nixon argued, the single greatest American foreign policy challenge of the end of the twentieth century.

A significant part of his strategy to advance this idea—and himself as its premier spokesman—was a major policy conference sponsored by the Richard Nixon Library and Birthplace, to be held in Washington in March. Nixon's speech was to be one of the centerpieces of the conference, and he intended to make the most of it. Knowing that he would use his speech to herald Yeltsin, he rejected the idea of inviting Gorbachev to speak. Further, Nixon understood that he would have to do something dramatic and sensational if he were to persuade Bush to change American policy.

The president did not help his situation with Nixon when he convened his own conference on aid to the former Soviet Union in Washington on January 22. With forty-seven participating countries, the conference quickly degenerated into a nonproductive photo opportunity. Nixon was incensed.

"First of all," he raved, "the Bush and Baker idea of U.S. leadership is to collect the world together and let them all talk. They're obsessed with the collective-action bullshit. Second, I think they're trying too hard to project that they're leading—like this aid thing is what they wanted all along. They did not. And forty-seven countries? They all want their piece of the pie. It's a joke."

I suggested that the conference could have been more effective with just four or five great powers participating. Nixon paused and bit his lower lip. "We need to take the lead. I don't just mean the United States. I mean," he said, pointing to himself, "*we* need to take the lead."

It was a revealing comment. Nixon clearly had begun to think about how and when he would address the question of aid to Russia. If Bush failed to act before the conference, Nixon would force him to act.

In late January, Yeltsin visited the United States for the first time since being elected president of the Russian republic. He got a warm and serious reception, leading Nixon to believe that Yeltsin had achieved the level of acceptance he needed to gain U.S. support for his initiatives.

"He must not fail," Nixon said on February 2. "And we can't let him. If he does, we'll see regressions across Eastern Europe, Russia, and even China. Look at what's happening to Yugoslavia. They're trying to reduce identities to the lowest collective level. But you *cannot* force it," he said, clenching his fist. "We've got to do something, or we're going to have a bigger mess on our hands."

When I asked how he planned to get the public's attention focused on foreign policy, he replied, "They *don't* care about foreign policy. But they should because if Russia goes down, all of this domestic crap that everyone is campaigning on isn't going to mean a goddamn. All of our resources are going to have to go into a new competition." He paused. "Look, I know that foreign policy isn't popular. But the president just has to talk about it. He's got to lead."

The end of the cold war brought reminders that the world is an imperfect place. The twentieth century survived two great political distortions: fascism and communism. When the hammer and sickle came down over the Kremlin, the twentieth century had beaten them both, and man's hope of a freer and richer future had become much brighter.

This did not mean a world at peace. On the contrary, it meant a time of instability as those who once were sheltered under a superpower's wing emerged to fight their own battles. No single country could shape a peaceful post-Communist world by itself. The United States had the necessary military power but too little of the necessary money. Japan had the money but not the will. Europe had some money, some military power, but not the cohesion. A coalition of the world's democracies, led by the United States, would have to do it.

Washington in particular had to remember that Russia was the heir of a proud and heroic tradition and that the collapse of the Soviet Union was a devastating blow to its national pride. The administration had to make clear in actions and words that it considered Russia an appropriate partner in world affairs, with legitimate security interests. A nuclear-armed Russia no longer needed the territorial buffers it traditionally considered so essential, so the resources that had been put into imperial expansion could now be put into economic recovery.

At the same time, Russia had to understand that new expansionism would exact a heavy price. A reactivated cycle of confrontation between Russia and its neighbors on one side and the rest of the world on the other would block any assistance. If, however, Russia respected the new situation and remained within its borders, a significant Western aid program would be in order.

Baker made an egregious mistake when he announced upon his return from Moscow in early February that the United States might give the Russians five billion dollars. The amount was clearly arbitrary and not connected to a plan for conditional disbursement. The statement, considered by Nixon to be highly irresponsible, not only confused an already chaotic situation but reinforced the idea that the administration's Russian policy was adrift.

"I think that one of the major reasons the book is doing so well is that Bush just doesn't have it to bring people to the mountaintop and offer a new vision for the world," he said on February 12.

The job had fallen to him. Nixon believed that Bush wanted Yeltsin to fail in his reform efforts in order to prove that he was right to cling to Gorbachev. A military coup was possible, and the alternative to Yeltsin would undoubtedly be less inclined to reform. The United States could wait no longer to act. On February 21, Nixon set his own plan in motion.

"If the situation gets any more desperate in Russia," he said, "the strong hand will have to return, and we will have no one to blame but ourselves. I have been out there talking, but no one in the goddamned administration is listening. Bush and Baker are still hung up on the Gorbachev thing, and even if Baker were inclined to do what I am advising, he still wouldn't do it because the idea originated with me. What else can we do?"

I responded with what I thought was the logical solution. "Sir, perhaps you should consider writing a policy memo to the man himself."

Nixon looked at me and asked, "To Yeltsin?"

"No," I said, "to Bush."

Nixon considered the option. He did not want to court embarrassment by confronting the president, but he had to find a way to force Bush to act in behalf of Russia without appearing to pressure him. Nixon drew upon his formidable diplomatic experience and decided to draft a memorandum not to Bush but to those whom Bush could not ignore.

Concealing his intentions, Nixon told me, "I will consider the idea. An approach *like that* may be worthwhile."

"If you do decide to go ahead with it, sir, you can then do a mailing so that it reaches a wider audience," I suggested, unaware that he had already reached a similar conclusion.

Two days later, he called me at home and said, "I have decided not to take this to Bush directly. Monica, he knows what to do. He's just not doing it. I am going to write a secret memo and distribute it," adding slyly, "if you know what I mean."

Over the next few days and in preparation for his appearance at the Nixon Library conference, whose theme was America's Role in the Emerging World, Nixon wrote a scathing essay, "How the West Lost the Cold War." He asked me to read it at different stages and offer suggestions on content and style. The final draft, however, was his product. On February 28, Nixon read the essay for a final time. He called me into his office and gave me a copy.

"There," he said, handing it to me. "That is your copy of history. Read it, and tell me what you think."

It was a devastating indictment of Bush's policy, which he considered hesitant in tone, trivial in content, and humiliating in its effect.

"While the candidates have addressed scores of significant issues in the presidential campaign," he began,

the most important issue since the end of World War II—the fate of the political and economic reforms in Russia—has been virtually ignored. As a result, the United States and the west risk snatching defeat in the cold war from the jaws of victory.

He continued with a stern warning:

We have heard repeatedly that the cold war has ended and that the west has won it. This is only half true. The communists have lost the cold war, but the west has not yet won it. . . . Today, the ideas of freedom are on trial. If they fail to produce a better life in Russia and the other former Soviet republics, a new and more dangerous despotism will take power, with the people trading freedom for security and entrusting their future to old hands with new faces.

This sense of urgency pervaded the rest of the memorandum. He compared the significance of the democratic revolution in the Soviet Union to Napoléon's defeat at Waterloo in 1815, the Versailles peace conference in 1919, and the development of NATO and the Marshall Plan in 1947 and 1948, some of the most defining moments in recent history.

"Russia," he wrote,

is the key to success. It is there that the final battle of the cold war will be won or lost. If freedom succeeds in Russia—if President Yeltsin's economic reforms succeed in creating a successful free-market economy— the future will hold the promise of reduced spending on arms, cooperation in coping with crises around the world, and economic growth through expanded international trade. More important, freedom's success will reverberate in the world's last isolationist strongholds of communism—North Korea, Cuba, Vietnam, and China.

After identifying the positive ramifications of democratic success in Russia, he outlined the dire consequences of its failure. The next three paragraphs began with urgent if-then scenarios.

If Yeltsin fails, the prospects for the next fifty years will turn grim.

Extreme Russian nationalism will dominate, bringing new repression.

If a new despotism prevails, everything gained in the great peaceful revolution of 1991 will be lost.

War could envelope the former Soviet Union, and emboldened new despots could threaten our interests worldwide.

If freedom fails in Russia, we will see the tide of freedom that has been sweeping over the world begin to ebb, and dictatorship rather than democracy will be the wave of the future.

Nixon then issued a desperate plea to the West to

do everything it can to help President Yeltsin succeed. . . . The bottom line is that Yeltsin is the most pro-western leader of Russia in history. Moreover, whatever his flaws, the alternative of new despotism would be infinitely worse.

Next, Nixon reviewed the modest things the United States and the West had done so far, including providing agricultural credits, humanitarian aid, and Peace Corps volunteers. "This," he wrote, "is a pathetically inadequate response."

He proposed a better plan: continued humanitarian aid, the creation of a "free enterprise corps" that would send thousands of Western businesspeople to Russia to help prepare the Russians for the mechanics of the free market, the rescheduling of the Soviet debt, greater access to Western markets for Russian exports, the provision of billions of dollars through the IMF for currency stabilization, and the creation of a single Western-led organization to evaluate Russian needs and coordinate all public and private aid projects.

Our allies could shoulder some of the burden, he wrote, but

to play in this game, we must have a seat at the table. To get a seat at the table, we must be ready to put some chips in the pot. The stakes are high, and we are playing as if it were a penny-ante game.

The gambling metaphor was deliberate: it reinforced the idea that the West could lose everything in terms of peace and prosperity if it did not act to improve the odds of success.

Nixon continued with grand doses of idealism and realism:

Opinion polls indicate that foreign policy rates only in the single digits among issues that voters consider to be important. . . . But the mark of great political leadership is not simply to support what is popular but to make what is unpopular popular if that serves America's national interests.

Further,

> Aid to Russia and other reformist republics of the former Soviet Union is not charity. We must recognize that what helps us abroad helps us at home. If Yeltsin is replaced by a new aggressive Russian nationalist, we can kiss the peace dividend good-bye. . . . Tinkering with the tax code or launching domestic initiatives will have little economic significance if the new hostile despotism in Russia forces the west to rearm. On the positive side, if Yeltsin succeeds, a free-market Russia will provide an opportunity for billions of dollars in trade, which will create millions of jobs in the United States. Most important, a democratic Russia would be a nonexpansionist Russia, freeing our children and grandchildren in the next century of the fear of armed conflict because democracies do not start wars.

He ended with an appeal to Bush's vanity:

> President Bush is uniquely qualified to meet this challenge. The brilliant leadership he demonstrated in mobilizing the coalition abroad and the American people at home to win victory in the Persian Gulf war can ensure that the cold war will not end just with the defeat of communism but also with the victory of freedom.

The memorandum was an exercise in defiance. It represented Nixon's refusal to disappear, his refusal to let his advice go unheeded, his refusal to accept defeat. His determination to be heard and obeyed on matters of national interest inspired tactics that were sometimes manipulative but always clever.

Nixon blended a unique combination of realism, pragmatism, and idealism into his message on Russia, but his arguments were not particularly original. That it was Nixon delivering the message, however, changed the tenor of the debate.

His objective was not to humiliate Bush but to protect him. With Democratic front-runner Bill Clinton emphasizing the state of the economy and other domestic issues, Bush was forced to answer Clinton's charges and play on Clinton's field. Nixon tried to give Bush political cover under which to take the initiative on Russia and preempt a "wishy-washy" nonresponse. By writing the memorandum, he tried to give the Bush campaign direction, vision, purpose, and a central theme around which it could organize itself and that could not be addressed adequately by Clinton.

The attacks of the memorandum were part of the highwire game of presidential politics. Nixon risked incurring the jealousy and resentment of those in the administration who were responsible for the nation's foreign policy. But Nixon had given them a chance to act and repeated warnings that he would not be silenced. When action was not forthcoming, he resorted to his trump card: by virtue of being Nixon, he could make the issue a top priority.

The newsworthiness of the memorandum was clear, and Nixon asked the staff to mail it immediately to several dozen prominent people. Those closest to the president received it first; policy makers, journalists, commentators, and others got it next. The obvious omission was the president himself. Nixon's strategy was simple and shrewd: surround Bush with Nixon's criticism and advice and force Bush to address it without confronting him directly. Nixon knew that his salvo could seriously damage his relationship with the president but decided that the situation in Russia was urgent enough to risk it.

"Bush won't be able to ignore us now," he said that morning. "No, this will definitely do the trick."

The trick would only work, however, if Bush addressed the criticism and then acted to correct the policy. Nixon's behind-the-scenes machinations were cleverly executed. His appreciation of the press's need to have a scoop and his willingness to deliver one right to their doorstep showed his mastery of the relationship between headlines and sources. Having spent his entire life in the political arena, he knew the perils of dealing with the press, but he also knew the opportunities in it. By making the memorandum scarce, he made it momentous.

The impact of the memorandum was not felt immediately. Those who received it first kept it, as Nixon had labeled it, secret. Nixon, however, had no intention of keeping it private. On March 3, he took a call from political consultant Roger Stone, who asked him if he wanted him to leak a copy of the memorandum. Nixon said yes, but Stone did not indicate how and to whom he would release it.

Kissinger called the next day to praise the memorandum, and he was followed on March 5 by Scowcroft, who thanked him for casting the argument so well, *The Wall Street Journal,* which wanted to publish it, and Ambassador Strauss, who thought so highly of it that he intended to bring it to Yeltsin's attention. Daniel Schorr of National Public Radio called me on March 9 to seek permission to quote from the memorandum. Nixon was delighted. With a small circulation, he had gotten exactly the effect he desired. Bush and Baker would see Scowcroft's copy, and the press would not be able to ignore it.

Nixon, meanwhile, wrote drafts of the speech he would deliver at the conference the next week. He was worried about the newsworthiness of the conference, even though Bush had agreed to attend and give a televised keynote speech.

"Conferences generally aren't worth a goddamn," Nixon had said early in March. "It will be a bomb without some controversy. Nobody pays attention to a bunch of talking heads. Action! That's what people pay attention to."

And action was what Nixon delivered. He had written a "secret" memorandum that criticized harshly the incumbent Republican president in the middle of a difficult reelection campaign. It would make news. It would attract attention to the conference. It would reinforce Nixon's role as the country's preeminent elder statesman. And it had the potential to change American policy on the most important foreign policy question of our time.

On March 10, the day before the conference began, *The New York Times* ran a front-page story that changed radically the course of American policy toward Russia and Nixon's relationship with the administration. In the article, by Thomas Friedman, major portions of Nixon's memorandum were reprinted along with positive commentary.

Suddenly, the debate over if and how to aid Russia changed character. No longer would it be acceptable for the president to ignore the situation. Bush was forced to address Nixon's charges—at Nixon's conference. Although Nixon had anticipated a positive response to his attacks, the front-page *Times* story and the ripples it generated were more far-reaching than he had expected.

I arrived at Nixon's hotel on March 10, a few hours after he did. He called for me almost immediately, pointed to the Friedman article on the coffee table, and grinned.

"What do you think?" he asked.

"I think you have a coup on your hands," I replied.

"Well, it will only be a coup if we prevent another one from taking place in Moscow," he quipped. "This caused a stir. No problem with the White House, though. [Chief of Staff Samuel] Skinner called to be sure that I wasn't breaking ranks. Scowcroft saw it and agreed with it; Bush did too. Those staffers he has are amateurs—nervous Nellies. Baker called State and the White House from Europe. He must be fuming!" He snorted. "He was worried that he was attacked in the memo. As usual, he's just worried about himself.

"No one had better pressure me to do a press conference. I won't. This thing stands out there on its own."

The gamble had worked, so far.

"When you do something like this," he said, "you rely on so many people and so many variables that you never know if it's going to work. You write the damn thing; then, you get it out. It's up to those who receive it to do something with it. You leak, but the leak may dry up right away. Friedman didn't have to address this at all, and the editors didn't have to put it on the front page. It's all a roll of the dice. You just hope for the best. In this case, it worked out, but the real test will come tomorrow night, when Bush will have to address it here—they're probably working like hell on another draft—and in front of this kind of audience, the kind of audience that knows I'm right."

The conference, held at the Four Seasons Hotel, attracted a stellar array of prominent policy makers, journalists, and academics. Former secretary of state Henry Kissinger, former secretary of defense James Schlesinger, former national security adviser Zbigniew Brzezinski, director of the Central Intelligence Agency Robert Gates, Senators Daniel Patrick Moynihan and Warren Rudman, Congressmen Lee Hamilton and Stephen Solarz, U.S. Trade Representative Carla Hills, Ambassador Vernon Walters, and General William Odom were among those scheduled to speak. The audience was just as distinguished.

At noon on March 11, Nixon delivered an address that drew upon the content of the memorandum but omitted its scathing indictments. Entitled "The Promise of Peace," it linked vision with policy on the Russian question and on the broader issues of American foreign policy and concluded with the scene of President Harry Truman meeting the early challenges of the cold war by asking for—and getting—aid from Congress to prevent Communist subversion in Greece and Turkey. The challenges of the end of the cold war required the same commitment.

"We responded magnificently to the threat of war then. Can we not respond to the promise of peace now?" he asked his audience. During the cold war, he continued, we united to prevent the expansion of what was evil. Today, we had to unite to advance what was good. No other country could lead the effort to ensure the permanence of the democratic gains in Russia and the other former Soviet republics. In a final rhetorical flourish, Nixon said, "This is our moment of greatness. It is our moment of truth. We must seize this moment because we hold the future in our hands."

He received a standing ovation. With a quick wave to his audience, he left the ballroom and waited for the panel on the U.S. relationship with the new Europe to assemble. The panel, chaired by Zbigniew Brzezinski, included Warren Rudman, Josef Joffe, and Alan Tonelson. Nixon hosted a different group of seven or eight people at his table during each of the panel discussions. I was invited to join him during Brzezinski's panel, and I took my assigned place to the right of Nixon. Schlesinger sat to my right, and a C-SPAN camera was positioned over our heads, trained on Brzezinski delivering his opening remarks.

Nixon, satisfied that he had given an important and well-received speech, was in a jubilant mood. He had done his job, and now it was up to Bush to answer his challenge.

About five minutes into Brzezinski's talk, I saw Nixon lean over and take from the center of the table a writing pad that the hotel had provided. Out of the corner of my eye, I saw him lift a pen and scribble something on the pad. He slid it over to me.

Fearful that the camera above us would pick up Nixon's actions, I turned the pad over before looking at it.

Nixon elbowed me. "Read it," he whispered.

I turned the pad back over and saw a simple question: "Are you having a good time?"

I nodded that I was indeed having a good time, and Nixon smiled. This gesture, perhaps more than any other, illustrated the Nixon I knew. He was at the center of one of the great foreign policy debates of the end of the twentieth century, when the president and leaders around the world would respond to a challenge he had put forth, and he was concerned with my well-being. It was a warm private exchange in the midst of a bruising public battle.

Nixon brought his good mood to the evening's black-tie reception and dinner in honor of Bush. Just before he was escorted to meet the president, Nixon called to me from his suite. He was fixing his bow tie when I came in, and he whirled around when he heard the door close.

"Is the tie straight?" he asked.

"It is."

"Good. You know, they say that every man looks handsome in a tuxedo. I don't know about that. I've seen some ugly ducklings in tuxes, and the clothes don't help them a bit!" He laughed. "Well, away we go. This is it. Either Bush steps up to the plate, or he doesn't."

Nixon hoped for the best but expected the worst. The day before, Bush had given a press conference to control the damage and contradict the premise of Friedman's piece—that Bush and Nixon were at sharp odds over how to proceed on the Russian question. Bush emphasized his "agreement" with Nixon and stressed that the United States had already done a lot in behalf of Russia.

Nixon knew that Bush was a cautious pragmatist who did not like direct confrontation. The memorandum was the most indirect direct attack Nixon could have launched, but the president, rather than answer Nixon's charges and seek to correct his policy, opted to circumvent them.

Nixon introduced the president and held his breath as he watched Bush lose the chance for a history-making diplomatic breakthrough. Bush acknowledged Nixon's foreign policy triumphs, perhaps not realizing that the comparison with his own record did not reflect favorably upon him.

Bush tried to agree with Nixon while dodging Nixon's arguments about aiding Russia. He spoke in general terms about the dangers of "isolationism" and "protectionism," the very themes that his challenger in the primaries, Patrick Buchanan, was using against him. American leadership was required, he said, because "turning our back on the world" was not acceptable. From my position several tables away, I could see Nixon nod gently in agreement.

He continued in Nixon's own terms: "We invested so much to win the cold war. Can we not afford to invest what is necessary to win the peace? If we fail, if we repeat the experience of the Weimar Republic, we will create new problems for our security and that of Europe and Asia. We must support reform, not only in Russia but throughout the former Soviet Union and Eastern Europe."

Nixon looked as if struck by a brief glimmer of hope. Bush just might dispense with politics and lead courageously on the Russian issue. He just might listen to Nixon. He just might earn his place in history by helping freedom win in Russia.

Instead, he backed down. He talked vaguely about "America's role in the emerging world," a phrase lifted directly from the title of the conference, and about the need for "an America that is vigilant and strong."

Then he sidestepped the opening Nixon had created for him: "Carrying out a leadership role in determining the course of the emerging world will cost money." He tried to soften the blow: "But like any insurance policy, the premium is modest compared to the potential cost of living in a warring and hostile world." And then, instead of outlining the costs and benefits of a visionary plan, he relied on warmed-over foreign policy lessons: "There is no distinction between how we fare abroad and how we live at home. Foreign and domestic policy are two sides of the same coin. True, we will not be able to lead abroad if we are not united and strong at home, but it is no less true that we will be unable to build the society we seek here at home in a world where military and economic warfare is the norm."

The arguments were circular and rhetorical. There were no dramatic foreign policy pronouncements, no new Marshall Plans, no strategic vision, and no seizing of any historical moments.

Nixon, disappointed but not surprised, stood and applauded along with the rest of the audience. I could see a smile frozen on his face; Bush had utterly failed him. It was at times like these when Nixon felt most frustrated with being out of power. Even when he furnished the policy, the arguments, and the political cover, his successors sometimes did not act. That Nixon could not act in their places caused him significant distress.

The crowd poured out of the ballroom, and Nixon, after bidding farewell to the Bushes, called for me.

"Come on in," he said, opening the door to the suite for me. "I just got up here, and I must say I need to let off some steam. Could you even *believe* that? I mean, could you even *believe* that performance?"

He paced but instructed me to sit. "What the hell was it? Never in my life have I seen a president step up to the plate, come so close, and then just completely strike out. I gave him everything he needed, including, incidentally, the political protection from *both* Buchanan and Clinton, and he didn't take the bait."

He put a fist to his stomach. "The guy's got no guts. He just doesn't have it. Do you think FDR would have struck out like that after Pearl Harbor? No way. Of course, that was a direct military strike at us, so the decision was easier, but here we don't have war; we have the chance to build peace. It's a positive thing, goddamn it, not a negative thing."

He looked at me. "What did you think? You worked on this memo. Weren't you disappointed?"

I was indeed. The memorandum and its message had consumed Nixon for several weeks. As he prepared to hear Bush's speech that night, he felt the same kind of apprehension he often felt on election nights: the outcome was unknown, the hope of a victory kept alive. With defeat came frustration and displeasure.

"When you go to sleep tonight, remember this," he said. "Presidents have some power; former presidents have none!" And unlike the frozen smile he wore at the end of Bush's speech, this time the smile he flashed was real.

The next morning, the conference continued with discussions of national security priorities, trade, and the U.S. role in Asia. The attention, however, was still on Nixon's challenge and Bush's failure to meet it. Senator Sam Nunn and Ambassador Strauss, both appearing on morning television shows, emphasized the need to aid Russia before it was too late. Every major newspaper covered the speeches, and most saluted what Nixon had done. "He is right," editorialized his old nemesis, *The Washington Post*. And *The New York Times* ran even more Nixon-memorandum and conference-oriented stories.

Nixon asked me to save all articles pertaining to the memorandum, his speech, Bush's speech, and their effects and delighted in seeing each one. He had more power than he thought: not only had he set in motion a chain of events leading to a change in the political reality, but he had, in a single stroke, offered the president a devastatingly effective campaign issue that he failed to use.

More important, the heavy coverage generated the beginnings of informed debate on the issue. To the extent that the discussions and columns led to political pressure that would ultimately lead to action, Nixon welcomed both sympathetic and dissenting views.

On March 16, as the debate continued to rage, someone sent Nixon a political cartoon featuring him shouldering a large globe. The caption read, "Nixon's back."

"Do you think this is positive?" he asked me, smiling.

The high politics of the last few days had been summarized neatly in a drawing. Not only was Nixon back, carrying the weight of the world on his shoulders, but he was leading where the incumbent president could not. The great unanswered question was the extent to which Bush would correct his policy.

Nixon decided to put his speech in writing and mail it to those who had not received the memorandum. As he edited the final draft, he said, "I think it reads better than it sounded. But the delivery was OK. It got the point across." The speech went out, and Nixon hoped that it would apply further pressure on the administration.

"My main concern now," he said on March 20, "is that the superhawks will not be willing to help Yeltsin because they want Russia to collapse totally."

He blinked. "I thought you'd be interested to know that I heard that the *Post*'s front-page headline is that the administration is going ahead with an aid program for Russia." He was clearly pleased. "No one had better stonewall this thing. It looks like we've had an impact after all. It depends, though, on what they have in mind. I can't believe that the *Post* put my credit on the front page. Isn't it something?"

I noted that Baker had now joined the movement for aid to Russia.

Nixon sniffed, "Yeah. Baker is going to claim the idea is his! Although I don't see how, with our message all over the place."

Nixon quickly became the lightning rod for every fear and hope associated with the Russian transition. Four days after the *Post*'s headline, he took a call from a frantic James Billington, librarian of Congress and Russian historian, who expressed concern that a new coup was imminent and that the United States needed to firmly back Yeltsin. Billington's concern became Nixon's.

"Whom should I call in the administration to pass this on to?" he asked. "Billington isn't an alarmist, so I'm inclined to believe him on this. The situation is desperate. I'd like to call Scowcroft, but I don't know."

"What about [Secretary of Defense Richard] Cheney?" I suggested.

"Maybe. But this sounds more like something Gates could deal with." He called the CIA director, who returned the call the following day.

"I'm sure this isn't news to you," Nixon told Gates. "But I think it's vital that we put out a strong statement supporting Yeltsin."

As he hung up, he said to me, "Gates is one of the best ones down there, but I still don't think this will do any good. If they don't listen and Yeltsin fails, the shit's going to hit the fan."

Nixon's worst nightmare was realized on March 28, when he learned that Bush had turned over responsibility on Russian aid to the State Department. He called me at home, utterly disgusted.

"Monica—Baker?" he asked. "*Baker?* Oh, boy. This thing is going to go right down the goddamned tubes. He has resented this issue from day one. I read somewhere that some lower State Department officials had agreed with me. Lower officials? Certainly not Baker! Of course, they wouldn't even be doing this if it weren't for us, right?"

He lowered his voice to a gossipy whisper. "I heard that the only reason Bush is giving a foreign policy speech on Tuesday is because Clinton is giving one on Wednesday."

"Everyone is trying to claim the Russian issue now," I said. "Clinton is correct to try to get to the right of Bush on this."

"I know," Nixon replied. "It's smart politically. But I'm so disappointed that Bush hasn't taken this on himself. He has left himself wide open on this score. And you know, Bush shouldn't be doing this kind of speech just anywhere. Clinton has to; he's the challenger. But this is the kind of speech that belongs in the Oval Office. He's president. He doesn't need to talk to the Cleveland Rotary Club!"

Kissinger, meanwhile, continued to vex Nixon. At the conference, Kissinger had warned strongly against an American policy based upon supporting one Russian leader and ignoring Russia's imperial history. With heavy emphasis on Eastern Europe's tragic history, Kissinger urged strengthening ties to Ukraine and the other republics to counterbalance Russia. Nixon had taken the floor at the conference and publicly disagreed with him, causing a minor stir. Kissinger, however, continued his theme late into March with a piece in *The Washington Post* that took issue with Nixon's "Russia first" approach.

The former president was furious when we met for an afternoon discussion on March 31. "He sets up straw men just so he can knock them down. I think he's vulnerable to the green monster because I eclipsed him on this issue. He just wants to be different so that he gets some attention." He waved the piece at me. "He should treat us better than this. I mean, he usually does. He's usually very good. But this, this is too much."

Nixon's frustration had less to do with Kissinger's argument than with Bush's failure to act at all. The world had benefited enormously from Russia's retreat from empire. For Nixon, Russian weakness was a threat to stability, not a blessing.

The president, meanwhile, decided to give his foreign policy speech on the same day that his main Democratic challenger was to give one of his own. Clinton was wise to talk about foreign affairs this early in the 1992 campaign. Stung by Buchanan's isolationist attacks and the criticism that he had emphasized foreign affairs to the exclusion of domestic ones, Bush had ignored the Russian issue until Nixon pressed him on it. By claiming that the United States did not have the kind of money needed to support such an aid plan, Bush refused to heed Nixon's warnings about chaos and dictatorship. The president closed his window of opportunity and opened one for Clinton.

On April 1, several hours before the president and his challenger were to speak, Nixon fielded separate calls from Scowcroft and Chief of Staff Skinner. Both attempted to head off any future criticism by Nixon of Bush by offering their "sincere thanks" for the "political blocking" the former president had done for the current one.

Nixon was satisfied but concerned about what he would hear in the consecutive speeches. "If either one mentions the Peace Corps, they've lost me."

Bush spoke shortly after eleven o'clock at a White House news conference. He said that "we have a major stake in the success of democracy" in Russia and elsewhere, and he proposed a $24-billion aid package, to be divided into four areas. The industrial powers would contribute $11 billion in bilateral aid, including commodity credits and humanitarian aid, with $2.6 billion coming from the United States; the IMF and World Bank would provide $4.5 billion, with $900 million coming from the United States; $2.5 billion in foreign debt would be rescheduled, none of it by the United States; and a $6-billion ruble-stabilization fund would be established, with $1.5 billion coming from the United States. Total American contributions would be $5 billion.

Lifting Nixon's words once again, Bush argued that if democratic reforms in Russia failed, "it could plunge us into a world more dangerous in some respects than the dark years of the cold war." And "the cost of doing nothing could be exorbitant. The revolution in these states is a defining moment in history. The stakes are as high for us now as at any time in this century."

He added defensively, "This isn't a Johnny-come-lately thing, and this isn't driven by election year politics." It was, however, driven by the pressure coming from his predecessor.

Clinton delivered his speech at the Foreign Policy Association in New York twenty minutes later. Aware that he was at a disadvantage when discussing foreign affairs, Clinton decided to risk it all. He delivered an aggres-

sive address that criticized harshly Bush's handling of international relations. He presented a vision of foreign policy based on democracy and
human rights, since Bush had "failed to provide a compelling vision to justify American engagement abroad after the cold war."

On the issue of aiding Russia, however, Clinton's proposal was very similar to the president's. He supported the idea of Western aid but scored a political point by using the memorandum to embarrass Bush: "Prodded by
Democrats in Congress, rebuked by Richard Nixon, and realizing that I have
been raising the issue in the campaign, the president is finally . . . putting
forward a plan."

In a single stroke, Clinton had chastised Bush and earned some credibility in the one policy area where he lacked it: foreign affairs. Bush needed to
offer a plan that went as far as Nixon wanted but not so far as to agitate his
critics. His dilemma expressed itself in contradictory remarks, such as "it's
not a tremendous amount of money" and "our commitment is very, very
substantial."

Though Nixon claimed that he did not intend to watch the speeches, it
was clear from his remarks to me that he had seen them.

"There was not one mention of a single coordinating body to manage
this aid package," he said, "or debt relief or initiatives by the private sector,
which is what is really going to be responsible for the success of the free market there. I can't believe Bush gave it to State. You've got to get it out of the
government," he said, stabbing the air with his finger. "You've got to get it
out of State. Baker will kill it."

He paused. "He didn't mention the Peace Corps, did he?"

"I hate to tell you this," I replied, "but yes, he did."

Nixon cringed. "Oh, boy! That's Baker too. We've got a major historical
opportunity here, and they're blowing it on the Peace Corps, for God's sakes.
How do you think Clinton did?"

I told him that Clinton gave a hard-hitting speech aimed at qualifying
himself as commander in chief. On the subject of aid to Russia, he sounded
more forceful and committed than Bush, although he also emphasized reliance on collective security.

"Except for the crap on multilateralism, the guy did all right," Nixon said.
"I can't see him in charge of foreign policy, but you know what? After Bush
and Baker, *anybody* might be better in there. Clinton has no experience, and he
might be reckless. But Bush has the experience, and he's still being reckless."

The next day, the dueling speeches dominated the headlines. William
Safire's column in *The New York Times* compared them and decided that
"Clinton came out standing a little taller."

Nixon agreed. He walked into the office that morning carrying his newspaper under his arm. He waved to me from down the hall and dropped the

paper. "Come on in," he shouted to me as he knelt down to pick it up. "The aid thing is headed down the tubes."

I followed him into his office and watched him arrange the paper on my chair so that it was turned back to the Safire column. He pointed to it. "Did you see it yet?" he asked. "He's right. Clinton did have the better speech. Bush may have had the stronger line on Russia, but his heart just isn't in it. That's it. It's the elite thing. And I noticed that the media deleted all references to Yeltsin. It goes back to their support of Gorbachev. Shrewd bastards."

The administration, meanwhile, claimed that it would have proposed an aid package even if Nixon had not advanced the idea first. Despite the late announcement, it said that the plan had been under consideration for months. Even Scowcroft only grudgingly acknowledged that Nixon deserved some credit for raising the issue and for selling the idea of aid to the public. Beyond that, the administration claimed the initiative as its own.

Nixon then decided that if the press asked him what he thought of the plan, he would endorse its original precepts but argue that it was not enough. It was the only way, he thought, to keep the pressure on the administration to follow through.

Many of Nixon's critics argued that the memorandum and the conference were executed by the former president with one objective in mind: personal rehabilitation. Since leaving the presidency in 1974, his central motivation, many believed, was not a selfless commitment to the nation but a quest for renewed political and historical significance. This was unfair, though not entirely inaccurate.

Nixon had invested much of his political life in winning the cold war. When the crucial time came, then, for the West to save its victory and no action was forthcoming, Nixon stepped in. He was driven by a need to remain a player on the world stage but also by the determination to see a favorable conclusion to the conflict that had defined his life.

He liked to recount a comment Winston Churchill once made to him: "I know what keeps a man young. It's power." Nixon sought power and influence out of office not for their own sake but for what he could do with them. His own rehabilitation was a secondary but no less important goal. Because Nixon acted in the country's behalf and because he based those actions on what he believed to be right, positive results inevitably redounded to him. Guiding American policy was done for its own sake; improvement in his historical standing was a benefit he courted in the process.

—

On April 6, Nixon traveled to Washington and briefed twenty-seven senators on the situation in Russia. We talked about the meeting two days later.

"I hit the debt-relief thing hard. I know we've been talking about the IMF, but most of the loans coming out of there would be used to repay bad loans made by Western banks to the Soviet Union, which, as we know, doesn't even exist anymore. The taxpayers would in effect end up repaying the Soviet debt. We've got to focus on areas where we can actually do some good, like transportation and getting their energy resources out of the ground, so they can get their hands on some hard money. We've also got to provide training in managerial skills. They don't know the first thing about business.

"I also said that they've got to get the goddamned thing out of State. They'll just screw it up, even though I see Baker's taking credit for it when he doesn't want to do it, even now. I'm going to continue speaking out on it because it's right and because it drives Baker right up the wall!"

He smiled and added, "I heard that Bush is considering a state dinner for Gorbachev when he comes next month. That is the most outrageous thing I've ever heard! The only nonhead of state to be honored was, and should have been, Winston Churchill. If they do that for Gorbachev, they've lost me."

"Haven't they lost you already?" I said.

He winked. "Why, yes, they have. But I mean, they'll *really* lose me!"

And then Nixon offered up an interesting, and revealing, historical parallel: "Remember Herbert Hoover and what a great job he did with Russian and European aid after the war? He had the misfortune of being president during the Depression, but look at what great work he did abroad out of office. He, of course, worked with the government; I'm working *against* the government."

Nixon's implied analogy with Hoover was revelatory. Both left the presidency under clouds of scandal, and both remained highly unpopular for years after their departures, but both went on to lead reconstructive efforts for former adversaries. Even more hopefully, for Nixon, Hoover's postpresidential activities led to a more favorable historical assessment.

In early May, Gorbachev, Nixon's "man of the past," began a two-week tour of the United States to raise money for his new cause, named appropriately the Gorbachev Foundation. Nixon was disgusted to see the fallen Soviet president embraced affectionately by the Reagans and attracting enthusiastic cheers wherever he went.

"They would never do this for poor Yeltsin," he said to me on May 6. "Never. Reagan has become a pushover when it comes to Gorbachev. And besides, the Reaganites argue that it was the arms buildup that caused communism's collapse. That's partly true, but the real reason was in communism's fatal flaw. Reagan and Bush were in the right place at the right time.

"And as far as Reagan's comments about 'Well I trusted him [Gorbachev]; that's why we were able to end the cold war,' it's ridiculous. Foreign affairs aren't about trust. They're about interests and power," he said.

Nixon, apparently, was in the right place at the right time for Gorbachev. The last Soviet leader called on Nixon in New York on May 13. Having seen the reception Gorbachev got from the Reagans, Nixon was apprehensive about the meeting.

"He's so used to being gushed over," Nixon told me about Gorbachev the day before, "that I don't think he's going to like what I have to say. But then again, he's a serious guy, so he may listen. Of course, he has no power and will have no effect on anything, so I hope this isn't just a courtesy call. But then again, people still come to see *me*, so what the hell!"

The morning of the meeting, Nixon called me into his office as he prepared to leave for New York. "Well, I'm off to see your friend! I've developed this line about aid to Russia that I think is pretty good, and I wanted to run it by you."

He cleared his throat. "Western governments are limited by budgets. Western businessmen are limited by opportunity. What do you think? I don't know. The idea needs some refinement, but there you go."

Upon his return several hours later, Nixon sat down with me in his office and related the conversation with Gorbachev, knowing that of the two deposed leaders, Nixon had the greater influence.

"I'm glad I saw him," he began. "The first thing he said was 'I read your speech from the conference. We have some disagreement, but mainly we agree. I would not have considered my trip complete without seeing you.' " Nixon smiled. "I told him what an extraordinary role he had played not just in Russian history but in the history of freedom. He appreciated that, and he firmly said that he was not planning a comeback. So I told him, 'If you are, don't tell anybody!' He laughed at that; I think he realized that it was some expert advice!" Nixon quipped.

"I told him that his historical legacy depends on whether or not Yeltsin's reforms succeed. Gorbachev knew that; he said that he wants Yeltsin to succeed, but he will criticize him when appropriate, which means, whenever possible.

"Gorbachev suggested that another coup may be possible by the Communist Party apparatchiks. I disagreed but listened to what he had to say on that score. You can't assume anything.

"He's so smooth. Gorbachev and Yeltsin are heavyweights. Not one American politician today can match them. Are you going to put Clinton up against Gorbachev? Please." He scowled.

"Gorbachev looked much better—rested, reenergized. I saw Raisa, who also looked great. She remembered my visit there in '86. Anyway, I'm glad I saw him, if only to get my point across that Yeltsin—the man of today and tomorrow—must succeed. Gorbachev is hoping in his heart that the guy fails, but if Yeltsin goes down, so does Gorbachev—historically, I mean. He's the one who set all of this in motion. And he will reap the rewards or suffer the consequences."

Nixon's meeting with Gorbachev had less to do with policy than it did with personality. Both were out of power, but both sought the attention of those who had succeeded them. Whereas Nixon had moved beyond the ideologies of the cold war, however, Gorbachev remained committed to his own ideologies. He was an unrepentant Communist, even after the philosophy itself had been irreparably destroyed. The most Nixon could hope for was that Gorbachev would leave the meeting with a better understanding of why American leaders were willing to assist Yeltsin's government when they had not been willing to support Gorbachev's.

Two months after his memorandum had ignited the debate over aid to Russia, Nixon again traveled to Moscow, to meet with Yeltsin and evaluate the state of reform. The day before he left, May 29, I wrote a note to him. It read, " 'It is better to be making the news than taking it; to be an actor rather than a critic,' Winston Churchill. You have, once again, taken the course of history into your own hands." Nixon took the note with him.

I heard nothing from him until June 5, when he called me from Paris. He was incredibly upbeat. "Monica! Hi! We're in Paris, and it's beautiful. We've had an exhausting schedule. I'm seeing Mitterrand tomorrow at nine, and I did the *Today* show this morning. Did you see it?"

I told him that I had seen it.

"What did you like about it?" he pressed.

I said that I was impressed by his answer to the last question.

"Oh, about my place in history? Yeah, well, I always like those questions because I say 'History may treat me favorably, but historians probably won't because most of them are on the left!' I can still stick it to them!" He laughed and told me that he would see me in two days.

Twenty minutes later, my phone rang again. "Monica, well, I have insomnia and jet lag, so I thought I'd fill you in a bit more. Baker tried to sabotage everything. You won't believe it. I can't tell you over these lines, but I'll fill you in next week."

Despite Baker's machinations, Nixon believed that his trip had been a success. He had seen Yeltsin two weeks before the Russian president would be in the United States. He had gotten a full measure of the reform process and its opponents. And he had foiled Baker.

"He forbade Strauss from seeing me to and from the airport and from holding a dinner for me," Nixon said to me on June 8. I sat down in his office and listened as he vented his frustrations with the secretary of state. "He did anyway, of course, which really must have driven Baker crazy! The meal was horrible, and it was like pulling teeth to get people to talk. I had to liven up the damn thing with a discussion of the American political scene. Strauss has been very good to us in terms of supporting our position on aid, but I don't know how long he'll want to stay in there. If he leaves, they should look for a young business type."

He shifted his attention to Yeltsin. "He despises Gorbachev. He took away his limo privileges; that was a great dig to the elites," Nixon said, flashing a wicked grin. "He commands the room. He's vigorous, emotional, a hell of a guy. He knows who was for him BC—that's 'before the coup.' He's a great politician, and he rewards who is for him. He said I was Russia's best friend. I told him that in the case of an emergency in Russia—say, if rioting breaks out—I would do my best to get the White House to send help—economic and humanitarian, not military.

"He sees right through Baker, but I think he gets along with Bush. I told him that if he plans to run for a second term not to tell anyone, and he smiled. He's got guts."

He shifted in his chair. "Moscow is totally depressing. There's no color there. The schedule was rough, and I was pretty tired, but we got it all in. I'm surprised we got as much coverage as we did; Baker put an embargo on the press, and because he's a story, they listen to him.

"Anyway, after seeing Gorbachev and now Yeltsin, I'm convinced that the Russians are in far better hands now than they were with Gorbachev. Yeltsin may not be perfect, but he believes in the right things. I'm going to draft a few suggestions for his visit to Washington next week that I want Dimitri to pass on to him and which I'll let you see."

Nixon's trip accomplished an important goal: he helped to set the stage for Yeltsin's state visit later that month. In all of his trip-related interviews, Nixon made it clear that Yeltsin was not just another beleaguered leader of a second-tier impoverished nation coming to America for money. Rather, Yeltsin was coming as the hope of a democratic Russia and as a partner in peace and prosperity. Nixon emphasized the importance of enacting the languishing aid package not out of altruism but out of hardheaded necessity.

In his memorandum to Dimitri Simes, Nixon suggested that Yeltsin use his state visit to the United States to present himself as a strong, charismatic statesman. For Yeltsin's consideration, he prepared some speech lines that stressed his position as the first freely elected president of Russia to address the U.S. Congress. Nixon also suggested that Yeltsin emphasize the partnership with the United States and the unlimited possibilities of peace and prosperity if reform in Russia succeeded.

Whether or not Yeltsin actually used the suggestions was beside the point; Nixon simply wanted to signal to the Russian president that support for his efforts extended beyond the president and the Congress.

On June 14, Bush called Nixon. Although Bush's primary concern was the electoral threat of Ross Perot, whom Nixon had seen three days before, Nixon used the opportunity to prepare the president for meeting Yeltsin. The memorandum had run its course; Nixon now issued direct instructions to the president.

"Well, this is what I told Bush," he said to me after the call. "Let me fill you in. I dictated a memo on the conversation—in full—which I will let you see tomorrow. He called at ten-thirty, and we talked for twenty-five minutes. It went that long at his request. It was the most substantive talk since the Gulf War." Nixon was clearly pleased. "We talked about Yeltsin, and I hit the Baker thing hard. I told him that Yeltsin likes *him* and will bring some surprises for him when he arrives this week, but he doesn't like Baker and will not work through him. Bush was silent, but he needed to hear it. Baker is his blind spot."

On June 16, the presidents of the United States and Russia emerged from the White House and stood together in the Rose Garden. Bush announced that they had reached agreement to reduce strategic weapons beyond the levels determined by START I and to establish a "senior group" to explore how to proceed jointly with a plan for a global protection system against limited ballistic-missile attack.

Yeltsin highlighted the significance of the agreement and announced that "we shall not fight against each other."

Nixon was pleased with the announcement's effect. "It was good. I think he could get a major lift from this if he milks it. But I must say that Yeltsin looks vigorous, much healthier than Bush."

The next morning, Presidents Bush and Yeltsin addressed a U.S.-Russian business summit, and Bush used the opportunity to argue in favor of the Freedom for Russia and Emerging Eurasian Democracies and Open Markets Support Act, or the Freedom Support Act.

"I will follow up in every way I can with the United States Congress to get them to support the Freedom Support Act," Bush said. "Let me be very clear to the American people: we are not supporting the Freedom Support Act simply because it benefits Russia. It is my view that the Freedom Support Act will benefit the United States of America and will benefit world peace and will benefit democracy and freedom."

Nixon continued to be satisfied. "So far, so good," he said to me after getting a transcript of the presidents' remarks from the White House. "The summit has gone well. I think it will help Bush in the short term—certainly not enough to go up ten points, because no one cares about foreign policy now. Yeltsin's revelation that Russia had information about the fate of some Vietnam POWs works to Bush's advantage, too. It's a scoop for him."

"It also proves that the wars of the cold war weren't just wars of national liberation, like the Soviets used to claim," I said, "but wars of Communist aggression sponsored by the Soviet Union."

"Absolutely right," he said, pounding his fist. "Well! Isn't that something? Everything we've said has been right, from Alger Hiss on down! Now look, Yeltsin is going to address the Congress—the first time a freely elected Russian president has done this. I want you to come over and watch it with Mrs. Nixon and me. It's a big moment; I don't want you to miss it."

I followed his limousine to the residence and walked through the front door with him. Mrs. Nixon appeared in the foyer, and the three of us rode the elevator up to his third-floor study. Mrs. Nixon asked the former president to move the straight-backed chair for her so she could sit more comfortably.

She then picked up a pillow from the sofa and walked toward me. "Monica, sit up for a minute. Dick straightens out my pillow every night like this," she said as she rearranged it behind me. "Now, isn't that better?" Nixon got up and put another pillow against the back of her chair, then went into the bar and came back with a glass of diet Coke.

"Anyone else want one? Pat?"

We declined and Nixon sat on the couch, fumbling with the remote control and pretending not to know which channel broadcast CNN. He found it, then promptly switched to see if the networks were carrying it live. They were not.

"Goddamned bastards!" he said.

Mrs. Nixon chimed in. "Disgraceful."

Yeltsin began to speak, and Nixon was entranced. The Russian president spoke of the new partnership between the United States and Russia, the new arms-reduction agreement, and the promise of real democratic and market reform in lands that had known only repression.

"He's a powerful guy," he said as Yeltsin continued. "He has very effective delivery, and he's a hell of an actor." When Yeltsin made statements that Nixon believed were not getting a properly enthusiastic response, he yelled to the Congress through the television, "Cheer, you jerks!" And he stood when the Congress stood at the end of Yeltsin's address.

"They *should* give him a standing ovation, for God's sake," he said, applauding at home. "That speech was a brilliant triumph."

"I agree," said Mrs. Nixon. "Dick, I never thought we'd see the day that a freely elected Russian president would stand before our Congress."

"I know," he replied. "Monica's young, but we've been around awhile. I didn't think we'd see the day either, Pat." The former president escorted the former first lady to the elevator, then wheeled around toward me.

"The Congress had better pass this Freedom Support Act," he said, walking back into the room. "Yeltsin came all the way over here, made a big concession on nuclear weapons, and he'd better get something for it."

Later that afternoon, Bush and Yeltsin held a final press conference in the East Room. Bush gave a lukewarm endorsement of the Freedom Support Act and could not resist campaigning: "We are prepared to move this package forward as swiftly as possible. . . . We are viewing this as a priority. . . . We have many domestic issues here, and we're going to keep pushing forward on them—economic growth, help for the cities. And we can do all of those and pass this Freedom Support Act."

Once again, Bush hedged. The aid package was getting lost in the discussion of the domestic issues that were dominating the presidential campaign. Nixon knew that the proposal had to stand on its own in order to generate the necessary support from the Congress. Bush, fearful of looking too preoccupied with foreign policy, linked the policy on Russia to his domestic initiatives and consequently diluted its importance.

Canadian prime minister Brian Mulroney called Nixon on June 24 to reassure him that Canada was contributing two billion dollars to the Russian-reform package. Nixon treasured his association with Mulroney, to whom he spoke quite often about foreign affairs. When Mulroney heard of the Nixon memorandum on Russian aid, he supported Nixon's message vigorously and ultimately became one of Yeltsin's foremost advocates.

"Mulroney's contribution is very courageous. Canada doesn't have a whole lot of money to throw around either, but at least he sees the importance of doing something," he said.

Nixon's frustration with Bush's inaction on aid to Russia had reached a newly intolerable level. The president did not follow his words at the summit with real leadership on the issue. The annual meeting of the Group of Seven industrial nations in early July presented a similar opportunity for Bush to showcase the American relationship with the new Russia, and once again Bush failed to capitalize on it.

This frustration inspired Nixon to begin to think about his tenth—and final—book. The presidential campaign was mired in important but parochial issues. The incumbent president and his main Democratic opponent were crisis managers and not visionaries. American foreign policy had become an orphan during the campaign, with little of substance said about Russia. The electorate seemed angry and disappointed but unsure about whom to blame. Nixon sensed a spiritual dislocation and a lack of community. The search for meaning was on, and Nixon wanted to address it.

In its earliest stages, *Beyond Peace* was designed to be his most philosophical work. He intended to address concrete foreign and domestic policy issues, but he wanted to couch them in a profound discussion of what it means to be an American in the late twentieth century. He believed that there was an acute and growing crisis in the American spirit that was producing ever greater cynicism, bitterness, and insensitivity. American society had grown soft, unresponsive, complacent, disjointed, and desperately materialistic.

An unraveling political system dominated by moneyed interests, low voter turnout, and a willingness to abdicate responsibility to a higher authority—whether it was the federal government or the UN—were symptoms of a grave political and social situation.

Nixon saw sweeping the country a ravenous spiritual hunger for something to believe in. The evidence of this hunger existed everywhere: the Persian Gulf War—short, uncomplicated, and of minimal risk—brought the country together instantly; Perot's six million volunteers and countless other supporters proved that Americans were not by nature apathetic. Given a viable, attractive choice, people would participate.

Americans wanted guidance, Nixon thought, but a guidance that accommodated their autonomy. He thought that he could communicate the need for strength, vitality, national unity, and individual responsibility to the rest of the country. The spiritual vacuum existed, he believed, in a pervasive attitude that we were entitled, by virtue of being the greatest nation on earth, to lives of unlimited wealth and a freedom unchecked. But, Nixon pointed out, political freedom does not mean a freedom from responsibility.

Freedom demands more, not less, from people. It demands that we gauge our own behavior, that we monitor our own institutions, make our own mistakes, and correct them. A democracy forces its members to make those decisions themselves and then live with the consequences. Freedom demands individual and collective discipline, relentless self-scrutiny, and a higher mission based upon goodness and virtue. Since human beings are fallible, the demands of freedom are easier to dismiss than to fulfill.

The question he wanted to address was simple but potentially unanswerable: was there anything, short of war, that was capable of bringing the nation together? He had observed that "war brings out the best and worst in men. Real peace will bring out only the best." Peacetime—an era marked by no overwhelming military or ideological conflict—should be a time of tremendous national unity.

Instead of coming together, however, we were coming apart. If the United States were suffering a crisis of mission at the end of the cold war, what was to be our new mission?

Nixon believed that the United States traditionally had waged war and fostered peace in order to extend the best possible life to the most people. If democracy were truly on the march, was that task winding down? As Nixon asked, "We responded magnificently to the threat of war then. Can we respond just as magnificently to the promise of peace now?"

The promise of peace means a better life materially—better and more jobs, better education, less crime and drugs, a cleaner environment, a government that responds efficiently to the people, and greater prosperity. But more important, the promise of peace means a better life spiritually, where faith guides the life of the nation.

At the end of the cold war, we knew we were a great nation, but were we a good nation? Nixon believed that government should elevate, educate, and inspire, not pander to the lowest common denominator. Before the American spirit could be restored, then, the American people needed to regain faith in their institutions. Nixon knew that he would have a difficult time addressing this, since many pointed to Watergate as the crisis that shook that faith, but he did not retreat from the challenge.

Our self-absorption was sending out powerful warning signals: trade and federal deficits, rising crime rates, crumbling infrastructure and education systems, a deteriorating environment, and a waning national spirit. Prosperity breeds contentment and a decline of will. Nixon believed that the United States had never been an ordinary nation. If it were to stay extraordinary, however, we now required something more.

The failure by the Bush administration to meet the greatest foreign policy challenge since the Second World War convinced Nixon that his views were right. Americans were as anchorless as their leader. With disappearing certainties, the need for meaning in political and national life was even more pressing. Nixon began thinking about the project in terms of addressing the decline of national community without attracting an inordinate amount of criticism for having contributed to it. It was during the summer of 1992, after the Russian-aid memorandum had run its course and *Seize the Moment* had been a success, that *Beyond Peace* began to take shape.

On July 27, he asked me to locate a copy of a speech he had given in Kansas City in 1971, in which he outlined his vision of an emerging multipolar world, based on the strength of Western Europe, Japan, China, the Soviet Union, and the United States. The speech was significant because the president had pointed to five power centers rather than the usual two; he had elevated Japan, China, and Western Europe from mere understudies to the superpowers to powers in their own right. Few remarked on the importance of the distinction at the time; "even Kissinger didn't see it or want to see it," Nixon said. The world remained bipolar militarily, but the future, according to Nixon in 1971, would be multipolar economically. The result would be the need for a far more complex and delicate foreign policy that went beyond the two-sided global balance sheet.

I found a copy of the speech, which he took from me and waved in the air. "Have you seen this?" he asked. "This was one hell of a speech. You want vision? This is it. And nobody in the media picked up on it. I know they hated to give me anything, but I still can't see how they could have ignored this. But the point is, Do you see anything resembling vision coming out of this White House?" He answered his own question: "No. And the reason is because they just don't see it. They don't see beyond their own noses. They have no idea about the workings of the world or the larger trends. If Russia succeeds, what a signal that sends to the Chinese and the Vietnamese! But no, they don't see it. Meanwhile, the world is crashing down around them."

On the last day of July, Strauss called to ask Nixon to use his formidable influence to persuade Republicans in the House to vote for aid to Russia. Nixon took heart. "The guy is trying, and he came to me. OK. I'll see what I can do."

He had planned to go to Washington that week, then decided against it. "The press will ask questions about Bush and the campaign, and I don't want to make any political statements at this time," he said to me on August 3. "They won't give a damn about what I say about Russian aid. The politics will overwhelm it."

Baker, meanwhile, moved to preempt any action by Nixon. He wrote an op-ed for *The New York Times* on August 5, in which he argued for supporting the Russian-aid initiative. Nixon was torn between giving Baker credit for writing the piece and knowing that he did it to dilute Nixon's influence on the issue.

"Can you believe Baker's op-ed?" he asked me early that day. "It was so turgid; it didn't have any enthusiasm; no oomph."

"But at least he wrote it," I said. "And at least he mentioned you."

Nixon raised an eyebrow. "Yes. I couldn't believe it."

A few hours later, Scowcroft called to ask Nixon to sign a letter from the former presidents to Speaker of the House Thomas Foley, supporting Russian aid before the vote on the issue, scheduled for the next day. Nixon was annoyed. He had worked hard during his post-presidential years to tower over his successors, and he resented being grouped with them. The issue, however, was crucial enough that he relented and signed the joint letter.

"It's kind of a rush job," he said, glancing at it. "But at least they used some of my lines in it. But really, to wait until the last minute on this issue? What an amateurish crowd." He handed the letter to me, and I faxed it to Gerald Ford's office for his signature. Nixon sighed, "If the Russian-aid bill fails tomorrow—not that this four-president letter will help—it just might be enough to topple Yeltsin."

The aid bill passed on August 6, and Nixon, relieved, offered an instant analysis. "It passed by a healthy margin, not that there should have been any debate on the damn thing. But Baker knew it would pass, which is why he wrote the op-ed. You don't think that if he knew it was going to go down, he'd be out there supporting it, do you? Please. He definitely snookered us so no credit would come our way. That four-president letter was a gimmick."

During a conversation with former secretary of state Alexander Haig on July 23, Nixon got some good news: Baker would be leaving the State Department to unofficially run Bush's lagging reelection campaign as chief of staff. Baker's new role meant that Nixon would have even less access to Bush, but as he said to Haig, "The best reason to get Baker to run the campaign is because it keeps him the hell out of foreign policy!"

Since Bush's chances for winning a second term were slim, Nixon knew that Baker would never again assume the helm of the nation's foreign policy. Lawrence Eagleburger, a veteran of the Nixon-Kissinger foreign policy team, replaced him, and although Eagleburger reported developments to Baker, Nixon felt far more comfortable knowing that a realist was in charge.

"I have to think about how best to use the time I have left," he said on August 31. "This may mean another trip to Russia. I know I said I probably wouldn't go back. But I have to stay on top of the situation there. Yeltsin will survive, but it will be very close. Passing the aid bill was fine, but what are they doing now? Nothing."

He sighed. "America used to be a great adventure, but not anymore. The big issues don't seem to matter anymore. This is what we're going to try to get at with the new project, right? I hope we can do it adequately. I don't want to do a half-assed job. I haven't told anyone else about it because I haven't convinced myself that we can tackle it. But people need a lift. We live in great times."

The presidential candidates in 1992 compounded Nixon's distress when they failed to address foreign policy during their televised debates in October. Nixon thought that this omission served Clinton well, since he was not forced to discuss matters with which he was unfamiliar, put Bush at a disadvantage, since his professed strength was international affairs, and did a grave disservice to the American people, who needed to know if their potential commanders in chief were responsible. Nixon, predictably, was disgusted by their lack of attention to foreign policy and, particularly, to Russia.

"The candidates aren't talking about what needs to be talked about," he said on October 2. "And when someone like Clinton does talk about Russia, he has completely missed the boat by being on that '60s kick of 'if we all got to know each other, the world would be peaceful.' The former Soviet Union does not need a democracy corps—all of these little political scientists running around there showing them how to take polls! No. Democracy is natural. It will happen. Free markets aren't natural. They need a free-market corps.

"They must appoint someone, like Paul Hoffman of the Marshall Plan, someone young and vibrant, to coordinate the aid and make it a priority. And not a foreign service type! They're good political officers but bad economic officers." He paused and lowered his voice. "Look, if you're going to do something controversial, do it all the way, not halfway, because you're going to take the heat for it anyway. Like in Cambodia; they would have blamed us anyway, so instead of taking out two Communist sanctuaries, I ordered them to take out all six. And there was no offensive that year.

"And another thing," he continued. "Those who are hog-wild on exporting democracy are irresponsible. I've never been big on that. We were criticized for dealing with authoritarian governments, but we were right. Sometimes you've just got to deal with the lesser of two evils."

He continued the theme on October 9, when we discussed what Nixon would have done differently had he been the candidate. "I would have hit the Russian-aid thing hard by saying 'I know it's not popular, but it must be done.' And it makes me sick to my stomach to see *The New York Times*—*The New York Times*, for God's sake—calling for force in Bosnia. Bush has allowed too many people to get to the right of him. They talk about changing the team in a second term, but they've got to win first!"

Nixon thought that Bush had missed a major opportunity to strike at Clinton by failing to command the Russian issue. If he had taken the lead, Bush would have reaped significant political rewards. Instead, he shortchanged himself and the country by playing on Clinton's turf: domestic policy.

As much as Bush's failures in foreign policy disappointed him, Clinton's inexperience frightened him. He had no training in how "the real world worked," demonstrated little interest in learning, and surrounded himself with advisers who were similarly preoccupied with domestic issues. The nation's foreign policy might be left dangerously adrift in a Clinton administration, though from neglect rather than mismanagement. But whereas Bush was resistant to Nixon's advice, Clinton perhaps could be taught and, indeed, influenced.

The day after Clinton's election in 1992, Nixon made his first overture to the president-elect. Having given up on swaying Bush, Nixon knew that if he were to have greater success with Clinton, he would have to set an early precedent for cooperation. He handwrote a note to Clinton that sought to open a direct channel of communication by congratulating him on running an excellent campaign and on overcoming adversity during the campaign.

By reaching out to Clinton immediately after the election, Nixon hoped to establish a positive working relationship with him. He knew that since they were on opposite sides politically on most domestic issues, his influence there would be marginal. His power to sway Clinton on the course of foreign policy, however, might be formidable.

He held out little hope, however, that Clinton would choose responsible and experienced realists to fill the important foreign policy positions in his administration. On November 6, he said, "On foreign policy, the guy is just too inexperienced. When Yeltsin called to congratulate him, he already looked in over his head. That's why he's got to appoint someone like [Senator] Sam Nunn or [Senator] David Boren to State and the CIA—someone good and responsible. And also," he said, tipping his hand, "someone I'd have influence with. Warren Christopher is weak. God help us if he's secretary of state. This is the [former secretary of state Cyrus] Vance crowd—irresponsible. Maybe Clinton will be more likely to reach out to me, but I see he's calling on Carter as an informal adviser. He wants to validate Carter's foreign policy and distinguish his own New Democrat style. I don't know if he'll call on me. Republicans are generally more gracious in victory than Democrats. They play hardball. Kennedy and Johnson never invited Mrs. Nixon and me to the White House. Never. I, of course, had Humphrey, Johnson—anyone who was alive. I don't expect that at all from Clinton. If he does, I will be very surprised."

The next day, Nixon saw an opportunity for Clinton. "The Russians need immediate debt relief. [Treasury Secretary Nicholas] Brady was so busy protecting his goddamned banker friends, and the Russians need a bridge loan. If Russia goes down, the loss will be on Bush's hands. And Clinton should blame him. Frankly, they deserve it."

He clenched his teeth. "And Carter—Jimma, as Rosalyn used to call him—going to Russia! He doesn't know anything about Russia, and Yeltsin knows that, but he's got to see him because he's got to work with Clinton. I'd advise Yeltsin to see him. But what bothers me is that they've elevated this trip to sort of a state visit—with Carter staying in the state house. Thinking of myself, I can't have it look like I'm injecting myself into the Clinton administration's policy. The goddamned media will say, 'Nixon is forcing his way in,' " which is exactly what Nixon intended to do. He did not want it to appear as if the former presidents were stampeding to Moscow, but the urgency of the situation there persuaded him to set aside his concerns and move again to position himself as the new president's foreign policy mentor.

On November 19, he wrote another op-ed for *The New York Times,* "Save the Peace Dividend." The piece was another "shot across the bow" to the president-elect and his foreign policy team. It began by flattering Clinton and giving him "high marks for aggressively addressing a number of important issues during the transition period. But," he continued in the tone of the Russian-aid memorandum, "the most important issue since the end of World War II has received minimal attention."

He urged immediate action on debt rescheduling, bridge loans, and private investment. "What's in it for us?" Nixon asked. "If Mr. Yeltsin survives, and freedom and democracy succeed in Russia, we will live in a safer world. We will also live in a richer world. . . . We will live in a freer world because the success of democracy and free markets in Russia will be an example for China and other dictatorships around the world to follow."

He argued that although the Clinton administration would be counting on a peace dividend to support its domestic initiatives, that money would not be available if the Russian democratic experiment failed and we were forced to wage a new cold war. It was a familiar argument and one that Nixon had repeated countless times, but now he had a new audience: Bill Clinton.

Nixon also decided to travel to Moscow again the following February. Clinton would find it almost impossible to ignore Nixon if the former president met with the Russian president in Moscow. "You will be pleased to know that I've decided to take you to Russia early next year, assuming Yeltsin survives, which I think he will. Paris, Moscow, Kiev—you should keep a diary every day. But it's a grind; you'll be working. You have Julie to thank. She convinced me that this is the year of the woman!"

He smiled. "You are so young and have so much to see. I traveled abroad in World War II and saw New Caledonia! But I only *really* went abroad with the Herter Committee forty-five years ago, and then as vice president, of course. Remember, though, most people go on trips thinking it will just be a junket. Not *my* trips. Be prepared to work."

On November 27, the day after Thanksgiving, I called Nixon at home.

"Monica? Hold on." I heard him pad over to the stereo and turn down the volume. "Sorry. I had some Christmas music on the record player. So, first, how was your Thanksgiving? You know, I like the traditional food, especially the stuffing and fresh cranberries. We went to Radio City with the kids, who had a ball, and we had lunch at Tricia's. David [Eisenhower, his daughter Julie's husband] is a movie buff, and he got *The Inner Circle.*"

"About Stalin?" I asked.

"Yes. It's very well done. Julie said, 'Monica has got to see this before she goes to Russia.' There's a love story in it, but it's still good.

"As you know, I'm going to London to give a speech next week. Julie is coming with me, which will be nice. It's off the record, which means I'm putting too much damn work into it. But I do plan to hit Russian aid hard; if the Americans aren't paying attention, maybe the British will."

Nixon brought his message across the Atlantic in early December and returned satisfied that the British would support efforts in behalf of the Russian democracy. He called me on December 8.

"Speeches are hard, hard work, particularly for those of us who deliver them without notes. In school, I was in some plays—my biggest role was as the innkeeper in [John Drinkwater's] *Bird in Hand*—and I had to memorize those lines. For my speeches, I can memorize, but it doesn't sound like I have. I think the more conversational you are, the better. [British member of Parliament] Jonathan Aitken said I was particularly effective when speaking to that high-level group in London. I focused on Russia without reading from notes. That's what makes the difference.

"I saw [former secretary of state George] Shultz on C-SPAN, and he was damn good on Yugoslavia. He said we must bomb the Serbs because they're the aggressors, and I couldn't agree more. They may have called me the mad bomber, but I believe that when you're dealing with dictators, and Communists in particular, the only thing they understand is force. I would have bombed the Serbs. There's no question in my mind. The administration isn't looking strong. They were hung up on Yugoslavia because of the Eagleburger and Scowcroft connections. But it's shocking: four hundred thousand people are going to die. What if they were Jews and not Muslims dying? It's a goddamned double standard and absolutely wrong.

"We have two options. One, we say we're neutral, but with the embargo we're really for the side with the most weapons, which is Serbia. We must get rid of the damned embargo. Or two, we should bomb the living bejesus out of the Serbs."

Policy inaction regarding Russia and the war in the former Yugoslavia continued to torment Nixon. Bush had shown a lack of strong, principled leadership by refusing to recognize the Baltic states when they broke away from the Soviet Union, by allowing the Communist Serbs to overrun their neighbors, and by failing to support the democratic transition in Russia. Serious neglect of large and small problems spelled disaster for Bush historically and posed immediate challenges for the new president.

If Clinton were wise, Nixon thought, he would reverse some of the damage done by Bush's failures by acting as soon as possible. The arms embargo could be lifted in the former Yugoslavia to establish a balance of force on the ground, and the United States could lead the international effort to aid reform. This was Clinton's chance to make his mark internationally, and Nixon moved to help him take advantage of it.

On December 22, the former president and I met in the morning. He was visibly upset that Clinton had neither issued a statement in support of Yeltsin nor indicated that Russian aid would be a priority.

"I've got to go to Russia. The Russians must realize that it's in their interest to talk to me, particularly when no one else in the West is talking to them.

"You'll meet Yeltsin, of course, for about fifteen minutes, to get a feel for his magnetism. But then I should spend quite a while with him alone. And I want you in the substantive meetings to take comprehensive notes. We'll see everyone."

By early January 1993, a meeting between Yeltsin and Nixon in Moscow had been confirmed. Nixon was encouraged but wary. "The parliament is bitching that Yeltsin is playing too much to the West and gave away the store on START II," he said on January 2. "He may not want to see us, although he should since I'm really his only friend in the West."

Three days before we were scheduled to depart, Nixon and I traveled to Washington to meet with the Russian ambassador to the United States, Vladimir Lukin, who briefed us on the progress of reform and the internal political situation, and with Clinton's ambassador at large, Strobe Talbott, who briefed us on the administration's position. As Nixon told me after Talbott left the room, "I am so disappointed that he was so wrapped up in the details of the U.S.-Russian relationship, like nonproliferation [of nuclear weapons], that he was missing the broader picture. If democracy and the free market fail in Russia, you can forget about the proliferation issues. First things first. Let's help get democracy stabilized first and the economy out of the toilet before we worry about that kind of stuff."

He shook his head. "I kept struggling to get him to see the mountaintop stuff, but he kept sliding back down into the nitty-gritty. All of Clinton's people are so detail oriented. Well, at least they aren't going to cause any problems for our trip."

"Sir," I said, "implicit in your remark to Talbott that you wouldn't criticize Clinton *on the trip* was that if Clinton does not step up to the issue in due time, you would go after him."

Nixon clenched his fist and slammed it on the armrest. "Whammo! And I am freer to do it with a Democratic president, and I *will*."

Nixon believed that it was crucial to hear "the administration line" and to reassure those in the administration that he would not contradict it when meeting with the Russians. The session with Talbott was a strategic courtesy designed to give Clinton time to consider how he would approach Nixon upon his return and what policy he would advance based on what Nixon found.

Nixon knew that the Russian people would survive, but he was not so certain about their nascent democracy. Either Russia would be democratic, re-linked by trade with much of its former empire, or it would be authoritarian, locked in nationalistic conflict with those same areas. If the latter situation developed, the democratic West stood to be discredited for decades to come.

So Nixon once again made his way to Russia, and this time I traveled with him.

———

On its approach to the Moscow airport, the small plane dropped precipitously, then suddenly began a quick ascent. I glanced at Nixon, who did not particularly like to fly. Both of his hands were wrapped around his armrests, his knuckles white; his gaze was fixed on the frigid terrain below and the snowstorm swirling outside the plane's window. As we began another descent, I could see his jaw clench tighter and his face grow pale. When the landing gear of our private plane finally met the ice-encrusted runway, Nixon closed his eyes in relief and pulled his hands from the armrests.

"Are they wearing hats?" he asked, breaking the silence with a question of diplomatic etiquette.

"Sir?" I asked.

"Hats," he repeated, "are they wearing them?"

I looked out of the window as the plane slowed and came to a stop. Assembled on the tarmac in the steady snowfall and below-freezing temperatures of early afternoon on February 9 were several Russian officials, including Foreign Minister Andrei Kozyrev, members of the Russian press, and Dimitri Simes. They were wearing hats.

Nixon quickly positioned his own fedora on his head, smoothed his coat, cleared his throat, and descended the stairs to greet his hosts. Kathy O'Connor, his administrative assistant, Joseph Crowley, his private security escort, and I followed, each of us arriving on Russian soil for the first time. The bitter cold forced quick greetings in Russian and English as we filed into our appointed government cars behind Nixon's ZIL limousine, and we began to make our way toward Moscow.

We passed the Russian White House, then the legislative home of the parliament; KGB headquarters; and the grand Bolshoi Theater. It was February, the depths of winter in Russia, and except for the illuminated red stars of Red Square, the city was bathed in a gray monochrome.

The Russian government had invited us to stay in their premier guesthouse in the Lenin Hills overlooking Moscow. Built by Stalin for diplomatic and social use in the late 1940s, the compound of guesthouses had been renovated but retained its original essence: high ceilings, game rooms, grand staircases, and secret meeting rooms. As we entered our quarters, Nixon quipped, "It's a hell of a place. But I don't think Stalin expected to put up an old cold warrior!"

The four of us stayed on the second floor of the same guesthouse. Nixon had a spacious suite in the center of the building, and the rest of the staff stayed farther down the hall, always under the watchful eyes of the three KGB-trained officers the Russian government had provided for additional protection.

Despite Nixon's objections, a meeting with a Russian official was scheduled for the afternoon we arrived. Tired and drawn, he did not want to see any Russians until he had recuperated and had time to review his informational briefings. Nixon was eighty years old, and although healthy, strong, and vigorous, he required a significant amount of rest. He told me, "I have always found international travel to be difficult, but it's even more grueling at my advanced age. That's why I only go abroad if I feel it's going to make a difference." Despite the great physical strain, he needed to prove to himself and the world that he could still shape geopolitics from international capitals. "As long as I am able to do it, I will," he said, but it was often at the cost of dangerous exhaustion.

Nevertheless, we traveled to the old Central Committee Building of the Communist Party of the Soviet Union to see Vladimir Lobov, a minister of industry in the Yeltsin government. As we stepped out of the cars, Nixon called me to his side and nodded to the building. "Look at this place," he said. "You know, I saw Khrushchev here in '59. It was a very different time, but the building hasn't changed, and I see it's still snowing."

Nixon, Simes, and I went to the third floor, where Lobov was waiting. Three secretaries sat at desks with several telephones that could accept only incoming calls, a quaint relic of communism, when orders were phoned down from a higher authority, who could not be called back to be questioned.

Nixon had a dynamic discussion with Lobov, primarily about the industrial sectors' tentative support of Russian president Boris Yeltsin. With their industries becoming increasingly marginalized, uncompetitive, and undermined by free-market reform, Lobov indicated that they might seek to replace Yeltsin with a coalition of industrial leaders. Nixon urged cooperation between the government and the special interests and patience with the reforms that, if successful, would benefit them all.

During the ride back to the guesthouse, he said to me, "It's hard to know what to say to these people. They're having one hell of a time. I just hope they make it. The problem is that I don't know if they can ride it out long enough for the reforms to take hold, like the Chinese have done. Look," he said, pointing to the buildings passing by the window. "This is what communism has done. It's all gray. It's all the same. And it's all depressing."

In February 1993, Russian democratic and free-market economic reform was beginning to generate both problems and opportunities. Yeltsin was firmly in control, despite increasingly contentious relationships with the Soviet-era parliament and his own vice president. The hardships of reform—including skyrocketing inflation, double-digit unemployment, food shortages, and rising crime rates—made Yeltsin a target for criticism, but he remained moderately popular, in part because no viable alternative had emerged.

On that first night in Moscow, Nixon invited Crowley and me to accompany him on a short walk around the guesthouse grounds. Highly disciplined and conditioned by routine, he insisted that he continue his walking regimen abroad; so, braced against the frigid temperatures, the three of us embarked on a midnight, midwinter stroll.

"Monica, whenever you want to talk in Russia, you must always do it outside, if you know what I mean," he said, rolling his eyes.

"Even in a newly democratic Russia?" I asked with some sarcasm.

"Oh, my God! I *know* about bugging. Democracies are the worst!" he laughed.

Since he had wanted to think about the next day's meeting with Yeltsin, we walked the rest of the way in silence. Crowley and I tossed some snowballs at each other, narrowly missing the former president, who bent down, made a snowball of his own and lobbed it at us.

"Enough fun and games," he said. "Monica, come here. Tomorrow we've got Yeltsin, which is the reason we came here in the first place. I want you to record everything you hear, see, and feel. It's important to write it all down as it's happening because if you wait, you'll forget. Your impressions will be important to you, and they'll be important to me when I get back to the United States and report to Clinton." He leaned toward me. "Remember, your first trip someplace is always the most interesting. Take it all in. Don't let anything get past you. And remember that just as you're watching them, they're watching you." Then he turned toward the guesthouse and walked slowly back inside.

The snow crunched under the wheels as our motorcade made its final turn onto the Kremlin grounds. Connecting streets had been cordoned off to allow us unencumbered access to the Kremlin. Slowly and silently, our cars moved around the labyrinthine passages until they stopped at a small doorway. Nixon's car, directly in front of mine, was approached by two men, who escorted him into the foyer. Our group followed Nixon into a small waiting room in Yeltsin's presidential suite overlooking Red Square.

"No cameras," warned the Russian chief of protocol, eyeing the small collection we had smuggled in. Nixon paced around us, mentally reviewing the points he intended to make to Yeltsin. He had spent two months preparing for this discussion, which would be one of the most significant contributions he would make to Russian-American relations during the Clinton administration. Understanding the reciprocal importance of Nixon's support, Yeltsin cultivated the relationship with personal correspondence and annual invitations to Moscow. Although Nixon never allowed personal relationships to taint diplomacy, he liked and respected Yeltsin. As he said, "Anyone who reaches the pinnacle of power in the Kremlin must have guts of steel."

Nixon saw much of himself in Yeltsin, which gave their association a remarkable depth. Like Nixon, Yeltsin was raised poor but possessed a relentless inner drive that propelled him to the top of the political ranks. Like Nixon, Yeltsin had a wily resilience that made him an enduring figure. Like Nixon, Yeltsin was a heavyweight—a smart, proud, tough, shrewd politician with a penchant for survival.

This was their third face-to-face meeting, and despite his great experience, Nixon was anxious. With his hands clasped behind his back, he paced by the window, stopping occasionally to glance outside. After a five-minute wait, we were summoned down a long red-carpeted hallway and into Yeltsin's office, where the international press pool was assembled. Camera lights and flashbulbs lit the room when the president and former president strode toward each other, hands extended and smiles beaming. Nixon turned and introduced me to Yeltsin, who clasped my hand with both of his and issued a warm welcome in Russian. Vigorous and imposing, he seeped charisma. Nixon called it "animal magnetism": a function of personal style, dynamism, confidence, and a flair for the dramatic. Yeltsin drew people in, made them listen, and projected strength even when he lacked it.

After their one-hour private meeting, an energized and upbeat Nixon secluded himself in his suite at the guesthouse to transcribe the conversation and his immediate observations, as well as those from his earlier meeting with Foreign Minister Kozyrev.

"Please, come on in," he said when I met with him several hours later. He pointed to the ceiling to warn that we may be overheard and asked me to sit across from him. "The meeting went just fine. Yeltsin is in control and more vigorous than I have ever seen him," he said for the benefit of whatever audience there may have been. "I would like for you to accompany me to the meeting with [Sergei] Stankevich this afternoon. As you know, he used to be part of the cabinet, and he's really a respected intellectual. I think you'll find it interesting."

"This morning was so important and probably took a lot out of you," I said, noticing that he seemed very tired. "Maybe we should consider rescheduling him."

"No," he said flatly. "I want to see as many Russians as I can in the short amount of time we have here. Otherwise, there's no point to being here. The most important meeting is out of the way, and now I can see Yeltsin's supporters and his detractors." He pointed to me. "That's how you get a true measure of the guy."

Stankevich backed Yeltsin, though with qualifications, and he warned that Russian "democracy" and "free-market economics" would not be based on the American, European, or Asian models, but would be a derivative of all three: "a fourth way." I took notes during the conversation and transcribed them for Nixon, as I did for all of the meetings I attended, in addition to preparing his more general background material. These memoranda served as Nixon's "memory banks" of ideas for the book, public speeches, and private conversations that would occur later.

When Nixon awoke from a nap an hour later, he summoned me. His suite was dark except for a dim light perched on a table in the corner of the room, and he was standing by a window, his famous profile outlined by the moonlight. When I addressed him, he spun around.

"Oh, hi," he said, stifling a yawn. "I had quite a nap; it must be the jet lag. Look, we have an extra day built into this trip, and I want to know if you would rather go to Prague or Budapest. I'll ask the others what they think, but I'd like to know what you think first. There is something to be said for Budapest—the Hungarians were the first to break away, but Prague is just breathtaking. Which will it be?"

He nodded in agreement when I suggested Prague. "OK, good. Now, you've got to go out and see Red Square, and I mean tonight. Just get one of these KGB guys to take you over there. You've got to see it at night, when the red stars are lit in every corner. And then, of course, there's Saint Basil's Cathedral, the GUM department store, and Lenin's mausoleum. Those you should see during the day, but you should see the square at least once at night."

Braced against the cold, I took Nixon's advice and went through Red Square, and when I returned to the guesthouse, I watched coverage of his meeting with Yeltsin on Russian television, prepared his briefings for the next day, slipped them under his door at two o'clock, and went to sleep, only to have him ask for me at six o'clock. He was irritable, padding around his suite in socks and casual, rumpled clothing. When he complained angrily that he lacked the necessary materials for the rest of the trip and lamented that the trip itself was not generating the proper media coverage, I explained that the Russians were scheduling meetings the day they were to occur, making it difficult to collect the information in time. He remained furious.

"I know Moscow is in disarray, but damn it, I have never felt so unprepared! Whatever is going on here is not enough. We have to be firm and *demand* the material we need," he fumed. "I can't stand having to depend on them for this stuff, and I hate like hell to delegate, but I have to, and it's just not working."

I explained that the Russians were resistant to providing us with supplementary material, and his expression softened. "I know you're doing the best you can under the circumstances. But Moscow is in total chaos, and I'm left out on a goddamned limb. Well, OK, nothing we can do about it; keep plugging away." He paused and then added, "We have Rutskoi this afternoon, and he's somebody I really needed to be prepared for. I have some basic information, and I know what the hell I'm going to say anyway, but you know what I mean."

At four o'clock that afternoon, we made the familiar trek to the Kremlin to meet with Yeltsin's fiery vice president, Alexander Rutskoi. Nixon knew that this hero of the Afghanistan war was more conservative, hard-line, and uncompromising than Yeltsin and harbored his own ambitions for the presidency. Unpredictable and unyielding, Rutskoi focused on building a core of support that he could use in a bid for the top job. He had his own agenda, refused to hide it, and could not be controlled, forcing Yeltsin to either accommodate or repudiate his own vice president.

Rutskoi enveloped Nixon in a massive bear hug and immediately lit a Marlboro cigarette. I sat next to Nixon and opposite Rutskoi, who often punctuated his points by leaning dramatically over the table. As he chain-smoked through the conversation, Rutskoi filled the room with booming intonations about the need for more government-sponsored "discipline" and "qualified leadership" in Russia.

"They are all afraid of my coming to power. Why? Because I will get things done—the right way," he shouted, slamming his hand on the table.

Nixon urged cooperation between the president and vice president but sensed that the advice would go unheeded. Rutskoi's separate vision for Russia—of centralized political and economic control—could not be reconciled with the Yeltsin government's reform efforts. Yeltsin had chosen Rutskoi as his running mate and now found himself running from him; it was a political problem that could escalate easily into an international one.

"Well! Rutskoi is really something, isn't he?" he said to me after the meeting, pointing again to the ceiling of his guesthouse suite.

"He's quite a force," I replied.

Nixon winked. "He's building backfires so he can seize power the moment Yeltsin falters. That's why our support is so important, and that's the point I've got to drive home to Clinton, because I'm sure that it's not just Rutskoi who's out there plotting. He's just more obvious than most." He walked to his desk and produced a yellow legal pad.

"I'm going to do some writing now on that conversation," he said, "but I'd like to get your opinions about Rutskoi later." He turned toward me. "I know this is rough going, and I didn't mean to get down on you this morning. I'm just not used to operating without schedules. Now, go on, and try to get some sleep." He closed the door behind me, and I retreated to my room to finish the memoranda of the day's conversations.

The days began to blur together on that fourth day in Moscow, February 12. We attended an early-morning meeting with the mayor of Moscow, Anatoly Popov, a midmorning discussion with an industrial leader, Alexander Volski, and a noon meeting at the Academy of Sciences. Nixon, obviously fatigued, turned much of the conversation at the academy over to Simes. He spent the afternoon alone in his suite, making notes and preparing for his next appointments, and I dashed to Arbat Street, the center of Moscow's burgeoning free market.

The energy and urgency of Russian private enterprise were undeniable. American rock music blared from every direction. Kiosks lined the streets, selling Russian-made shoes and dolls, clothing, and Soviet-era souvenirs. And the new Russian entrepreneurs, willing to endure the subzero temperatures to promote their wares, negotiated prices in American dollars. The early lessons of supply and demand generated chaos, but on that dark street on that frigid afternoon, Russian capitalism was taking root. Primitive and undisciplined, it was nevertheless the beginnings of an economic revolution.

Nixon was asleep when I returned to the guesthouse. I had summarized the day's activities for him and had begun briefings for the next day when he emerged from his suite and padded down the hall into our staff room. With sleep still in his eyes, he looked at us blankly and lurched to the left, steadying himself on a chair before he could fall.

"Well, I am *tired.* And a little woozy," he said, glancing around the room. "It looks like we have a good base of operations here. At least we have that going for us. Well, we have a long day tomorrow, so I think I'll go back to bed. And remember, it's Lincoln's birthday, so don't work too hard." He smiled, turned on his sock-clad heel, and left us.

Early the next morning, Nixon pulled me aside and said, "Monica, what we will do today is just as important as seeing Yeltsin," referring to the scheduled visit to Moscow's Central Market. "It is *crucial* to get out and meet the people, talk to them, and listen. The leadership talks about reform; the people are living it. They always tell it like it is."

The Central Market was a sprawling, bustling commercial center. People jostled past, the wealthier making purchases, the others simply looking. Fresh bread, meats, fruits, vegetables, and flowers graced every corner. Voices loud and small filled the air as purchases were made, refunds given, and prices negotiated. Nixon was recognized as soon as he walked in, and when a *Today* show camera arrived on the scene, the marketplace erupted in mayhem.

Through it all, Nixon focused solely on his conversations with ordinary Russian citizens. To each of them, he posed the same question: Was life getting better under political and economic reform? Most replied that their own lives had remained the same, unaffected by the government's machinations; others said adamantly that their lives had gotten worse; and a butcher pleaded desperately to Nixon, "Please, sir, if you do not help us, we will have communism again, and that we cannot bear."

Approached by many respectful well-wishers, Nixon accepted both compliments on his leadership and gifts from their marketplace booths. Exhilarated, he suggested we visit Arbat Street so he could see firsthand the dynamic free enterprise I had described to him so enthusiastically.

Unfortunately, the scene was not as I had experienced it. The street had been raided an hour earlier by police searching for illegal vendors and was now deserted. There would be no positive outpourings here, no adulation, no valuable interactions. Nixon, irritated and disappointed, stormed to his car.

Upon our return to the guesthouse, I joined him for his meeting with the reactionary legislator Valery Constantinov. A fierce Stalinist, Constantinov urged Nixon not to support Yeltsin: "That is the best way to help Russia." Nixon disagreed and offered his own interpretation of events in Russia but knew that his powers of persuasion were lost on Constantinov. Seventy years of hard-line communism would not be replaced easily, particularly when those with interests in holding on to the ideology remained in positions of power.

Following a lengthy interview for Russian television, Nixon met with member of parliament Valery Armbatsumov, the chairman of the Foreign Relations Committee, at the Russian White House. Nixon seemed energized by the discussion of Russian foreign policy, particularly with regard to the other former states of the Soviet Union, the "near abroad," and Russian-American relations. Armbatsumov was a centrist who did not agree with the fully pro-Western foreign policy advocated at the time by Foreign Minister Kozyrev. Nixon agreed: "Russia has its own interests, and even democratic partners will disagree."

After we left the meeting, Nixon said to me, "He's right, you know. Yeltsin must not toe a completely pro-Western line, or he will be undermined by extremists like Constantinov and even moderates who support him. Politically, he must be 'Russia first.' There are those in the United States who don't understand that, but they've got to. In order to survive, he's got to put Russia's interests first, or the others waiting in the wings will kill him." He looked at me. "And that could be literal or figurative."

Early the next day, we boarded our plane for Saint Petersburg, and during the short flight from Moscow, Nixon briefed me privately on his meeting with Yeltsin.

"Yeltsin is as vigorous as ever. He's at his best during crises, and God knows he has enough of those! He's still preaching democracy, although political pressures have slowed down the process. When I told him that the U.S.-Russian relationship depends on how Russia conducts itself abroad, he reassured me that he remains committed to a nonaggressive foreign policy, particularly with regard to the near abroad.

"He is tough, decisive, and sometimes ruthless; he has to be to survive. Emotionally, he seemed stable, and he told me that despite the widening rift with Rutskoi and the parliament, he had enough support to keep reform on an even keel. What matters most is that he has met the test when the stakes were highest.

"He ended our talk by telling me how much he appreciated my consistent support and said that I was the best friend he had in the West." Nixon then gave me the yellow legal pad on which he had scribbled his initial impressions of the Yeltsin meeting. As I read them, he said, "I have made notes like those after every significant meeting I have had since I entered public life. It's important for historical purposes."

Fortunately, the landing at the Saint Petersburg airport was much less turbulent than the one in Moscow. A small Russian delegation waited for us to deplane and joined us for the drive into the city, where the great structures were painted the most vivid blues, yellows, and greens. Monuments to Peter the Great and Lenin lined the entrance to the city, and the grand Hermitage, the winter palace of the czars, loomed before us. Nixon, riding in the car directly in front of mine, turned around and pointed wildly to the Hermitage to be sure I did not miss it. With graceful architecture and vibrant color, the city defied the bleak sentence handed down by winter.

Nixon's first meeting was scheduled to be a round-table discussion with Saint Petersburg's top businesspeople, chaired by Mayor Anatoly Sobchak. Nixon, preferring one-on-one private meetings, appealed unsuccessfully to Simes to change the format. Sobchak, he was told, was proud of the entrepreneurial spirit reigning in Saint Petersburg and wanted to showcase its leaders. Nixon conceded reluctantly.

Mayor Sobchak, an energetic and dynamic man, bounded down the ice-covered steps of his residence to greet Nixon and our small staff. As we stood in the darkness of late afternoon, Nixon introduced me, and Sobchak, noticing that I did not have a scarf around my neck, asked, "Why aren't you equipped for the cold?"

Nixon turned toward me and answered, "She's one of those indestructible types."

"Like you, Mr. President, yes?" Sobchak asked, and Nixon laughed as we climbed the stairs.

Fortunately for the former president, who was extremely tired, most of the discussion was led by the Saint Petersburg entrepreneurs, who regaled him with stories of successful private enterprise in a country still held hostage by the Communist mentality. They told him of developing private businesses despite bureaucratic red tape, organized crime, and limited international support and appealed for greater trade and investment from the United States.

The next morning, I arrived at Mariinsky Palace as Nixon's second, more private meeting with Sobchak was beginning. This discussion focused on the business of governing the city, from deterring crime and encouraging free-market activity to striking out from under Moscow's control. This talk was much more productive for Nixon, who was now rested and better adjusted to the rigors of daily travel, and for Sobchak, who used it to get advice from the former president and offer appreciation for Nixon's efforts in behalf of Russia.

"Only you truly understand, Mr. President," Sobchak sighed. "Others in the West talk about helping Russia; you are willing to do it."

At Simes's suggestion, we added Riga, Latvia, to the schedule. When the Soviet Union dissolved, ethnic Russians living in some of the other fourteen newly independent states alleged mistreatment by those governments, particularly in the Baltic region. Simes believed that it was crucial for Nixon to bring a message of tolerance to one of the Baltic states, preferably Latvia, where basic civil rights were allegedly being denied to Russians. Nixon agreed, and we were shuttled to our government guesthouse accommodations overlooking the Baltic Sea.

The first official function in Riga was a small, semiformal state dinner hosted by President Anatoliys Gorbunovs in honor of the former American president. Gorbunovs suspected the reason behind Nixon's visit, and conversation was tense. Nixon talked generally about Latvian independence, political and economic reform, and the current Russian perspective, but the social atmosphere precluded serious discussion. Frustrated by the lack of substantive talks, he followed dinner with a long, recuperative walk on the beach with Simes, after which he spoke with me.

"State dinners are grueling wherever you are. You have to make conversation and keep it light. That was never one of my favorite things, and it takes a lot out of me," he said wearily.

The next morning, we arrived at the Latvian capitol to discover that the prime minister was dissolving the government and would not attend his scheduled meeting with Nixon, who flew into a rage.

"Goddamn it! I did not come all the way out here to be stood up or to see second-tier people," he fumed at Simes. "I am not staying another minute. Let's go. *Now!*"

Simes tried to calm him, but Nixon, accepting no excuses, bolted for the door. Rushing after him, I saw him explode once again as Simes informed him that the Latvians now insisted on a press conference.

"What?" he cried in disbelief. "No, I am *not* doing a press conference. For God's sake, I didn't see the prime minister, so what the hell am I going to say?"

After finally being persuaded by Simes to talk to the press, he gave them a short interview, and then we boarded the plane for a return trip to Moscow. Nixon traveled in silence, now more disgusted than furious.

On the tarmac, our government cars idled, ready to whisk us to a hastily arranged meeting with Ruslan Khasbulatov, the speaker of the Soviet-era parliament, the Congress of People's Deputies. Khasbulatov was Yeltsin's political nemesis and, like Rutskoi, a scheming reactionary determined to replace him. By seeing Khasbulatov, Nixon would be granting him a measure of legitimacy, but he believed in talking with the opposition while they were still just the opposition.

With the ordeal of the morning's episode behind him, Nixon invited me to accompany him to the meeting with Khasbulatov. In the diplomatic Gold Room of the Russian White House, Nixon was introducing me to several Russian officials when a rush of footsteps passed and a voice announced "the speaker." Khasbulatov entered the room and walked toward Nixon. With an unexpected shove, a burly KGB officer grabbed me from behind, lifted me off the floor, and moved me several feet away from Nixon so that he and Khasbulatov could have a proper introduction. Moments later, I was permitted to greet Khasbulatov and take my place next to Nixon on the American side of the table.

Khasbulatov was intense, sharp, tough, and articulate. At the time, I recalled in my notes that "he used compromising rhetoric but I sense he's unyielding." Khasbulatov claimed adamantly that he wanted to work with Yeltsin but that the Russian president was accelerating reform when it should be slowed to allow it to be "responsibly" executed. Though he argued for a more moderate approach, Khasbulatov wanted the reform process reversed.

"*You* know about checks and balances," he told Nixon in a clever twist of phrase. "We in the parliament are providing checks to the president's policies when we think he has gone overboard."

Nixon firmly told Khasbulatov that Russian reform need not be Polish-style "shock therapy" but an appropriately paced program of increased political participation and decentralized economics. Khasbulatov, like Rutskoi, wanted to restore centralization and Soviet-era discipline with authoritarian rule from Moscow, preferably under him. Cloaked loosely in their diplomatic jargon were personal ambitions to govern Russia, constituting what Nixon believed was a movement toward usurpation.

Immediately after the meeting, we arrived at a new hotel overlooking the Kremlin. After spending an hour in his suite writing, Nixon invited me to appreciate his full view of the Kremlin and to take the caviar the hotel had left for him. He was developing a speech that he would deliver the following night to a large group of prominent Russian officials, including former prime minister Yegor Gaidar.

"I let them know that I only want a standing microphone for this speech," he said. "I'm delivering it without notes, and I do not want a podium. I'm probably spending too much time on this damn speech as it is, and it's probably too long with the translation, but what the hell. I might as well do it right." He walked to the table and handed me the caviar. "For the road," he said.

At home in the United States, Nixon never attended the dinners or other social functions prior to his speaking engagements. To keep the material clear and fresh in his mind, he arrived precisely when he was scheduled to speak and kept the socializing to a minimum. Abroad, however, he could not always control the circumstances, and on this last night in Russia he had to endure a lengthy reception and dinner before speaking. The sight of the podium that his Russian hosts brought in at the last minute sent him into a tailspin.

Despite his irritation, the thirty-minute speech was well delivered and well received. His discussion of the new U.S.-Russian partnership and the need for a successful Russian reform process was met with a standing ovation, but back at the hotel he was critical of his performance. When I gave him a positive review, he just shrugged and replied, "Well, you know, you plug away and hope to make an impression. The translator wasn't the best, but I think it went all right. But I must say that when I saw that goddamned podium being brought in, I thought I'd lose it." He walked to the window with the Kremlin view and stared at the fortress walls towering in the nighttime sky.

"I won't be back," he said erroneously, "but you will. Remember looking at this view when you do." And with that, he wished me a good night.

———

We left Russia as we had arrived: in the midst of a swirling snowstorm. As the plane climbed into the air, the falling snow seemed to mask even the reality of the landscape.

We landed in Kiev, Ukraine, for a brief diplomatic stopover. Russian-Ukrainian relations had become increasingly tense, stemming from conflicts

over the border status of Crimea and the evaporation of the Russian oil supply. Ukraine was in a precarious position. Wary of possible Russian expansionism yet reliant on Moscow for material resources, it was seized by fear
and dependency—ingredients for an intractable security dilemma. And
Russia, dependent on Ukraine's agricultural products, could not afford the
market prices Ukraine now charged. "If we lose Ukraine," Lenin once said
about the Soviet Union, "we will lose our heads." Russia's reliance upon
Ukraine, though less severe than Ukraine's reliance on Russia, generated
conflict that threatened to erupt militarily. Ukraine could not live with Russia, but Kiev also could not live without it.

Nixon wanted to send a signal to Moscow that Kiev was geopolitically important to the United States and that the West was monitoring their relationship. He asked Simes and me to attend his meetings with President
Leonid Kravchuk and Prime Minister Leonid Kuchma. Upon arrival at
Kravchuk's presidential suite, our party was immediately separated and
shown into different rooms. I waited until Simes found me, and we joined
Nixon for the first fifteen minutes of his meeting with Kravchuk. The shrewd
and serious Ukrainian president told Nixon about the volatile state of Russian-Ukrainian relations, indicating that their acrimonious relationship of
mutual dependency was fueling escalating military tensions. "The Russian
bear is always there," Kravchuk said, holding up both of his hands in the air.

Kuchma's remarks reflected similar apprehensions about Russia but focused primarily on the staggering political and economic reform process.
"We cannot accelerate reform until we can stand on our own, and we will
not be able to do that until we have a normal relationship with Russia," he
said. Ukraine had not even achieved the modest level of reform that Russia
had, and Nixon left the country disappointed with the slow pace of reform
but with an unexpected appreciation of its geopolitical predicament.

Poland, by contrast, with success at rapid reform and without a significant border on Russia, showed the true colors of independence.

During the cold war, Nixon had called the nations of Eastern Europe
"captive nations," bestowing a powerful image of victimization upon the region. Forty-five years of Soviet political, economic, and military control had
erased national identities and replaced them with tyranny and repression.
Despite the rule by force, the Eastern Europeans refused to be silenced. In
Hungary in 1956, during the Prague Spring in 1968, and in the shipyards
of Gdańsk, Poland, in 1980, they struggled gallantly to reclaim their countries.

Evening was falling as we landed in the gray slush at Warsaw's military
airport. With my Polish heritage in mind, Nixon insisted that I ride through
the streets of the capital to the hotel with him.

"During the cold war, as you know, I was in Poland, and Warsaw used to look like Moscow," he said. "Gray, dreary, and depressing—the Communist way. Now, just look at the vitality and energy! Now we see that we're really in the West. My God! Warsaw has become a different world; it has come alive!"

His amazement carried over into his remarks later that evening at a formal dinner given in his honor by the Polish foreign minister. In an emotional toast, he recalled his 1959 visit to Warsaw, when thousands of Poles defied a government warning and lined the streets to greet him.

"Even then," he said, "I knew something miraculous would happen in Poland."

Of the three countries we visited that day—Russia, Ukraine, and Poland—each was experiencing its own miracle. Russia and Ukraine were still weaning themselves from communism, but Poland was already reaping both the rewards and the problems of reform in progress. The contrast was striking: each country represented different stages of the same overwhelming process.

The next morning we proceeded to Belvidere, the presidential residence, to meet with Lech Walesa. With his defiant leadership of the Solidarity movement in Gdańsk in 1980, Walesa had become the symbol for Eastern European resistance to Soviet-installed communism and a mythic hero with its success. His unparalleled popularity vaulted him to the presidency, where he was often bored with presiding over reform and frustrated by declining approval ratings.

As a protocol officer announced the entrance of Walesa, I stepped quickly away from Nixon and watched the boisterous and magnetic Polish president greet him, then promptly light a cigarette and launch into a monologue about potential Russian expansionism. Nixon tried to reassure him and turn the talk toward the status of Polish reform, but Walesa remained focused on Russia and the need for increased Western aid.

"Poland gave the West a great gift—political and military victory in the cold war," he said emotionally. "The West will not take this gift, and you can't force anyone to take a present they don't want." No longer supported by Russia to the east and not yet accepted by the West, the countries of Eastern Europe had become orphans. Walesa, expressing the abandonment felt by most of the Eastern bloc, implored the United States to fund greater assistance or face grave consequences.

"Walesa was a great revolutionary," Nixon said to me later, "but we shall see if he is up to governing. In most cases, the revolutionary seldom makes a good leader. It's like campaigning and governing: two different things requiring very different talents." He had no such doubts about Prime Minister

Hanna Suchocka, who reviewed the intricacies of Poland's economic transition and was willing, as he put it, "to bite the bullet on reform."

After a brief but dynamic press conference with the Polish media, Nixon invited his staff to join him for a midafternoon stroll through Warsaw's Old Town, which was rebuilt after its destruction during the Nazi occupation. But when he saw that there were few people outside with whom he could interact, he turned back to the car disappointed.

At midnight, Nixon was awake and called for me. His room was dark except for a small light streaming from a foyer desk lamp.

"Mr. President?" I asked, clutching my notes as I walked into the suite. There was no reply.

I heard some papers being shuffled in a corner office and moved through the darkness in that direction. Wearing pajamas, a tightly wrapped bathrobe, slippers, and eyeglasses perched on the tip of his nose, he sat at a desk, writing furiously. He looked up, startled to see me.

"Oh, hi. I couldn't sleep. Look, tomorrow we go to the Czech Republic, and by morning I need these additional research items from you," he said, handing me a paper scribbled with his notes. "This trip has gone fine so far, and I don't want any screwups now."

I turned to leave, and Nixon stood up, his tone softening. "I just want Prague done right. You know, we really can't have anything go wrong."

"I know," I said. "No problem."

"It's just that I figured that I'd get these things out of the way," he said. "Well, you know you can do this research tomorrow. You don't have to do it tonight. Here, let me turn on some lights so you don't kill yourself on the way out." He walked me to the door and closed it quietly behind me.

We arrived in Prague as a morning snowfall was ending. When the plane came to a stop, Nixon announced, "Prague will take your breath away."

What was once the Iron Curtain was now the baroque châteaux, the medieval villages, and the verdant river valleys of the Czech Republic. The streets were animated by small musical bands entertaining passersby, clusters of vendors, and puppeteers undaunted by the winter weather and by the colors of newfound freedom. It was a Saturday, and life in Prague had the relaxed tenor of a holiday.

Simes and I accompanied Nixon to his meeting with one of President Vaclav Havel's closest economic advisers, Vaclav Klaus, who spoke primarily about the pace and scope of the free-market reforms. Like Poland, the Czech Republic was experiencing both the benefits and the complications of a successful reform process. Simes and I posed several questions to Klaus to relieve Nixon of some of the diplomatic burden and were surprised to learn that the Czechs, like the Poles, feared renewed German expansionism more than Russian imperialism. I wanted to discuss the matter with Nixon as we traveled to the next meeting, with the Czech president, but I saw that his eyes were closed in either thought or sleep.

Havel had been a popular dissident playwright during the cold war, and his works were reputed to have inspired the resistance movements of the late 1980s. As the unrivaled leader of the peaceful Velvet Revolution that overthrew communism in Czechoslovakia, he was lifted to the new presidency on a wave of public gratitude and presided over the amicable split with Slovakia. Like Polish president Lech Walesa, Havel was a revolutionary now charged with governing, but he was an artist before he was a politician.

As we crossed the Vltava River, I could see our destination, the Prague Palace, rise above us. We drove up the hillside, past isolated cottages in scattered patches of forest, until we reached the entrance to the president's residence. The diplomatic waiting area was quiet, serene, and understated, leaving us quite unprepared for what we were about to encounter in Havel's office.

The Czech president rose from a chair as we entered, cigarette dangling from his lips. Sporting casual clothing and disheveled hair, Havel smashed the cigarette into a crystal cup and walked around the black minimalist furniture and a giant red sculpture of a water pipe to greet Nixon, who seemed a little disconcerted by the avant-garde setting.

Havel immediately lit another cigarette and reclined on a velvet sofa; Nixon sat across from him in a baroque velvet chair, and Simes and I took our places next to him. As their conversation began, I noticed a large impressionist painting of two nude women hanging directly over Havel. I glanced quickly at Nixon and saw him notice the painting. He stopped short in midsentence, and his eyebrows shot up.

Havel, oblivious to the effect his artwork was having on his American guests, spoke philosophically about the end of Soviet-imposed communism, saying "Gorbachev remains a captive of socialism; Yeltsin has liberated himself." Nixon, recalling Havel's past as a dissident playwright, said, "The twentieth century was a lost century for Russia artistically. Seventy years of communism extinguished the great Russian artistic flame. But in Czechoslovakia, under communism for forty-five years, that flame never died because of brave, talented, and principled men like you." Havel waved his cigarette in appreciation and returned the compliment with high praise for Nixon's cold war leadership. Trailed by a cloud of smoke, Havel then walked us out to the quiet waiting room, where his creative presence seemed misplaced.

"Monica! Wasn't that painting something else?" Nixon chuckled when we returned to the hotel. "I'll be damned! Imagine! A president having that hanging in his office! I must be of a different generation because I couldn't believe it!" He hooted again with laughter and truly relaxed for the first time since we had come abroad.

"Well! It looks like I've slept for thirteen hours," he said the next morning, when he woke at eleven o'clock. "I really needed it, but I hope I didn't cut into your Prague time," he said. "I'll tell you what. To make up for the fact that I've kept you here all morning, I will take you for a guided tour of Prague. How about that?"

Accompanied by several Czech security officers, we began a two-hour walking tour of the city. Nixon, thoroughly rested and bundled against the cold, insisted that our first stop would be the famous Wenceslas clock.

"I hope you like it after the damn buildup I've given it," he said as we stood waiting for the hand-carved characters within the clock to perform. "The whole city is just like this clock: magical, full of surprises. The spirit of this place is remarkable. Of course, the shops that you see all around here weren't here during my previous trips, and because of the Prague Spring the Czech Communists were the fiercest in the Eastern bloc. But the place has just stayed beautiful."

Nixon then made his way to a cathedral, climbed the steps, and found the main doors locked. He located an open side entrance, led us into a small empty chapel, then broke away from us and approached the altar, clasping his hands in prayer. Suddenly, he turned back, walked to a pew, and in a highly uncharacteristic spiritual display, knelt and bowed his head. Moments later, he rose and in silence led us out.

When word spread that Nixon was strolling through Prague, he was overwhelmed by autograph seekers and well-wishers. He enjoyed an unqualified respect and admiration abroad that he was often denied in the United States, and he savored it. He posed for pictures, told jokes, and fielded questions with good-natured aplomb.

Our next stop was the old Jewish Memorial, a hauntingly beautiful testament to the thousands of Czech Jews sacrificed through the decades. As we climbed its winding staircases, Nixon shook his head sadly.

"The Communists shut down all of this," he said. "Denying the history— that was their idea of how to succeed. They thought that if they just shut down the history, they could start from scratch. As we know, it doesn't work that way. Prague, of course, is one of the most beautiful cities in the world, and it was preserved because Czechoslovakia folded when the Germans came through. Poor Warsaw was destroyed—burned to the ground because the Poles fought back. But now so much has changed. Life has come back to these countries. They've really climbed out from the depths of the cold war."

We flew to Paris on February 21 for the fifteenth and final day of the trip. Nixon had contracted a cold, which was getting worse, but he insisted on keeping his appointment with French president François Mitterrand and treating us to a final dinner in Versailles.

Before he went to sleep that night, he padded into our makeshift office, wearing navy-blue flannel pajamas, matching robe, and slippers.

"I was about to turn in when I thought that I'd just like to thank you again for all that you did on this trip. Here," he said, handing us a bottle of Dom Pérignon champagne. "The hotel left it for me, but I can't drink it." He turned and entered his darkened bedroom, closing the door behind him.

Early the next morning, Nixon met with me to confirm his afternoon appointment and review his talking points. When he saw that I was staring at his attire, he stood up and smoothed out his cardigan sweater.

"When you saw me in my pajamas last night, you probably thought you had seen it all. Not so! This is my Jimmy Carter look," he cracked. "What do you think?"

"Well, as long as you're comfortable," I said.

"Well *that* was a hell of a political response! My God, you're learning!" He laughed and, with a nod, dismissed me.

He emerged two hours later in his suit, ready for his meeting with Mitterrand. Whenever he traveled to Russia, he made a point of stopping in at least one Western European capital to survey the state of Europe and the views toward its powerful Eastern neighbor. After Nixon's private meeting with Mitterrand, we left for the airport. His cold was beginning to overwhelm him, and once he was seated on the plane, he scanned the contents of his briefcase, wrote some notes about the meeting, and closed his eyes. About an hour later, he called me over to his seat and reviewed his conversation with the French president.

"Mitterrand seems supportive of Yeltsin, but he was totally for Gorbachev, and that is affecting his view of Yeltsin," he said. "Those in the United States who claim that Yeltsin is finished are irresponsible; they're just trying to prove that they were right on Gorbachev. Mitterrand doesn't go that far, and he wants Yeltsin to succeed; of course, the Europeans would be on the front lines if Yeltsin fails.

"When I told him that some observers in the United States believe that Eastern Europe should be a buffer zone, he was incredulous. 'Where did such an odd idea come from?' he said. 'Eastern Europe has always been a part of Europe, except for the period when Europe was divided by the cold war.' He, of course, is big on European integration and would like to see Eastern Europe brought in at an appropriate time."

He put the notes down and removed his eyeglasses, wielding them in his hand for emphasis. "This trip was enormously successful. We had a bit of an organizational problem in Russia, but we won't have that problem next month in Asia. When we get back to New Jersey, however, I want you to develop a list of heavyweights—senators, congressmen, journalists, academics—whoever *you* think that I should see when we return. After a trip like this, it's important to share your observations with the people who matter and hope that someone listens."

As we flew into the night over the Atlantic Ocean, the small cabin grew dark, and Nixon pulled a blanket around him and fell asleep. I had been asleep for some time when I was awakened by a tap on my shoulder.

"Monica?" Nixon whispered.

"Yes, sir!" I whispered, bolting upright. "What's wrong?"

"Oh nothing. Are you sleeping?" he asked. "Well, you were. I'm sorry. Go back to sleep. I just thought we'd talk about the China trip, but we can do that later." He moved back to his chair and lit his overhead light to read the copy of E. H. Carr's *The Twenty Years' Crisis* I had lent to him.

I looked around the cabin. The rest of the group remained asleep, and since I was now fully awake, I stole over to the insomniac. "We can discuss the Asia trip now," I told him.

He looked at me over the top of his eyeglasses and smiled. "I didn't mean to wake you, but I want to be sure that you start collecting the background materials I'll need for Korea, Japan, and China. That trip is only five weeks away," he said. "It will be my last trip to Asia, and I want it to go smoothly." He glanced out the window and into the darkness. "And who knows when I'll be back to Europe."

"Sooner than you think," I said.

He closed the book in his lap. "Everyone is exhausted," he whispered, looking around the dim cabin, and as he shut off his overhead light, he said softly, "Yes, it has been quite a trip."

The landing at Teterboro Airport in New Jersey woke all of us. Nixon sat upright and fumbled through his briefcase, stashing notes, books, and eyeglasses. The rest of us collected our belongings and began the strenuous process of deplaning. It was midnight, and the snow and ice covering the tarmac made it difficult to distinguish between our Teterboro and Moscow arrivals.

Nixon stood alone at the bottom of the plane's stairs, waiting for his staff to follow so that he could thank each one of us. I suggested that he move out of the cold and into his idling limousine. Walking together, we reviewed the significance of what we had learned during the trip and how he would communicate it to the rest of the country.

As I opened the door to the car for him, I offered my thanks for inviting me to accompany him. In the darkness, I could see him place his briefcase inside the car, step halfway in, then turn toward me. Slowly he raised his hand to his forehead and accepted the gratitude with a small salute. As the limousine carried him away, I stood alone on the tarmac and quietly returned the salute.

———

Upon our return on February 22, we learned that Clinton had arranged to meet with Yeltsin. Nixon was surprised. "I thought he'd be crazy to meet with world leaders so soon after the election since he was elected to take on the domestic stuff," he said over the phone on February 25. "But it's smart. Shows he's presidential. And at least he's thinking about the goddamned issue.

"I see that Clinton and Yeltsin have announced a summit for April 4. He'd be wise to talk to me before that . . . I don't know if he will call on me. He should, but the newspeople are slobbering all over him, so he may not want to alienate them by talking to me. We'll see."

Three days later, Nixon felt that Clinton had been influenced by his trip to Russia. The president was reported to have proposed a three-hundred-million-dollar increase in the amount of aid pledged to Russia, prompting Nixon to reply, "That's pennies."

"He probably did that to preempt any criticism from you on the issue," I said.

"True, but it's still tokenism. He needs to do more, and if he doesn't, I will come after him. All of this other crap he's consumed with—gays in the military, health reform—none of it matters compared to having to fight another cold war."

As he worked on another op-ed for *The New York Times* on the Russian situation, he took a call from his good friend Senator Bob Dole late in the afternoon of March 2.

"Dole told me something very interesting," he said to me after the conversation. "He said that Clinton may go to [Senator] Strom Thurmond's party next Tuesday, and Dole told him that I was going to be there and that we should meet prior to it. And Clinton—I don't know how serious he was—said, 'Well, I guess I'll call him on Russia or something.' We'll see. The guy overcommits on everything. I doubt he'll call."

The irony was that it was Dole, the man who would challenge Clinton in 1996, who facilitated Nixon's extraordinary close working relationship with the president. And as much as Nixon wanted Dole to be the next president, he needed to work with the current one in order to secure an effective American policy toward Russia. If Clinton acted on Nixon's advice, not only would he advance U.S. policy interests, but he would be helped politically.

Clinton called Nixon several hours after Dole did. That initial conversation began a surprisingly constructive relationship between them—surprising most of all to Nixon. He believed that since they were of two different political parties and two different generations, Clinton would not be inclined to call on him. And even if he were, Nixon thought that since Mrs. Clinton had worked for the House Watergate Committee, she would prevent the president from reaching out to him. Nixon was wrong.

Later that evening, he left a brief message on my answering machine: "I just had a forty-minute conversation with your friend who lives in the White House."

The next morning, Nixon summoned me to his office, eager to share what had been discussed. I found him sitting in his corner chair, twirling his eyeglasses, and smiling. "Have a seat," he said to me. "Well, it was a surprising thing, but your prophecy was correct. He did call. I waited five minutes on the line, and then eight minutes, and they couldn't find him. The White House operator asked if he could call me back. At about ten minutes to ten o'clock, he called again. Frankly he sounded very tired, and—most surprising—he confided in me; he said things that he absolutely would not want made public. I wonder if his wiretaps are working!

"He was very respectful but with no sickening bullshit. To give you a quick overview, he only spent one third of the time on foreign policy, mostly Russia, but he asked about China also. He said that he was worried that his defense cuts may be too steep; of course he may have just said that because I'd be against cutting defense too much. But he likes to talk, and he was candid on aid to Russia. I gave him the highlights of what we found. He asked what I thought of Yeltsin, and he said he admired his guts for seeing him when Clinton was a candidate. After all, Bush was president. He admired the fact that Yeltsin was so straightforward; I told him that with Yeltsin what you see is what you get. He said that he has spoken to Yeltsin twice and Yeltsin sounded worried. Clinton suggested that they meet earlier than the April 4 date, but Yeltsin wanted to wait until after his struggle with the parliament had been resolved. He said that Yeltsin told him to see me."

Nixon raised an eyebrow. "That was something! But Clinton asked me, 'Will he last?' I told him that it will be a very tough thing. And he won't survive unless he has U.S. support. He is the best politician in Russia, the most popular—and elected. We cannot leave any distance between the United States and him. He asked about sending technical assistance and so forth. But what is amazing is that two thirds of the conversation was about domestic policy."

He bit one end of his eyeglasses. "He said it was a tough call as to what to do. I told him that I am almost solely concentrating on foreign policy, because I didn't want him to feel that he had to listen to me on that score; we are, after all, on different sides of most domestic issues. So I reassured him that I don't engage in partisan politics anymore but that any criticism I give is meant to be constructive. He appreciated that."

Nixon continued, "Anyway, it was the best conversation with a president I've had since I was president. Better than with Bush, because Baker was always looming around, and I *never* had such a conversation with Reagan. Clinton wanted to be reassured. It was never a dialogue with the others. I used to have to force things into the conversation with Reagan and Bush. This was a different cup of tea. . . . This guy does a lot of thinking."

Clinton had risked criticism from within his own party by talking to Nixon, and he did it anyway. The former president was impressed. "I think that his call is significant." He stopped, put his glasses on the end table, and folded his hands. "He invited me to the White House.

"In twelve years, neither Reagan nor Bush *ever* put me on the White House schedule or put a picture out. We would get the story out on occasion, but you know . . ."

Just as Nixon was considered the only president who could open diplomatic relations with China, Clinton was the only one who could bestow upon Nixon the kind of public credibility he so desired. A baby boomer Democratic president inexperienced in foreign affairs had little to lose and much to gain by seeking advice from Nixon. Because enough time had passed since Watergate prematurely ended Nixon's presidency and because Nixon remained a serious contender on the international stage, Clinton saw no political liability in consulting him. Free of the political baggage Republican presidents carried in dealing with the scandal-damaged former president, Clinton willingly used Nixon both as a sounding board and as a source for advice.

The next day, I entered Nixon's office as he was dictating his thoughts on their conversation, and he waved me in.

"I tried to get it through to him that he needs to spend more time on foreign policy because—well, look, he's starting to be criticized in the press for it, and he must tend to it before a crisis forces him into it. Besides, foreign policy is just more interesting. As long as he is talking to me, he'll be OK. If he relies on his Carter-type advisers, he will run into trouble."

He had dinner that evening with former ambassador Robert Strauss, after which he related their conversation to me. "Bob told me that he had just spoken to Clinton, who told him that his conversation with me was 'the best conversation he has had as president' and that he learned more from his talk with me than from all of his advisers. Clinton is trying to learn, and he told Bob that he wants my recommendations on Russia. He told him that the letter I sent him after the election was the most moving he received. Now, the guy could just be full of crap, but at least he knows how to be diplomatic! In any event, Clinton is a listener, and my sense is that he has a profound fear of failure. It took guts for him to call me, but maybe those guts came from that fear."

Nixon continued to court Clinton by publishing his next op-ed in *The New York Times* on March 5. The original title, "President Clinton's Historic Opportunity," was changed to the more powerful "Clinton's Greatest Challenge," and Nixon opened the piece by lobbing that challenge directly at the new president: "If [Clinton] demonstrates the same leadership qualities in addressing the major foreign policy issue of our time, he can secure his place in history as a great president. That issue is the survival and success of political and economic freedom in Russia."

Nixon continued by identifying the obstacles to that process, including astronomical inflation and crime rates, plummeting living standards, and violent ethnic conflicts. There were, however, positive signs that signaled the promise of reform: increased privatization and growth in private industries, a free press, fewer shortages, and a workforce increasingly responsive to economic incentives. He urged an immediate increase in Western financial aid to Russia, a restructuring of its debt, and a single coordinator to organize the flow of money, goods, and services to the country. Nixon wrote, "It would be tragic if, at this critical point, the United States fails to provide the leadership only it can provide."

Like the 1992 Russian-aid memorandum, this piece made a familiar argument and used flattery to persuade the president. The difference was that the new president might be far more open to the suggestions than the previous one had been. Nixon deliberately played on Clinton's insecurity in foreign affairs and his need to be respected abroad as well as at home. Most important, Nixon pandered to Clinton's vanity by implying that if he just listened to him, he could place himself in the ranks of the great presidents. The maneuver worked, at least initially.

Several days before he went to the White House, Nixon said to me, "If you can think of anything I need to tell him—although most of it is in the *Times* piece—let me know."

I suggested that he tell Clinton that the Eastern European leaders with whom he met were more fearful of an American withdrawal from Europe and a resurgent Germany than they were of an authoritarian government in Russia replacing the fragile democratic one. Nixon agreed that Clinton should be told, although, he added, "The Germans are of course not a threat, but he needs to take the Eastern Europeans' concerns seriously."

Nixon met with Clinton at the White House on March 8 and stayed in the capital for two additional days to deliver a highly anticipated speech on the House floor. The events were covered extensively and positively, and Nixon returned to New Jersey on March 11 triumphant.

He sat behind his desk, beaming, as I walked into his office. I sat in my usual chair, and he moved into the corner to sit across from me. "This trip," he said, smiling, "was probably the best one I have had to Washington since

I left the presidency. The House speech was really something. I did it from the well, because I wanted to talk *with* them, not at them. I told them that the last time I was there was forty-three years ago, when I briefed the chamber about the Alger Hiss case. Who would have thought I'd be back in 1993, talking about a democratic Russia? They loved it. And I said that I heard [General Douglas] MacArthur speak after he was recalled by Truman from Korea. He said, 'Old soldiers never die; they just fade away.' I said, 'Old politicians sometimes die, but they never fade away.' The place roared! Oh, boy! It was really something."

He recrossed his legs on the ottoman and continued. "The meeting at the White House was the best I have had since I was president." Nixon related his initial interaction with the president and the first lady and then told me what he told Clinton about "issue number one: Russia.

"I told him that on Russia the risk of action is great but the risk of inaction is greater. He took it. He was also very interested in China. He told me to tell the Chinese that he's an OK guy, because he's nervous about what they think of him. I told him to hit the Japanese hard on aiding Russia and to hammer them all on the IMF. He brightened up when I told him about the grain-barter deal. He made a note when I said that Russia must develop an entrepreneurial class and do it at the grass roots—that's the Peace Corps mentality, which is why he picked up on it. He also agreed that it will take more money than what he put forward."

Nixon continued, "He also said that the domestic issues are very difficult." He lowered his voice. "Monica, history will not remember him for anything he does domestically. The economy will recover; it's all short-term and, let's face it, very boring."

When I asked if he sensed that Clinton was getting frustrated with domestic politics, he replied, "Yes! He's getting more interested in the foreign policy stuff because he realizes getting the domestic stuff through is just very hard—pretty thankless too. For the last six months of the Bush administration, foreign policy was an orphan. Clinton has got to seize this."

Nixon clearly appreciated the political risk Clinton took by seeing him so publicly. "I think that Clinton showed real guts by having me there. And I think we could work together on the Russian thing and on whatever he wants. I got a good sense from all of it."

Nixon had set the stage for a productive and cordial working relationship with the sitting president, whom he considered highly intelligent and amenable to hearing his advice. Not only was Clinton eager to learn from Nixon, but he seemed willing to give Nixon far more influence in shaping the nation's foreign policy than had either Reagan or Bush.

As Nixon considered his next move, the unrepresentative and antireform Russian parliament voted to strip Yeltsin of some powers and assume more of its own, leading some in the West to speculate that the Russian president was losing control to an ascendant and unelected congress. "These people [in the press] are overreacting," Nixon said on March 12. "The Russians are just jockeying for power. And I see some idiots are saying Clinton shouldn't make the mistake Bush made and overinvest in Yeltsin the way Bush did in Gorbachev *and* Yeltsin! That's pure horseshit. That was a choice between Gorbachev and Yeltsin, communism and democracy. What are we talking about?"

He paused. "I'm very concerned about Yeltsin's future after the showdown with the parliament this morning. These bastards in the press want him to fail to prove they were right. Yeltsin needs an economic czar and a good political adviser. I should be over there telling him how to handle this goddamned illegitimate congress."

I asked him if Yeltsin should consider dissolving the congress, "subverting democracy in order to save it."

"I couldn't agree more. Emergency rule—ruling by decree—is probably necessary to keep reform moving." His anger exploded. "What is the matter with the goddamned State Department assholes? Don't they see this? Why aren't they supporting Yeltsin? I'm going to call Simes and tell him to pass the word to Yeltsin to cancel the April referendum. He must not call elections when his numbers are down and the economy is in the pits. He will lose, and if he does, he'll have to resign. It's too much of a gamble."

After the evening news that night, he called me to fret about CBS's "gloomy" story on Yeltsin's future. He asked, "Do you think they're doing it to embarrass me?"

I told him that the situation in Russia was desperate enough to warrant news stories warning of a potential collapse of the Yeltsin government.

"I know. It's just that I—well, I don't regret going out on a limb for Yeltsin. If the press wants to say 'I told you so,' then so be it."

A few days later, he was shocked to hear that the administration had considered the idea of sending American troops to Moscow to support Yeltsin's government. "You can't send American troops to *Russia*, for God's sake. They already have a huge military with its own agenda, and when we went against the Bolsheviks, it was a disaster. Besides, we can't be in a position to interfere in their internal affairs—and *militarily?*" he shrieked. "Oh, my God!"

The United States needed a broad approach to Russian developments that avoided entanglement in Russian political battles. With the obvious exception of the extreme nationalists, the United States could tolerate a variety of groups in power with different proposals for economic and political reform. To insist that Russia always act, at home and abroad, according to a U.S. government formula would have been destabilizing and wrong. Demanding policy perfection exacted too high a price, for the Russians, the Americans, and the rest of the world.

The underlying reality was that the second Russian revolution would not be complete until the Soviet-era constitution and the unelected members of parliament from the old order were replaced. New elections would ensure that all sides were on equal democratic footing, and by supporting the reform process, the United States could improve the electoral chances of the reformers.

On March 18, Nixon took the unusual step of drafting advice to Yeltsin on how to manage the conflict with the parliament. He wrote a brief memorandum to the Russian president in which he told him that he had had extensive consultations with Clinton, members of his administration, and the congressional leadership about assistance to Russia. He indicated that he found strong bipartisan support in Congress for substantial aid to Russia and that there was "no doubt" that Clinton was committed to developing a comprehensive aid package.

This would be jeopardized, however, by reports of increased political instability in Russia. He urged Yeltsin to avoid a confrontation with the Russian congress until at least after his April 4 meeting with Clinton in Vancouver. He told Yeltsin that he would be stronger politically in dealing with the Russian congress in June, after a successful summit with Clinton and after getting possible additional support from the Group of Seven industrial countries.

He asked me to fax his advice for Yeltsin to Ambassador Lukin in Washington, who would then forward it to Yeltsin. It was an extraordinary political maneuver. Since interference in another country's internal politics could be not only inappropriate but counterproductive, advice given to a foreign leader had to be offered delicately. The situation in Russia between the president and the parliament was so acute, however, that Nixon was compelled to step in.

Toward the end of March, Nixon grew pessimistic that the American president would act more forcefully on Russian aid. Despite Nixon's repeated exhortations, Clinton had acted only in a limited way. Canadian prime minister Brian Mulroney called Nixon again on March 19 to tell him that he had just spoken to Clinton and urged him to convene an emergency G-7 meeting on the Russian situation. The problem was that even if Clinton were inclined to move forward with a more aggressive plan, there was no single person outside of the government with the ability and the stature to act as a coordinator.

"I got the sense that Clinton was committed to doing more on Russia, but I hope he wasn't just telling me what I wanted to hear. Bush and Baker suffered from a great lack of creativity in foreign policy; it was a damn shame that they were in charge at the end of the cold war. But here Clinton has a historic chance to do something, and I don't see it happening. I'm dictating a memo to Dole on the Russian thing. Maybe he can do something," he said as he retrieved his handheld tape recorder from his briefcase. "Somebody had better listen to something."

The next day, Nixon was annoyed to hear that Yeltsin had declared "special rule" until after the upcoming April 25 referendum on his presidency. "He did not take a word of my advice," he said, pounding his desk with his fist. "Maybe he didn't get my memo. I don't know. I told him to avoid a confrontation with the parliament, and he's doing it anyway. But the problem is that he's more and more isolated, and he's getting bad political advice. He's rash, emotional; he acts from the heart, not the head. And now he's surrounded by advisers who are just as rash. Everyone has to keep their heads on this.

"I'm very impressed by the way the White House and Clinton have handled this [conflict with the parliament]. They kept steady, supported Yeltsin, and even [communications director George] Stephanopoulos handled it extremely well. He's much better than [Bush press secretary Marlin] Fitzwater. His answers were crisp and to the point. It's important not to say too much.

"I hope I wasn't given a bum steer on this memo to Yeltsin. But I wish I knew what happened: either he got it and paid no attention, or he didn't get it at all."

Bush, Clinton, Dole, and Yeltsin had all been targets of Nixon's direct advice on Russia. None had taken significant action based upon it. That his suggestions had gone unheeded inspired rage, disappointment, and frustration, but it did not stop him from continuing to make them.

Clinton held his first press conference on March 23, and Nixon was "very impressed" with his performance. "He handled it very well, not just on Russia, where his statement in support of greater aid was strong and correct, but on everything." The day after he met the press, Clinton called the former president, and Nixon shared his view of the conversation with me during a late-afternoon meeting at the residence.

"At about two-thirty, I got a call from Clinton, and we spoke for about twenty minutes. He came for straight advice—no bullshit. I sense he was really panicked about what to do on the Russian thing. I told him that I thought what he's done so far has been outstanding and that he must meet Yeltsin carrying a significant aid program. I reiterated that it's a risk to support Yeltsin, but if he goes down without U.S. support, it will be far worse. He must see Yeltsin alone—no secretaries of whatever or other assholes along. If I had waited for the bureaucracy, we never would have had the China initiative.

"He gave me the four policy options on Russia that he has, two of which are ludicrous. And you can't do anything at the ministerial level. I sent him a fax on this, which I think is pretty good. I told him that he must deliver a real program, and he must stand up for Yeltsin unequivocally. He must enlist the G-7 at the presidential level to make the package big enough. He should meet Yeltsin in Vladivostok and then go to Tokyo and stroke the Japanese. They should be doing more for Russia."

He paused. "He asked if I thought he should talk to Kissinger. I couldn't tell him not to, and although Henry is brilliant, that's just what he wants. So I told him to talk to Scowcroft first. Anyway, he's probably seeking advice from others, so I gave him a bit of additional advice. I told him that when he talks to others, he must *tell* them what he is going to do and *then* ask for their advice, because if you ask first, then do something else, they'll be upset. Clinton likes to talk to everyone, but when you do, your thinking gets watered down. But how do you like that?"

Nixon was a realist and knew that Clinton sought his advice for his own benefit, not for Nixon's. But Nixon, aware that his position close to Clinton's ear guaranteed him access and influence, flattered Clinton as Clinton flattered him. It was a mutually beneficial relationship: Clinton got much-needed foreign policy advice from the nation's elder statesman, and Nixon got a measure of public credibility and access to the president. And every time Clinton wove his advice into speeches and remarks about Russia, Nixon became even more confident of his ability to influence the new president.

He was also relieved to hear that Yeltsin had survived an impeachment vote in the parliament, bringing tens of thousands of people into the streets in support of him. "Even if the congress votes against him, he should ignore it," Nixon said on March 28. "And we should not be sending foreign advisers over. He's having a hell of a time with the hard-liners, and they will kill him if they think he's selling out to the West. By the way, I heard that Clinton is considering [former vice president Walter] Mondale for the ambassadorship to Moscow. That will be an enormous mistake. He doesn't know a thing about the economic side.

"I'm concerned that the administration will focus not on dollars but on people, like the Peace Corps, which isn't worth a damn. The Japanese withdrew their objections on aid to Russia, but we've got to go after them, too. Yeltsin's showdown with the parliament was a draw, but at least he survived it. That constitution is a sick joke; we all laughed at it during the cold war. But overall, the administration has been OK on all of this, particularly when we consider that Clinton didn't know a tinker's damn about foreign policy when he was elected, and the only thing he knew about Russia was what he learned when he went over there as a guest of the KGB!"

Despite Clinton's professed commitment to aiding Russia, he remained transfixed on the American economy and other domestic issues. Nixon, therefore, felt the need to refocus the nation's attention on foreign policy by traveling to the Far East. Relations with China, Japan, and Korea were suffering from benign neglect, and Nixon sought to tend to those crucial relationships *and* argue in behalf of Russia. He decided to execute this balancing act from the Pacific Rim in the hope that the administration would realign its priorities.

As we flew to Anchorage en route to Tokyo on April 3, Nixon told me that he had taken a call from Anthony Lake, Clinton's national security adviser and a veteran of the Nixon-Kissinger national security team. Nixon put on his eyeglasses and removed from his briefcase a yellow legal pad on which he had made notes of the conversation. "I told him that I appreciated their gutsy call on Russia, and he said that it couldn't have been done if I hadn't taken the lead. He brought up some things he wanted me to discuss with the Chinese—primarily on human rights—so that they can go after those who oppose MFN [most-favored-nation trading status]. Also on Russia, he said that the top-level G-7 meeting was still a live idea." He put the legal pad back into the briefcase and removed his glasses. "I don't like—or was not impressed by—what he did on Vietnam or to Kissinger," he said, referring to Lake's disavowal of Nixon's Vietnam policies, "but I've got to get along with these people, and he was very helpful."

The summit between Yeltsin and Clinton took place while we were in Alaska, and Nixon was interested in the tone of the meeting and how effectively Clinton managed Yeltsin. I reassured him that Clinton seemed to deliver to the Russian president a much-needed vote of confidence.

"If Clinton continues to step up to this and follows through, Yeltsin just might survive," he said. "And Clinton will have a triumph of historic proportions."

The trip to Asia diverted Nixon's focus temporarily from Russia, but on April 25, three days after his return, developments in Moscow again commanded his attention. Yeltsin survived a referendum with 70 percent of the popular vote, and Nixon was ecstatic. "As a political man, I didn't think he'd win this big! And he won on continuing reform. After seventy years of communism, it's thrilling to see them voting, and voting right. To listen to our goddamned media, you'd think he lost the thing. None of them wanted him to succeed. And they played it so pessimistically; I think back to 1956, when they said [Adlai] Stevenson was gaining. Stevenson!"

"And in 1960—" I began.

"Yeah, when they said Kennedy would win in a landslide."

"And McGovern," I added.

"Seventy-eight percent of the media voted for McGovern," he said.

"The seventy percent of Russians who voted for Yeltsin are his Silent Majority," I said.

"Damn right. Defying the media," he said.

The next day, he took another call from Clinton and related the substance of the conversation to me. "You will be pleased to know that I got another call from Clinton today," he began. "He thanked me again for taking the lead on aid to Russia, and he was delighted with the [Russian] election results, although he agreed with me that the media have been disgusting by downplaying Yeltsin's victory. Naturally, I'm not for Clinton, but I will side with him when the media pack comes after him. Anyway, I told him—again—that it was a gutsy call on aid but the right one, and he said he'd just talked to Yeltsin; Clinton said [Yeltsin] was pleased with the aid program, but he was having difficulty getting the goddamned bureaucracy to carry it out. And these are his own people! But they have a socialist mentality and move like snails. I told him that I completely understood. Look, if we had relied on the bureaucracy, we never would have gone forward with ninety percent of what we accomplished with regard to China, Russia, Europe, and the Middle East.

"Well—the main reason he called was to ask what I thought about Bosnia. It's obvious that he's leaning toward lifting the embargo and using limited air strikes against the Serbs. I told him that I agreed, but whatever he decided I'd support. He's on the right track with this since we have got to have a balance of force on the ground before a peace agreement is even an option, but I didn't want to push it in case he goes with something else. To reinforce this point, I told him that you can only negotiate at the table what you win on the battlefield, and I said that if the Serbs aren't stopped, they may go after other parts of Yugoslavia. He made a good point. He said, 'Yes, or in other parts of the world.' He is tilting toward action and thought that Britain and France would go along. I also told him that he cannot win the war there, but he can provide a correlation of forces that may bring some sense to their heads.

"He listened," he continued, "but who knows what we will hear tomorrow? He's very susceptible to pressure from the press. And it burns me up to see that [*New York Times* columnist] Tony Lewis—who went through a male change of life over our bombing in Vietnam—is for our involvement in Bosnia. With a Democratic president, I guess military intervention is OK." He grinned.

"Oh, I also told Clinton that Yeltsin should attract private investment like China has, and he said that he wanted to talk to me about China at a later time, so that's in the mix."

"Clinton is very clever," I said.

"He sure is," Nixon said. "But what exactly do you mean?"

"Well, by mentioning China at the end of the conversation, he leaves you tantalized, waiting for the next call—and prepared once it comes."

"Of course," Nixon said, nodding. "The guy knows how the game is played."

The former president also knew how the game was played, and he played it well. Since Nixon had made himself indispensable, Clinton relied on him. On May 1, Nixon remarked that the one thing that would reflect favorably on Clinton would be that "he bit the bullet on Russia."

"Assuming," I said, "that he follows up and gets the Congress to pass the program."

"True," he said, "but even so, at least he did it." He paused and added knowingly, "And I hope he has a better appreciation for the gut-wrenching decisions presidents have to make, like the kind he protested against when I was in there. I doubt he'll do anything on Bosnia. The libs in his party are after him to do something, but I don't think he will.

"You know, in a few days, on May 8, we will celebrate the anniversary of the second hardest decision I had to make, the first, of course, being the resignation. It was the bombing of Haiphong [in 1972]. We were worried about the Russians. It was an extremely difficult decision. No one—except for [Treasury Secretary John] Connally, really—was with me. [Elliot] Richardson was ready to resign. Kissinger was waffling. I don't think Clinton has it in him to make the tough call.

"I remember so well when [CIA director Allen] Dulles came to see me during the Cuban missile crisis. I put all of this in *Six Crises*. He told me he told Kennedy 'not to let it fail.' My God, you've got to go all the way or [do] nothing. Clinton must not go halfway on Bosnia. All of this Hamlet-like deliberating makes him look weak. We've got to get our allies, the Congress, and the people to go along. Instead of *telling* them what we are going to do, he's looking for their permission! This isn't leadership! He doesn't scare anybody, and neither does Christopher. Hillary inspires fear. You've got to put fear in these people or scare them with silence—just don't say anything and leave it uncertain. But I find his vacillation on this frankly shocking."

Nixon became concerned that Clinton's statements to him in support of Russian aid and stronger action in the former Yugoslavia were empty promises made to placate him and preempt criticism. He was, Nixon feared, just telling him what he wanted to hear. Nixon knew that Clinton was a master of political expediency, but he did not intend to be used. If Clinton were simply nipping potential dissent in the bud, then Nixon would respond with a harsh indictment not only of Clinton's policies but of his methods.

—

"I don't know what the United States is going to do in the post–cold war world," he said on May 17. We had been discussing the new book Nixon had decided to call *Beyond Peace,* since peace as an end in itself was no longer enough to inspire policy. "Our purpose is by example—not in Bosnia. It's too controversial, and I don't know what the hell they're going to do. Maybe you could look at the Kansas City speech. No," he said abruptly, "I don't want to get into that. None of the assholes in the media paid attention to that speech—only Mao did. No one else got it.

"This book is certainly going to deal with Russia, which is still issue one, regardless of what the administration does or doesn't do, but we need to get at the more profound reasons of *why* it's important and what it means for America and the world. It's the mission thing, OK? Can we do it?"

"Well, if you can't do it," I began.

"That's a cop-out," he replied. "Think about it. Can we—and I mean with all of the attacks we are going to take—do it?"

Nixon was afraid that Clinton's indecisiveness and failure to lead were robbing America of the extraordinary power, leverage, and credibility it had done so much to achieve. The new book would try to restore some of the guiding principles that had been lost. Nixon began to devote significant time to it by the middle of the year and told me on June 1 that he wanted it to be the most "personal" book he had written, "apart, of course, from *The Memoirs* and *In the Arena.*

"I want this book to be all me, and not just policy prescriptions, which will make it weaker. We want this to be challenging, uplifting, raising questions. It should get to the nitty-gritty of what it means to be an American now, without war. What are the challenges we face beyond merely maintaining peace? Is there anything that can bring the country together beyond war? What is its moral equivalent? I don't know if we can answer them; I don't know if they can be answered at all. But we're going to try.

"I want it to have three main themes: One, after a war, where do we go from here? Two, we have a crisis of spirit or whatever you want to call it. And three, what will it take to make the United States an example?—without getting into the particulars, although I do want to kick the hell out of multilateralism since the UN isn't worth a damn and the Clintonites seem hooked on it.

"I want you here as a sounding board for this project. As you know, *Six Crises* I did myself. It reads like me. It was rugged. On *Memoirs,* I had help from [Frank] Gannon and Diane [Sawyer], who did a hell of a job. We had Ray [Price, Nixon's White House director of speechwriting] on *The Real War* and some of the others. *In the Arena* was all me, and you know the arrangements for *Seize the Moment,* since you played a role. This book should be the most personal in terms of what I believe for America, since it will probably be my last book. I may have one more in me, and I think this is it."

Six days later, we met again at the residence to discuss ideas for the new project. Nixon was relaxed and anxious to begin preparing an outline. As he requested, I brought a copy of Allan Bloom's *The Closing of the American Mind* with me to the meeting. Nixon was seated in his study on the third floor when I arrived, poring over some of his notes.

"Come in, come in," he said as I came to the top of the stairs. "Are you ready for our bull session? I find these sessions when we just toss out ideas very helpful in the preparation of a book. It really gets the mind moving."

Nixon began a stream-of-consciousness recitation that covered diverse subjects, some of which would be part of the book and some of which were simply on his mind at the time.

"I don't go for this exporting democracy crap," he said. "Democracy doesn't belong everywhere. Not all societies or cultures are meant for it. It's just not advisable.

"Look at the Russians. They could never sustain our type of democracy or even the Asian type. And they shouldn't. They need to find their own way, a way that will work for them.

"The point is that the United States needs to lead. To those who say that we are not worthy to lead, I say, 'That's bullshit!' Who else is going to lead? No one. You know what I mean.

"We've got to avoid all this loose talk about democracy and capitalism. Although I like the phrase 'democratic capitalism,' some of our friends go nuts when it's mentioned."

He picked up the Bloom book. "You see this?" he said, pointing it at me. "The first two or three chapters are gangbusters. Then it falls flat when it gets into the heavy philosophical stuff. I want to avoid that." He put the book back down.

"Looking at what happened in the last election—Perotism didn't just happen in a vacuum. I was disturbed to see that the religious right gained so much momentum. They can contribute very positively to the party, and I'm glad that they're on our side. But some of their positions, like outlawing abortion, are just too extreme for the United States. They must not be permitted to take over the party or the country. They are too hung up on the individual kooky things. I admire their principles but don't think that they should be necessarily put into policy. This is where I must put distance between myself and my old friend [Patrick] Buchanan.

"This country still has great things to achieve. Cold materialism isn't enough. What would the world be like without the United States? It would be a world in terror. [Woodrow] Wilson, whom I admire for many reasons, thought leadership could be done solely by moral power. That's what the [Henry Cabot] Lodge reservations were about. And that, of course, led to the isolationism which was so disastrous in the '30s and led to the big war.

"Speaking of war, you know that it has to be cast in idealistic terms, or there is no way the people are going to support it. In Korea, we were fighting the Commies. In Vietnam, it was harder to get the message across. In the Persian Gulf, we had to send a signal to aggressors. War *is* a great enterprise, only because it brings people together in a common mission. We must find its substitute. We're here for another purpose, something more. Peace must be only a foundation. What we are really looking for is what the title of the book suggests: What is our mission beyond peace?"

Nixon's ruminations were both concrete and philosophical. He was searching for a meaning to America's role internationally in a world without a definitive conflict. When war dominated, peace was an end in itself. This was no longer the case. Conflict between nations would always arise, but Nixon wanted to ensure that America had something beyond merely sustaining peace upon which to base its existence. Even if he could not propose a solution, at least he could raise the issue.

His next flurry of thoughts and ideas came on June 23.

"I dictated a memo on [E. H.] Carr which is relevant to today's problems," he said, looking drained and tired. "One point I do want to stress is that the roles of people are different, and they should be, just like governments. I want to knock down the bull that the only important role is in the public sector. That is not true. The guy in the factory is just as important as the bureaucrat in the goddamned EPA. Government is a good calling, but it's not a higher calling. And with Hillary gassing around about the [*Tikkun* editor] Michael Lerner crap—the politics of meaning or whatever the hell it is—we have to avoid what Eleanor Clift correctly criticized Hillary for—soggy, sentimental bullshit.

"We want to tackle the deep issues, but without all the mushy stuff that goes nowhere. But this book has to be controversial and not just play to the audience."

Several weeks later, on July 7, he continued the theme during a book meeting at the residence in the morning. "Well, I want strong, vigorous, picturesque prose at the beginning of the book to grab people. Look at the G-7 meeting: if Bill Clinton is the most popular leader there, the world is in a hell of a shape.

"I'm going to cut up the UN, but you have to say they're good even though they don't mean a goddamned thing. We won't get into the America First crap. But if we don't get into policy specifics, it might get flabby, but how can we avoid the ethereal sentimentalism of Hillary? The one thing we have to watch is to be criticized for 'where's the beef?' It has to be substantive *and* philosophical. How do we invigorate our values? Through family, church, and—God help us—the schools? Hillary and Lerner float out there, but she's on to something. There is a spiritual vacuum here, which I want to talk about without getting into malaise, but that's not the whole story. The end of the cold war left us without a mission to replace it.

"I want to go no-holds-barred on policies that have been ineffective: Reagan's, Bush's, and my own. I have great affection for them personally, but I'm no longer bound to support what they did.

"It's like the religious right. The issues they put out there, like abortion, stirred up the voters like the Panama Canal did—remember that? It was a good issue but the wrong thing to win on. On abortion—I had to deal with it during my presidency, and I said that government is not to provide the funds to encourage it, but women should have the choice—well, I didn't say 'choice,' though that's what it was about. The argument wasn't as developed then.

"And I'm for gun control, because when I shot a gun for the only time when I was in the navy, I didn't hit anything! But really, you need gun control.

"The civil rights thing is crucial too. I was better qualified on civil rights than Kennedy was; he didn't really care. During my vice presidency, I was lonely in arguing for voting rights. Eisenhower was very conservative about that. But I said that eighty percent of the world is nonwhite, and we had to think of what we did here in terms of its impact abroad. There still is too much racism in this country.

"I also want to take on [Ross] Perot. He's wrong to be against NAFTA [the North American Free Trade Agreement], and on majoritarianism—is he going to take a poll on TV for more wildlife for turkeys or some goddamned thing? No, that's not what this country is about."

And with great prescience, he predicted some political results: "In '94, we should pick up five to six Senate seats, and it will be a considerable Republican year. Look, in '46, we won the House and the Senate with the Eightieth Congress. In '48, with the Truman upset, we lost both. In '50, I won, and Taft won in Ohio, and we gained in the House. In '52, we won both with Eisenhower. Today we should make gains in both in '94, with the potential to go over the top in '96. And this means that the end of the cold war will ultimately have to be managed by Republicans. Both parties have screwed it up so far, but with this book I want to direct my message to the future leaders of this party and the country. The end of the cold war is serious business."

He folded his hands in his lap. "I remember going to Capitol Hill to sell foreign aid, and I did it well, but only when I related it to the Soviet threat. We must take on those who claim that the cold war should never have been fought because communism was bound to collapse anyway. Evil ideas will inevitably fail, but until they do, they can do great damage. And they must expand to survive. That's why containment was right; we prevented the subjugation of Western Europe and stopped attempts to expand into the third world. Détente just softened the bastards up; let's face it. Communism must be pure to survive. The moment it compromises, it fails.

"Back in the early '60s, Khrushchev was saying 'We'll pass you,' and then this country went crazy with *Sputnik,* which gave Kennedy his crap about the missile gap. There was an economic competition, though we didn't know how weak they were at the time. There was a military competition. But these were things we could measure. Now, we don't have that. Nothing is clear, and that's why the challenge is greater. That is the meat of the coconut.

"[Senator Henry] 'Scoop' Jackson—my friend—was a cut above the others. But most liberals didn't have their hearts in fighting the cold war. I remember when Kennedy and I were in Congress voting for Greek-Turkish aid, we'd get hundreds of postcards saying 'Send food, not arms.' People must have policy set in idealism.

"Think of [Friedrich] Engels's quote 'It is necessary to change the world.' Change is sometimes good, sometimes bad, but we should never just change for the sake of change. The challenge we face now, of peace, is greater than what we faced in '45. That one could be met simply with more economic and military power. Today we face these soft concepts of values. The leadership class has failed us. America's head isn't screwed on right, but its heart is still OK."

Nixon began to weave these themes into his early drafts of *Beyond Peace.* His specific recommendations on Russian aid had gone unheeded by two presidents, leaving him frustrated. He decided that his energy would be better directed toward the broader philosophical questions facing the country. If Nixon could not influence policy during the end of the cold war, he might at least influence the thinking that would shape the new era.

On September 4, Nixon began editing his full draft of *Beyond Peace.* He was satisfied with its content though concerned that it would attract criticism he would be ill-equipped to answer.

"Producing something like this is like having a baby, although I've never had one! That's what I said after I did the Silent Majority speech. I said, 'The baby has been born.' Anyway, I'm concerned that our critics may justifiably say, 'Who is this guy to talk about the crisis of spirit when he contributed to it with Vietnam?'—which they always blame us for, although they shouldn't—'and Watergate?'—which was a child of Vietnam."

I reassured him that the crisis began before Vietnam, Watergate, and the end of the cold war and needed to be discussed by someone who *had* in some way contributed to it.

Nixon nodded. "Maybe you're right. Maybe it does require somebody who had something to do with it to write about it credibly. I don't know. And frankly, I don't really care about the criticism; it will just make the book more interesting to people. And I *need* to do it. I really need to do it."

"For yourself or for the country?" I asked.

"Both," he replied.

In mid-September, he directed his attention temporarily back to the situation in Russia. His fears that Yeltsin would not survive politically were replaced by fears that he would not survive physically.

"I'm very concerned about Yeltsin's health," he said on September 18. "Dimitri says his drinking has gotten very bad. He said Strobe Talbott tried to get Lukin out of Washington; he was strong but apparently not pro-American enough. Talbott should stay the hell out of that kind of stuff. The corruption under Brezhnev and Gorbachev was in the perks and salaries; now they don't have anything. Everything is for sale, so they steal. And it's a mess. It's a wonder Yeltsin has held on for this long, no thanks to us. But if something happens to him physically, we're really screwed."

Two days later, Yeltsin dissolved the unruly, unrepresentative, and antireform parliament, which declared the action unconstitutional and moved to impeach him. Led by Chairman Ruslan Khasbulatov and Vice President Alexander Rutskoi, the parliament seized control of its seat, the White House, and proclaimed defiantly that it was rebelling against the state.

Nixon agreed with Yeltsin's action. Since the congress was an enemy of reform, Yeltsin had to once again suspend democracy in order to save it.

The next week, however, Yeltsin began moving troops toward the White House. Khasbulatov and Rutskoi remained in the building, ordering troops loyal to them to seize whatever they could, including control of Moscow television. As the situation escalated, Nixon again sided with the Russian president.

"These commentators in the West who say that dissolving the congress was unconstitutional are crazy. What the hell! That's a Communist-era fraud! They're treating that document as if it were legitimate, which it is not. Christopher is wasting his time talking about human rights, but Clinton gets high marks for coming out strongly for Yeltsin at the beginning. I must say that I get some of the credit there too, because at our meeting at the White House that's all we talked about. What the [Princeton professor] Stephen Cohens of the world miss—those who bash Yeltsin for acting extraconstitutionally—is that he is the most pro-American in his foreign policy. The others are anti-American, so what are we talking about? These are the same type of people who believed Hiss! That burns my tail.

"And oh, the way the media calls him Mr. Yeltsin when he's a president; well, I know it's sort of a petty thing, but it's important. But at least Clinton has stood up for the guy. I give him credit there."

Yeltsin tested that support on October 4, when he ordered the tanks to fire upon the besieged parliament building. Khasbulatov, Rutskoi, and other Yeltsin detractors were seized and imprisoned. One hundred forty-seven Russians were killed, and hundreds of others were wounded. The peaceful revolution was no longer peaceful. Nixon, however, remained committed to Yeltsin.

"I don't think Yeltsin went too far," he said. "They started the violence. They are old-line Communists. No way they are going to give up without a fight. Yeltsin needed to take decisive action, and he did. I heard that seventy-two percent of Muscovites support Yeltsin and just nine percent support the parliament. How about that? Goddamn our press! They've gone after him for everything from closing down the press to firing opponents. What's wrong with that? I love it." He threw his hands in the air and smiled. "Fire the bastards! Fire all of them!"

Clinton must have sensed Nixon's sympathy with his position, because he called the former president again on October 8. Although most of the conversation concerned the U.S. military involvement in Somalia, Nixon told me that "he said he'd been working on Russia and Japan. . . . I congratulated him on Yeltsin, and he said there were some who felt he shouldn't go as far as he has to support him. At least he's standing up on that. It was a good conversation, but he sounded troubled and hectic."

The crisis in Russia, coupled with the intractable situation in Bosnia, a commitment to help restore democracy in Haiti, and the inherited engagement in Somalia, had forced the "domestic policy" president to focus on international problems, and Nixon sensed that "the guy doesn't have the fire in the belly for it." Clinton had hoped that the world would remain intact during his presidency and that war would be a non-issue. He was wrong, and he turned to Nixon once more on October 19.

"The point of the call, I suppose, was Haiti," Nixon told me after the conversation. "It's clear that he's driven to distraction by the foreign policy stuff. Today, he just sounded irritated, but he was great with me and even said how nice it was that he had me to talk to about these things. The guy knew his stuff. He's a quick study. If he could only learn—" He stopped. "Well, I guess the presidency is a little late to be learning foreign policy. He doesn't know foreign policy, but he's smart enough to reach out."

Nixon informed Clinton that he was considering another journey to Russia. "When I told him I planned to go to Russia, he didn't react," he said to me. "He may be planning a summit or something and didn't want to tell me. I don't know. He calls me, but I don't know if he listens. I hope I got across that Haiti and Somalia are peripheral issues and don't amount to a tinker's damn compared to Russia; Russia is the big one."

He continued sarcastically, "Monica, shall our next fact-finding trip be to Haiti?" He laughed. "Well, it *is* warmer than Russia!"

Clinton did indeed plan to travel to Russia, and the White House made the announcement several days after his conversation with Nixon. Clinton's popularity had suffered a significant decline, and polls indicated that the public was losing faith in his ability to manage the economy and international affairs, prompting Nixon to speculate that the Russia trip was "totally political. He needs a victory, but even this could lose for him." During the cold war, presidents could always rely on a summit with a Soviet leader to improve their standing with the American people; now, however, with the people turning inward and concerned more about the economy than national security, the president was not guaranteed to benefit at home by toasting foreign leaders.

Nevertheless, Clinton decided that a summit with Yeltsin in January 1994 would allow him to stroll across the world stage, engage in a bit of high diplomacy, and appear presidential, which might improve his job-approval ratings. He needed to gain some stature abroad, particularly after he admitted publicly in mid-October that when it came to foreign policy, he often wondered, "Who's on first?"

Nixon laughed and said, "My God! I can't believe it. You never admit that—even when you don't know anything. I think he blew it when he blamed the British and the French for his weak foreign policy. *The Economist* calls for a whole new team. They're right, you know. Christopher has to go. Bush is out there defending himself on everything from Russia to Somalia, and of course so is Baker. Jeez God! Clinton must be going crazy with having to put health care and the rest on the back burner for foreign policy!"

Clinton did, however, see some benefits to setting aside the contentious domestic issues for the spotlight of the international arena. Not only could he distract voters from his waning popularity, but he might actually improve U.S.-Russian relations.

Nixon's own trip to Moscow was postponed because the Russians could not guarantee a meeting with Yeltsin. Nixon, unwilling to travel around the world for a meeting that might not take place, unpacked in late October and remarked that it was better to see Yeltsin when it would be "productive. The word is that he has very high highs and very low lows, like most leaders. He just knocked out the parliamentarians, got a summit with Clinton, and came back from a successful trip to Japan. That high has now produced a low. He's way down."

He shook his head. "How did I survive? It takes an iron will not to get way down. Besides, I'd rather go when I can have the most impact. [Vice President Al] Gore is going in a few weeks, which is a big mistake to go so close to Clinton's trip in January. And then there are the elections in December in Russia. No, it's too cluttered this time, too much going on. Let's just wait."

Meanwhile, he had a crisis of confidence about the new book. He thought that the profound themes we had discussed were not addressed adequately and perhaps could not be. On November 5, he suggested to me that he "flush the project." I was incredulous. He had invested so much of himself in its development that it would have been tragic not to complete it. Nixon remained unmoved.

"I'm just thinking out loud here. Look, I'm realistic about life and death. I don't want to spend the four or five years I have left grinding through this goddamned book. And I cannot produce an inferior product. The reviewers—who never like what I say anyway—will say, 'Nixon's lost it.' No, I won't do it. I should be doing things that satisfy me and that I think are good enough to put out there. I should do things that are good for me, not fun in that sense but things I enjoy. I'm still interested in this project—it's timely and it's needed. But I'm not sure I'm doing it right. I don't mean to bring you down, but I want you to think about it."

I advised Nixon to continue to work on it, edit it, polish it. He did, partly because he had only halfheartedly believed his own argument and partly because he was not, as he said, a "quitter." He had made a commitment to see it through, even if it meant grumbling as he did it.

On December 3, as he refocused on the book, he heard from Simes that the administration planned to announce a new Russian-American condominium during the January summit between Clinton and Yeltsin. Nixon was aghast. "Dimitri tells me that Talbott is on this kick that they want to make the Yeltsin-Clinton summit an extravaganza, calling it a 'partnership for peace,' which is silly and destroys NATO. They want this to be the major foreign policy accomplishment of the administration, as if they did it with their own little hands. It's all PR. I remember that the Russians—well, Brezhnev, during our third summit on the Black Sea—said the United States and Soviet Union should have a condominium, excluding, of course, China. He said the others don't matter. Here we have a weak Russia, and now they want to exclude Europe and China. Amateurs! Bad, bad policy," he said, as if scolding the policy itself.

A call from Kissinger on December 7 reinforced this point. "Henry says that the U.S.-Russian partnership Strobe Talbott is conceiving—and by the way, journalists shouldn't be making foreign policy—is ridiculous. It sticks it to the Chinese, the Japanese—and the Europeans of course are shattered." The administration was trying to lay the groundwork for a new relationship with Russia based on vague pronouncements of partnership but without the concrete help it really needed. It was a diplomatic substitute for real aid.

The failure of the West to provide long-term substantial aid to the democratic forces in Russia resulted in the rise of extreme nationalists like Vladimir Zhirinovsky, who was elected to the congress on December 12. Zhirinovsky—a volatile man known for his anti-Semitic and xenophobic remarks—argued for everything from the military restoration of the great Russian Empire, including Alaska and part of California, to nuclear war with the United States.

Three days after Zhirinovsky's election, Nixon despaired. "I hope it's an alarm for the West. But what the hell! None of the aid we pledged got there. It's been pathetic. And Gore, who is over there now, did something really stupid. He denounced Zhirinovsky. Now the guy's bad, but you don't say it! You might have to work with him regardless of how awful and repulsive he is. Anyway, at least this development puts an end to the 'partnership' thing."

The backsliding evident in Zhirinovsky's election was a vivid example that the end of Soviet communism did not guarantee an irreversible move toward liberal democracy and capitalism. The Russian government and a considerable part of the Russian population had unrealistic expectations that the new, nonaggressive conduct of foreign policy and adherence to the recommendations of international financial institutions would bring billions in Western aid. With these hopes frustrated, the backlash was inevitable.

In Moscow, the feeling was that the administration's willingness to help Russia was a device to keep it down. This unfair but real perception worked against everyone in Russia, including Yeltsin, who believed in a strategic partnership with the United States. If allowed to stand, that perception would continue to generate candidates like Zhirinovsky and turn the partnership into another adversarial relationship.

———

Nixon's final year, 1994, began with a review of Clinton's trip to Moscow. "First of all, he's going over there to promote this 'partnership for peace,' whatever that's supposed to be. Such woolly-headedness! I feel so sorry for those poor Eastern European leaders. What can they do but accept this partnership when what they really want and deserve is full NATO membership?

"Secondly, Clinton is playing this trip like a fine instrument, which I guess is what he went over there to do. He went to a market; of course, it was an expensive one, not the kind I went to, with the average Russians. But that's OK; that's what he wanted to do. But he's got to think of image, of how it's going to play there with the average Russians and over here with average Americans."

Clinton's summit with Yeltsin accomplished little except to reinforce the idea that the United States would support the democratic transition in Russia as long as the financial commitment was limited. Despite Clinton's assurances to Nixon that he would provide assistance, he again failed to make good on his promise. Imagery meant nothing when the nationalists and the Communists were on the rise.

During the first week in February, Nixon and I did a final edit of *Beyond Peace*, the two main themes of which were brought to the fore by the end of the cold war: the need to support Russia and the need for the United States to define a new mission for itself. On February 9, he read the entire manuscript "cover to cover, and I'm delighted. It's really something. It pulls no punches. I can't believe I'm saying this after almost tossing it out the window, but I think it's good. I really do. But I won't read it again. I never do after turning it in. You think, 'Why didn't I do this differently?' I'm not into second-guessing."

With the book completed, Nixon prepared for his final trip to Russia. On February 24, he told me that he would be going "at an interesting time. I'll be seeing Zhirinovsky and others. Of course, the administration will like that because they can't see him alone, so they want me to! Clinton might call before the trip, but it really doesn't matter. They are supportive of it, and how can they not be? God's sakes, we *made* the issue!"

He held up two fingers. "There are two groups screaming about ending aid to Russia: the libs and the media, who want Yeltsin to fail so socialism will come back, and the far right, who say Russia will never change and want the enemy back. And if things go to hell, someone like Zhirinovsky could come to power, although it's a long shot."

Nixon had the opportunity to warn Clinton about impending disaster in Russia when the president called on March 3. Instead of the self-satisfied enthusiasm he had displayed after previous conversations with Clinton, Nixon was downbeat. "I got a call from Clinton this morning, as expected," he told me with a weak smile as we sat in his office. "We spoke for about fifteen minutes. . . . He wanted to know what my itinerary was going to be in Russia. I told him that I was going to see the opposition: Rutskoi and Zhirinovsky. He thought that was great because his people can't see them. He was worried about Ukraine, as he should be. He said he was glad that I'm going to see [German chancellor Helmut] Kohl; he said Kohl was one of America's best friends."

Nixon continued, "But you know, at least we are getting support from the administration on our trip. Remember Shultz? He gave us nothing. And

Baker instructed the embassy to treat me as just another businessman. Insulting. At least this administration has treated me the right way."

Nixon left for Russia on March 4 and called me twice from Moscow two days later. "I know how much you love this city. I wish you weren't in school," he said, referring to my graduate work at Columbia University. "The stopover in London was well worth it. It was beautiful. They are further along in spring than we are. The crocuses and forsythia are out, blooming like mad. We went with Jonathan Aitken to the London revival of *Carousel,* which I saw for the first time twenty-five years ago.

"The press met us in Moscow, and I talked to them about how it's the first time in thirty-five years that I will be seeing freely elected parliamentarians, as well as the opposition."

I told him that Gore had given Nixon's trip great support that morning on *Meet the Press.* "Good," he replied. "They are with us. Tomorrow I see Rutskoi, since Yeltsin is out of town; we may go to the Black Sea to see him."

The decision to see Rutskoi first proved to be fateful. Rutskoi was Yeltsin's longtime nemesis and the director of the recent armed insurrection against the government. For Yeltsin, Nixon's choice to meet with Rutskoi before meeting with him was an egregious affront. Not only had Nixon violated Yeltsin's personal trust, but he had bestowed on Rutskoi a measure of legitimacy. The Russian news agencies carried images of Nixon and Rutskoi engaged in an apparently warm and dynamic conversation, despite the fact that Yeltsin and his band of reformers—those whom Nixon was ostensibly there to help—considered Rutskoi an enemy of the people.

In another move that added insult to injury, Nixon met with the head of the Russian Communist Party, Gennadi Zyuganov, the very next day. He represented the party that had only recently come back from being outlawed for crimes against the people, and yet Nixon saw him before seeing Yeltsin. Simes, who was traveling with Nixon and coordinating the events, did not stop him from seeing these men first, and both paid the price.

On Wednesday, March 9, Yeltsin lashed out at Nixon. "The former American president met with Rutskoi and Zyuganov," he said angrily, "and he was coming here to meet with me. How can one come to a country and look for dark spots? Let him know that Russia is a great country—and to play with it this way, I want one thing today and tomorrow another—that won't work now. No. After this, I will not meet him. And the government will not meet him." Yeltsin then revoked all of Nixon's transportation and security privileges and canceled all of his appointments with members of the government. The Russian president had been betrayed, and Nixon, himself so sensitive to slights, should have anticipated the consequences.

Instead, he was shocked and tried to regroup. Rather than allow himself to be intimidated by Yeltsin's fury, he decided to remain in Moscow, carry out whatever still existed of his schedule, and issue a strong statement indicating his continuing support for the Russian president.

Clinton, meanwhile, came immediately to Nixon's defense. He claimed that it was not "the end of the world" and said that he would not "overreact to the fact that he met with some people who are in the opposition to the president." Indeed, as Nixon had indicated to me prior to his departure, the administration was relieved that he was going to see the opposition.

My phone rang at nine o'clock the evening of March 9. "Monica? I can't believe that I got through to you. I just punched in your numbers and hoped for the best! Well, it's five A.M. here, but I've got insomnia, so I thought I'd call and fill you in. Yeltsin, of course, had had a few when he erupted at me. That's well-known. But we got some good news coverage and managed to get through to the White House. Clinton gave a good statement; of course, he *had* to. I understand that both he and Dole sent Yeltsin notes urging him to see me. Both of them have been *very* good. Seeing the opposition has always been my practice. These are the men who will be running for the presidency. It doesn't matter if Yeltsin won't see me. We are not canceling this trip. We will see everyone else we came to see."

Nixon was on the defensive but sounded relaxed and a little tired. He had traveled around the world to meet with the Russian president, made a dreadful mistake by seeing the president's enemies first, and after evaluating the damage, decided to stay in Moscow to justify the mission and perhaps his own actions.

"I had a bad twenty-four-hour stomach virus here. In forty-five years of travel, I only had this once before, in Hong Kong. I was very sick, in very bad shape, but I'm all right now.

"I managed to walk through Red Square, and I was reminded of the time I did it with Khrushchev thirty-five years ago. We went into the GUM department store to buy a hat.

"Anyway, I can see where Yeltsin's coming from, but I'm just not going to let it bother me." It was, however, clearly bothering him.

The next day, he phoned me from Moscow again. "Moscow calling!" he bellowed into the phone. "I really don't think that it's as bad as it sounded. Yeltsin has a flair for the dramatic, as you know. But I do take some responsibility. It should not have been this way. I want you to call Tricia because she was very discouraged by the coverage.

"Dimitri is putting together a whole new schedule, and I must say we are flying by the seat of our pants. Tomorrow I'm seeing the head of the women's party! I knew you'd like to hear that!

"The embassy provided cars for us, and the White House—well, I must give them credit. They stood up on this."

Nixon decided to take the high road publicly and show no outward signs of frustration, disappointment, or anger. Instead, at a reception hosted by the new ambassador, Thomas Pickering, Nixon praised both Clinton and Yeltsin as "partners in freedom throughout the world. . . . Democratic Russia, under the courageous leadership of Boris Yeltsin, gave the knockout blow to Soviet communism. I came here as his friend and I remain his friend. I wish him well."

The words were designed to serve several purposes. First, they constituted a diplomatic apology to Yeltsin and his reformers. Second, they signaled to Clinton an appreciation for his support. Third, they diverted attention from his own mistake. And fourth, they showed that he could remain above the fray of a seemingly petty incident. Nixon, however, knew that the incident was not petty and would not be easily forgotten, and he moved to contain the damage.

He did some damage to himself on March 13 and called me from Moscow. His voice sounded steady but weak. "Well, I fell in Red Square and scraped my knee and hit my rib. It hurts when I breathe. I don't know what happened. I just sort of lost my balance and slipped. First the flu, then Yeltsin, now this. I guess the stars just weren't with me this time around!" He reassured me. "I'm all right, though."

Yeltsin, having heard Nixon's carefully worded apology, relented. He permitted members of the government to see him and dispatched a representative to tell him directly that he considered the matter closed. The Russian president did not, however, request a meeting with Nixon but returned to the Black Sea, where he said he was needed after the death of his mother-in-law. Yeltsin had deftly accepted Nixon's apology, declared a truce, and salvaged his pride.

"You know," Nixon continued from Moscow, "the whole affair was badly handled. But I have to say this, and I want you to remember it: controversy is the key. We needed the controversy—even though we don't like it when we're in the middle of it—to generate interest. Right? It's indispensable." Continuing the Machiavellian argument, he added, "Most things aren't worth doing if you don't draw attention to them. Sure, the purpose of traveling around the world was to see Yeltsin. But if this whole thing had never happened, if I had seen him as scheduled and that was it, there is no way the world would have even known I was here. Maybe we would have gotten some coverage, but you know what I mean. Now everyone knew I was here; Clinton and Dole stood up for me. The controversy brought attention to the need to help these poor bastards. And the controversy might bring results."

Nixon called me a final time from Moscow on March 15 to tell me that the speech he delivered the day before to the Duma, the lower house of parliament, was "the first for an American and the most covered event in Moscow, apart from the Yeltsin flap, which wasn't pleasant but made the trip newsworthy. I'll fill you in on the speech when I get back. And by the way, this trip isn't over yet."

That was a cryptic reference to Nixon's scheduled meeting with the ultranationalist Zhirinovksy. He called me from London the following day. "I know it's been twenty-four hours since you've heard from me and you can't believe it!" he laughed. "But I wanted to tell you that the Zhirinovsky conversation was the most interesting. I have information no one else has, because I cross-examined him in a subtle way. It was really something. We worked it out so that there were no photos of the meeting, because you know what effect that would have had. He's a piece of work."

Nixon returned home on Sunday, March 20. He phoned me at eleven o'clock in the morning and asked me to come to the residence so that he could give me "a rundown of the trip." I arrived in the early afternoon and found Nixon standing in his study, looking tired and relieved to be home. He had poured two glasses of white grape juice and placed his notes next to his chair. As he handed me a glass of juice, we toasted his return, and he added, "And to a trip full of scandal!"

We sat down, and Nixon retrieved his notes. "This was a very good trip. The highlight was the speech to the Duma; I told them that they must stay on the course of reform and not sway from it. I told them that there is no going back because while communism is dead in Russia, God is now alive. That's a line that they were shocked to hear but loved.

"Yeltsin is in very bad shape, physically and politically. He's just uncontrollable. [Ukrainian president Leonid] Kravchuk, who always had been pro-Yeltsin, said he won't last. I asked, 'How? Either through a coup or losing reelection?' And he said, 'Neither. They'll just surround him and make him a figurehead with no real power.' It's begun already. Kravchuk is still shrewd. He said Zhirinovsky couldn't win a national election, but the Zhirinovsky phenomenon could succeed with someone less outlandish and, frankly, crazy. He's explosive but skillful. I don't think he's going anywhere, certainly not to the presidency, but what he represents is very powerful— you know, the feeling that Russia has lost its greatness and needs to recover its former glory. That message has a lot of appeal to a defeated power. Look at Germany after the First World War. No, we have to be very careful of him and the people out there like him.

"The reformers are too young yet to rule Russia, but they're coming along. I haven't lost faith in them. I found some of the same sentiment in Europe. Kohl is very impressive. He's totally supportive of Yeltsin. The British aren't; they're aware of what's happening.

"I know Clinton was very good when the whole thing with Yeltsin erupted, but I don't want to see him or Talbott. The administration is immersed in Whitewater, and I need to put some distance there, for both of our benefits. I already got a few questions as to how Whitewater and Watergate are similar. I'm not answering it. You agree?"

I agreed but suggested that he consider preparing a written memorandum to Clinton to preempt any gesture on the administration's side for a meeting. Nixon rose at four in the morning on March 21 and dictated a lengthy letter to the president. "I should report only to the man, anyway," he told me later that day. "I was brutally honest in this memo; I told him he needs a new ambassador in Kiev because the situation is very dicey. I don't want to tell the State Department idiots because they won't do a damn thing. Maybe if he hears it from me, he'll get on the ball. He'll need a foreign policy victory since this Whitewater stuff is dominating the news."

Nixon also drafted his final op-ed piece for *The New York Times.* Entitled "Moscow, March '94: Chaos and Hope," it abandoned the optimistic view of his previous essays that democratic and free-market reform was taking root in Russia. He dispensed with flattery and painted a dramatic picture of Russian chaos and decline:

> "The Russia I saw on this trip is a very different nation from the one I visited just a year ago. Optimism about the future is being replaced by pessimism. A strongly pro-American attitude has in many cases become disturbingly anti-American. Boris Yeltsin is still a political heavyweight but he is no longer a superman.

He moderated his previously uncompromising support of the Russian president:

> Yeltsin has lost much of the mystique from his historic role in the destruction of Soviet communism. He may be finding that history is against him. Over the centuries, revolutionary leaders have not been good nation builders. But it would be premature to write Mr. Yeltsin off because of his frequent absences from Moscow and his increasingly erratic conduct. . . . The United States should treat him with respect and work closely with him.

He gave assessments of key opposition leaders, including Zhirinovsky, whom he called a "holy fool," Rutskoi, and Zyuganov. He stated that the "most disturbing development" he found was the dramatic change in Russia's foreign policy. Foreign Minister Andrei Kozyrev had changed his "emphasis on universal human values and commonality of interests with America to a renewed Russian superpower role and the need for Moscow to chart its own course."

He warned that the future of NATO should not be "sacrificed for the sake of Russian sensitivity." The Partnership for Peace should include a guarantee that NATO expansion into Eastern Europe would occur gradually, without jeopardizing Russian interests. "Russia must not be given a veto over a NATO decision to expand," he wrote.

He ended the piece with a more sober spin on his familiar argument:

> Clinton would be well-advised to order an immediate, comprehensive review of aid to Russia and the other former Soviet states before Congress forces him to do so. The survival and success of political and economic reform are not only in the interest of the Russian people. They are in the interest of peace. . . . It is a miracle that the new Russian revolution still shows promise. The reformers may fail even with our help. They will certainly fail without it. Mr. Clinton deserves bipartisan support on providing adequate aid to the forces of freedom in Russia. But,

he added with a dash of the language of détente,

> this support should be hardheaded, without illusions about Russian conduct and without the sacrifice of U.S. interests.

On the morning it appeared, March 25, Nixon waved the paper at me. "Do you see this? I have been barking up this tree for two, almost three goddamned years now. Does anyone pay any attention? There hasn't been any aid sent, no support given to the Russians. I guess that answers my question." He shook his head. "I do these things because I can't afford not to do them. But I don't think it's worth it. These things—trips, op-ed, whatever—are too much work for nothing."

The administration did, however, restructure its aid program, perhaps because Nixon had recommended a thorough review. Russia would now receive 35 percent of pledged aid instead of the original 65 percent, with the rest going to the other former Soviet republics. And perhaps thanks to the alarm Nixon rang with regard to the situation in Ukraine, the administration decided it would get seven hundred million dollars.

"None of it means anything," Nixon repeated, "if no one follows up."

Yeltsin, meanwhile, expressed an interest in seeing Nixon, who called me on April 7. "Simes said that Yeltsin is worried about his international image and wants to get well with me, so he wondered if I would come to see him. I said if he puts it in writing, I'll go, but I'm not going to risk having the same thing happen. He must be responsible for committing to a meeting. How do you like that?"

Nixon was delighted by this turn of events. Not only had Yeltsin expressed regret about the previous episode, but he had now actively appealed to him. The Russian president reached out to one of the few Western friends he had left, someone who had reached out to him over and over again, without hesitation and despite criticism. Nixon would make a renewed commitment to help Yeltsin, but only if that support were reciprocated.

This was the last exchange between the Russian president and Nixon before Nixon's death on April 22. The final "shot across the bow" to the American president came in *Beyond Peace,* published the week he died.

———

He had decided, months before, when editing the manuscript, that while he would disagree strongly with many of Clinton's domestic policies, his criticism of his foreign policy would be measured and evenhanded. Clinton's proposal to nationalize health care was fair game; his policy toward Russia, much of which was built on Nixon's advice, was another matter. As expected, he attacked multilateralism and reliance upon the United Nations as "naïve," the concept of exporting democracy as dangerous and misguided, and the brutality in the former Yugoslavia as an "unfortunate and unnecessary foreign policy failure."

When he focused on Russia, however, Nixon did not criticize Clinton directly but emphasized the urgency of the situation as he had in his previous writings. The well-known argument rang out. "No other single factor will have a greater political impact on the world," he wrote, than "whether political and economic freedom take root and thrive in Russia and the other former communist nations." He leveled the challenge, once again, directly at Clinton. "Today's generation of American leaders will be judged primarily by whether they did everything possible to bring about this outcome. If they fail, the cost that their successors will have to pay will be unimaginably high."

Although he urged continued unwavering support for Yeltsin, whom he still considered to be the best hope for reform, he rejected a personalization of foreign policy. This was a departure from his previous line, which urged unquestioning support for Yeltsin. He stressed the need to reach out to the younger Russian reformers, who would be ultimately responsible for the success or failure of the process.

*Beyond Peace* was Nixon's parting shot, to Clinton and other American policy makers, to Yeltsin, his reformers, and his opponents, and to the historians who would judge him. His well-known prescience made him someone worth listening to; his experience made him an indispensable source of guidance for those, like Clinton, who lacked even the most rudimentary knowledge of international politics.

It was to Nixon's credit that he saw a confluence of circumstances and seized them: the collapse of communism and the state that pioneered it; the search for a "new world order" in the wake of the resulting chaos; and the inauguration of a new president with no foreign policy credentials and an interest in appealing to partisan opponents. Nixon cobbled together for himself a position as the president's foreign policy mentor. It would have been an ideal situation if Clinton had acted more aggressively on Nixon's advice, but at least Clinton had listened to him and responded favorably, something that Bush had failed to do. In that regard, Nixon had succeeded: the sitting president, a baby boomer Democrat, had turned to a former president, a controversial Republican, for advice and, to some extent, had taken it.

The end of the cold war presented so many rich and unexpected opportunities for Nixon. Since he neither predicted nor anticipated its swift and peaceful conclusion, he was not fully prepared for what it delivered to him: a chance for vindication, a confirmation of his role as an elder statesman, renewed prominence on the global stage, and another opportunity to make policy from the world's capitals.

That Nixon had begun his political career at the beginning of the cold war, established his conservative credentials as an anti-Communist, led the country through a critical period of the cold war with a creative policy of détente, and then lived to see the end of it, was remarkable. The defeat of communism and the victory of freedom were immensely gratifying developments. He knew now, as he had known forty-five years ago, that he was on the right side of history. Like all of the presidents during the great ideological struggle, he had fought for the right principles.

Nixon's responsibilities, however, did not end when the hammer and sickle descended from its perch over the Kremlin in 1991. Rather than declare a personal victory and sink into retirement, Nixon began the daunting task of defining the new era and policies that might guide it. He counseled assistance and patience, flexibility and vision. The current generation of leaders could not be taught vision. But if Nixon could inspire them in some way to take action to preserve the victory, his job would then be done.

The frustration he felt when Bush ignored his advice or Clinton listened to it, then failed to follow it up came from a need to see his successors act as he would have. He was determined not to allow his successors to claim the victory for themselves or lose it. He was convinced that we were witnessing not the end of history but the beginning of a new and uncertain era, which required his leadership as much as the previous era had. His books, speeches, op-eds, and public and private memoranda were part of his effort to regain the power to influence the course of events.

One mission had been completed; another one had begun. The end of the cold war had vindicated everything Nixon stood for and gave him the opportunity to begin anew. Nixon was determined to remain not only relevant and progressive but indispensable to the leaders of the world as they charted their new courses.

During his lifetime, Nixon had seen the First World War, a weak isolationist peace, the Second World War, and a cold war marked by several hot wars. He knew that the new peace would be far different from anything the United States had known this century, a peace resulting not from the end of a hot war but from the internal collapse of the adversary. The very uniqueness of the situation gave Nixon the chance to continue to make his mark into the twenty-first century. Swaying the nations of the world was what he *did:* it was an inevitable mission, an essential part of his calling and life's work. The end of the cold war allowed him to transform himself once more, from a cold warrior to the foremost advocate for helping the new Russia. It was not a surprising development, considering that the one belief that drove him throughout his life remained the same: that freedom would prevail over tyranny.

# CHAPTER 2

# NIXON IN CHINA

I will be known historically for two things," said Richard Nixon on April 11, 1993. "Watergate and the opening to China. One bad, one good. It's not fair, considering that we worked so hard on so many other things, like détente with the Russians, the war on cancer, the EPA. . . . But those two things are going to stand out, and that's the way it is."

The comment came as we stood on the deck of the small ship built for him and Chou En-lai on West Lake in Hangzhou, China. I accompanied Nixon on his final trip to China, and our hosts in the scenic resort town had insisted on a midafternoon cruise. The boat listed sharply to one side as it moved slowly away from the dock. The former president, waving to throngs of cheering Chinese on the shore, stumbled in the direction of the lurch and grasped for the railing. As the boat steadied itself and assumed a slow and even pace toward a far shore, he regained his balance and cast a worried look in my direction. Placing one hand across the other along the railing, he walked carefully with me to the bow, where he could clearly view the Chinese countryside.

"I don't mean to be pessimistic, but Watergate, that silly, silly thing, is going to rank up there historically with what I did here," he continued, waving one hand expansively in the direction of the high-rise buildings that dotted the mountainous landscape. "Look at this," he said to me. "None of this was here when I took this boat tour in 1972. Most of it wasn't even here when I was here in '89. The growth of this place is really unbelievable. And you know," he said quietly, "I like to think that I had something to do with it."

The achievement of which Nixon was most proud was his 1972 opening to the People's Republic of China. With a single diplomatic stroke, Nixon had opened American relations with China and the eyes of the Chinese to the world, and the world would never again be the same.

In 1967, a year before his election, he wrote an article in *Foreign Affairs* that hinted at his intentions toward China. He wrote that "taking the long view, we simply cannot afford to leave China forever outside the family of nations, there to nurture its fantasies, cherish its hates, and threaten its neighbors. There is no place on this small planet for a billion of its potentially most able people to live in angry isolation." But he also urged for the short term "a policy of firm restraint, of no reward, of a creative counterpressure designed to persuade Peking that its interests can be served only by accepting the basic rules of international civility" so that China could gradually be welcomed "back into the world community—but as a great and progressing nation, not as the epicenter of world revolution." This was to be both a qualifying requirement and a standard of conduct: if the Chinese decided to "turn their energies inward rather than outward," they could look forward to a constructive partnership with the United States.

When he wrote that piece, China was still an aggressive power and a serious threat to the security of its neighbors. Soon after taking office in 1969, Nixon directed an exploration of the possibilities for a rapprochement with China. It began with a series of private diplomatic exchanges, a chance for both nations to circle each other without risking humiliation or confrontation. By the time Nixon took his first historic trip to Beijing in 1972, China was still repressive at home, but except for its brief invasion of Vietnam, it no longer posed a direct military threat to its neighbors. That allowed Nixon to alter global politics by engaging China.

It was ironic that Nixon, after having built his political career on the solid and politically profitable foundation of anti-communism, would as president initiate détente with the Soviet Union and rapprochement with China. A pragmatic realist, Nixon knew that the constraints the Vietnam War placed on our resources and will to act would require a less aggressive approach to dealing with the Soviet Union; the situation demanded a creative policy of containment that required neither belligerent rhetoric nor a lot of money. During and immediately after Vietnam, Americans would not tolerate additional confrontation.

Nixon recognized the domestic constraints and designed American policies toward the Communist powers that encouraged cooperation and emphasized a similarity of interests and goals. It was a remarkable balancing act that many argue only Nixon, with his anti-Communist credentials, could have performed successfully.

Détente was a complex arrangement of pressures and incentives designed to modify the Soviets' external behavior until the United States could recover enough from Vietnam to pursue a more aggressive policy. Rapprochement, on the other hand, was meant to be a foundation for a long-term working relationship with the Chinese.

When Nixon went to China in 1972, there was a lot of speculation as to why he seemed to change his hard-line position of opposing recognition. Some suggested that he wanted to use China as a counterweight against the Soviet Union and to enlist its support to end the Vietnam War. Others suggested that he had finally determined that Chinese communism was not as odious as he had previously believed. Both of these views, Nixon often said, were wrong.

"I didn't go to China because I finally saw the light or any other crazy idea," Nixon said on September 18, 1991, during a late-afternoon meeting at his residence. "I went to China because I saw a change in our interests and in theirs. It brought us closer together, in spite of the fact that they were Communist and we were democratic. Both of us were concerned about the threat to China and the rest of Asia by an aggressive Soviet Union.

"At the time, China looked around and saw itself surrounded by potential enemies," he said, pointing a finger in the air. "To the north was the Soviet Union, with troops aligned on the border. To the south was India, friendly with the Russians and a potential nuclear power. To the northeast was Japan, an economic powerhouse and a traditional enemy. But across the Pacific, the Chinese saw the United States: an ideological opponent but with interests opposed to those of the Soviet Union, its most serious and immediate threat. So the Chinese saw the benefits of working with us. They had to choose between ideology and survival. They chose survival. It was that simple.

"We, of course, needed a good relationship with the Chinese regardless of the Soviet threat. I would have gone to China even if there had been no threat from the Soviets. It was essential to develop a new relationship with the Chinese *then*, you know, when they were weak and still open to it, rather than waiting until they were strong and didn't need us anymore. That's why I did it, and it was the right thing to do."

Nixon saw immense potential in China: an intelligent and industrious people, vast natural resources, nuclear capabilities, and a history of power politics. Alienated from the Soviets, the Chinese stood alone, though not by choice. When Nixon approached them in the early 1970s, the timing was right for a workable partnership with the United States.

During Nixon's final years, two arguments came to the fore: one, that the United States no longer needed a close relationship with China since the threat of Soviet aggression had evaporated, and two, that the Chinese no longer needed the United States to protect them against possible Soviet aggression. Again, he said, both views were wrong. In an era without a definitive enemy, China and the United States needed to cooperate with each other for reasons totally unrelated to the Soviet Union or Russia.

At the beginning of the century, when Friedrich Engels refined the theory of communism, he set out to "change the world." He was referring to the power of the Communist ideal: enforced social equality, cradle-to-grave security, and the promise of world supremacy. Intellectually contagious and ostensibly egalitarian, communism seduced the Soviet Union and, later, China.

After its great and tragic experiment, however, communism collapsed in its pioneer state and exists now only as a cover for repressive political rule in China. But although China lacks the military might and intellectual allure that Soviet communism once had, it began an enormously successful quest for something even more important: economic power.

"Before I went to China in '72," Nixon said on October 1, 1991, "somebody said that Mao's first question to me would be 'What is the richest nation in the world planning to do for the most populous nation in the world?' Let me say this: during my five days of meetings with the Chinese, not once did economic issues *ever* come up. Not once. They were only concerned with the strategic issues and the military power of the Soviets. Twenty years later, economic issues are almost all we talk about. Communism there is meaningless in terms of economics; what they are pursuing is capitalism, but as they say, with a Chinese face."

Historically, economic power has been the precursor to military might and global influence. During the last ten years of Nixon's life, he watched China post annual growth rates of over 10 percent, thanks to Deng Xiaoping's economic reforms and opening to the West. With more than one billion people, China was on its way to becoming the world's second largest economy, with global reach in terms of its own market and as a major exporter. One fifth of civilization would be lifted out of poverty in spite of, not because of, communism. The Soviet Union never reached those kinds of economic heights, despite Khrushchev's shoe-banging promises to "bury" us.

During his four visits to China between 1976 and 1985, Nixon saw the country evolve from one of the world's most reactionary, doctrinaire Communist strongholds into one of the most progressive in reversing communism's economic tenets. Long before Gorbachev brought glasnost and perestroika to the Soviet Union, Deng Xiaoping lifted the dead weight of Marxism by opening the economy to the forces of the market. He gradually liberated the economy and prices, first by encouraging farmers to grow for profit, then by inviting foreign investment in light industries, which in turn created the explosive growth in coastal areas that spread quickly inland. Capitalism crept in, profit by profit, until it became an irresistible and irreversible force. Once that happened, China left behind its policy of self-imposed isolation and quickly became a major geopolitical power center locked into the global economy.

Nixon did indeed have "something to do with it." Diplomatic contact made economic and cultural contact inevitable. The communications and technology revolution made it possible for a billion Chinese to see vivid pictures of what the free world had that they did not: political choice and economic prosperity. It was only a matter of time before they would demand them for themselves.

In the spring of 1989, two parallel events—the Sino-Soviet summit and the pro-democracy demonstrations in Tiananmen Square—cast into question the future course of China's foreign policy and domestic reform and the future of the Sino-American relationship.

The normalization of relations between the Soviet Union and China did not alarm Nixon. Relations were restored not because of a shared ideology but because of a shared border, a Soviet retreat from Afghanistan, and a Vietnamese withdrawal from Cambodia. Moscow, Nixon believed, could not offer Beijing foreign investment, advanced technology, or a working economic model. The Chinese needed to work with an economic partner, not an economic basket case. If the United States continued to give the Chinese an economic stake in good relations, the Chinese would hold up their end in a constructive relationship.

The events of June 4, 1989, however, changed the tenor of that relationship. A million peaceful demonstrators gathered in Beijing's Tiananmen Square to demand political reform. Initially composed of students and intellectuals, the crowds soon drew workers and others demanding democratic change, and the protests spread quickly to over two hundred provincial cities. The régime arrayed a military force to intimidate them into backing down. When the demonstrators refused to move, the government cracked down, killing at least thirteen hundred Chinese and wounding ten thousand more. Another ten thousand were taken into custody, most of whom were sentenced to prison or hard labor on state work farms and some of whom were executed.

Unlike the killing of peaceful demonstrators in Lithuania in 1990 by Soviet Black Berets, the massacre in Tiananmen Square happened in full view of international television cameras. The live images of courageous pro-democracy demonstrators defying army tanks were beamed into the White

House, the Kremlin, and millions of homes around the world. Offended by the use of excessive force, the unjust sentences handed down to the protesters, the propaganda and misinformation disseminated by the Chinese leadership, and the lack of remorse expressed by those leaders, the U.S. government immediately suspended all high-level contacts with the Chinese.

After the brutal repression in Tiananmen Square, some observers concluded that Deng's progressive reforms would be reversed in a crackdown on the economic freedoms that led to the demonstrations for greater political freedoms. They did not recognize that the power and profits of the marketplace were already entrenched. Hard-line reactionary decrees could not turn back what not only had already become a foundation for a better life economically but also held the potential for a freer life politically. The new revolution had begun.

In the immediate aftermath of the massacre in Tiananmen Square, some argued that the United States should terminate all relations with China, impose economic sanctions, and isolate it until it reversed its repressive policies. Nixon, however, knew that ending the Sino-American relationship rather than fixing it would bring devastating results, to our interests and to theirs.

He did, however, believe that the brutal actions of the Beijing régime deserved the universal condemnation they received. The United States initiated a termination of all arms sales, a suspension of most senior-level discussions, an extension of visas for Chinese studying in the United States, and an offer of humanitarian assistance for victims of the violence. This, according to Nixon, was a proper, calibrated response, since additional sanctions, including a total economic boycott, would have been counterproductive and would have defeated the purpose of keeping the demand for reform alive.

In 1989, three weeks after I met Nixon for the first time, he once again took the Sino-American relationship into his own hands. In his most dramatic trip to China since 1972, he went on a mission to repair its badly frayed relationship with the United States. During his six days in Beijing, from October 28 to November 2, 1989, he had twenty hours of one-on-one discussions with Chairman Deng Xiaoping, Premier Li Peng, General Secretary Jiang Zemin, President Yang Shangkun, Foreign Minister Qian Qichen, Education Minister Li Tieying, Propaganda Minister Li Ruihuan, and the mayor of Shanghai, Zhu Rongji.

During our first conversation, on October 2, he did not reveal his intention to make the trip. He did, however, stress the need for patience and hardheaded realism. "You've got to talk tough to the Chinese and let them know that the United States will not sit by and watch the Chinese government slaughter its own people," he said. "But you must do it in private. Our differences can be bridged if the discussion is behind the scenes, but they'll only be made worse by tossing them around in public."

Nixon believed that he was the only who could do it. The Bush administration walked a fine line between reacting to the outrage of the massacre and wanting to stabilize Sino-American relations. The president was subject both to domestic political pressures to sanction the Chinese and to diplomatic pressures to work with them. Nixon thought that he was the only American with the stature, experience, and respect of the Chinese to carry a blunt message of displeasure and cautious optimism that the relationship could be rebuilt. He traveled as a private citizen, as he always did, unencumbered by politics and the need for diplomatic posturing. Only Nixon could match the realist wits of the Chinese leaders, warning them of the dire consequences of their reversion, and only Nixon could return with a sober, hardheaded, and realistic report for the American president.

News coverage of Nixon's trip was extensive and positive. *The New York Times* credited him with "putting his reputation to good use," *Newsweek* reported that "both Washington and Beijing viewed him as a go-between," and the headline in *The Boston Globe* read BEIJING BOWS TO A NIXON HARD-LINE. The news reports indicated that at a banquet hosted by Premier Li Peng, the enforcer of the crackdown, Nixon said, "The cultural, political, and ideological differences between us, Mr. Premier—you are a Chinese communist who believes in Leninist rule, and I am an American conservative who believes in capitalism and democracy—are too great to permit a common understanding of the tragedy." In responding to a toast by President Yang Shangkun, he continued, "China's leaders now appear to claim that how they rule their country internally is nobody's business. Most Americans deeply believe, however, that international standards exist to guide the conduct of leaders everywhere." But, he added, "another tragedy would be the death of a relationship and of policies that have served so well."

With a few sharp remarks, Nixon made the points more effectively than the administration had through traditional diplomatic channels. It was a powerful visit: Nixon expressed the depth of outrage over the events in Tiananmen Square and managed to put an optimistic spin on the future of the Sino-American relationship. He came as a friend, not as a hostile critic, and delivered both a warning and a promise: if China turned back its repressive policies, it could look forward to a prosperous and strategically beneficial relationship with the United States.

On November 23, a month and a half after my first meeting with Nixon, I went to my mailbox on the campus of Colgate University and found a bulky envelope from the office of Richard Nixon. Inside was a letter to me from the former president and a copy of a memorandum he had written after his trip to China three weeks before. Entitled "The Crisis in Sino-American Relations," the seven-page personal and confidential memorandum was a condensed version of an eighteen-page report he had written for President Bush that included his evaluation of the Chinese leaders, their policies, the prospect of a reversal of the repressive policies of the Tiananmen Square era, and recommendations to improve the relationship between the United States and China.

He wrote that his "highly candid" talks with the Chinese leaders covered the political and economic situation in China, the crisis in Sino-American relations, and other international issues, such as the Chinese assessment of Gorbachev, the revolutionary developments in Eastern Europe, and the status of third world hot spots such as Cambodia and Afghanistan.

"Sino-American relations are in the worst condition they have been in since before I went to China seventeen years ago," he began. The tragic events in Tiananmen Square were seen by the Americans and the Chinese from completely different perspectives—a gap, he said, that was "totally unbridgeable." The Chinese leaders with whom he met insisted that the crackdown was necessary and justified and that the American response was an unacceptable intrusion into their internal affairs. They refused to call the use of excessive force on June 4 a tragedy and insisted on terming it an "incident." Further, they believed that sanctions and moral condemnation coming from the United States, with inadequacies of its own, were groundless and hypocritical. Nixon wrote that if we used the same approach as that of the Shanghai communiqué—acknowledging both our differences on the crackdown and our common interest in building a partnership in spite of them—we could move beyond the stalemate.

He argued that if we allowed those differences to permanently damage a relationship that has benefited the Chinese, the Americans, and the "cause of peace and progress" in Asia, we would compound the tragedy. The events, he said, must be kept in perspective. In 1972, when relations were first opened with China, our differences were enormous: we disagreed on Vietnam, Korea, Japan, and Taiwan, and on ideology. But we recognized that despite the irreconcilable differences, we had one common, overriding interest: the need to develop a policy to deter an aggressive and expansionist Soviet Union that threatened us both. Today, Nixon wrote, with the diminishing Soviet threat and the possible end of the cold war, we had to find the "glue that can keep us together."

Nixon then posed a question: Why was the renewal of a cooperative relationship in our interest? First, assuming that the cold war was coming to an end and the Soviet Union posed little threat to the United States and China, we still had a strategic interest in rebuilding a positive relationship with China. Gorbachev, Nixon warned, was not a "closet democrat, a philanthropist, or a fool." His goal was to mend communism, to coax it into being a leaner and more efficient system. Though Moscow posed less of a threat, a potential Soviet-Chinese relationship could be used against us. The Soviets talked to the Chinese, but we did not. Now that the suspension of high-level contacts had served its purpose of sanctioning the Chinese, high-level talks should be resumed.

Further, China was a nuclear power with which we needed to work on nonproliferation issues and without which we would have no leverage in trying to prevent the sale of nuclear technology to international hot spots.

If the balance of power were to be maintained in Asia between China, Japan, and the Soviet Union, a strong, stable China with close ties to the United States was essential. Peace could not be maintained in Korea, the Taiwan issue could not be resolved peacefully, and peace could not come to Indochina unless the United States and China were responsibly engaged.

Nixon argued further that with China inevitably becoming a major economic power, we should not "rule ourselves out" and leave that huge potential market to the Japanese and Europeans: "Is the door which we opened with such high hopes seventeen years ago to be closed?"

Nixon then turned to China's stake in a positive relationship with the United States. Although Gorbachev's approach of initiating political reform without economic reform had dominated the news, Deng's economic reforms had delivered explosive growth. But both economic and political reform would fail over the long run, he wrote, unless they were put into effect together. If Deng's economic reforms and opening to the West survived him, the pressures for political reform would inevitably mount. The leaders with whom Nixon had met assured him that the economic reforms were irreversible but knew that they faced an important choice.

At a banquet hosted by the premier on October 30, Nixon posed that choice directly to his hosts: Would China turn away from greatness and "consign itself to the backwater of oppression and stagnation?" Or would it continue to venture forth toward progress, peace, and justice for its people?

The United States, he wrote, could not and should not be in the position of interfering with the choice that only China could make. But if the United States continued to isolate China, the reactionaries would be emboldened and the forces for change would be silenced. Contact and cooperation, Nixon stressed, were essential if those who supported Deng's reforms were to prevail.

Nixon suggested that both sides take specific steps to heal the rift. China, he recommended, should rescind martial law, provide amnesty for peaceful demonstrators, work to resolve the dispute over dissident Fang Lizhi, who had sought refuge in the U.S. embassy, and invite students, businesspeople, scientists, and tourists to visit and contribute to China's emerging private sector.

The United States, for its part, should eliminate the economic sanctions, resume government assistance to those who wanted to invest in China, and continue the financing of major Chinese projects by international financial institutions.

The timing and "choreography" of the steps each side would take toward restoring relations were crucial and could only be agreed upon through private diplomacy at the highest levels. In a passage reminiscent of his 1967 *Foreign Affairs* article, he wrote, "To leave the present and future leaders of China isolated, nurturing their resentments and even hatred of the United States," is senseless. The Great Wall of China, he wrote, is very thick. Although it is difficult to be heard when you are on the inside, "it is impossible to be heard when you are on the outside."

Nixon emphasized the friendship between the American and Chinese peoples and the eagerness of the Chinese leaders to join us in rebuilding a constructive relationship. Striking back at hard-line Chinese leaders with further sanctions might be gratifying, but basing policy on emotionalism was folly. The reactionaries in Beijing believed that since they had survived for centuries without contact with the West, they could do so again. What they did not realize, and what those in the United States who argued for isolationism did not realize, was that because of the technological revolution, no nation could exclude itself from the rest of the world. The United States needed to engage China in a constructive dialogue before China chose to have that dialogue with someone else.

Finally, Nixon reported that despite the differences, he was more optimistic about Sino-American relations now than he had been in 1972, because then the two nations were brought together by fear of conflict with a mutual adversary and now they were joined by hope for economic progress and peace.

This Nixon memorandum, unlike the notorious 1992 memorandum on aid to Russia, never made the news. It did not criticize the president during an election year. It did not attack current American policy in scathing terms. It did not propose any revolutionary courses of action. Rather, it offered a sound strategy for dealing with the Chinese that was as simple as it was difficult: encourage peaceful change by keeping the economic door open and by keeping discussions and disagreements over sensitive issues honest but private. It would be a delicate balancing act, but the United States needed to work with China as an equal partner, not as a bitter enemy.

Cooperation could work slowly in fostering change, but isolation would not work at all. The strategy of patience was the best way to promote a long-term relationship with China that was as much cooperative as it was competitive. Nixon warned that Beijing was focused on building the one thing that the Soviets neglected and that, ultimately, was the key to military strength and global dominance: economic power. It was wise to maintain a constructive relationship with the Chinese while they were still amenable to having one with us.

"It would be a mistake for us to do anything that would result in the weakening of the private Chinese economy," he said on January 23, 1991. "An open economy provides the greatest pressure for political reform, and believe me, the next generation is far more Chinese than they are Communist." During this first extensive conversation between us about China, Nixon focused exclusively on his 1989 trip.

"I think back to that trip, just a few short months after Tiananmen Square. What a time it was! You know, almost everybody warned me not to do it, not to go. They said that my critics would have a field day by saying that I was trying to save the China opening, you know, by going over there. That's not how I saw it at all, but that's how many people told me it would be perceived. I agreed with them to the extent that I worried about being seen tipping glasses with those who had ordered the crackdown. But there was something even more important involved here: I needed to do what I could to restore the relationship because it was so important to both countries.

"No one knew that Bush had sent a secret delegation to China; *I* didn't know, and I know why Bush kept it from me: the same reason we didn't tell anyone about our secret negotiations with the Chinese. You just don't want any screwups. That was fine. But it didn't matter because I would have gone anyway. The American people needed to see me go over there to do publicly what the administration could not do."

When I asked if he felt uneasy bringing his blunt message to the Chinese, he replied, "No, not really. I knew it would be difficult for me to say those things, but they needed to hear them. I knew it would be difficult for them to give me the standard line about not tolerating any interference in their internal affairs when they had just killed over a thousand of their own people. They knew how I'd feel about that. Of course, look at what happened at Kent State. Those kids *were* Communists, and the National Guard was defending itself. But it still wasn't right. You simply cannot put down dissent with lethal force. You can't kill people just because they disagree with policy.

"You know, during Vietnam we had hundreds of thousands of demonstrators in the streets every day, paralyzing entire cities. Now, I can sympathize with the Chinese leaders in terms of wanting to restore law and order. But there is an enormous difference between democratic law and order and Communist law and order. We just put up with the demonstrators; the Communists cut them down."

I asked if he believed that the Chinese understood his point about tolerating peaceful demonstrations for political reform, and Nixon replied, "Of course they did. The Chinese are very wise and very sharp. They knew exactly what I was saying. What they didn't understand was that they can't profess to base their foreign policy on strategic interests only and then base all of their internal actions on ideology. If you're going to deal with nations with opposing ideologies for cold strategic interests, then you've got to expect that those nations will object when you use ideology as a justification to use force to hang on to your own power."

"So how did you make this point to the Chinese without causing more damage?" I asked.

"When I talk to the Chinese, I don't worry about offending them. What needs to be said needs to be said. You try to do it as diplomatically as possible, of course, but without worrying about stepping on toes. Look, they killed some of their own people. They needed to hear that the United States will not put up with that quietly.

"I went over there with three goals in mind," he continued, counting them off on his fingers. "One, to show the leaders that even China's best friends were outraged by what they had done; two, to refocus their attention on international politics; and three, to begin a discussion with them on the future of our relationship."

When I asked if he thought he was the only one who could accomplish all three goals, he answered, "Well, I'm not sure about that, but probably. No one else out there could really do it—you know what I mean. Bush can't for obvious reasons. Kissinger is a friend, and he goes over there and does some very good things, but he wasn't president. It was just the right time for me to go and take on the goddamned issue.

"You know, my meeting with Deng Xiaoping was probably the last one I will have with him. He's pretty old, even older than I am," he said, laughing, "but I really don't think that I will ever go back. That was probably my last trip to China.

"But in any event, it was a very strange situation. He was very frail, in a hell of a shape, really, but his mind was still sharp. He had fallen apart since I last saw him, maybe four years before. But his hearing was terrible; he had two translators near him, one to make a record of the conversation and another to scream the translation in his ear. It ended up being a three-hour conversation. We covered so many things.

"I starting out by saying that I have observed Sino-American relations for close to two decades. There had never been a worse crisis in our relationship than the one we were experiencing. Even friends of China were criticizing them. I said to him that we had to look at those differences and repair the damage done by the actions of the Chinese leaders.

"Deng's answers were far more subtle than those of some of his colleagues, who blamed the United States for everything. No, Deng said that in order to put the recent past behind us, *we* needed to take the first step. China, he said, was weak and small while the United States was strong and big." He smiled. "Imagine that! He said that if he did not maintain respect for China, then he should step down. Of course, he was just playing the victim, but I tried to make him understand that he can't have it both ways. China cannot want to benefit from relations with other nations, especially us, then not listen to what we have to say about human rights and other issues."

Nixon argued, then as in 1972, that the United States needed to be patient in charting its course. China was one of the five major geopolitical power centers, a point he addressed in his 1971 speech in Kansas City. It was a nuclear power. It was the most populous nation in the world. It was a key player in the regional conflicts involving Afghanistan, Cambodia, Korea, and the Middle East. It was absolutely crucial for the United States to maintain close ties with China in order to promote cooperation on bilateral issues such as trade and nonproliferation.

We had to accept the fact that our relations with other countries were determined primarily by what they did outside, not inside, their borders. Although Nixon began to alter this realist notion to emphasize a universal respect for human rights, he believed that our policy toward other nations should be based primarily on how those nations behave internationally. The best way to pressure closed societies to reform was to engage them. If the choice were between dealing with an odious Communist Chinese régime now and encouraging reform over the long term or isolating the Chinese now and stifling reform, the former path was the correct one.

"You know," Nixon continued, "when I met with Jiang Zemin, who is now the general secretary and Deng's apparent successor—although who knows—I gave him a list of sixteen steps China could take immediately to demonstrate its willingness to deal with the human rights issues. Some of them they took, like lifting martial law—and by the way, martial law almost always backfires, as we saw in Poland. But you know, they did other things, like release some students who were out there demonstrating, reinstate the Peace Corps program, though God only knows what the Peace Corps is up to over there, and lift the sanctions against Voice of America. It took guts for them to do that. They know with every tie they loosen, their power becomes more and more difficult to hold on to."

I mentioned the precedent of Eastern Europe and the impending collapse of the Soviet Union, and Nixon agreed that the warning signals surrounded the Chinese leadership. "The Chinese know perfectly well that communism is collapsing all around them. This is why Deng was such a visionary. He saw years ago—and I mean *years* ago—that communism does not work economically. And unless you want a revolution on your hands, which is what happened to the leaders in Eastern Europe, you've got to reform. Now, he also understood that people are less likely to revolt if they have full stomachs. So he came up with a formula that allowed the Communists to hold on to political power but let loose on the economic side. People started making some money—not much, but some. The economy started growing. People wanted a piece of the pie. There's no turning back on that score. But since they can't really call their system Communist, they can't hide behind that justification anymore."

"You mean in terms of rationalizing what they did in Tiananmen Square?" I said.

"Exactly."

No longer was it possible for the Chinese leaders to balance easily the benefits of market economics with totalitarian political rule. In order to stave off a meltdown of the kind that brought the end of the Soviet Union, they scrambled to preserve their political power and continued to invoke Karl Marx, Vladimir Ilyich Lenin, and Mao Tse-tung even as they found that ideology was made increasingly irrelevant by free markets, privately run businesses, joint ventures, and family farms. And they exhorted their subjects to guard against the "peaceful evolution" toward capitalism even as they gave away control of the economy.

Marxism, however, still had its uses in China. The party still exercised an unchallenged monopoly of power over the people. The idea of the "people's democratic dictatorship," with which the leadership justified suppressing dissent for the greater good of the majority, held fast. The state-run enterprises, despite the boom of the private sector, remained the major source for the party's wealth. But the high-wire act of the leadership in balancing economic openness and political repression threatened to come crashing down. It produced a tension that exploded in Tiananmen Square and would blow up again if not addressed.

"Within twenty years, China will move to democracy," Nixon said on May 31, 1991. We had been discussing the chapter on the Pacific Rim for *Seize the Moment,* and he indicated that he wanted the book to emphasize the need for the United States to exercise patience in its policy toward the

Chinese. "You can't rush them. The Chinese look at history and the future in terms of centuries, not decades, the way we do, because they're so much older as a culture. I know it's tempting for us to want to see democratization come to China right away, like this," he said, snapping his fingers, "right after Tiananmen Square. It doesn't happen that way. It did in Eastern Europe, but only because communism was imposed there by the Soviet Union, and when the Soviets didn't use force to keep it in there, it collapsed. The Chinese are playing a different ball game."

When I mentioned that communism could not work without its basic economic principles, Nixon replied, "Communism is too far gone in the Soviet Union to try now to have a mixed Chinese-style economy. But the Chinese knew what the Russians didn't: that economic reform had to come first. Of course, Gorbachev never intended to lose his empire, but the point is that you can't make communism economically more efficient. It doesn't work." He paused. "It has to be scrapped. This is what the Chinese have done. They have scrapped the economic side in order to hold on to the political side. This is why the hard-liners in China, like Li Peng, *want* to isolate China and the reason why they want the United States to isolate them. Then their political power is ensured. They won't have to worry about all of this corrupting Western influence."

I remarked that since China lacked much of the ethnic strife that had plagued the Soviet Union, the pressure for reform would not build as quickly there as it had across the Soviet empire.

Nixon considered the point. "There is something to that. And you know, the Chinese feel that they are having the last laugh after Gorbachev basically brought down the Soviet Union and after years of being its junior partner in the Communist bloc. Although now that they have compromised on the economic side, we can't really call them Communist, can we?"

On June 21, Nixon had a chance to pose a version of the question to a fourteen-member Chinese delegation that included Han Xu, former Chinese ambassador to the United States, the president of Beijing University, and the Chinese ambassador to the Soviet Union, who was dressed in a Mao suit and sandals. They came to Nixon's New Jersey office to discuss the future of Sino-American relations with the man who had begun them almost two decades ago, and I attended the meeting.

Nixon began by stressing the necessity for continued engagement: "China must move ahead in its own way, but you must realize that economic reform will inevitably lead to political reform. You must lead the new revolution toward greater openness or be left behind."

He turned toward the president of Beijing University: "I know that you've had some problems with student demonstrators. I can sympathize with you!

But you must be patient with them. They have been given more opportunities, and they demand more opportunities politically."

The Chinese responded by saying that they needed to impose "stability" and "order" if any progress were to be made, to which Nixon replied, "There is a difference between order under the rule of law and order imposed through force. If you wish to benefit from relations with the United States, then you must also listen to what we say about how you treat your own people.

"Americans are very concerned about human rights. We do not like to see innocent people killed, particularly when they were just asking for a greater voice in how their country is run. We are also concerned when the Chinese government sells sensitive weapons technology to states like Iran. We believe that doing so is irresponsible and destabilizes the delicate balance of power in the region.

"Now, I am not among those who believe that the United States should impose excessive sanctions upon, and isolate, the Chinese. I believe that it is in both of our interests to continue a close and constructive relationship, where both sides can comfortably discuss their differences and search for common ground. The relationship is too important to disregard."

He offered them some historical perspective. "For twenty-five years before 1972, we had no contact whatever with the Chinese government—no trade, no diplomatic relations, no student or tourist exchanges, nothing. China was still a completely closed society. Since our opening, the Chinese have astonished the world with their progress in granting economic freedom and opening their society up to the free world."

He ended on an optimistic note: "During the cold war, the United States and China were brought together by our fears, fears of an aggressive Soviet Union. Today we need new economic incentives that will help to hold us together by our hopes, hopes of greater prosperity and peace."

The Chinese listened intently to Nixon despite his sometimes unpalatable message. As he did in Beijing, Nixon spoke frankly: the United States would continue to raise the human rights issues until China moved to correct them. He would always protest such violations publicly and privately. He made clear, however, that the relationship did not turn solely on human rights. Those who supported an open Chinese economic policy were as concerned about human rights as those who wanted to revoke that policy. The main objective was to find a policy that would ultimately convince the Chinese leaders to provide more political freedom and end human rights abuses. Implicit in Nixon's remarks to the Chinese delegation was that China needed the United States more than the United States needed China, but both countries did in fact need each other.

During the summer of 1991, Nixon wrote most of *Seize the Moment*. Although the events in the Soviet Union commanded his attention, he emphasized the need to make the chapter on Asia, "The Pacific Triangle," relevant, controversial, and important.

"Come in, come in," he said to me as I entered the residence for a book meeting on August 15. Nixon was standing in the doorway, waiting for me, holding a bottle of Chinese mao-tai. "Do you see this?" he said, closing the door behind me. "I just found it upstairs. It's mao-tai, and it will kill you. It's so strong that it will burn your esophagus going down. I remember being at those banquets in '72, and the Chinese drank this stuff like it was water. I could only take a sip. It's powerful stuff. Of course, now I can't drink anything at all, so I'm giving it to you."

"You're giving me something that can kill me?" I laughed.

"You're young, you can take it!" He put the bottle on the foyer table. "You can pick it up on your way out."

We went upstairs to Nixon's study, where he had assembled background materials for the chapter. He moved to his chair and picked up his eyeglasses, which he pointed at me. "This book is going to have to be controversial if it's going to amount to anything. It's very hard to take issues like Japan and China, which have been written about over and over again by everybody, and liven them up. But we've got to find a way," he said, clenching his teeth. "I can write about China without a problem. Of course, unlike the Soviet Union, there's no earth-shattering drama going on there. Reform there is much slower and more gradual—the Chinese way, you know. So I'm just going to talk about what I've always talked about: the need for patience and cool heads, on both sides."

He pointed the eyeglasses at me again. "I remember so well in 1972 we left a satellite TV unit behind when we left. It was used by the American press when we were there, but it turned out to be a Trojan horse because it brought images and news from the West right into China. There were maybe a few hundred thousand TV sets in China at the time. Now there are millions. The point is that when the Chinese saw what life was like in other countries—and let's face it, they were looking at what we had in terms of material wealth—they wanted it. Deng saw this coming and had the foresight to open up the economy. If they are going to continue this progress in terms of allowing economic reform to spill over into demands for political reform, we have to keep our contact going. That's the only way. And it means no suspension of high-level contacts and no revocation of MFN."

Nixon felt very strongly that most-favored-nation trading status should continue to be extended to China despite the annual bruising debate it inspired in the Congress. The designation permits countries to trade normally with the United States and is restricted only in the cases of nations that openly sponsor terrorism, such as Libya and Iran. Those who argue to revoke China's MFN status contend that its human rights abuses should preclude it from benefiting from normal trade with the United States. Advocates of continuing China's MFN privileges, like Nixon, argue that the best way to promote human rights reform is by engaging the Chinese through trade and other contacts.

"I know that the libs out there get a lot of political mileage out of yelling to revoke MFN." He put on a mock scowl. "They say, 'Those bad Chinese! We know how to hurt them—hit them in the pocketbook.' And their supporters cheer, and some of their constituents do too. But they couldn't be more off the mark. All of this grandstanding on human rights is atrocious. Yes, we have to care about how they treat their own people. And yes, we should tell them when we disagree with what they've done. But hitting them in the pocketbook is not the way to do it, particularly if we want them to improve their human rights record.

"If you take away MFN, what kind of leverage have you got?" he asked, throwing up his hands. "None. You might as well close the book on any hope for political reform and human rights. Economic freedom will spell death for the dictatorship, maybe not as quickly as we would like, but it will happen. So while the Chinese leaders are concerned with making their country rich, we should be concerned with waiting out the inevitable results. That's it in a nutshell."

For Nixon, China's economic power made lectures from the United States about human rights unwise and largely irrelevant. Even the most reactionary hard-line Communists, who supported the crackdown in Tiananmen Square and were opposed to political reform, had no choice but to endorse the free-market economic policies that had delivered such spectacular economic growth.

In *Seize the Moment*, Nixon decided to set China in what he called the Pacific triangle—a precarious balance of power among China, Japan, and the Soviet Union. American engagement with all three corners of the triangle was crucial—balancing them, stabilizing them as they competed, and maintaining a zone of peace among them. Traditional ambitions, maneuvering, and clashing interests made the Pacific a potentially dangerous region. If the United States remained engaged, particularly with China, peaceful political change would soon match the regional economic boom.

On October 1, Nixon met with the U.S. ambassador to China, James Lilley, who told Nixon that he saw three levels of leaders in China: the "immortals," led by Deng; the current group of hard-liners, in their sixties; and a group of more reformist-minded leaders, in their forties, who, he thought, represented the future of China. Nixon was fascinated by his evaluation and asked me to write it out for his review.

After Lilley left, Nixon called me into his office. "Terrific analysis, don't you think? The guy is on the ball, not like some of these other foreign service–type jerks who run around and drink champagne and mao-tai and don't know a goddamned thing. No, this guy is serious. He knows and respects the Chinese. He's good. Bush is lucky to have him over there. I'll tell you—once the old men die in China, you're going to have one hell of a power struggle between those who want repression and those who want reform. It may be only a matter of time before the army turns on the people again, like it did in Tiananmen Square and like the Soviet army did."

When I asked if he thought that Chinese communism would be able to survive without delivering political reform, Nixon shrugged. "It's true that if given the choice between votes and food, people will choose food every time. But once those needs are met, they'll rise up and ask for the votes. This is what the leadership is afraid of, and they should be. We like to think that all of this, all of these revolutions in Eastern Europe and now in the Soviet Union, are for freedom, and to some extent they are. But it's really for a better standard of living. It's really for greater prosperity—more money, more things. They've given the people TVs and telephones and so forth, so they should be able to hang on for another maybe twenty years."

Nixon fiercely guarded his proprietary relationship with the Chinese. As he watched his successors and their representatives visit Beijing, he routinely derided the trips as "flops" and ridiculed their failure to extract concessions from the Chinese. Only he could command their attention and respect. Only he could join the two nations together in honest discussion. Only he could hear the Chinese line and fully understand it. And only he could persuade them to listen openly to the American position. In Nixon's mind, only he could deal successfully with the Chinese. He exploited that position, using it to advance not just Sino-American relations but his own standing politically and historically.

*Seize the Moment* was published in early January 1992, and Nixon spent most of the month giving interviews in support of the book. He knew that the questions would focus on the end of the Soviet Union and on the upcoming race for the White House, but he hoped to focus at least some attention on Asia and the crucial importance of a positive relationship with the Chinese.

Bush, meanwhile, began the year with a trip to Asia. Nixon thought it would allow him to highlight his foreign policy skills and look presidential at a time when his poll numbers were falling. Instead, the president took the American economic problems abroad.

Nixon was aghast. "I cannot believe that Bush is in Japan whining about our economy. He should not look like he's running for reelection when he's abroad," he said as we arrived in Washington on January 6 to promote the book. Two days later, in an interview with CNN's Larry King, Nixon hid his disappointment with Bush's trip.

"I realize that some are knocking the trip because they feel that it's too commercial. . . . Let's understand one thing. There was a very unfortunate statement—which the president didn't make, but somebody in his Cabinet did—to the effect that the recession may have been caused, to an extent, by the Japanese. That's nonsense. . . . We've got to look to ourselves and then look to them," he said, careful not to criticize Bush for traveling with automobile executives and pointing out that three fourths of the trade deficit with Japan was in cars and car parts. "There then comes a reason to try to get the Japanese to make some sort of arrangement where we could sell more to them and maybe cut back on what they sell to us. I don't like that idea. I'm a free trader. . . ."

Just as some got political mileage from calling for the revocation of MFN for China, others got it by criticizing the Japanese for unfair trade practices. And just as Nixon advised a policy of patient engagement with the Chinese, he counseled it with the Japanese. Both relationships were too important to the United States and to the stability of the region to be sacrificed on the altar of haughty self-righteousness or impatient overreaction.

"It does not make sense," Nixon had said on August 16, 1991, when discussing the Japanese section of *Seize the Moment*, "for the United States and Japan to circle each other like sharks. We're allies. We have to face the fact that the Japanese are among the smartest people in the world. Look at what they have accomplished since World War II: they've built a powerhouse economy out of devastation. And ninety-five percent of Japanese graduate from high school, while only seventy-five percent of Americans do. We need each other, not only economically but in terms of keeping peace and trying to get political freedom to expand.

"With Japan, it's the security issue. They need our military guarantee as a shield against China, Russia, and Korea. China, of course, needs us to guarantee that Japan won't return to an aggressive foreign policy. Every Asian nation is scared to death of the Japanese because of what happened in World War II, even though they pose no threat now whatever. But if the Japanese do perceive a threat, they can go nuclear in about two minutes. That's why all of the powers want us in there—in Asia, I mean, and in Japan in particular. It keeps spending on arms way down. If we left, can you imagine the kind of arms race that would take place? My God! It would spin out of control and probably lead to a war."

He shifted in his seat. "The economic side is, of course, just as crucial. They could never survive without access to our market. No way. And our exports to Japan are going to increase regardless of what the so-called experts say, and we will be even more dependent on theirs.

"But look around Japan: they're surrounded by potential threats. The Soviet Union is falling apart, China is becoming a military and economic giant with nukes, and North Korea is trying desperately to get them. Japan will not go nuclear unless it's threatened, and even then it'll turn to us before it does anything. That's why if we leave, the whole place—not just Japan but all of Asia—will fall apart. Wars, arms races, trade wars—you name it."

I found a handwritten note from Nixon on my desk the next morning, comparing the 6 percent of gross national product the United States spends on national defense with the 1 percent Japan spends. Japan, he wrote, should "drastically increase its foreign-aid" budget by 5 percent to match what the United States spends. Since it was politically unfeasible and undesirable for Japan to increase its defense budget, Nixon believed that it should increase its foreign-aid budget to counter the widely held impression that its economic-assistance programs were designed to help only the Japanese.

"They should be doing more for everybody," he said on September 25, 1991, as we sat talking in his office about Japan's financial contributions to the fighting of the Persian Gulf War. "They're so rich and yet so selfish when it comes to spending on other countries. On the other hand, we practically give away the store, but that's another story. But look, they should use foreign aid for what we do: to improve the chances for peace, economic progress, and political stability wherever they see an interest in having that happen, like the Middle East. For God's sake, they are totally dependent on oil from the Middle East, and they barely contributed anything to the war. They should be financing the Arab-Israeli peace process. What a great opportunity for them to get involved there! And once the Russian thing straightens out, those who want democracy there are going to need all the help they can get."

He leaned forward. "Listen, if Japan wants the rest of the world to take it seriously, it's going to have to pony up the money. Peace doesn't come cheap. Neither do good, solid alliances."

On November 10, he continued the theme. "When economic times are bad, finger-pointing is popular. That's just politics. But let's look at the situation for a minute. We have a huge trade deficit with Japan, and it grows every year. They refuse to let some of our goods in. We have an enormous budget deficit. Their economy is slowing. They save; we spend. Both of us have big problems. The point is that bashing the hell out of each other does absolutely no good. You can see this in the way we deal with the Chinese.

You've got to work with them, not against them. Remember, they're our friends. Getting them to lower their trade barriers and contribute more in terms of burden sharing is not going to happen if we keep hitting them over the head. No, as TR used to say, 'Carry a big stick,' but don't use it unless you absolutely have to. And I don't think that we absolutely have to unless they invade somebody or something.

"It's the same thing with us. Do you really think that the fine men in the Congress will be more friendly to the Japanese if the Japanese bashed us every day in the Diet? Of course not. OK," he said, pressing his hands together, "so no managed trade and no trying to even the score by subsidizing American industries or blocking Japanese goods. The answer is not more government regulation but less. The answer," he said, pointing a finger in the air, "is for both sides to see that we are worthy competitors, not vicious enemies. It's got to happen on some level, or forget it."

Nixon's main concern was that Japan would continue to have power without purpose. For too long, it enjoyed being an economic giant with few of the attendant responsibilities. Japan had to assume an international role commensurate with its economic superpower status. It had to play a more active role in the international financial system, particularly the World Bank and IMF. It had to help to reduce the third world debt. And it had to increase significantly its "untied" aid to strategically important nations.

Nixon believed that Japan's enormous GNP could support a drastic increase in its foreign-aid budget. The issue was whether Japan would be willing to use its financial power to stabilize global money markets and expand into a truly free-trade system even if it meant sacrificing short-term business interests. Japan clearly wanted a higher international profile. But before it could be considered for a seat on the UN Security Council, it had to behave like other democracies on the council, which meant it had to have more open markets, more open financial systems, and more open checkbooks.

Nixon was aware that increased Japanese activity internationally could produce a nationalistic backlash. The Japanese were likely to resent American pressures for "burden sharing" when the United States refused to take the necessary steps to revive its own economy and to accept more "power sharing" in determining the broad strategic goals of the bilateral alliance. And although the United States could not induce generosity, it could try to convince the Japanese that if they wanted to get more abroad, they had to spend more abroad.

Bush's failure to get that message across to the Japanese during his trip in early January 1992 was the main reason why both conservatives and liberals panned the visit. The liberals argued that Bush was not tough enough on the trade issues, that he should have issued ultimatums to the Japanese, and if they had not responded adequately, he should have retaliated. The liberals argued further that Bush's "trade mission" was a reelection move that back-fired. Facing a recession at home upon which his Democratic opponents were capitalizing, Bush traveled to Asia, talking about "jobs, jobs, jobs," and returned with few concessions. Foreign policy, they argued, was no longer Bush's strong point. The conservatives argued that Bush's pandering to the Japanese was another example of his indecisiveness. Since he failed to ex-tract concessions, protectionist Democrats could now claim that Bush tried unsuccessfully to play their bullying game with the Japanese. Consequently, the president paid a heavy political price. His free-trade credentials tar-nished by talking about "managed trade" and his stature diminished by traveling with automobile executives, Bush returned home looking pan-icked and defensive.

"Bush should have made it a 'high road' trip," Nixon said on January 7 as the president continued his tour of Japan. We met in his Washington hotel suite before going to ABC News to tape *Nightline.* "I don't mean to be down on the guy, but all of this petty crap he's consumed with over there, like talk-ing about jobs and car parts—my God! And to go over there with [Chrysler chairman Lee] Iacocca, who's a loose cannon anyway—well, what a mis-take." He shook his head. "Presidents are supposed to leave the negotiations of the details to their subordinates. That's the point of having a Cabinet and secretaries and undersecretaries and the entire bureaucracy. But for Bush himself to get out there and talk about this stuff—hoo boy! Bad, very bad. I could talk about the details, but Bush should stick with the mountaintop stuff: talk about trade but diplomatically; talk about the regional balance of power; talk about the importance of keeping our relationship together with-out the threat from the Soviets. If he's so desperate for reelection already that he's playing to the voters from Japan, then we're going to have a hell of a time in November."

He opened his briefcase and put on his eyeglasses. "I was going through some old files and came across these two pieces," he said, handing them to me. Both were from *The Economist.* The first focused on Japan's interest in negotiating the return of the four small islands off northern Japan known as the Northern Territories. Nixon wrote underneath that the forward-thinking Japanese were "romancing" Yeltsin while Bush was calling him "a boob!"

The other piece discussed the boom West Coast states were experiencing by trading heavily with Asia. Nixon circled the opening paragraph, which included a quote from railway magnate Henry Huntington in 1912: "Los Angeles is destined to become the most important city in the country, if not the world. Its front door opens on to the Pacific, the ocean of the future. The Atlantic is the ocean of the past."

Nixon pointed to the articles in my hands. "These pieces are absolutely right. The first one, about the islands, hit it on the head. We shouldn't be insensitive to Japan on this issue; those islands are, after all, occupied by the Russians. And as far as the other piece goes, the Pacific is where most of the ideas, money, customers, workers, and partners are going to come from from now on. There's no way around that."

In early February, Nixon received an invitation from the Japanese government to visit Tokyo. He considered the idea until the Japanese indicated that they would pay for all expenses associated with the trip. Nixon immediately declined. "I cannot have the Japanese paying for my trip," he said on February 11. "It was a generous offer, but I don't sell the office for money. Never have, never will. Besides, it's just not the right time for me to go to Asia. Maybe next year, but not now." He paused. "Maybe China next year, too. I'll take you. You must see these places in order to understand them. And you've got to see the Chinese Communists—tough as nails, far more ideological than the Russians. But maybe next year the timing will be right for the Chinese to hear my message again that communism gave everyone an equal share of poverty and the free market gives everyone an equal opportunity to improve their lives. Bam!" he exclaimed, slamming his fist on his armrest. "They're finding that out, but it may be time, in a few months, for another little visit."

Despite the fact that the collapse of the Soviet Union and the struggle of the democratic forces there had commanded Nixon's attention through 1992, he decided in early 1993 that following another visit to Russia he would travel to Asia. The election of Bill Clinton and his selection of what Nixon considered a "weak" foreign policy team led Nixon to believe that Clinton would need all of the foreign policy help he could get. Nixon decided to tend to the crucial relationships with the Asian powers, submit his evaluations to the new president, and position himself as Clinton's foreign policy mentor, particularly on China.

"You know, Clinton is such a disaster in foreign policy—because he doesn't know anything and, frankly, doesn't care—that I'm afraid he is going to send our China policy right down the tubes," Nixon said on November 8, after Clinton's election. "I mean, he is really going to screw up China beyond belief. All of these libs around him will push him to revoke MFN, which was hard enough for Bush to hang on to, and he was pro-China! Clinton is so susceptible to pressure on issues that he doesn't know much about, which is just about everything in foreign policy, and I'm really afraid for China. He's got a bunch of know-nothings around him who are looking to make an example out of China because of the human rights thing. These are the same people who believe in the Peace Corps and the UN. I can just see it now: they're going to run around screaming 'human rights, human rights!' and push our relationship with China back to pre-1972 times. I've got to do something because I'm not going to sit quietly and watch Clinton screw it up."

Nixon feared that Clinton's reputation for bold liberal activism would extend to his handling of relations with China. Seeking to placate those in his party who clamored for a more aggressive and adversarial approach to China, Clinton might link trade issues with human rights, thereby alienating the Chinese, suspending constructive high-level talks, and retarding economic growth on both sides. If Clinton were looking for a foreign policy issue with which to "express himself," as Nixon put it, the former president worried that it might be China.

"There is no one around him to tell him *not* to go that route," Nixon continued on December 20. "Christopher—forget it. Lake? Well, he knows but probably won't stand up to the president on this score. Talbott's got his problems worrying about Russia, which, after all, is still issue one. But China could become issue one if we do the wrong thing."

Nixon then made an executive decision. He would travel to China in the early spring of 1993, draw the president's attention to the issue and to the region, and report back to him right before the annual June vote on MFN status. The timing of the trip was crucial. Nixon intended to counter the pressure building on Clinton from within his party to punish Beijing for human rights abuses by carrying back an honest evaluation for him, not only on the status of economic reform but on the need to continue an open and constructive relationship with the Chinese. Clinton needed a heavy dose of realism to see a bit of gray amid the black and white he was seeing in the advice of the foreign policy idealists around him.

On Saturday, January 2, 1993, I went to Nixon's residence to pick him up and bring him to the office for a lengthy meeting. As I turned the corner into his driveway, I almost ran him down, because he had walked right into the car's path. Nixon, oblivious to the near miss, got into the passenger seat.

"Hi!" he said. "Happy New Year! Sorry to have you come get me like this, but the house is full with the grandchildren and not exactly quiet. You can't really hear yourself think. And the limo is in the city, picking up Tricia, I think. Anyway, thanks for the lift."

During the five-minute drive to the office, Nixon told me that he wanted to go on a short vacation to the Caribbean but had difficulty finding a travel companion. "Julie and Tricia are always great to go with, but they have their own families, you know. Bebe [Rebozo] and Bob [Abplanalp] are terrific too, but they can't always go. I can't really go by myself . . ."

I laughed. "It's just so ironic, because millions of people around the world would love to go on vacation with you!"

Nixon smiled. "I know. That's the problem!"

We sat in his office and reviewed plans for the first trip he would take that year. "If Russia in February happens, great. You've got to see the place. I will not go over without a firm commitment from Yeltsin. But if that trip falls through, my alternative plan is to go with you and Bob, Bebe, and Ray [Price] to China, Korea, Japan, maybe Taiwan. The Chinese won't like that, but they also know I'm the only heavyweight and friend supporting MFN. Anyway, we'd stay over in Hawaii. I want you to see that, and I know how much Bob, Bebe, and Ray would love to go. We were supposed to go a few years ago, but I got sick and we didn't, and they were terribly disappointed. It would be more of a personal trip than anything, but I've got to get Clinton thinking clearly on China.

"You must see the Great Hall of the People and the Great Wall, of course. It's one of the most spectacular countries on earth. It's just so old, and there's so much richness there, in the people and in the culture. You'll be overwhelmed. Then, of course, there are the Communists. They sit there," he said, crossing his legs, "and talk a good Communist line, but they know that the economic reforms have totally overtaken them in terms of any control they used to have over the economy. But you've got to meet a real Commie; you've studied them enough!"

We left for Russia on February 7, and as we flew from New Jersey to Paris on the first part of the trip, Nixon called me over to his seat. His shoes were off, and a yellow legal pad sat in his lap.

"Have a seat," he said, patting the empty chair next to him. "I know we've got Russia on the brain, but I cannot help but be worried about China. Clinton will be protectionist on China; that's the price he paid for support of the so-called middle class and the libs out there. He'll listen to Nancy Pelosi, who's a jerk," he said, referring to the California congresswoman who strongly opposed extending MFN to China, based on its human rights record. "This is why we've got to get to China before he makes up his mind on MFN. If he's getting pressure from the left to revoke it, why, we'll give him pressure from the right to keep it!"

Upon our return from Russia, Clinton called Nixon for the first time, for a lengthy conversation and to extend an invitation to the White House. On March 5, as the former president prepared for the meeting, he talked with me about his conversation with Clinton, their impending meeting, and China.

"Clinton asked me why the Chinese have ten percent economic growth. I said that there were three reasons," he said, counting them off on his fingers. "One, Deng started with agriculture, which Gorbachev didn't do and the Russians still haven't done. Two, they have political stability, which is unfortunate because political stability is too high a price to pay for growth without freedom. And three, because they're Chinese. Clinton understood it."

As Russia fell apart, China prospered, and the next day, Nixon elaborated on one of the reasons why. "The Chinese have always been merchants. When I told Clinton that they did it because they were Chinese, this is what I meant: they have always been highly industrious, and when Deng opened the floodgates of the market, the Chinese responded immediately. Farmers *wanted* to make a profit. Others rushed at the chance to make some money by running their own businesses or by getting into joint ventures with Western firms or by just selling stuff on the street. The Russians haven't really taken to the market: they are so down on it because of an ingrained skepticism about inequality. The Chinese never had that problem.

"The point is that the Chinese jumped at the chance to make a buck. They don't flinch from hard work. When Deng opened up the economy, he really opened it up. There were no controls put on it the way the Japanese do. They just let it all go crazy," he said, waving his hands around.

"Of course, there is the problem of corruption that always goes along with rampant growth. They've got to try to clean it up, or they're going to have a big mess on their hands.

"But look—there are so many ethnic Chinese outside of mainland China—in Hong Kong, for example—who turn around and invest in China. It's a powerful, powerful thing. The Chinese have all this growth because they're Chinese, and that's the way it is."

As Russia struggled with the messy distractions of democracy, China focused on instituting a brand of "socialist capitalism" that harnessed the energies of the Chinese people in its drive to be an economic and military superpower in the next century. The Russians had tried to decree prosperity in a final reaction to the death of communism, but the Chinese regulated their growth gradually, and it paid off. Their ambitions were clear to Nixon: they wanted to replace the Soviet Union as the foremost challenger to the United States. If we were to meet that challenge, we would have to maintain a good relationship with them.

Nixon was almost completely consumed with Russia's difficult transition from communism to democracy and free markets, yet he knew that if foreign policy had been an orphan in the Bush administration, it would be completely ignored by Clinton. His steady stream of op-eds on the Russian situation brought some attention to the subject, but he did not want it to be at the expense of Asia. Nixon's mission was to tend to the crucial bilateral relationships with China, Japan, and Korea in the hope that the administration would then develop solid policies for working with them.

On March 13, Nixon called me at home at seven in the morning. "Monica! It's a goddamned blizzard!" A foot of snow had fallen, and the former president, deprived of his early-morning walk, was holed up in his study. "Mrs. Nixon and I have our candles and flashlights ready. My God! What a storm.

"Well, I've been putting together some material for our Asia trip. Do you realize that it's three weeks from today? Time is flying by.

"I spoke to Bebe and Bob, and they are so excited about going. You are going to love traveling with them. They are great kidders. You haven't met them yet, have you? Well, you're in for a surprise!"

Charles "Bebe" Rebozo and Robert Abplanalp were Nixon's oldest and dearest friends. Loyal, unassuming, self-made, generous, and witty, Rebozo and Abplanalp were devoted friends and fierce advocates. For decades, they stood by Nixon, through triumph and tragedy, the making of history and the revising of it, the moments in the spotlight and the quieter times. They had always been there for him, ready with a joke, a story, or a sympathetic ear. Comrades in the brutal arena of Nixon's political life, Rebozo and Abplanalp never asked for anything; they did not want perks or favors, the glare of political celebrity, or the power to influence. They just wanted Nixon's friendship, and they got it, unconditionally.

It has been often said that Nixon liked their company because rather than challenge him intellectually, they provided unquestioning support for him. This misses the very point of their relationship: it was about friendship, not politics. It was about having people around, apart from family, whom Nixon could trust absolutely and who could provide a safe haven in the simple shelter of silence. Rebozo and Abplanalp were the rare confidants, allies, and faithful friends who could always make Nixon laugh and give him a gentle crutch of companionship when he needed it most.

"I know how much all of you are looking forward to this trip. It will be very interesting for you in particular because of your interest in the region. You haven't seen the world until you've seen China."

"We'll be in the middle of the high tensions on the Korean Peninsula, unless a war breaks out," I said.

"War! That's the best time to go!" he replied.

At Nixon's request, I assembled State Department briefing papers on China, Japan, and Korea, newspaper clippings, and other background materials, from which he made extensive outlines and notes. He studied economic growth rates, trade numbers, current political conditions, official and unofficial profiles of the region's leaders, the state of bilateral relations between those countries and the United States and among one another, regional military spending, and proliferation and human rights issues.

On March 31, three days before we departed, Nixon called me to the residence for an afternoon meeting. I found him reclining with his feet up, several papers in one hand, and a pen in the other. "You know what's really amazing?" he asked. "Since Deng came to power in 1978, per capita GNP has tripled in China. Tripled! And since they have so many people, do you know what that means? They are becoming an economic superpower. And fast! No wonder the Japanese are worried." He tapped a page. "In 1992, the ten billion dollars that China attracted in foreign investment was the same amount attracted by the United States. Not bad for a Communist country!

"Meanwhile, Japan has hit a major economic slump. Of course, those are just the cycles of the market: up, down, back up; recession, boom. It happens that way. The Japanese just haven't seen it in any significant way—you know what I mean. But they still save a hell of a lot more than we do, and they invest more. We're such a disposable society." He raised his eyebrows. "Don't like it? Sick of it? Why, throw it away! Spend now! Don't save! You could be dead tomorrow! This is how we think, and then we wonder why the Japanese have such a powerhouse economy."

When I asked him about the prospects for a regional security alliance for Asia, he paused before replying. "I know what the line is: that since the cold war is over, the need for the U.S. to be there is eroding. But we have to understand that suspicions pre-dating the cold war are still there. Look, the Japanese and Koreans can't stand each other, the Japanese and the Russians fear each other, and so do the Japanese and the Chinese. We have human rights disputes with China and trade disputes with Japan. Korea is still split into two. So you've got this very complex and potentially dangerous situation in Asia: four great powers and the regional ones all looking for money and influence. It may be necessary to find some kind of a new security arrangement to make sure that China can be brought in peacefully—and so can Russia, by the way."

"Can it be done?" I asked.

"Well, I don't really know. Maybe. We can cooperate when it comes to trade, so maybe we can when it comes to security. But as I've said, we're the only ones on the block that have never waged a war of aggression. None of these Asian countries trust each other. They may not trust us, but at least they know that we're not going to send tanks over there and roll over them.

"If a security arrangement does go through, the U.S.-Japanese relationship has got to be the anchor. There's no way around that."

With shared principles on economic development, the growing primacy of geoeconomics, increasing pessimism over war and its costs, and expanding trade, advocates for a new regional security alliance said it was now possible. Nixon, aware that America's presence and security guarantee stabilized the entire area, was wary about relinquishing any control to a multilateral organization: "If I get any questions on it, I'll hedge."

On Saturday morning, April 3, I drove to New Jersey's Teterboro Airport and boarded our aircraft. I greeted Ray Price, Bebe Rebozo, and Bob Abplanalp, who immediately had the former president laughing. Nixon's mission, though lacking the urgent drama of his trips to Russia, would be important for him historically and politically. The fact that he was accompanied by his two dear friends and Price, whom he respected and admired enormously, was an added benefit.

We landed in Anchorage and had dinner that night with the governor, Walter Hickel, and his family. Though tired, Nixon delivered his standard but incisive analysis of the Russian transition: "Yeltsin will make it, but it will be a very close run thing. We must help him in whatever way we can. The media are such snobs on Yeltsin that they never run favorable stories on him, ever. That's because they were all for Gorbachev and the idea that communism could be saved. So they ignore the populist—Yeltsin—and only cover him when they have to and hope he fails. It's been disgusting. Monica," he said, turning to me, "you think Yeltsin is going to survive, don't you?"

I replied that I thought he would survive because he not only stood for the right things but had a strong political character.

"That's right," Nixon said. "He's a fighter. Fighters always come out on top, even when it doesn't look that way."

After bidding good night to the governor, Nixon wanted to take a walk. It was late, and he was exhausted, but he insisted that I accompany him and his security escort, Joseph Crowley, on a short but brisk stroll that seemed to energize him.

"Look at how they sparkle out here," he said, pointing to lights in the distance. "The colors—well, you saw them today—are just spectacular. Everything up here is either white or green or blue. I know people love New York, but after seeing this, we've got to wonder why we go back to the goddamned place. Sometimes it's even warmer here than it is where we are."

He buttoned the top button of his coat and pulled his collar close to him. "What did you think of Hickel? He's a hell of a guy. He was with us, you know, and stood up very well for us. He's an environmentalist, but it's hard to be governor of Alaska and not be. Look at all of this beauty! But he understands the foreign policy stuff; he's just more interested in the domestic side, which is fine. He's responsible and a damn good governor.

"But what I said about Yeltsin is true. The media only cover him when they absolutely have to, like if he wins a vote of no-confidence or something.

Otherwise, they just hang him out to dry. Well," he sighed, "I guess we can't expect much more from them. I only hope that Clinton stands up with Yeltsin tomorrow and gives a strong statement for the guy. He's *got* to do it."

Early the next morning, Nixon asked me to summarize the Sunday-morning talk shows. I told him that Talbott had delivered positive remarks about the Clinton-Yeltsin summit, and Senator Lloyd Bentsen and Ambassador Strauss were highly supportive of the Russian president. Nixon clapped his hands together. "Good. It's about time, goddamn it. I want you to write them notes telling them that you were impressed by their support of Yeltsin. They'll know that it came from me if it comes from you. They love to hear the good stuff because usually they just hear when they're getting the hell beat out of them."

We left Alaska en route to Tokyo later that day. As we approached the international date line, Rebozo and Abplanalp assembled all of us for a "ceremony," which included some jokes and a toast to our journey. To put us in a festive mood before landing in Asia, Abplanalp opened a suitcase and distributed fortune cookies to the group. Nixon opened his and smiled. "Monica," he said, handing me his fortune, "Read mine—out loud."

I read it first to myself and understood why he wanted me to read it aloud. "Your mentality is alert and analytical," it said. "You see," Nixon said, "obviously not written by one of my enemies!"

After we landed in Tokyo, Nixon called me in to his suite before retiring for the night. "Here," he said, handing me some materials that he had finished reviewing. "Hold on to them, but don't lose them. I'm pretty tired, so I'm going to bed, but if you're not too tired, you should really get out and see the city. It's such a metropolis. Of course, you can't see everything in a day, but you should go to the imperial palace if you can."

He yawned. "I say to you again I'm glad that we aren't bound by the embassy. People wonder why I go abroad without having the embassy or State control it. It's because I can just do whatever the hell I want. I know I'm hard on the embassy and foreign service people, and they don't like us because we don't use them. But," he said, "they cramp my style."

After a hearty laugh, he continued. "I had a good talk with [Ambassador] Michael Armacost. He's smart, a little arrogant, but that's OK. He knows the Japanese, and he's a good diplomat. Of course, there really aren't the type of political issues that come up with the Japanese that come up with other countries, but he's got all of the economic issues. He can handle them and do it well. I'm glad I saw him."

Nixon seemed well rested the next morning when he called for me again. "I want you to come with me to the meeting with [Prime Minister Kiichi] Miyazawa. You must see diplomacy at its highest levels; that's the only way to learn. Miyazawa is a very impressive guy. He was a protégé of [former prime minister Shigeru] Yoshida, of course, who built modern Japan. He was in the Finance Ministry, so he's a money guy. But he also knows world politics. It will be interesting for you to see. I'll take Ray into these meetings too, because he's so interested in the diplomacy and the whole region. They [the Japanese] gave me only a half an hour with him, which means fifteen minutes of conversation, with translation, but that's fine. I'll keep my comments on the big picture."

Nixon then departed for a private meeting with former prime minister Yasuhiro Nakasone at Nakasone's office, and when he returned to the hotel, he picked up Price and me for the meeting with Miyazawa. We were escorted into the prime minister's official residence, where an international press corps was waiting. Following opening remarks by the two principals, the press left the room, and Nixon and Miyazawa had a spirited discussion about the future of Japanese-American relations.

Nixon said that despite the differences the United States had with Japan "on the economic side," referring to the trade deficit, we had interests that bound us together. "We must not let the differences obscure the common interests," he said. "We are both democracies. We are the two strongest, richest free-market economies in the world. After the return of Okinawa, we had no territorial disputes left over from World War II. And we are both trading nations with a common interest in promoting free trade and in resisting protectionism. That's why managed trade may be a temporary and politically expedient way to go, but it's not in the long-term interests of the United States or Japan."

Staring straight ahead, Miyazawa replied that the Japanese economy was more open than it had ever been and that trade was flowing as freely as it possibly could without unduly damaging Japan's economic interests. Nixon, sensing that his powers of persuasion were limited on the trade issues, changed the subject with a blunt suggestion.

"While Japan is a very generous donor in terms of foreign aid, it should consider increasing it, particularly when it comes to Russia. Every free nation has a huge stake in a nonaggressive democratic government in Russia. Now, Japan's reluctance to do more is understandable because it is concerned about the Russians' not returning the four islands, which they should do, following our example on Okinawa. But on the other hand, it makes no sense to take that position with the Yeltsin government, because the alternatives to him will be far worse. Japan will never get back those islands from any of the nationalists waiting in the wings."

"I know," said Miyazawa. "I have read 'Clinton's Greatest Challenge,' " referring to Nixon's *New York Times* op-ed on the need to aid the democratic forces in Russia.

"If Japan considers sharply increasing its aid to Russia," Nixon replied, "not only will that signal to the rest of the world that it is ready to play a major role internationally, but it would also give it the right and duty to play such a role."

Miyazawa listened but did not answer Nixon's point directly. Instead, he moved to diplomatically safer ground and reiterated his belief in a strong bilateral relationship with the United States and the need to find the common ground that Nixon had mentioned.

When we arrived back at the hotel, Nixon wanted to meet with me. "Well, there you go," he said as I walked into his suite. "The Japanese never change. Tough as nails and so polite about it. He doesn't give an inch. Boy, is he strong and charismatic—a very able guy. But I think I made my points pretty well. What did you think?"

I told him that it was clear that Miyazawa had listened to him but unclear as to the extent to which he would act on anything Nixon said.

"I know," Nixon replied. "The Japanese are like Cheshire cats. They never show you what they're thinking, not like the Russians, who are very emotional and will let you know, right there and then, if they don't like what you have to say. The Japanese never show their hand. That's classic diplomacy. You'll see that with the Chinese too. Very controlled, listeners more than talkers. But that's OK because it gives you a chance to say what you need to say.

"But the point is that a greater global role for Japan is inevitable. I hope that I got across that only by working together can we improve the chances for peace, prosperity, and stability in the Pacific. The Japanese already know that, but it's nice to have someone like me reinforce it once in a while."

Nixon smiled. "Let's see now. You have already met Boris Yeltsin and all the leaders in Eastern Europe. You've met a Japanese prime minister. In a day or two you'll meet the South Korean president. And then you'll meet the Chinese Communists. They're *really* tough." He smiled and closed the door behind me as I left.

The next day, April 7, I met with Nixon in his suite at nine in the morning. He was restless and agitated. "I didn't sleep much last night, and I really needed to. Look, I've got tea with Madame Aso, who, as you know, is Yoshida's daughter. Then we're off to Korea. I just don't know if we've spent enough time here. Japan is so important, but who else could I see? What else could I say?

"Miyazawa is subtle, tough, and shrewd. He was head of MITI [Ministry of International Trade and Industry]; they're tough sons of bitches. [Lloyd] Bentsen could handle them, but very few others. Our CEOs are ruthless, but very few in our government are that way. It was apparent, though, that he was shook up by my column [on Russia]. They know what they have to do; they just don't want to do it."

Later that day, during the flight to Seoul, Nixon asked for my assessment of the trip to Japan. I told him that despite his limited time with the prime minister, he had made some very effective points.

Nixon replied, "I think it was effective. Frankly, he needed to hear it, particularly on the Russians. You agree?"

I agreed, and Nixon looked out the window of the plane. "You must never get tired of these places, even if you come back a thousand times. This is your first time here, so it's all new and exciting. But when you return, you must look at these places as if you were looking at them for the first time."

He cleared his throat. "You will always remember this trip because you met the people in power. But what is even more important is to meet the people in the street, like we did in Russia. We will have time to do that in China. That's the most important thing. Besides, leaders don't make up nations and cultures; the people do.

"When we land, I'm going to review my notes for Korea and then sleep, so I may not see you again until tomorrow, when we meet with Kim [President Kim Young Sam]. How are you getting along with Bob and Bebe? Aren't they great fun to travel with? They relieve some of the stress of all this diplomacy. I haven't been able to spend much time with them yet, but once the big meetings are over in China, I'll be able to."

I saw Nixon the next morning, after his private breakfast with former president Roh Tae Woo. "He's very impressive," Nixon said of him. "He takes the long view. The Koreans have always put up good statesmen. You'll see that in Kim this morning. Because the peninsula is split and the border so militarized, the leaders in the south have to be good. It's like Israel that way: surrounded by enemies, so they generate tough, good leaders. Korea is one of those places where the United States has a vital interest in seeing peace and stability. The North Koreans are isolated now that the Soviet Union doesn't exist; they're desperate and, frankly, nuts."

The meeting with Kim was longer and more wide ranging than the one with Miyazawa. At the Blue House, the residence of the president, Nixon met with him alone first while Price and I waited in the state dining room. After a half an hour, they emerged and joined us for lunch. Hang Soo Joo, the foreign minister, Jong-Wonk Ching, secretary to the president for international affairs and national security affairs, and Kyung Jae Lee, secretary for public affairs, completed the group.

Nixon walked the president over to Price and me. "Mr. President," he said. "There are three generations represented on my side of the table. Myself," he said, pointing to his chest, "Mr. Price, who was in the navy during the war, and Miss Crowley, who was born the year I was elected president." The Koreans laughed. "But we are united in seeing Korea as an economic miracle and one of the United States' best allies."

Kim began by commenting that he thought highly of Yeltsin and questioned a report that indicated that some Republicans disagreed with Clinton's aid package to Russia.

Nixon replied, "There will be opposition to every issue that comes before the Congress, but I believe there will be strong bipartisan support for the plan. When I returned from Russia several weeks ago, I met with many members of Congress, and I am confident that they will support the plan. Foreign aid is never popular, but if it is known as an investment in peace and prosperity, it will be supported."

Kim termed Clinton's decision on Russian aid "very bold" and added, "I think that Japan's decision to go forward with some aid despite the Kuril Islands [Northern Territories] issue is also bold."

Nixon said that it was difficult for the Japanese because of the Russian unwillingness to return the islands, but "if Japan contributed as much proportionately to what South Korea has already contributed, it would be a major investment.

"The Russian transition is a gamble because it's unprecedented. It's a miracle that the Yeltsin government is still standing. But communism was such a failure they will never go back, particularly now that thirty percent of the workforce is private. Our support is right and necessary; we want to see the ideas that have worked for us win in Russia."

"The two most uncertain places in the world are Russia and North Korea," Kim said.

"I agree," Nixon replied. "The North Koreans have such unpredictable political leadership. Many thought the Soviets were evil, but none thought they were crazy. We cannot say that about the North Koreans. It is the most closed, secretive society in the world. In the short term, we are concerned about having the north comply with nuclear inspections; in the long term, we must get them to open up because this will cut short the life span of totalitarianism. Consider China."

"I agree," Kim said. "The most important foreign policy issue for the south is to get the north to agree to inspections and join the Nuclear Nonproliferation Treaty. I am also concerned with how much power will be transferred from [North Korean president] Kim Il Sung to his son."

Nixon indicated that the nuclear issue was the most immediate problem for the United States and the world. If the north moved forward with its nuclear program, it would frighten the south and Japan, causing them to react with their own military buildups.

"The north is an outlaw nation," Nixon said. "It is unacceptable for it to have nuclear weapons. This is an issue of the highest priority for the United States, and it should be for China because China is also a nuclear power and should not welcome any other regional power getting the weapons. We all have differences as tough economic competitors. Each country, however, must be concerned with proliferation, especially in North Korea. Now, Mr. President," he said, clasping his hands together, "what points should I convey to the Chinese, because I'm not in the government, so I can afford to be irresponsible!"

Kim laughed, and Nixon continued, "The economic issue must not be linked to other issues on China policy. The Chinese are interested in another Marxist government in Korea, but they are more interested in economic developments, which would be dealt an enormous blow if the United States revoked MFN. Clinton has said that he would reexamine China policy, but if China does not join the international community against North Korea on the nuclear issue, China can forget about MFN in the Congress."

Kim agreed with Nixon's points but expressed more concern about the north's continual insistence that the United States pull out of Korea than about the explosive economic growth of China.

"The United States should not consider pulling out of Korea," Nixon said. "We must explore ways to reduce the tensions between north and south. There are some pragmatic forces in the north, and the régime is endangered by the communications revolution and the spread of ideas. Look at Albania: there was a totally closed society that could not resist the flow of ideas and finally opened up; the North Korean leadership will not be able to resist the pressure once the people are exposed to life outside their borders. Normalization is indispensable to this process."

Nixon concluded the discussion by recalling his first goodwill visit to Korea in 1953, when he was greeted on a cold November day by countless schoolchildren waving American flags. "I knew that Korea would succeed," Nixon said. "And you have set a great example for others in the region and in the world to follow."

Immediately after the meeting, Nixon decided to visit a Seoul department store to see the free market at work. As we toured the store, Nixon said to me, "Look at all of this stuff! It shows you what the market can bring to the people even if the prices are a little high yet for the average person. But look, you didn't see this kind of stuff in Moscow. It will come, assuming that they stay the course." He stopped. "Look around. There is a great vitality to this town. They really have made an economic miracle. And I'll tell you something else: they have shown real guts in giving aid to Russia. They have a fraction of the economic power of Japan, and they've given so much more proportionately. If the Japanese showed the kind of courage that South Korea has, Russia would be in far better shape."

After another brief walk through the gardens surrounding our hotel, we left Seoul and landed in Beijing. As we drove through the streets of the Chinese capital, we could see thousands of people moving through the city, riding bicycles or donkeys, driving cars, or walking. Enormous signs advertised Beijing for the Olympics in the year 2000. American pop music played over car radios. Everyone seemed to be in a hurry even though it was late in the evening. It was a scene of controlled but lively chaos.

We were escorted to a compound of government guesthouses patrolled by armed guards and surrounded by ponds and gardens. Nixon disappeared down the hall and into his suite. "Monica?" I heard him call.

I walked down the red-carpeted hallway until I reached his door. It was open, and I could see him looking out of a window down to the patio below. "You asked for me?" I said.

He whirled around. "Yes, yes," he said. "Come in and look at this. Look at all of this. This is where I stayed in '72. Can you believe it? It's just as magnificent now as it was then." He walked slowly to the desk, which was lit from behind, and ran his hand over the top of it. Then he moved to its chair, sat down, and looked up at me. "This is where I wrote the Shanghai communiqué. This is where I did it all. It was a lot of heavy lifting. A lot has changed since then, but that breakthrough was probably the most significant accomplishment of my presidency." He paused. "Well, I just thought you'd like to see where it all happened."

He stood up and walked me to the door. "How are your quarters? Just remember when you go to sleep tonight that you are in the capital of the most dynamic country in the world."

The next day, April 9, Nixon sent our entourage to tour the Forbidden City. Beijing was experiencing a major windstorm, which blinded us to the magnificent sights with great blasts of dust and wind. When we returned to the guesthouse, Nixon was surprised by our windblown appearance and requested that we "clean up" before leaving for lunch with the foreign minister, Qian Qichen.

The luncheon was more of a gesture of courtesy to Nixon than a substantive meeting, and though Nixon broached topics such as China's relationships with the United States and Japan, most of what Nixon had come to China to say was reserved for his conversation later that afternoon with Premier Li Peng.

Li Peng was a doctrinaire Communist who had begrudgingly accepted Deng's reforms. Cast as a brutal reactionary after the Tiananmen Square massacre, Li kept a lower profile internationally but kept strict control over his own power and over the society. Dissidents were sent to jail without legitimate trials or were executed. Propaganda continued to flow. And although the free-market reforms had thrown off the dead hand of communism, Li made certain that the urge for any political freedoms stayed suppressed.

At five o'clock, Price and I accompanied Nixon to his meeting with Li at Zhongnanhai, the office of the premier. Nixon greeted him in front of the press and introduced Price and me, adding, "She went with me to Russia a few weeks ago." Li looked at me and said, "Do you speak Russian?" When I told him that I did not, he replied that he had studied in Moscow and then, waving the cameras out of the room, asked us to sit down.

He began by saying that it was a great pleasure to meet Nixon again, an "old friend of China." He asked for Nixon's analysis of the situation in Russia because, he said, he did not believe that the government was providing materially for the people.

"When I was in Moscow a few weeks ago, I saw everyone in and out of the government," Nixon said. "I also saw plenty of goods in the stores, although the prices were high. Progress is being made in Russia, although not at the rate of China. Economic reforms have gone forward at the cost of some political instability, but they are irreversible. There will be no return to communism. President Clinton, to his credit, took the lead among the G-7 on assistance, and it is vital that the Yeltsin government survive, because of its nonaggressive foreign policy. Every one of the alternatives to Yeltsin will adopt an aggressive foreign policy."

He continued, grounding the need for Yeltsin's survival in China's immediate interest: "Chou En-lai was concerned about an adventurist Russian foreign policy. Yeltsin's democratic government is not a threat; it is in the interests of both China and the United States that that government remain in power. Yeltsin's successors would seek a greater Russia, apart from political or economic ideology."

Li responded that Russia was in "chaos" and stated categorically that China would not interfere in its internal crises. China wanted a "good-neighbor policy" with Russia regardless of who was in power in Moscow.

"China will be safe with Yeltsin in power," Nixon continued. "I give him over fifty percent odds to survive. Despite the economic problems, Yeltsin remains the popular man in Russia; he has a special chemistry with the Russian people that Gorbachev never had. Both were born peasants. Gorbachev became a man of the world; Yeltsin stayed a man of the people. China should have a friendly neighbor to the north; it should not be expected to support that democratic government, but it should welcome it."

Li replied that Yeltsin had a successful visit to China the previous December, during which they talked about increasing trade. And aware that Nixon was Yeltsin's foremost advocate in the West, Li admonished, "The United States should not place its hopes on one man, because Yeltsin's popularity has dropped."

"We should not tie our policy to one man," Nixon answered, "but rather to what he stands for and what we want and what China should want: a nonaggressive Russian foreign policy."

"Even if the West gives Yeltsin's government more aid," Li replied, "it can only be symbolic because he must take some practical measures to improve the economy," measures, he implied, not unlike those China had taken.

Nixon then raised the issue of Sino-American relations. "We face a different situation today than we did in 1972. It was vital then for the United States and China to have a special relationship because of Vietnam and the Soviet threat. I came to China with no illusions that China would help on Vietnam, but the American people supported relations with China because of the Soviet menace. Now we are in a new era, and we must find reasons to continue our relationship.

"China is a great regional and global power and on the verge of becoming an economic superpower. On June 3, as you know, the Congress will vote on MFN status for China. President Clinton is under pressure to attach conditions to MFN because of campaign promises to be tougher on China and because there are many who are anti-China in the Congress. But I am convinced that Clinton wants good relations with China. I think, however, that China should be willing to offer some reassuring actions in human rights and nuclear proliferation in North Korea to avoid giving those who are anti-China ammunition to revoke MFN."

Li looked down at his hands, and Nixon continued. "I do not mean to intrude in China's internal affairs, but as one who opened relations with China twenty-one years ago, I feel it would be detrimental to both countries if the relationship were disturbed now over these issues."

Li cleared his throat. "Russia may still be a threat because it still has massive nuclear arsenals," he said, "and no other nation has ever conquered Russia, including Napoléon and Hitler. The world must be aware of Russia's nationalist tendencies. On a high pillow, you can have a good sleep, but the West cannot sleep well. Clinton has focused on the American economy as China has focused on hers. They are mutually complementary."

"In the United States, most leaders do not think long term," Nixon said.

"The United States needs more leaders like President Nixon," Li replied.

Nixon nodded and took another approach. "President Clinton is cutting our defense budget because there is no longer a Soviet threat, but I oppose any U.S. withdrawal from Asia. If Japan loses American support and protection, it will have no choice but to go nuclear. China will face a very difficult situation if that is the case."

He shifted gears. "There is another issue which I would like to discuss with the premier. The United States has an eighteen-billion-dollar trade deficit with China—"

Li cut him off. "That is an absurd figure."

"Does the premier trust our CIA?" Nixon asked.

Li smiled. "The commerce secretary has not done his homework because the trade balance is equal."

Nixon raised an eyebrow. "Well," he responded, "this is an important issue because there is at least a perception of significant trade deficits with Japan and China."

"If MFN is revoked," Li said in a calculated answer, "Hong Kong will suffer. The United States should not give up its stake in the market by revoking MFN."

"I agree," Nixon said.

"The United States and Japan are rivals," Li said, trying to sow discord, "but the United States and China are economic partners. Chinese exports to the United States are cheap and of high quality, and if the United States does not import them from China, it will from other nations, where the workmanship may not be as good. Please convey to President Clinton that what he said during the campaign does not matter; we watch what he does and says now. We are willing to cooperate."

Nixon then turned his attention back to North Korea. He asked Li point-blank, "What is China's policy toward North Korea's nuclear-weapons development, and can you influence them to sign on to the NPT [Nuclear Nonproliferation Treaty]?"

Li shifted in his chair. "North Korea has good relations with China, but China will not interfere in their internal affairs."

When Nixon pressed him about the North Korean weapons program, Li replied that the United States would need to deliver proof of such development before he could ask them to halt it.

Nixon ended the conversation by telling the premier that he would oppose strongly any effort in the United States to attach conditions to MFN or to otherwise "destroy the relationship."

Nixon's meeting with Li was not nearly as contentious as his 1989 meetings had been with him and other Chinese leaders. Enough time had passed since the Tiananmen Square tragedy to allow Nixon greater latitude in discussing the positive aspects of the relationship as well as his concerns over proliferation and human rights. Li had assumed a greater measure of power since Nixon saw him in 1989, having defeated prime minister Zhao Ziyang in an internal power struggle. Nixon remarked that he had left China after his visit in 1989 "guardedly optimistic" about the future of Sino-American relations. This time, he *entered* his meeting with Li guardedly optimistic and

left encouraged that the hard-line premier had not just listened to his arguments but perhaps understood them.

Back at the guesthouse later that night, he called for me. The door to his
suite was closed, and I knocked. There was no answer. I turned the knob and
opened the door. "Mr. President?" I called out into the darkness. A soft light
at the far end of the room became brighter. Nixon sat in the corner of the office area, legs propped up and hands folded in his lap. "Sir?" I asked. "Is
everything OK?"

He waved to me to enter. "Yes, I just had my eyes closed so I could think
about today's conversation. Here, sit here," he said, moving his legs from the
ottoman and pushing it out to me. "Well, you saw a real Commie in action.
He was such a demagogue. You saw how he made the points. Of course, I
was able to make my own in my own way. But the guy is tough as nails. He's
a Communist through and through. You can see the steel in him," he said,
making a fist. "But he, like the others, have had no choice but to accept the
economic reforms because deep down they know that they're the only goddamned things keeping them in power. If the people weren't making money
or if they were hungry, they would have risen up against the Communists
long ago." He leaned forward, lowered his voice, and pointed to the ceiling.
"Remember what I told you about the Russian guesthouses?" He put his finger over his mouth. "Watch what you say."

Nixon sent his traveling companions to see the Great Wall the next day,
April 10. He stood at the entrance of the guesthouse, watched us get into
our cars, and waved as the motorcade pulled away. I turned around in the
car and saw him cross his arms as he watched us pull out of view. "I've been
to the wall," he had said. "Everyone should see it at least once. But I can't
spend two hours in the car each way to get there, particularly when I have
the meeting with the president [Jiang Zemin] this afternoon. But you go;
you will be amazed. It's one of the most spectacular things in the world, that
and the pyramids, of course."

Upon our return from the wall, we joined Nixon for a visit to a Beijing teahouse. As soon as he climbed out of the car, he was enveloped by hundreds
of Chinese, all applauding and waving wildly. He made his way through the
adoring crowd into the teahouse, where we were treated to performances of
Chinese traditional martial arts, dance, and song. Nixon swayed to the
music and cheered the artists, obviously relishing the adoration and respect
being showered on him. Caught up in the frivolity, he picked up a tam-
bourine and tapped it in rhythm to the music, then got up and walked onto
the stage, where he posed for photographs and signed autographs.

From the teahouse, we proceeded to the Great Hall of the People, where
Nixon led us on a walking tour up the grand staircase and through the banquet room where Chou En-lai and he had made their toasts celebrating the

historic achievement in 1972. Nixon broke away from our group and moved slowly to the stage. He walked up the stairs and stood silently in the middle of the stage, looking out on the empty chamber. Several minutes passed before he spoke.

"This is where we did it," he said softly. "This is where we toasted the agreement to open relations between our two countries. It's empty now, but in 1972, what a crowd we had! This room was filled to the brim with people, all celebrating the breakthrough with us." He paused. "That was quite a time."

From the Great Hall, we walked through Tiananmen Square, where Nixon said, "This is the center of it all: pro-democracy demonstrators crushed, openings to the world, the beginnings of the free market, bringing growth and wealth and, ultimately, pressure to change what Mao began. If Mao could see China now—my God, he's probably rolling in his grave!"

I accompanied Nixon later that afternoon to his meeting with President Jiang Zemin. The former president, aware that Jiang was considered to be Deng's chosen successor, decided to make many of the same points to him that he had made to Li, with the same balance of warning and optimism.

Jiang began the discussion by welcoming Nixon warmly and recalling his historic 1972 visit. Nixon congratulated him on reaching the presidency and remarked that relations between the United States and China had improved since his last visit, in 1989.

"I hope," Nixon continued, "that the president may be able to build new relations with the new American president based on cooperation. Many people have speculated as to why I came to China in 1972: to end the Vietnam War, to balance the Soviet threat, and so forth. Now, however, with the end of the cold war, we need a new basis for Sino-American relations. What many have failed to realize is that I would have come to China without Vietnam or the Soviet threat. I came because China is a great nation that will play a decisive role far into the future. Cooperation between our two countries is indispensable to keeping the next century a century of peace.

"As you know, every year the Congress has very close votes on whether to extend MFN status to China. We have another vote on June 3. President Clinton will be under pressure to attach conditions to that status because many in the United States are opposed to MFN for China because of the human rights issues. I am confident, however, that President Clinton will develop a good relationship with the president [Jiang] because both of you are good with people. I hope that that new relationship is not poisoned by any difficulty on the MFN issue. I would urge the president to consider taking some actions in the human rights area that would remove pressure on President Clinton to attach conditions to MFN."

Jiang looked straight ahead. "I appreciate your straightforwardness. History has shown that you have always taken the long view, and that is appreciated.

"When I became president of China, President Clinton sent me his congratulations and demonstrated an understanding of the need for positive bilateral relations.

"I do not see a fundamental conflict of geopolitical interests between China and the United States, but a continuing lack of understanding between us could lead to significant problems. We should pursue greater contacts and exchanges between our two countries."

Nixon replied, "An unfortunate fallout of Tiananmen Square was the termination of all executive-level contacts and at the congressional level. They must be restored."

Jiang nodded in agreement. "Like you, I came up from the people, worked as an apprentice, then as director of a factory, and then into the government. We think similarly," he said, conveniently ignoring the fact that Nixon was an American conservative and he was a Chinese Communist. "Maintaining MFN is beneficial to both countries, and China has taken many positive measures to work to that end. China continues to open up and work toward a socialist market economy," he said, again ignoring the irony of his phrase.

Nixon continued, "I raise the human rights issue as a friend, and I always supported MFN when it came up in the Congress. It would be detrimental to both economies if it were denied, but the pressure on President Clinton will be enormous. He can change his views if China gives him an incentive to do so. It is essential that President Clinton develop good relations with China now. Both of you have a historic opportunity to build a new strategic and economic relationship."

Jiang expressed his own desire to build this new relationship and added a relatively favorable appraisal of Yeltsin.

Nixon concluded, "There are four great nations that will determine the future of the Pacific: China, Russia, Japan, and the United States. The closer the relationship between them, the better. The United States must not withdraw its forces from the region or risk seeing greater instability. This is why a good relationship between the United States and China is indispensable."

Jiang stood and applauded Nixon as he escorted us to a banquet he was giving in Nixon's honor. The Chinese president showered Nixon with praise during his many toasts and emphasized Nixon's unique position as an honest broker between the United States and China.

When we returned to the guesthouse, Nixon sat down with me in his suite and said, "Back when Bush asked me about him, I just said that I don't think we need to worry about him. I'll tell Clinton the same thing. Right now he's just following the party line. After Deng dies, if he even survives the succession struggle, he may not be as formidable a player. But you know, Jiang has more spirit in him than Li does. He's stuck being general secretary of the Communist Party, which, as communism declines in China as an economic force, will mean less and less."

He sat bolt upright. "Well! You've had quite a day: the Great Wall, the Great Hall of the People, Tiananmen Square, dinner with the president. It almost feels like 1972 again!"

The spirit of his successful meetings with the leadership seemed to invigorate him, and as we boarded a chartered Air China flight to Hangzhou the next morning, he was relaxed and joked with the flight staff. After takeoff, Nixon walked from his seat back to mine and sat down next to me. "How are you doing, after meeting all of those Communists? You saw Li, a tough son of a bitch. A real Communist. Ruthless. The president—Jiang—is not. He's smart but doesn't quite have the steel we saw in Li. If Li also survives the succession struggle, he may be the real power. The Chinese are very different from the Russians. The Russians drink, smoke, laugh; the Chinese never do, not in diplomatic conversations. But they are so proud of their economic progress, and they should be; they have made enormous strides because they bit the bullet on economic reform."

He leaned in closer to me. "You heard them discount Yeltsin. They are *terrified* that he will succeed, because that will mean the death knell for them. The reform bug will spread like you have never seen it before. So I set my remarks in terms of their self-interest—why *they* should want to see Yeltsin survive, and that is for a nonaggressive foreign policy, which Yeltsin is for and which the alternatives to him are not. You heard Jiang—they want good relations with the Russians because they share such a huge border. Well, if Yeltsin goes down, his successor will send more troops to that border faster than you can imagine."

He changed the subject. "Can you believe that we have gotten almost no Western media coverage? Now, say what you want about the Chinese media, and they're censored to hell, but at least they gave us some play. Why is it? Is it—this trip—irrelevant? No. Maybe the Chinese are keeping them away."

Nixon was distressed that the American media had not given his trip the attention he thought it deserved. Unlike his trips to Russia, which always attracted coverage, his mission to China failed to rate a substantial mention in the major American papers. Nixon was clearly disappointed: "They should pay attention, but they won't."

In Hangzhou, we boarded the boat built for Chou and Nixon in 1972 and enjoyed a tour of the lake. When Nixon broke away from his Chinese hosts to talk with me on the deck, he said, "What do you think? Isn't this spectacular? None of these high-rises were around in '72. The progress that they've made has been incredible." He stared out over the waves to the landscape beyond. "This is China's big tourist area, apart, of course, from Beijing. People come from far and wide to see this: the boats, the cherry blossoms, the bustling energy. You can see that there are some private shops, but lots of color. When this is over, I want to get out among the local people. The Chinese are so warm and friendly."

With their unconditional affection for him in mind, the former president plunged into a crowd in downtown Hangzhou. Masses of people swarmed around him, clapping, shaking his hand, reaching out to touch him. Nixon himself was almost lost in the crush.

"It's very heartening to be treated that way," Nixon said after his rendezvous with the crowd. "The recognition factor is so high, and they just seem to appreciate what I have done." It was a physical *and* a historical recognition. The Chinese expressed an admiration and respect for him that were denied to him at home. Just knowing that somewhere in the world he was revered absolutely gave him a sense of gratification and vindication. On that warm day in China, his post-presidential activities took on a new meaning: he was a hero to the Chinese, a man appreciated, listened to, and heeded. He sought respect, and he got it in China.

We proceeded to the Hangzhou Botanical Gardens, where Nixon posed for photographs next to the sequoia he had planted with Chou in 1972, to the guesthouse where they negotiated the Shanghai communiqué, then returned to the hotel, where Nixon wanted to speak with me. He seemed relaxed and content.

"How did you like that 'people bath'?" he said, chuckling. "It's always good to get out and see the real people, but in China you will always be mobbed because you're an American."

"Or because you're President Nixon," I said.

"That too," he said, smiling. "But they're so grateful that I helped to open their country to the rest of the world. And I'm grateful that they've appreciated that. I know that it's sort of a walk down memory lane for me; I hope it wasn't boring for you.

"You've learned a lot that you will put to use when you are advising on foreign affairs or when you're involved yourself. The Chinese people are good people; it's their government that stinks. Their free market is pretty primitive, but you've got to start somewhere, and if anyone can do it, the Chinese can."

When I asked if he thought that what China needed next was the political reform that would anchor its economic progress, he answered, "Of course, but it's not going to happen. Not anytime soon. Twenty, maybe thirty years and we may see some movement on that score. I don't think sooner, although when Deng dies, you never know what could happen. The Chinese have never been much good at succession struggles. But the up-and-comers are still socialist, just pragmatic. It's going to take a generation, I think, for China to move toward democracy in any meaningful way. But remember, China thinks in terms of centuries; for them, thirty years is like a hiccup."

With these remarks, Nixon placed himself on the record with his prediction for real democratic progress in China. Socialism with a Chinese face was ultimately untenable. The free market was rapidly lifting more than one billion people out of poverty and into the global middle class. The Chinese were pursuing prosperity with passion in an economic revolution bubbling from the bottom up. Nixon knew that the reforms were unstoppable. While the political leaders in Beijing talked about ideology, everyone else in China talked about commerce.

Nixon believed that the next upheaval would not be driven by students and intellectuals demanding a greater political voice but by the new middle class insisting on more prosperity. The leadership would be forced to accommodate them rather than shoot them because, as Taiwan and Korea showed, economic success often produces a more tolerant and pluralistic society, less inclined toward violence and more inclined to compromise.

The Chinese government scrambled to keep up with market activity that kept slipping ahead of its control. Political control would begin slipping away as well when those who were benefiting from economic choice started demanding political choice. Nixon's prediction that real democratic progress would come to China in twenty years was based on the idea that it would take that long for the demand for political freedom to match the momentum of economic progress.

On April 12, we arrived in Shanghai, a sprawling, bustling free-market metropolis. Nixon made his way through several adoring crowds as we toured the city with our Chinese hosts, who took us to Nanpu Bridge to witness the port's economic development, the Shanghai Securities Exchange to see the beginnings of their stock market, the Jinjiang Hotel to visit the site where the Shanghai communiqué was signed, and the American consulate, where Nixon made a few remarks about the breathtaking economic growth.

On the return trip to the hotel, Nixon had our motorcade stop abruptly on a crowded street. From the car behind his, I could see his door swing open. He stepped out and stood on the floor of the car, holding on to the roof for support and waving to the thousands of Chinese who cheered wildly for him. He tried to step out of the car, but the crowd pushed in, and fearing for his own safety, he ducked back into the limousine.

"Well! Wasn't that something?" Nixon asked me when we returned to the hotel. "The Chinese understand the magnitude of what we did in '72 because they're living the results every day.

"And the Americans at the consulate seem to be very good. They seem to know China. I was impressed with them. But you know, I often think, 'If only the Russians could do what the Chinese have done . . .' " He stopped. "Well, that's a different story."

When we landed in Guangzhou the next day, Nixon visited an outdoor market, where he was able to "mingle with the people and experience the real sights and sounds and smells of China," and the Guangzhou economic and technological district.

"Did you see what is happening here? You've got an international port of call that could be as busy and as wealthy as Hong Kong pretty soon," he said before we left for dinner with Guangdong governor Zhu Senlin. "Hong Kong is right next door, and if Guangzhou plays its cards right, it will be the next Hong Kong. You see these politicians in Guangzhou. They're more like American politicians than the Communists you saw in Beijing. They just ignore what Beijing has to say, or at least bribe them to be left alone. In any event, what they have here that other regions of China need is private foreign investment, mostly from Taiwan and Hong Kong. They've got these successful free-market zones, which are really making a way for capitalism to spread throughout the rest of the country. You can see it everywhere: neon lights, stores, cars—you name it. I even saw people today talking into those wireless phones . . ."

"I had a man try to sell me one on the street," I said.

"You see? Capitalism is everywhere, but so is the corruption. They have a terrible problem with that, but if you're going to have a free market, you're going to have the dirty stuff going on. They have got to find a way to deal with it, or it could really destroy what they've done so far."

He tapped me on the nose. "Be careful of these people approaching you trying to sell you things. Not everyone out there is nice."

On April 14, we left Guangzhou for Shenzhen on Train Number 5, in a special car reserved for our party. Nixon sat with me for part of the trip so he could point out the "real China" passing by our windows. "Look," he said, "people shadowboxing! I tried that once; you can imagine how it turned out!" As we sped past oxen pulling carts in the rice fields, Nixon said, "Can you believe that this is the same country you just saw in Guangzhou? China is just so many things: cars and oxen, wealth and poverty, communism and capitalism, the old and the new. I don't think that any other country has this many contradictions right now."

He paused and looked out the window. "I'm concerned that we are too condescending to the Chinese. Sending professors over here? Please! Most of our professors are Marxists anyway," he laughed. "What could they teach them that they don't already know or are already rejecting? There's a hell of a lot we could learn from them. We're no model society!"

"Some want the United States to try to build a universal culture," I said.

He turned to me, horrified. "You mean like Americanize everything? Oh, God! That's not only wrong, that's a crime."

"I heard from somebody in Guangzhou that when the Chinese decided to build the hotel we stayed in, they brought in an American manager, who gave all the Chinese workers American names because it was easier for him," I said.

Nixon's jaw dropped. "No! Why, that's goddamned insulting! I can't believe it. Who did he think he was? Coming over here, to one of the strongest, richest, oldest, proudest cultures in the world and stripping them of their identity? Oh, my God. That's bad," he said, shaking his head. "Nobody should let that happen: not us, and not the Chinese.

"You know, all of this development seems like a seamless thing, but pretty soon the modern parts are just going to overwhelm the other in a tidal wave."

"A tidal wave of money," I added.

"That's right," he said.

After a brief stop in Shenzhen, we traveled by motorcade to the border crossing into Hong Kong. We were detained for over one hour at the gate while border officials examined our passports. Nixon jumped out of his car and began pacing. "What is taking so long? All of our papers are in order, goddamn it." He gestured wildly, then turned toward my car, shrugged, and got back into his own.

When we finally arrived in Hong Kong, Nixon was mobbed by the press as he tried to enter the hotel and almost fell as the reporters pushed to get closer to him for a quote or a photograph.

"My God! How did I survive that crush?" he said when I met with him an hour later. He stood in front of a mirror, straightening his tie. "They almost killed me! They've got a very aggressive press corps here. But only use the press when you have something to say. I didn't mind them; they have a job to do, but so do I.

"Anyway, you'll see what a teeming place Hong Kong is. Look at this," he said, walking with me to a window from which we could see the bustling port. "There is an energy here that you won't see anywhere else in the world. Really. Here it is late at night, and ships are moving through the port by the hundreds. The streets are still crowded."

He turned to me. "Are you tired?" I was. "So am I. It's been rough going over the last few days. And then of course I get here and get roughed up by the press. Well, better to be in demand than not. And since I cannot be in a position to ask for an interview, I'm glad they're coming after me."

Nixon spent the next day putting the finishing touches on a speech he would deliver to the Nixon Library during a stopover in Los Angeles on his way home. We talked again in the morning.

"I see that the G-7 may go forward with new money for Russia. Half of it is for debt rescheduling; that should be a given," he said. "That should go to them anyway. It's bullshit—smoke and mirrors."

"I heard Bentsen encourage the Japanese to do more," I said.

"Good! It's OK for me to say it, but others should be saying it as well. They *should* be doing more.

"I know I've said this before, but I'll say it again: our foreign service people are the pits. They're all bad. There are exceptions, but most come from the elite schools and the social set and don't know a damn about foreign policy. They're all liberals, Democrats. Usually they don't do too much damage, except if they're posted in a country going through a major transition, like China or Russia. Then we have real problems.

"The poor Russians have spent over seventy years under communism. They don't have the traditions to build a democratic society on. They just don't. China, of course, doesn't either, but they have the economic basis for it, which is the most important thing."

He looked right at me. "Tell me, you're going to get out and see Hong Kong, aren't you? I'm going to stay in the room all day and work on this speech. Bebe tells me that you are all going to take a ferry to Kowloon and shop around. Have a good time, but be careful. And be sure to take it all in."

I did not see Nixon again until we boarded our plane later that night and flew across the Pacific, landing in Hawaii on April 16 for a two-day layover.

"I am down about this library conference," he told me the morning of April 18, when we met to discuss the speech he was preparing. "It doesn't mean a thing. News flows from east to west, never west to east. Having it in California was a mistake. It won't get any press in the East. This is basically for the professional conference goers, who are mostly the arrogant types. And the audience for this thing is small, damn it. I wish I didn't have to do it, but I do."

I reassured him that his remarks did matter, particularly to such an influential audience.

"The other former presidents try to have an influence, but they just don't; you know what I mean," he replied. "Reagan tries; Ford doesn't really. Carter started out with great fanfare with that group that was supposed to stop wars. That didn't amount to anything.

"This conference—well, I know it's meant to be something, but I just don't think it will amount to much. And I'll tell you right now that I'm working too damn hard on this speech. I've made nine drafts, too many for something that's not going to be covered. And another thing: it was a mistake to concentrate only on Japan for the conference. It should have been Asia after the cold war. The whole focus is wrong. The Japanese are important, but let's address the whole region. Well, in my speech, I'm going to focus on all of Asia anyway, so what the hell."

Nixon left Hawaii on April 18 to fly to California, and I flew back to New York to return to my graduate-school studies. I called him in Los Angeles on April 20, the day before he was to deliver his speech at the library. "Monica! Are you awake?" he asked.

"Yes," I said, "but I did sleep for sixteen hours."

"Good! I used to go like that when I was a little older than you. I'd go two or three nights without sleep during a campaign. You aren't at your best when you are like that. But you, coming back from Hawaii, had two red-eye flights in a row. No wonder you're exhausted.

"Listen, tomorrow I give this speech. I'm done preparing for it. I'm not putting another second of work into it. I'll bring you the transcript when I get back. [California governor Pete] Wilson is introducing me, which is good, and then I'm going to deliver the goddamned thing and get the hell out."

Nixon returned to New Jersey on April 22, and I met with him at the office the next day. He stood by the window, hands clasped behind his back. I must have frightened him when I entered the room, because he turned with a start.

"Well! We've been gone so long from here I almost forgot what this place looks like," he said as we sat down. "What did you think of the trip?"

"I think the trip was successful," I replied. "You got across the points you wanted to make to the Japanese, the Koreans, and the Chinese, and they listened. It's important that you return to Asia, particularly when you think that the next century will probably be the Pacific century."

"I know, but I'm very disappointed about the lack of coverage. The media is so sick. In my case, it's hopeless to try to get coverage. They just blocked us out. They won't cover me unless I do or say something controversial."

"The trip was worth doing, though, because leaders appreciate the fact that they can talk to you, and you to them, in a straightforward way," I said.

"They don't really have to deal with the diplomatic bullshit," he said.

I told him that since he was one of the few Americans who could deal with the Chinese in good times and bad, he needed to return to the region often to maintain the relationship between the United States and China.

"That may be," he replied. "But when you don't get the coverage, you don't get the message out. I'm down on this trip. It was sort of a dud, if you know what I mean. My speeches were good, but nobody paid any attention. They are a hell of a lot of work for nothing. But, as you say, I was good on the person-to-person exchanges in China, but as a public figure I wanted to end China on an up note, and it was not. It's important to recognize that when something doesn't go, don't repeat it. I don't mean to sound mean or to depress you, but you know what I'm saying. I'm my own best critic.

"From now on, with regard to television, I'm only going to do properly controlled situations. Since they didn't pay attention when we were in Asia, screw them."

Nixon was frustrated that the media not only had failed to cover him adequately when he was abroad but had failed to pursue him upon his return. Nixon in China made historic headlines in 1972; Nixon in China made dramatic headlines in 1989. Nixon in China in 1993 made few if any headlines.

He took it as a personal defeat and wondered if his message on Asia were irrelevant or if he were becoming a mere historic novelty, a leader who had outlived his usefulness but insisted on traveling around the world. Nixon, trying to avoid that perception at all costs, ensured that his trips were serious and substantive. Even as he encouraged his staff to see the sights, he remained ensconced in his suite, reading, studying, and writing. Those serious endeavors were not active or controversial enough to be covered, and Nixon was left to make his own news. "I gave up on the media years ago," he said but did not really mean it.

The trip to Asia was a success since Nixon achieved all of his objectives. He told the Japanese that the United States remained concerned about unfair trade practices but wanted to continue a positive security and economic relationship. He told the South Koreans that the United States would do what it could to ensure stability on the peninsula. He told the Chinese that the United States was gravely concerned about their human rights abuses and their willingness to sell nuclear technology to rogue nations. He maintained his special relationship with the Chinese. He gave the Clinton administration political cover to deal with sensitive economic and human rights issues. And even without press coverage, he positioned himself to advise the new president on Asia.

Nixon, of course, never intended to fade away. He knew no other life except the one in the arena. He knew no other way except traveling the world, trying to influence American policy. He knew no other role but that of statesman, and he used it even when it was a quiet role, not in the spotlight but guiding it.

Nixon used his speech to the library conference on April 21 to warn once again about the consequences of a failure of the democratic experiment in Russia, then turned his attention to what he had found in Asia. While there had been substantial economic reform in China, he said, there had been hardly any political reform. In order to encourage progress on political reform, the United States needed to continue China's most-favored-nation status. Just as Bush was correct to veto attempts to revoke it in the past, "I hope President Clinton will do exactly the same if it comes to his desk after June 3, when he has to make that decision." Nixon had clearly begun his campaign to pressure Clinton publicly to maintain China's unconditional MFN status. He even gave Clinton the political ammunition to wield against those in his own party who wanted to revoke MFN: "In our dealings with the Chinese, we should emphasize our concern on the [human rights] issue diplomatically, but we should not go so far as to weaken the private sector, because the growth of economic freedom in China is the best way to produce political freedom."

He urged his audience to keep up a positive relationship with the Japanese: "Don't let the differences obscure the common interests." Warning that American criticism of Japan ran the risk of feeding both a defensive arrogance and outright resentment, he said it could backfire into a trade war or a collapse of the security arrangement. In negotiations with Japan, he implied, our goal should not be to diminish Japan's economic power but to improve our own.

After an impassioned defense of our worthiness to lead, Nixon concluded the speech with a question: "What is America's mission today?" He related William Pitt's response after being toasted as the savior of Europe after Nelson's victory at Trafalgar: " 'I return you many thanks for the honor that you have done me. But Europe will not be saved by any single man. England has saved herself by her exertions and will, I trust, save Europe by her example.' " Nixon continued, "Today the world will not be saved by any single nation. But America can save herself by her exertions and will, we trust, save the cause of peace and freedom in the world."

Ultimately, Nixon was satisfied with the trip, since it apparently impressed upon his successor the importance of a realistic and responsible policy toward the region. As the June 3 vote approached on extending MFN to China, however, Nixon grew concerned that Clinton would revoke it under pressure from those wanting to punish China for human rights violations. Despite the former president's willingness to run interference for Clinton on the issue, the president did not seek out his advice.

"That's because he knows exactly where I stand," Nixon said on May 12. "If he hasn't made up his mind, or even if he has, he's not going to come to me to hear otherwise. This has me worried. If he decided to go ahead with MFN, he would have called me, pleased as punch that we agree. He hasn't. And he hasn't called me to line up votes for him. This means that he's either going the other way or hasn't decided.

"The Chinese take it for granted that it's a done deal that they're going to get MFN. I hope they listened to me on that score. This guy [Clinton] is playing a different ball game. He's under a lot of pressure to revoke it, and he won't stand up to Pelosi and [Senator George] Mitchell." He scowled. "Frankly, and just between us, I almost wish he'd screw it up, and all those business leaders who were for him would see what a mistake it was to elect him. But no, I really don't want to see it go that far. Our relationship with the Chinese is just too important."

Eight days later, he continued to fret. "If he lets Pelosi control foreign policy, he'll have a hell of a mess. If the administration is leaning toward slapping conditions on MFN, they are playing with dynamite. The Chinese will say, 'To hell with you,' and they should."

He continued, "I remember when I was running for Congress, I got excellent advice from an older member, who told me never to ask an older politician for advice unless I was prepared to take it. That's why he hasn't asked me. Adding conditions will be a terrible mistake, and I will make it known what I think if he does it. China is a giant, and the United States can't be screwing around with it. The nuclear-weapons sales are an important issue, but trade must be separated—make it a *political* issue. If he doesn't step up to this, I swear I will go public against him."

Fortunately for Clinton, however, Nixon did not have to "go public" against him. The president ultimately recognized that free trade and the benefits it brings to the American economy, to our relations with other countries, and to the forces of democracy and free-market economics were too important to sacrifice on the altar of partisan politics. Nixon's argument seemed to hold sway: economic choice would ultimately lead to a demand for political choice if the door to trade with the United States remained open.

Clinton refused to attach conditions to China's MFN status and announced that he would "delink" its human rights record from the trade issues. Just as Nixon had suggested to me, Clinton made the human rights issue a political issue, separating it from trade and allowing both to be dealt with exclusively.

Nixon thought it was an inspired—and courageous—decision. Previous attempts to deny MFN had not only made China more recalcitrant but had also threatened to hurt the fifty-billion-dollar trade flowing between the United States and China. By reinforcing trade ties, Clinton argued, the United States would be in a better position to influence China on human rights. Clinton had decided that Nixon was right.

In early July, the first family traveled to Tokyo for the annual gathering of the heads of state of the Group of Seven. Nixon dismissed it as "a nothing thing" and derided the resulting communiqué promising greater economic cooperation as "fluff."

When I met with him on the morning of July 9 at the residence, he tapped his copy of *The New York Times* with a pen as I sat down.

"Well, I see that another G-7 meeting has bombed," he said. "They're good for nothing, except to get all of the leaders together for a nice picture. You know, two things struck me watching that group waltz around. One, with the exception maybe of Kohl, Yeltsin is the only one who towers on the world stage."

"In spite of, not because of, the fact that he leads a troubled nation," I said.

"Yes," he replied. "And two, the G-7 are rich but stagnant. None of these countries have economies that are really booming, and none come anywhere near the growth of China and the Asian tigers, like Singapore and Thailand. The most economically booming country is China, and it wasn't even represented at the summit."

"So Russia and China—two developing countries—are the ones to watch," I said.

"If they play their cards right," he said, "they will be the future."

"Do you think an alliance could develop between them?" I asked.

"It's possible. They could even include Japan in that," he said.

When I mentioned that all three—Russia, China, and Japan—had totalitarian traditions, he replied, "It's something that we really have to watch, or we are going to face a very dangerous situation someday."

After watching the evening news later that night, he called me to fume about the coverage Clinton got at the summit. "No wonder no one watches the damn networks anymore," he said. "God, the news is bad. It's all entertainment, not really news. And the news they do give you is so slanted to the left that it's just outright biased. Anyway, [NBC's Tom] Brokaw really built up Clinton and Hillary in Tokyo, saying Hillary was a real heroine to the young women. Now, what the hell. When we were there in 1953, women were nothing, and Mrs. Nixon went out among them and talked to them, and the damn media never gave her any credit. Why?"

"You were in the wrong party," I said.

"That's it," he replied. "How did CBS play it?"

"They credited Clinton's visit as a success," I said, "probably because he talked about domestic policy, not foreign policy."

"When the president's abroad, you want him to do well, and he'll get a little lift out of this. It won't last, though. The summit didn't amount to a goddamned thing. The only thing that Clinton did right was give Yeltsin special attention. That was great. But I just can't see how you can hold an economic summit in Asia and exclude China. Just as managed trade with Japan would be a disaster because they'd kill us, continuing to ignore China will also be a disaster.

"And look, the Indians and the Chinese are starting to turn toward each other as a result of the end of the cold war. The Soviet Union traditionally supported India, and we were with the Chinese and supported Pakistan. Now it's all coming apart. It's a mixed-up bag!"

I asked him if he thought that the Chinese leadership feared that the Chinese people would get ideas from India's brand of democracy, and he shrugged. "I don't know," he said. "They probably do worry about that."

"How would the Chinese manage a billion votes?" I asked.

"It's a hell of a problem," he replied. "It would have to be one man, one vote. China is a state. India should never have been a state; the British made it one. They have a hard time managing all those votes. With that many people, it's very, very hard."

In late September, another development caught Nixon's attention. The International Olympic Committee decided to award the hosting duties of the 2000 games to Australia, turning a deaf ear to China's massive campaign to have them in Beijing. Nixon was distressed by the news.

"This will have a very negative impact in China," he said on September 23. "They have politicized this beyond belief, and it's wrong every time they do that. The Chinese are so proud. You saw the signs promoting the Olympics everywhere when we were there. They shouldn't play politics with it. It's a terrible double standard and an insult to them."

Nixon shook his head. "A country of one billion people, a culture here way before any of us, and we're scolding them. Oh, boy. It burns my tail. How stupid can we be? Not many can handle the diplomacy with the Chinese. I could, Kissinger could, but everybody else? Well, it's not easy. You can understand the Chinese and not understand them at the same time. But one thing we've learned from watching their economic growth is that it comes from the people. The government—in China or anywhere else, for that matter—really has very little to do with the actual success of an economy. It's the people."

Prosperity could not be ordered from above. It had to come from the risks taken by those below. The people made the sacrifices, risked losses, and reaped the profits. One by one, the Chinese people were building a free-market economy. And one by one, they would make China a huge state of middle-class entrepreneurs. The only thing left of Marxism in China was a relentless withering away of the state, only not as Marx had anticipated. It was a revolution of a different sort, of laissez-faire capitalism, which would eventually lead to democratization. The masses were gaining control of daily economic life in the steady, quiet victory of the individual. No longer did "the people" mean pawns in the Communist experiment; "the people" now meant those leading the capitalist march to prosperity.

"There really isn't a third world anymore," Nixon said on January 15, 1994. "Think about it: there are only two. Wealth divides Eastern and Western Europe, the northern and southern nations, and of course China. If China can get its economic growth to spread inland and affect the lives of average Chinese, China will have an achievement of immense proportions."

As Nixon sailed across West Lake in Hangzhou and stood upon the stage in the Great Hall of the People, he was aware that he did indeed have "something to do with" China's modern development. He landed in a closed society in 1972 and left an open one; he returned in 1989 to warn the Chinese about the consequences of human rights abuses and left a better friend of China; and he made a final trip in 1993 to evaluate the state of economic reform and left amazed by its progress.

Nixon's visits to China were a special event for Nixon's successors, for the Chinese, and for Nixon himself. American presidents had a reliable and experienced emissary in Nixon and benefited from his advice; the Chinese saw him as an old friend with whom they could speak and be understood; and Nixon had the chance to protect and advance his own historical achievement. Opening relations with China would be, as he recognized, one of the two things for which he would be best known. He could not control how Watergate would be perceived historically, but he could control how he would be remembered with regard to China.

He often said that without the United States, the Pacific triangle—China, Japan, and Russia—would be like a three-legged stool: unstable and potentially dangerous. The United States had to be the stabilizing fourth leg—a regional balancer, honest broker, and security guarantor. Nixon took it upon himself to be the caretaker of American relations with the Pacific powers because they needed the attention and the cultivation only he could give. When Nixon said that the United States needed to play the leading role in Asia and had far better qualifications than any other nation to do so, he was also saying that *he* needed to play the leading role and had the best qualifications to do so.

Nixon took his unparalleled experience with Asia into the 1990s, continuing his proprietary relationship with the Chinese and smoothing relations with the Japanese and the Koreans. As Nixon observed during his final trip to Asia, there was a universal desire to achieve the better life that the developed world promised. War and conquest no longer led to economic prosperity, and grand experiments of social engineering led to poverty and misery. Even the Chinese Communists recognized that despite its faults, the free market was an engine for growth and an escape valve for political pressure. They saw that successful economies were expressions of a people's will, spirit, intelligence, and resourcefulness, not the results of a vast collective.

Nixon, the old cold warrior and unabashed conservative free-marketeer, saw much of Asia transformed. That he lived to see his opening to China manifest itself in great economic growth gratified him; China was "the biggest of them all," and his stewardship of Sino-American relations brought rewards for both countries and, indeed, for him.

The new revolution was about wealth, not promises of egalitarian justice. In 1972, Nixon opened the door to China and let in the idea that a better way existed beyond the vows of communism. It did not involve any grand theories or dramatic proclamations about changing the world but involved the gradual escape from deprivation and isolation to prosperity and global community. The Chinese leaders, like most other Asian leaders, took the path Nixon had laid out and were now reaping the rewards. Nixon had had "something to do with it," and in his own way he changed the world.

# CHAPTER 3

# THE PERSIAN GULF
# WAR

On the morning of August 2, 1990, the former president walked into my office, leaned over my desk, and announced, "It looks like we have another war on our hands."

Hours earlier, Iraq had sent tanks across its border with Kuwait, seized oil reserves, sent the Kuwaiti leadership into exile, and effectively took control of its smaller neighbor. Diplomats scrambled for condemnations, the oil markets trembled, and commentators issued instant analyses and recommendations. It was an old-fashioned invasion, and Nixon savored its unexpected political, military, and diplomatic challenges.

The invasion proved once again that the Middle East—a seemingly remote region usually described in terms of religion, oil, or terrorism and the source for the constant stream of reports on the continuing "peace process"—can instantly capture our attention and demand our resources. The last fifty years in the Middle East have been punctuated by crises, most of which required the resolution capabilities of the United States. Since the partition of Palestine after World War II, the Arabs and the Israelis have fought five full-scale wars, one every decade—1948, 1956, 1967, 1973, and 1982—and have been involved in countless skirmishes and minor military clashes. Although the cold war did not inhibit that conflict, it did deter other regional threats; without superpower-imposed discipline, potential aggressors might be more tempted to act. As Nixon remarked on the morning of August 2, "I should have seen this coming."

He believed that despite being the culturally rich cradle of civilization, the Middle East was a cauldron of simmering ancient religious and political hatreds, important to the United States for its oil, its regional instability, and our relationship with Israel. "Conflict has engulfed the Middle East for two thousand years," he said the day of the invasion. "We can do some things at the margin, but nothing the United States can do will change that. It's up to the direct parties involved, not us." Because of the region's enormous strategic significance, however, the United States has a continuing obligation to protect its own interests by promoting greater stability.

During the cold war, the dynamics of the Middle East were defined by the strategic dance of the Soviet-American competition. Nixon believed that the Soviet Union sought relentlessly to establish a significant presence in the Persian Gulf. World War II was barely over when Stalin made his first foray into the region, and the Soviet wartime occupation of northern Iran led to the formation of the Soviet republic of Azerbaijan, a Kurdish people's republic under Moscow's control. When the Soviet Union pushed toward Greece and Turkey to try to gain better access to the Persian Gulf, Congressman Nixon voted for the aid program that allowed President Truman to repel the threat. During those decisive postwar years, oil became crucial to the stability and survival of a fragile, recovering Western Europe and to the Soviet grand strategy of destabilizing the area and gaining widespread regional influence.

Israel, however, posed a different challenge. Nixon believed that the United States would always have a critical interest in its survival and security. Although not formal allies tied by a security agreement, the United States and Israel were bound by something more profound: a moral commitment. "Israel will never be betrayed by the United States," Nixon told me in 1990, "and it shouldn't be." The unspeakable horrors of the Holocaust commit the United States and all other justice-seeking nations to the moral and physical support of Israel. With virtually no natural resources, it has built an industrial economy that competes successfully in the global market. Its military is among the best in the world. And despite over forty years of war as the target of destruction by its neighbors, Israel is the only working democracy in the Middle East. Because of our unwavering commitment to Israel, its democratic system has survived, many Arab governments recognize its existence, and the peace process continues despite occasional setbacks.

Nixon argued, however, that our foreign-aid budget could not continue to be distorted by allowing Israel to claim one quarter of all available money. American aid to Israel and Egypt, the two top recipients, consistently makes up over half of our entire aid budget. Nixon believed that the sum should be reduced drastically so we could support the other nations in which we had a strategic interest, particularly Russia. By subsidizing the militarization of the Middle East, we were limited in the help we could offer to the struggling democracies of the former Soviet Union or Asia, leaving our vital interests there vulnerable. To rectify the foreign-aid imbalance, the United States needed to move the peace process forward so that Israel's security could be maintained without the high cost to the United States.

Nixon believed in negotiating from a position of strength; the United States could press Israel in the peace process, and Israel could make a deal while it was still stronger than its neighbors. Even with our friendship, Israel could not survive forever surrounded by enemies bent on its destruction. The only way for the United States to protect Israel before it was threatened was to lead peacemaking efforts, even if our influence were only, as Nixon said, marginal.

For Nixon, the major threat to our vital interests and to peace in the region stemmed from the radical régimes in Iraq, Iran, Syria, and Libya and from the terrorist groups they financed within and outside the region.

Saddam Hussein's lengthy rule in Iraq was marked by unmitigated brutality and rogue military power. He crushed domestic opposition, slaughtered Iraqi opponents around the world, and expanded his influence throughout the Middle East through terrorism and intimidation. Iraq, with 11 percent of the world's proven oil reserves, possessed extensive military resources despite a debilitating war waged with Iran through the 1980s and the efforts of the United Nations to contain its nuclear-weapons program.

The foundation for the Iraqi invasion of Kuwait was laid during Iraq's eight-year war with Iran. By the war's end, in 1988, Iraq owed more than fifty billion dollars to other Arab states and Western banks. Kuwait had lent Hussein fifteen billion dollars, and most of the borrowed money was spent on augmenting Iraq's military machine. Hussein had demanded that Kuwait write off its massive war loan to Iraq and help increase the world price of oil by not pumping in excess of the Organization of Petroleum Exporting Countries (OPEC) quotas. This excess, coupled with a general international oil glut, had lowered world prices and had, according to Hussein, caused Iraq to lose fourteen billion dollars in oil revenues. He went searching inside the Kuwaiti border for oil, claiming that the reserves belonged to Iraq.

On July 26, 1990, OPEC ministers met in Geneva and agreed to lower production in order to raise prices. Five days later, delegates from Iraq and Kuwait met in Jidda, Saudi Arabia, to settle the border dispute while Iraq massed one hundred thousand troops on its border with Kuwait. The military intimidation followed a promise by Hussein in July to Egyptian president Hosni Mubarak that Iraq would not use force against Kuwait as it had ten years earlier with Iran. On August 1, Iraq's delegation walked out of the negotiations in Jidda. Iran, its longtime enemy, watched from across its own border with Iraq.

The invasion proved that constructive American relations with the stabilizing influences in the region, such as Turkey, did not take the place of an effective military deterrent presence. There were no substitutes for American power, a lesson Nixon had learned with the collapse of Vietnamization and the fall of Saigon in 1975. The United States was the only Western power with the military resources to project force and deter advances by radical régimes. As Nixon wrote in his 1980 book *The Real War,* "The leaders of Saudi Arabia, Oman, Kuwait, and other key states must be unequivocally reassured that should they be threatened by revolutionary forces, either internally or externally, the United States will stand strongly with them so that they will not suffer the same fate as the Shah of Iran."

Nixon strongly advocated enhanced rapid-deployment sealift and airlift capabilities for putting American troops into the Persian Gulf and the formation of a limited defensive strike force in Saudi Arabia to deter potential threats. A drastic cut in the defense budget would have seriously hindered our ability to protect our interests in the Persian Gulf and elsewhere. A hollow military could not secure continual access to the oil supply, and a weak United States could not contribute to a more stable Middle East.

Nixon argued adamantly for being prepared and for projecting the appearance of being prepared. We had to have the will to use force when necessary, and we had to be ready to demonstrate that will. We would court risks by defending our interests in the Persian Gulf, but we would invite greater risks if we failed to do so. We had to have the material resources and the resolve to use them, and we had to be able to respond quickly with military power, diplomatic artistry, and a bold strategic formula. This was the essence of Nixon's philosophy on American power as he watched Iraq invade Kuwait in 1990.

His nonchalant reaction the morning of the invasion revealed the seasoned cynicism of a leader who had handled numerous crises in the war-ravaged Middle East. "Never tell your enemy what you will do, and never tell him what you won't do," he said on August 8, 1990. When I walked into his office that morning, he was pacing, hands clasped behind his back. "I have been through this kind of thing so many times. It is crucial that Bush not waver in public. He should be tough as nails in whatever statements he makes," he said, pointing at me. "In a crisis, a good leader should always say, 'No comment. We haven't ruled out any possibility.' Keep them guessing. That's the only way to do it. Uncertainty—*that* is the key to getting the advantage, particularly early on in a crisis."

Nixon believed in the rationality of irrationality: by behaving in unpredictable ways, a leader might persuade potential adversaries that the costs of challenging him will be unimaginably high. Erratic statesmanship can send a signal to would-be aggressors that they will tempt disaster by provoking an uncertain response. Nixon knew that this was an invaluable tactic and used it in negotiation and crisis; he was skeptical, however, that President Bush could or would use it, particularly in dealing with the Middle East.

During the first few weeks after the Iraqi invasion of Kuwait, Nixon often posed a deceptively simple question to me: "War or peace?" I usually responded with an academically sterile answer: the end of the cold war initiated a new era in which war was viewed as increasingly immoral, untenable, and prohibitively costly; diplomacy would prevail, and war would be averted. As Nixon listened to this response, he often smiled and raised an eyebrow, aware that war was possible and, in fact, likely.

Had Hussein pursued his military advantage and invaded Saudi Arabia immediately after Kuwait, there would have been no military power in the area that could have stopped him. The American military response would have been limited to air and missile attacks by the *Independence* aircraft-carrier task force in the Persian Gulf and B-52 bombers stationed on Diego Garcia Island, almost three thousand miles away, in the Indian Ocean.

Fortunately for the United States, however, Hussein did not advance against Saudi Arabia. The immediate calm following the invasion allowed Bush to initiate Operation Desert Shield for the defense of Saudi Arabia and its oil-producing neighbors. Working with Secretary of Defense Richard Cheney and the chairman of the Joint Chiefs of Staff, General Colin Powell, Bush ordered fifty thousand air, sea, and ground forces to bases in Saudi Arabia and sent three aircraft-carrier groups into the region with "four simple principles": to cause the "complete withdrawal of all Iraqi forces from Kuwait"; to restore "Kuwait's legitimate government"; to preserve the "stability of the Persian Gulf"; and "to protect the lives of American citizens abroad." Since U.S. extended deterrence in the Persian Gulf had already failed, Bush moved this military power into the region to serve as an immediate deterrent to further Iraqi aggression.

Critics voiced opposition to the operation almost immediately. Isolationists and others who opposed the use of force argued that since Western Europe and Japan were now more economic competitors than geopolitical allies, the United States should refrain from action and depend, like the rest of the world, on sanctions by the United Nations. Their view was that the United States could better bear the brunt of OPEC price extortion than either Western Europe or Japan, and we should allow them to manage the crisis without American intervention.

According to Nixon, however, the isolationists failed to see that UN-directed action was more symbolic than substantive. The only way to roll back Hussein was to stop him with the only thing he understood: military force, led by the United States. Even though we would suffer less than our allies from OPEC's extortion, the adverse consequences for all nations would jeopardize a stable world order. Nixon argued that our allies should contribute significantly to the defense of common interests, but that in itself did not reduce the American commitment.

On September 5, Bush telephoned Nixon about the newly tense situation, and Nixon promised him a written memorandum of advice. Nixon wrote through the night, produced three drafts, and the next morning asked me to read the final draft, which directed Bush to use the military without hesitation, diplomatic avenues with subtlety, and the United Nations without illusions.

It was a thoroughly realist document. He began by telling Bush that it was important to recognize the motivations of the major players. Although it was useful for "PR purposes" to agree with those who proclaimed the triumph of the UN's "high ideals" in opposing the use of force to resolve conflicts, Bush had to recognize that the leaders involved were motivated by their national and material interests and not by those ideals.

He identified the players and their motivations one by one. "Gorbachev's heart was with Iraq. His head was with us," he wrote. The Soviet economy was in desperate condition, and given the choice between his traditional ally, Iraq, and the West, he chose the West.

The Arab motivations were even clearer: "The 'Arab world' is a misnomer. Most of the Arabs hate each other, even more than they hate the Israelis," he continued. The Syrians loathed the Iraqis, and the Saudis feared them. The Egyptians felt that their leading position in the Arab world was threatened by Saddam Hussein, and none of the oil-producing nations wanted him to have the power to dictate OPEC policies.

Nixon then couched our interests in purely realist terms. He cautioned that we should not be too "sanctimonious" about why we began to move troops into the region. Again, for "PR purposes" we should emphasize our opposition to the use of force to change boundaries, but, he continued, if India or China had tried to "gobble up" Nepal, no one would have suggested seriously that we commit military forces to contain the aggressor.

Even this early in the crisis, Nixon argued for "removing [Hussein] from power and, at the very least, eliminating his war-making capabilities" and cautioned against "engaging in any high-flown rhetoric about trying to bring 'democracy' to Kuwait." Bush, he advised, should avoid getting into the politically untenable position of encouraging our Arab partners to submit their fate to the masses in democratic elections.

Further, Nixon urged Bush strongly against enlisting the Soviet Union as a diplomatic mediator. Despite Gorbachev's "new thinking," Nixon did not believe that the United States should change its forty-year-old policy of keeping the Soviet Union out of the Middle East. With the Soviets out of the way, Bush could focus on maintaining the support of our allies, although that objective should also be conducted pragmatically: if Bush had to decide to use force, he should do so without regard to whether our "allies" would support his decision. Once he made the decision to use force, all that would matter would be "whether it works." The allies will support it if it does, and "even our best friends will jump ship if it doesn't." Above all, Nixon argued, the United States must lead any efforts to protect the oil interests in the Persian Gulf and to turn back the act of aggression committed by Iraq, lest other potential aggressors be tempted.

Nixon closed the memorandum with a morsel of sharp partisan advice. He told Bush that he had heard someone suggest that he should launch a military attack in October in order to ensure Republican victories in the off-year elections. "No advice could be more stupid," he wrote. Regardless of what Bush did between then and November, his popularity was so incredibly high that good candidates would win but poor ones would lose. "A military operation," he concluded, "would have only marginal effect."

I flew to Washington on September 6 to hand-deliver Nixon's pragmatic and hawkish advice to Bush in the White House. Since the president was traveling, I gave the memorandum to his personal assistant, who guided me through the darkened, deserted, and deafeningly quiet hallways of the White House. As we entered the Oval Office, she excused herself to take a telephone call, and I stood alone in front of the president's desk in a silence broken only by the exaggerated strokes of a grandfather clock. His aide rejoined me and directed me into Bush's private study off the Oval Office, where I saw a vast collection of his beloved country-music tapes, recordings of Churchill's speeches, Millie's dog bed covered with shed hair, and an empty "in" box. The serenity of the White House that day belied the international crisis enveloping it. Nixon, fearful that Bush would not meet the challenge with adequate force, tried to nudge the president into acting as he would have acted.

The crisis in the Persian Gulf put into bold relief Nixon's deep frustration with being out of power, particularly during times of acute crisis. "Sometimes I see such screwups, and I can't believe it, but I also can't do much about it," he said to me on October 13. "I did what I could when it was my time in there, but now all I can do is offer advice. If they take it, fine; if they don't, what can I do?" Normally, Nixon would not present such advice unless asked, but the Iraqi invasion was a serious enough crisis that he had planned to offer Bush unsolicited advice if Bush did not come to him first.

Since the president favored compromise over confrontation and diplomatic threats over threats of force, Nixon advocated an aggressive approach toward the Iraqis, hoping to push a temperamentally reluctant Bush to pursue the right policies. Nixon believed that Bush had condemned the invasion as harshly as he did only because British prime minister Margaret Thatcher was with him in Aspen, Colorado, on August 3 and had "put the spine into him." Bush needed to be provoked to act. Nixon made the advice more palatable by peppering it with flattering references to Bush's leadership, but his suggestions were always undeniably clear. Being out of office meant that Nixon could not hold the reins of power, but behind the scenes he could still influence those who did.

On September 7, Brent Scowcroft called Nixon to thank him for his "very thorough and insightful" memorandum to Bush and to inform him that the president would be delivering a message to the American people on the status of the crisis early in the next week. Bush's decision to move significantly more military matériel and personnel into the Persian Gulf required a direct public explanation, and the president spoke from the Oval Office on September 11. The next morning Nixon sent him a three-word note: "A home run!"

He called me into his office and showed the note to me before he folded it into its envelope. "It's short but sweet. The memorandum was for advice purposes. This note suits another purpose: to buck the guy up. He needs some encouragement. He's surrounded by critics and people who don't want to step up to this. He needs to be reassured that he's doing the right thing."

Nixon required reassurance as well, and as I sat with him after Scowcroft's call, he reread his memorandum to Bush several times to be sure that it did not contain anything that could be misinterpreted. Satisfied that it conveyed an appropriate message, he followed it with a steady stream of communications to Scowcroft, knowing that the general was a reliable conduit to Bush.

Nixon commended Bush and James Baker for using diplomatic channels wisely and for assembling an imposing military force. They lined up widespread international support for the trade embargo against Iraq and for Desert Shield. More than a dozen nations agreed to send military and financial assistance, including Great Britain, France, Canada, Japan, Australia, Egypt, Saudi Arabia, and Syria. Bush saw the diplomatic and military coalition as the product of the new world order; Nixon saw it as a bonus for predetermined U.S. action. Despite being a stunning diplomatic achievement, the coalition would give supplemental support for a course of action that could only be led by the United States.

Although Bush continued to deploy significant military facilities in the region, Nixon sensed that he was too sensitive to the Soviet reaction and relying too much upon the diplomatic component. This could easily be perceived by the Iraqis as a lack of American resolve, which in turn could lead them to dig in. Nixon feared that Bush was conveying "indecisive leadership" by appearing too eager to accept a quick diplomatic solution, thus imperiling not only the U.S. military threat but the president's own political standing. Perception was the key, and the adversary had to be persuaded that the United States was intent on using military force should Iraq not reverse its aggressive action.

On September 14, Nixon sent an urgent note to Scowcroft that reinforced this point. He wrote that he increasingly doubted the possibility of a diplomatic settlement and that as soon as the necessary military forces were arrayed, Bush's only choice would be to resort to military action after delivering an ultimatum to Hussein. Most important, according to Nixon, such action would be a warning shot across the bow to potential aggressors: "By USING force now in this crisis would mean that our THREAT of the use of force in a similar crisis" elsewhere would be so credible that potential aggressors would be more inclined to pursue their goals through diplomatic means than through military means.

On election day, November 6, 1990, Nixon expressed his discontent with Bush's seeming uncertainty. When I asked him if he thought Bush were still unsure about using the military forces deployed in the region, he smiled and said, "Well, he's not consulting me." Although Bush *had* tried, unsuccessfully, to call him the previous weekend, Nixon's desperation that events were being guided without him overflowed in a burst of frustration. "For the military to be considered credible, we have got to bomb the hell out of them," he said, pounding his fist on his desk. "We can't think in terms of casualties or hostages. And I'll tell you another thing: if Bush falters even an inch on this, Hussein will dig in, and every goddamned dictator in the world will have a field day. We simply have to do what it takes, criticism be damned. If we don't, who will? No one. What is the point of talking about being number one if we don't use that power? This is so clear cut, such an issue of right and wrong, that I can't believe that everyone is just pissing around. What are we going to do, debate Hussein until he leaves Kuwait?"

The United Nations, meanwhile, decided to take action, passing Resolution 678 on November 29, which authorized the member states to use "all necessary means" to uphold and implement the earlier Security Council Resolutions 660, which condemned the aggression the day it occurred, and 661, which imposed a trade embargo and financial sanctions on Iraq and promised "to restore international peace and security in this area" unless Iraq complied fully with the resolutions on or before January 15, 1991.

Nixon reacted to the UN move by waving his hand dismissively in the air. "The UN vote is helpful but really not necessary. I've always believed that the United States should use the UN when necessary but not be used by it. The authorization grants some international legitimacy to what we're doing, but we'd do it anyway. At least, I *hope* we'd do it anyway. With Bush, you never know."

Nixon disregarded collective security as a hopelessly idealistic and pathetically impotent idea with a terrible historical track record. Both the United Nations and its predecessor, the League of Nations, failed to prevent enormously destructive wars and tragic losses of blood and treasure. As a realist, Nixon believed that conflict was an immutable fact of international life and that any permanent collective effort to restrain aggression and punish transgressors was doomed to failure.

"All of this collective-security nonsense is a pile of crap," he said on November 30. "Anyone who believes that a body like the UN can act decisively on anything is not only misguided but hasn't been paying attention for the last forty-five years. The people who are out there screaming 'Let the UN handle it' don't know anything about the real world. They think if we can all just get to know each other, there would be no more war. 'Let's understand each other,' they say. My God! How naïve can you be! Conflict comes up *not* because adversaries do *not* understand each other but because they do!"

He shook his head. "The UN is good for one thing: it's a valuable place to talk, to gas around about whatever issue is on the burner. But there is no way in hell that it can ever substitute for real power and American leadership. No way. And Churchill was right when he said that no state would relinquish its power to the United Nations or any other collective body. Period. That's the reality. And that's why we've got to do these things on our own."

For Nixon, only the United States had the comprehensive combination of political, economic, and military power to take the lead in defending and extending freedom and in deterring and rolling back aggression. Germany and Japan lacked the military resources despite their formidable economic power. Russia and China lacked the established economic power despite their potential military might. Only the United States had a full portfolio of power resources and the credibility to act as an honest broker internationally. Nixon reminded Bush of this and continually emphasized the need for strong unilateral action whenever the president was being pressured to adopt a new "assertive multilateralism" based on UN leadership.

Some argued that the Security Council vote to allow the use of force against Iraq, with an abstention from China, seemed to indicate that collective action was indeed possible in what Bush termed the new world order. Alliances could form and be sustained until an international action was successfully completed, bringing together disparate interests and contentious adversaries in the name of a common mission.

"Nonsense," Nixon said on November 11, 1990, dismissing this notion out of hand. "National interests will never be secondary to collective ones—not now, not ever." He sat opposite me in his office, sipping a diet cola. "We think this episode is so special because it's happening at the end of the cold war. Do you know what the significance of that is? Nothing besides timing. The alliance against Iraq is just a coming together of similar interests at one point in time. That's it! The United States, Great Britain, France, and Germany have oil interests to protect and want to roll back aggression; the Soviet Union has a strong interest in acting with the West to get the financial support it needs to survive; Israel, of course, needs the American security guarantee; and Syria sees a rare opportunity to align with the United States. So there it is: self-interest, not collective interest."

To allow the invasion to go unchecked would have been disastrous for all involved. Only China, which abstained from the Security Council vote to protect its Iraqi arms market, and Jordan, which claimed neutrality but leaned toward Iraq, resisted the anti-aggression bandwagon. All, however, looked to the United States to see if it would act to protect its interests. When it became clear that it would, the alliance came together, and its members followed the leader. The former president's mission was to ensure that the current president maintained that leadership.

Nixon always believed that military missions had to be explained and detailed repeatedly if an administration were to gain the widespread domestic support it needs to sustain them successfully. Nixon learned this lesson the hard way, from the American engagement in Vietnam: any U.S. intervention requires domestic support at the most and minimal dissension at the least. If the country is torn internally, the external mission will suffer. A conflict could galvanize domestic support for its leadership, but only if the engagement is short, successful, and waged with the preponderant amount of force needed to win.

"The invasion of Grenada and the bombing of Libya were really nothing things, compared to real wars like Vietnam. But they helped Reagan tremendously and lifted the spirit of the country," Nixon told me on November 13, 1990. "If you go in and nail the bastards without losing your own men, you can go a long way politically. The only problem is that with military action, you never quite know how it's going to go. But once you make the commitment to do it, you've got to go in there and bomb the hell out of them with everything you've got. There can be no hemming and hawing or hand-wringing," he said, wringing his hands in mock indecision. "Make the goddamned decision, and do it. We're not talking about Vietnam here. But we're also not talking about Grenada either. It will be longer than that, but for God's sakes we've got the technology. Why the hell do we spend all of that money on high-tech weapons if we don't use them when we need them? Keep it as short as possible; the short operations always work best. We saw that in the Reagan years." More extensive missions with longer lead times, such as the Persian Gulf operation, required a proper explanation for the military action, which despite Bush's Oval Office speeches and Baker's dramatic diplomacy Nixon felt had not yet been given.

"You know as well as I do that the American people will not go for it unless you put it in idealistic terms," he said when we met on October 28. "You can't just go out there and say 'Hey, we're going to war.' You need to tell them what it's about, over and over again. They don't have to accept it, but they do have to understand it. And since Bush isn't doing a goddamned thing to explain it to the people, I've got to do it. There are some people out there who still might listen to me," he said, and he began to think about how he would help Bush make a persuasive case for the use of force.

Nixon knew that Americans would commit support to an overseas mission only if it were defined in positive and transcendent terms. Without an idealistic justification, it can be interpreted, criticized, and undermined as Machiavellian realpolitik, high politics exercised without morality. The American people would not tolerate such morally bankrupt activity; good and evil, right and wrong, had to be evident if the public were to support an intervention.

Bush may have had this in mind when he declared in early November that Saddam Hussein was comparable to Adolf Hitler, sending Nixon into a bout of frustration. "Did you hear about the Hitler analogy?" he asked as soon as I entered his office on November 12. "Well, that was a mistake. I know what he was trying to do, but boy did he screw it up. OK, it created an image, but what a hell of an overstatement! Saddam and Hitler? What are we talking about? Of course, Hitler is considered a hero in the Arab world because they are both enemies of the Jews. But you really can't compare the two. Hitler caused a world war; Saddam is just a bully on the block with a pile of weapons," he said, shaking his head. "Bush went overboard, and I mean overboard!" Bush had tried to invoke an image of absolute evil to create a momentum of support for the military buildup, but his extreme example became more of a parody than a rallying point.

As the deployment progressed, Bush and Baker continued a frenzied pace of diplomatic maneuvering. The Soviet Union was experiencing its final year of upheaval, and the president and secretary of state sought to protect their investment in Soviet president Mikhail Gorbachev by welcoming every Soviet-sponsored initiative in the Gulf. Just as Gorbachev felt he needed Bush to survive, Bush felt he needed Gorbachev in power to vindicate his own long-standing advocacy of the Soviet president.

Nixon knew that the Soviets were playing a dual role in the Gulf. They offered the United States and the anti-Iraq coalition diplomatic support and at the same time refused to recall their military advisers in Baghdad and continued to covertly funnel military supplies to the Iraqi army. Since the Iraqi army was the Soviet link to Iraq and its guarantor of stability at home, Gorbachev would not risk alienating it. Nixon also suspected that since the Soviets had increased their arms shipments to Iraq the previous year, they had implicitly encouraged the invasion of Kuwait to deflect attention from their own internal crises and to provide an opportunity to align themselves with the United States that could lead to much-needed financial rewards. By playing both sides, the Soviets hoped that the crisis in the Middle East might help to resolve the crisis they faced at home.

Nixon, meanwhile, became increasingly disturbed by the diplomatic dance that accompanied the military deployment. He feared that Bush and Baker would seize each new Soviet diplomatic initiative in order to avoid a costly war and help to rescue a drowning Gorbachev. For Nixon, personalizing international politics was one of the most disastrous mistakes a statesman could make. International relations was the realm of power, not personality. Leaders could like each other, but allowing personal sentiments to cloud calculations of national interest was dangerous and naïve. Statesmen change; interests do not. Nixon knew that Bush genuinely liked Gorbachev, but he worried that the president would allow that friendly relationship to supersede any independent American course of action. After almost every Soviet peace initiative, Nixon immediately warned Scowcroft not to allow Bush to be seduced by the personal diplomacy.

"Bush has got to get away from the personal side, particularly with Gorbachev," he said on November 14 when we met at his office. "He is so taken in by that, and it could not be a worse mistake. And it's not just Bush. Baker and the rest of them are guilty of this too. I must say that I am nauseated by the incessant gushing over Gorbachev by Bush and Baker in this goddamned crisis. This is just another example of their tendency to personalize everything. Backslap, tell a joke—they think that this is what foreign policy is all about. No!" he said sharply. "It's made of interests, and that's all."

By November, the number of American troops had increased to more than two hundred thousand, and then, in a move that surprised his opponents, Bush doubled the size of the force on November 8, giving it an offensive capability as the January 15 UN deadline for Iraq to voluntarily leave Kuwait came closer. Nixon, who consulted often with former secretaries of state Henry Kissinger and Alexander Haig, believed that the deadline was artificial and never should have been announced since it would allow Iraq to play numerous diplomatic games and permit others to exploit the time to suit their own agendas. When the UN authorization was approved, he said simply, "It's a profound mistake to let your enemy know when you will strike."

On November 30, Bush made a major diplomatic overture to Hussein and prepared to send Baker to Baghdad. In a fit of rage, Nixon spun toward me as I stood with him in his office. "That's such a blunder," he exploded. "Don't pander to the enemy. Diplomacy has its place, and this is not it. My God! What in hell is going on down there? Don't they know that this will backfire right in their faces?"

When I suggested that the administration was taking the action not because it wanted it to succeed but because it needed to show the American people that it had explored every diplomatic option before using force, Nixon shot back, "No, they want it to succeed all right. They don't want to have to use force. I used it when necessary, and Reagan wasn't afraid of it either. But Bush is another kind of animal. Conflict is not his thing. He would prefer that Baker go to Baghdad and come home with a neat solution."

By this point in the crisis, Nixon knew that force was required if the U.S. commitment to reversing the invasion were to be credible and that a diplomatic resolution would have been both counterproductive and dangerous. Diplomacy was useful to signal to the domestic constituency that the administration pursued peace even as it prepared for war as long as the will to use force without hesitation remained in place. Sending Baker to Iraq provided Hussein with a legitimate diplomatic escape route that, if taken, would neither resolve the immediate crisis nor deter other aggressors. As Nixon repeated to me on December 3, "To be credible, you have to bomb the bejesus out of them."

Nixon also believed that the military action should come sooner rather than later. "Let me tell you something about using the military: the longer you wait, the more difficulties you are going to face. Of course, domestic and international support will fall off, but it's the leaders' responsibility to bring those polls back up," he said, and I then informed him of a particularly effective interview given by Kissinger the day before. Nixon held up his right hand, then picked up the telephone receiver and asked to place a call to Kissinger. When I excused myself from the room, Nixon waved me back into my chair.

"Henry!" he bellowed. "Do you feel lonely? You are the only hawk out there! I didn't see the interview, but my foreign policy assistant did, and she said you were terrific. And by the way, don't do any more interviews; you've said your piece. Either they listen or they don't." Kissinger responded, and Nixon continued.

"The Baker trip is a terrible mistake. The Iraqis aren't stupid. Do we have to go over there with the UN resolutions and read them to them, for God's sake?" Kissinger responded again, and then, shooting me a quick look, Nixon said, "Here, Henry, I'll have her tell you herself what she thought of the interview," and he thrust the receiver at me. As I told Kissinger that he seemed to be the lone spokesman for the use of force, Nixon began waving wildly at me and whispering instructions about what to tell him. When this brief three-sided conversation was done, Nixon retrieved the receiver and bid farewell to Kissinger.

"I'm glad you told Henry what a great job he did," he said to me. "He needs to hear it because it was true and because he needs the encouragement to get out there and keep saying the right things. Imagine! He's the only one out there doing anything constructive on this. Everyone else is a coward." He shook his head. "Poor Henry. He's out there fighting like hell for this, and Baker goes over to Iraq to screw it up. Bush should listen to Kissinger. After all, he knows more about the Middle East in his sleep than most of these other clowns running around Bush will ever know."

Nixon's relationship with Kissinger had a long and complex history. Kissinger, the quintessential academic, earned a doctorate from Harvard in 1953 with a dissertation that examined the classical nineteenth-century European balance of power. Having been instructed in the academic theories of conflict and cooperation, he adopted realism as the most judicious way of looking at the world and took a hardheaded approach to dealing with both allies and adversaries.

By contrast, Nixon's graduate education was in the law. His understanding of international relations came directly from experience, not from the classroom. While in the Congress and later as vice president, Nixon traveled extensively abroad to learn how the real world worked. Kissinger's foreign policy education was formal and credentialed; Nixon's education was achieved in the field. But once Nixon was elected president and had selected the Harvard professor as his national security adviser, the politician and the academic became complementary partners in policy making. Ideas and decisions flowed between them, driven by both mutual respect and heated intellectual rivalry. Even when they held two of the most powerful offices in the world, they competed because the academic was also a bit of a politician and the politician was also a bit of an academic.

They were two towering egos clashing in an intense and public competition for the international spotlight. Kissinger had won the Nobel Prize for his role in completing the cease-fire agreement with the North Vietnamese, but Nixon had won two presidential elections. Kissinger proposed innovative ideas, but Nixon had the power to bury them. Kissinger could leak damaging information to the press, but Nixon could fire him. Kissinger had been secretary of state, but Nixon had been president. Both had propensities to high drama and low politics, for using the reins of power and for using each other.

By the end of his life, however, Nixon knew that there was more to gain from courting Kissinger than from alienating him. Nixon had always appreciated Kissinger's insights on international issues, most of which were identical to his own, and he used Kissinger as a sounding board when policies with which he disagreed were being made. They shared frustration with being out of power but reveled in the ability to affect policy with a well-placed word or a strategically timed column. Nixon discussed ideas with Kissinger, looking for his concurrence, and Kissinger asked Nixon to use his stature in ways that helped them both. More important, however, the former president and the former secretary of state spoke to hear their own views accepted by the other.

Nixon held a far more unfavorable view of Bush's secretary of state, James Baker, who he thought was a smart but elitist businessman with no understanding of the workings of global politics. The resentment, however, flowed both ways: Baker was offended by Nixon's ability to go over his head to Bush directly and supersede his authority to guide American foreign policy. Nixon believed that Baker was making self-serving and dangerous mistakes; Baker believed that Nixon was overstepping his bounds. Their mutual disdain produced little communication between them and private, if not public, criticism of each other.

On the forty-ninth anniversary of the bombing of Pearl Harbor, December 7, 1990, Nixon delivered a well-received speech at the Plaza Hotel in New York. Although it focused primarily on the developments in the collapsing Soviet Union, the speech argued for the quick and comprehensive use of force against Iraq. Nixon had the address transcribed the next morning and mailed it to everyone on his standard list of three hundred policy makers and commentators, hoping to convey his message to a broader audience and keep Kissinger company in the lonely field of those supporting the use of force. It achieved its objective when Jeane Kirkpatrick quoted it in her column in *The Washington Post* the following week, leading Nixon to believe that the speech had been an ideal policy tool.

Several days later, Nixon heard that Bush was sending Robert Gates, the deputy national security adviser and future director of central intelligence, to brief all of the former presidents on the same day on the activities in the Gulf. Offended that he was not receiving special treatment from the president, he turned down the visit from Gates because he did not want to hear the standard administration line when he felt that he had, at least in part, written that line.

"Would you even believe that Bush would send Gates to see me on the same day that he was sending him to talk to Ford and Carter and Reagan?" he asked me incredulously. "I mean, my God! I have given this administration so much in terms of public and private advice and giving them cover to do what the hell they wanted in the Middle East and supporting every move they have made. And here's Bush treating me like the others? No," he said, slamming his hand on his armrest. "I will not do this. Giving me the line when I know the line inside and out! Insulting! The others may need to hear the line, but I don't."

Nixon's disappointment with Bush's behavior now matched his doubt that the president would use force to resolve the crisis. By the end of December, he saw expediency in Bush's and Baker's diplomatic charade with the Soviets, the Iraqis, and the UN and believed that the administration was sacrificing long-term American interests for short-term gain.

"Baker wants a deal at all costs," he said on December 18, waving his hands in the air. "I'm just afraid that Bush is getting bad advice. Massive air strikes are needed to take out the logistical supply lines, communications, and the military-industrial complex; then let's see if Saddam wants to negotiate—not before. If we cut a deal without force that the Israelis find unsatisfactory, they'll bomb Iraq on their own. But it's not Israel's responsibility to remove the threat; it's ours."

Five days before Christmas, his fears were allayed. Scowcroft called to tell him that barring a complete Iraqi withdrawal, the president had decided to use the military option. Satisfied that all diplomatic avenues had been explored and that the Iraqis would continue to be intransigent, Bush could now justify going to war. He had finally come to the decision that Nixon had made several days after the invasion.

"The administration is not going to like this," he said on January 3 as he reviewed a draft of a piece he had written on the U.S. role in the crisis, which would appear in *The New York Times* on January 6, 1991. Entitled "Why," the essay was a firm rationale for our presence in the Persian Gulf and laid the political foundations for the possible use of force.

He began the column with a statement he thought Bush should have made long ago: "It is time for some straight talk about why 400,000 young Americans spent Christmas in the deserts of Saudi Arabia and why in less than two weeks the U.S. may be once again at war." He argued that although the war would not be about installing democracy in Kuwait or punishing Hussein's cruelty, it would be about two major issues—one material, one political.

The material reason was identified bluntly: "Had we not intervened, an international outlaw would today control more than forty percent of the world's oil. We cannot allow Mr. Hussein to blackmail us and our allies into accepting his aggressive goals by giving him a choke hold on our oil lifeline."

The second reason was even more profound: "We can be sure that if Saddam Hussein profits from aggression, other potential aggressors in the world will be tempted to wage war against their neighbors." If, however, the United States succeeded in removing Hussein from Kuwait "and in eliminating his capacity to wage war in the future," we would have the credibility to deter aggression elsewhere without sending forces.

Those who advocated nonmilitary means to settle the dispute, such as the continuance of sanctions and diplomacy, were wrong for several reasons. First, "while the Iraqi people suffer the effects of the sanctions, Hussein will direct his resources so that the Iraqi military will not." Second, sanctions would weaken us more than Iraq because of the political difficulty of maintaining the alliance abroad and support for the troop commitment at home. Third, while sanctions might work, "military force will work."

He concluded that "a bad peace is worse than war because it will inevitably lead to a bigger war," and with a flourish of Wilsonian idealism he argued that it was a "highly moral enterprise" and "a war about peace."

"Have you seen the column?" he asked when he called me the morning it appeared. "I think it makes the points pretty well. Bush has only done the bare minimum to educate people about this thing. You cannot send people's sons and daughters out to the middle of the desert and not tell them, day in and day out, why. This piece does that in a few good paragraphs. Bush may know what he's doing, but he's not reassuring anybody."

When I asked him how he thought Bush might react to it, he replied, "I don't know. I didn't think he'd like it because I was the one making the points. For that reason, of course, we *know* Baker didn't like it! But Bush may have appreciated it because I did some of the heavy lifting with this piece, which is exactly what he needed help with."

The article, aimed at Bush, Baker, Scowcroft, Gorbachev, Saddam Hussein, the Congress, and the American people on whose support the mission relied, was Nixon's only formal public statement on the crisis, and it apparently reached its audience. Scowcroft called the day after it appeared to commend, concur with, and thank Nixon for doing the political blocking for Bush just before the Senate vote on the use of force.

Two days after the article ran, Kissinger told Nixon that it was a "major contribution" to the debate on the American role in the Gulf, and Haig delivered testimony to the Senate Committee on Foreign Relations that reiterated Nixon's arguments. The column achieved what Nixon had hoped: it resonated among policy makers and opinion makers and generated the momentum needed to use force effectively.

Nixon, however, spent his seventy-eighth birthday, January 9, 1991, worrying that Baker's last-minute diplomatic meeting with Iraqi foreign minister Tariq Aziz in Geneva might produce a weak settlement. It was better, he believed, for the United States to remove the Iraqi threat before it grew to more dangerous proportions than to accept a bad deal that would just postpone the confrontation. When I informed him that afternoon that the Baker-Aziz talks had collapsed, he clapped his hands together in relief.

"Good," he said. "Baker may have wanted a deal, but I know that the White House didn't want one. How could they? Hell, if the Iraqis weren't negotiating in good faith, why should we?"

As the January 15 UN deadline approached, Nixon had another concern: that the United States and our allies would allow Hussein to exploit any hesitancy on our side to use force. In response to the possible scenario in which Hussein might issue a preemptive strike against American targets in Saudi Arabia or Israel, Nixon said, "He will never go for Israel. He's not that crazy. Israel has nuclear capabilities and will not hesitate for one second—*not one*—to use them and blow him off the map." In response to the potential scenario in which Hussein might withdraw partially from Kuwait on January 16, technically not complying with the UN resolution and saving face but making it difficult for the United States to attack, Nixon shrugged his shoulders and said, "It's possible."

During the Senate debate on January 10, 11, and 12 on authorizing the use of force in the Gulf, Nixon became exasperated. Those who opposed the military option under any circumstances argued for continuing sanctions, saying that nothing in this crisis, particularly not oil, justified sending American troops into harm's way. Their isolationist argument disquieted those in the administration who had already committed American troops and credibility. Baker, having failed at his brand of personal diplomacy with Aziz and hearing the Senate arguments disapproving of the administration's intention to use force, took an uncharacteristically blunt stand against Iraq to try to influence the Senate vote. Most of the major media outlets gave extensive coverage to a few small pockets of pacifist protesters to try to do the same. The night before the vote, Nixon called me to predict the results: "I thought I'd like to go on the record with you now and say it will be fifty-two to forty-seven for the use of force. As you know, before World War II, the draft was in by only one vote. It doesn't matter how close it is as long as the damn thing goes through."

Early the next morning, after the Senate had authorized the use of force by the margin Nixon had projected, he called me to revel in his "right on" prediction: "Well, my prophecy was correct! I knew those responsible members of the Senate would come through," he cracked. "Boy, what a tiresome goddamned thing." He believed that the president should be able to act without congressional approval, just as the United States could act without UN support: both were useful but neither was necessary.

He asked me to locate the text of the 1973 War Powers Act, passed into law over his veto, which stipulates that the president must consult with Congress before intervening with our forces in an armed or potentially armed conflict. He is then allowed to continue the intervention for sixty days without congressional approval and another thirty days if he certifies in writing that the safety of our military personnel requires it. If the Congress does not by that time authorize his actions by a declaration of war or other legislation, the act requires a withdrawal of our troops.

As I handed him a copy of it, he snatched it from me and waved it in the air. "This is one of the worst pieces of legislation I have ever seen. It hamstrings the president in a time of crisis and allows our enemies to take advantage of that. Fortunately, it hasn't really been effective. But I'll be damned if the president is going to bend to the whims of the Congress when it comes to international emergencies. Remember what de Gaulle said about parliaments? That they can paralyze policy but they cannot initiate it? Whammo! They can debate issues until they're blue in the face, but debating and acting are two different things. There is no way in hell that Congress is going to have the power to initiate policy when we've got missiles or tanks coming at us."

As the Senate debated the use of force, the Soviet Union, knowing that the United States was distracted by the crisis in the Gulf and the looming UN deadline, cracked down violently on the independence movement in Lithuania. Bush and Baker, consumed with the Persian Gulf and still concerned with protecting Gorbachev, hesitated to react, sending Nixon into a fit of frustration.

He received a phone call from Scowcroft at six-twenty on the evening of January 16, informing him that Bush had just given the order to begin the air offensive against Iraq. Twenty minutes later, the aerial bombardment of Baghdad and other Iraqi targets began, illuminating the sky with precision-guided missiles and electro-optical guided bombs. Bush addressed the nation on Desert Storm later that evening in a speech that Nixon thought overemphasized the importance of the United Nations. But the people had to hear from the president, and the address itself was a simple announcement that the offensive against Iraq had begun, an appeal for domestic support, and a salute to the international coalition that had sustained the American effort.

In the late afternoon of January 17, the first full day of the war, Nixon called me into his office to rail against the United Nations and the so-called new world order. He pounded his clenched fist for emphasis: "I want to hit the UN hard in this book [*Seize the Moment*]. No one should have the idea that after this war the UN will suddenly be this great body for world leadership. Every parliament stinks, and the UN is the most uncontrollable, unfair parliament of all.

"And another thing—this 'new world order' doesn't amount to a tinker's damn. I mean it. Every time we see the end of some kind of era in the world, we call it a new world order. Bullshit. The world is a dangerous, unpredictable place; force will always have to be used; and collective organizations, whether it's the UN or whatever, will never work when it comes down to protecting national interests. And it *always* comes down to national interests. The only collective body that ever worked was NATO, and that was because it was a military alliance and we were in charge."

Later that evening, I heard a radio news report that eight Iraqi Scud missiles had hit Israel, and I reported the development to Nixon, who was shocked that his earlier prediction had been wrong. "I honestly didn't think Saddam was crazy enough to go after Israel. Maybe he wants to drag Israel in, but he's got to realize that that's a dangerous game. He probably feels he has nothing to lose."

Although the war was directed against Baghdad, it had as much to do with the protection of Israel and Saudi Arabia as it did with the punishment of Iraq. By launching attacks against Israel, Iraq could turn American attention and resources away from the battle within its own borders and force the United States to react to the threat to Israel as well as to the threats to Kuwait and Saudi Arabia. If it could accomplish this by lobbing a few unsophisticated Scuds at Israel, then Iraq could direct the conflict. Hussein gambled that American support would dwindle and the international coalition would fall apart if he could just hold out long enough and bring Israel into the war.

Israel absorbed the random Scud attacks and deferred to the United States for the military response. Knowing that it was difficult for Prime Minister Yitzhak Shamir to take the attacks passively, Nixon commended his restraint: "It's all he can do to just sit there. He's got to be climbing the walls. But if Israel gets involved, we are going to have a hell of a mess. Shamir is willing to trust us, and that's great, particularly when the hard-liners in the Knesset have got to be giving him hell. But he's willing to hold back, and that's gutsy." An Israeli response would have played into Hussein's hands and further complicated the allies' regional strategy; by allowing the United States and our allies to respond, Israel denied Hussein the second front he desired.

Immediately after the aerial bombardment of Iraq began, Bush's approval ratings started to climb. By January 23 his approval rating was at 85 percent and rising. Nixon dismissed the numbers as "misleading and obviously inflationary" and sensed that they would give Bush a false sense of invincibility. "I know Bush," he said, sighing. "He and the others down there are riding high on this eighty-five percent and won't be open to suggestions." Nixon then held in reserve a memorandum of advice on current and postwar strategy that he planned to send to the president: "I'll wait until his numbers start to come down, when he's more humble." Five days later he sent it to Bush.

He began by saluting Bush's leadership, telling him that his astronomical approval ratings were "richly deserved" and that although Kennedy reached those heights after the Bay of Pigs situation—a foreign policy disaster—he reached them with a major foreign policy victory.

Nixon then instructed Bush to remain firm during the next "testing time," when some of our allies would urge him to order a pause in the military assault so peace negotiations could begin: "I am delighted that you have indicated that you will categorically reject such proposals."

Next, he delivered the historical analogy meant to persuade Bush to continue a hard line: "I was rereading last night a diary note I made after having breakfast with LBJ in the fall of 1969. He spoke bitterly about the advice he had received, which led him to order bombing halts, including the one immediately before the election which almost won it for Humphrey." After frightening Bush politically, he offered the lesson: "He said, '[Ambassador Averell] Harriman told me at least twelve times that if I called a halt the North Vietnamese and Vietcong would stop shelling South Vietnamese cities. But nothing happened. Every one of the bombing halts was a mistake.' "

Nixon then drew the inevitable parallel to Hussein and encouraged Bush to stand firm in his commitment to continue the war until all military and political objectives were achieved. He closed the note with another flattering reference to Bush's leadership and sent it with the hope that it would help Bush resist pressure for a premature cease-fire.

Baker, however, needed Nixon's lesson more than Bush did. In a frantic attempt at U.S.-Soviet solidarity, he and the new Soviet foreign minister, Aleksandr Bessmertnykh, delivered a joint communiqué on January 29 calling for acceptance of their peace plan and a cease-fire in Iraq. Nixon was outraged: "What the hell is Baker doing? Including the Soviets in this now is a major mistake. They armed those [Iraqi] bastards, keep military advisers in there even as we're prosecuting the war, and are looking for a way to save face with Hussein and get themselves into the Gulf. And we took the bait. They used to talk about an imperial presidency, but my God! This is an imperial State Department!" Shaking his head, he concluded, "Baker is way out of line."

The White House apparently thought so as well and issued a clarification, hoping to unmix Baker's mixed signal and reiterate its commitment to a full prosecution of the war. Nixon learned that Bush was annoyed with

Baker for undermining his authority by offering publicly a peace proposal sponsored by the Soviet Union. In a remarkable act of insubordination, Baker had disregarded existing policy and forced the president to issue a repudiation. Having had his own damaging experience with freelancing subordinates, Nixon felt that Baker himself should be sacrificed if Bush were to be served well.

"Bush should fire him over this," Nixon fumed the next day. "And I mean now and not a moment later. To put the president in that kind of a position is unacceptable. He's just drooling to be president, and he's already acting like he's got the goddamned job! Elections? Who needs them!" he said sarcastically, tossing his hands in the air. "Why, just overthrow the guy who's already in there by doing what the hell you want!"

Fortunately, neither the Baker-Bessmertnykh proposal nor the numerous subsequent peace initiatives flowing out of Moscow were adopted. Gorbachev, trying to salvage a peaceful image in the wake of the bloody crackdown in Lithuania, project loyalty to third world Arabs, and maintain the Soviet-Iraqi axis, directed his foreign minister to negotiate with the Iraqis and deliver a steady stream of cease-fire proposals. To Nixon's relief and perhaps in part because of his advice, Bush rejected the Soviet initiatives and reiterated his commitment to a thorough and successful completion of the war.

On February 15, the Iraqis, sponsored by the Soviets, proposed numerous conditions under which they would withdraw from Kuwait. British prime minister John Major denounced them as outrageous and "a bogus sham," and Nixon agreed, though he braced for a possible Bush collapse. The media coverage of the Iraqi proposal, however, suggested that peace was at hand.

"The way the media is covering this, you'd think the war was over!" Nixon said, exasperated. "They want to make any peace proposal a self-fulfilling prophecy."

For Nixon, the Soviet overture was a tactical diplomatic charade designed to delay the ground war, maintain Moscow's relationship with Iraq, continue its dialogue with the third world, and have Gorbachev emerge as a peacemaking hero.

"I hope that these Soviet motives are now apparent to Bush. He's got to see them for what they are, or at least Scowcroft does, and then we're OK. I hope to hell Bush doesn't buckle," he said.

I replied that I thought Bush was considering the plan as a political stalling tactic but that our allies would apply the brakes to any administration inclination to act on it. Nixon's concern was that the initiative had started a peace process, but I argued that the war had irreversible momentum.

"You're more hopeful than I am," he replied. "I've been around this lap before. The 1972 Christmas bombing brought the Soviets to the table anyway. Saddam is secondary; we need to watch the Soviets."

They continued to push their peace plan, and on February 18, Bush had to finally choose between saving Gorbachev and defeating Saddam Hussein.

"I'll bet they are having a hell of a meeting down there tonight," Nixon remarked. "Wouldn't you love to be a fly on the wall and watch the fur fly over this one? Boy, we used to have some lively conversations when we were in there! But if I were there now, I would tell Bush that the Soviets will replace Saddam's losses secretly anyway; hell, they could do it in five minutes. So just keep pressing on, for God's sake."

Bush, however, did not call on him that night because he had already reached a decision. He rejected the Soviet plan because it linked any Iraqi withdrawal from Kuwait to an Israeli withdrawal from the occupied territories. It was a substantial gamble for the normally risk-averse Bush, since it could have split the fragile coalition, alienated Gorbachev, and put distance between the United States and the Soviet Union. Nixon speculated that Bush may have even resented the Soviet initiative because it complicated the diplomacy, the military action, the coalition, and the U.S.-Soviet partnership. But the administration had failed to consider that Gorbachev was serving his own interests, as he was entitled to do, and assumed incorrectly that he would look after our interests as well.

"Well, you were right on Bush," Nixon said to me on February 22. "I didn't think he would, but he's going to stand firm. I just talked to Scowcroft." The second deadline for Iraq to withdraw from Kuwait, February 23, was eighteen hours away, and the ground troops were preparing to move. Nixon had tried to call Scowcroft earlier, but the general was with Bush, reviewing the president's speech on the Soviet peace plan. I watched Bush deliver the speech and reported to Nixon that Bush called the Soviet initiative "useful."

He was incredulous. "Oh, for God's sake!" he said. "It wasn't useful. It was manipulative and deceptive, but I guess he had to say something positive to keep from dumping on the Russians completely. Well, at least he's not going to fold. That's the most important thing. I hope Cheney is in there, since he's the only hawk, and he's not just hearing from Baker."

Nixon's worst fears were realized on the morning of the second deadline: Bush was with Baker at Camp David, without Secretary of Defense Cheney and without Scowcroft, who remained at the White House. He called me with the news. "Goddamn it! Baker has Bush's ear, and that's a disaster. Of all the people for Bush to listen to, he's got to turn to Baker? Oh, boy. Baker will go for peace at any price, and I'm afraid that Bush is still susceptible to that kind of crap."

Two hours later, he called me again with the word from Scowcroft: "You will be pleased to know that the ground war will go ahead today. I heard from Scowcroft that [General H. Norman] Schwarzkopf has the OK. This must kill Baker, but the big losers are the Soviets. They really backfired with this one." Their peace plan efforts had been roundly rejected, and the Iraqi-Soviet connection remained intact. Bush called Nixon at six o'clock in the evening on February 23 to tell him that the ground offensive, Desert Saber, was scheduled to begin in two hours despite Soviet efforts to prevent it. Nixon was relieved and mildly surprised that even in Baker's company Bush had remained committed to the use of force.

Kissinger called Nixon three days later, equally astonished. He reported that when he had been at the White House for dinner the evening before, Baker repeatedly called Bush away from the table, pressuring him to accept the Soviets' plan. Nixon thought that the behavior was "outrageous" and told Kissinger, "We would have fired his ass," perhaps not consciously aware that that would have meant Kissinger.

Nixon feared Bush's propensity to believe in the purity of Gorbachev's motives, and this was reinforced by Kissinger: "Bush half-believes them; Baker does totally." I mentioned to Nixon a CBS News Poll indicating that 80 percent of those polled thought that the Soviets were "up to their old tricks" with their plan. "Bush had better watch *that* poll," he said. "In fact, that's the only poll he should watch."

I came to my desk early on February 26 to find an essay written by former president Jimmy Carter ripped from *Time* magazine. Nixon had scribbled my name on top, followed by two exclamation points. Entitled "Don't Reject a Cease-Fire," it argued that holding out for complete surrender as an alternative to any peace negotiations would guarantee a long, destructive war, fracture the alliance, and destabilize the region. Nixon was appalled. Not only was Carter grossly incorrect, but publishing this advice during the ground war was "totally irresponsible."

Nixon called me into his office and, upon seeing the article in my hand, fumed, "Can you even believe it? Look at this crap! Give it to me, please," he said, taking it from me. "What the hell kind of essay is this? I can't believe that he would send such a disastrous mixed signal when we are so close to finishing off Iraq. Our troops are out there fighting like hell in the middle of the goddamned desert, and he has undermined what they're trying to do. If Carter had a problem with the war, he should have told Bush privately, not publish it in *Time*."

Once the war was under way, our adversaries and our troops needed to see a consistent signal of domestic support, not dissension coming from a former president.

The ground assault lasted only one hundred hours. The Iraqis were driven out, and Kuwait was fully liberated, but Kuwait had been badly damaged by the occupation, with many things of value stolen, pillaged, set ablaze, or shipped to Iraq. On February 27, Bush announced that Iraq had agreed to a cease-fire, and the war was over.

Nixon was distressed. "There are a number of problems with this cease-fire coming now," he said when we met again in the afternoon. "And they're classic problems in the aftermath of a war. First, what is the fate of Hussein? It's a grave mistake to leave him in power. Second, there was no word directly from him on this cease-fire, so why should we let up? And third, what the hell are the Soviets up to over there?"

Nixon believed that although the military and political objectives had been achieved—Iraq was forced from Kuwait, and the Kuwaiti régime was restored—the United States should have kept the pressure on Hussein and left him unable to rebuild his armed forces and resume his dictatorship. These concerns were borne out almost immediately after the cease-fire, when Hussein used his surviving forces to violently suppress separatist rebellions by the Kurds in the north and Shiite Muslims in the south.

Meanwhile, a minor disagreement erupted between Bush and Schwarzkopf after the formal end of the war. Schwarzkopf, like Nixon, suggested that Iraqi forces loyal to Hussein would have been left much weaker and less capable of crushing the uprisings if the ground offensive had continued. "Frankly," Schwarzkopf said, "my recommendation had been . . . to continue the march. We could have made it . . . a battle of annihilation." Bush responded that there was total agreement among his war advisers as to when the war should have ended. The difference of opinion, however, illuminated some problematic policy questions.

First, there was confused debate over what the American role should have been in Iraq immediately after the war. The Bush administration argued that our role was limited to deciding upon the terms of a permanent UN cease-fire and that our mandate had been simply to evict Iraq from Kuwait, not to quell Iraqi infighting.

The Iraqi rebels, however, claimed that the internal revolution was an extension of the war begun by the U.S.-led coalition, and therefore we had a responsibility to support their cause. They claimed correctly that Bush had personally called upon the Iraqi people to rise up and overthrow Hussein and that since they had acted upon that advice, they expected American assistance.

The administration countered that Bush's comments were intended only to emphasize to Iraqi society that the United States would never maintain normal relations with Iraq while Hussein remained in power. Bush was inviting a coup, not a revolution, and consequently we had no debt to the rebels.

The chaotic situation in Iraq that this debate spawned indicated to Nixon that we should have advanced to Baghdad while we had the Iraqi troops in a rout, removed Hussein, and destroyed more military hardware.

The second point of debate was the question of whether our policy was caught up in its own contradictions. We called for Hussein's overthrow but opposed Iraq's dismemberment; we called for the Iraqi people to rise up against Hussein, but we were unwilling to help them do the job; and if we did not assist the rebels, Hussein would stay in power, and normal relations would be impossible, but if we did help them, we would involve ourselves in their civil war.

Nixon argued that the United States should have removed the source of the turmoil root and branch, and it was the secretary of state, he believed, who advocated this unfortunate premature cease-fire: "I'll bet it was Baker who pressured for this, telling Bush that the Soviets would crack the coalition if we didn't go for a cease-fire now." He was appalled to learn that Baker was planning an immediate trip to Moscow to bestow upon the Soviets a role in the cease-fire that they did not deserve.

The rebel uprisings in Iraq *were* the logical extension of the American-led war against the Iraqi people's oppressor, Saddam Hussein, but the United States was not prepared to deal with the consequences. The Kurds wanted their own state, apart from Iraq, and the Shiites demanded protection for their own minority, and both faced brutal suppression by the rearming Iraqi forces. The Iraqi violence against them was not launched over a border, as it had been in Kuwait, but within the border, and the two groups were left to defend themselves without the protection and support of the United States. On April 15, Nixon did a live interview with CNN's Bernard Shaw, during which he said what many others were thinking: "We should get the CIA to take out Saddam."

Had we removed Hussein, the minorities in Iraq would not have faced the brutal denial of rights to which they were now subjected. But Turkish president Turgut Ozal argued persuasively to Bush that a stable Iraq under Hussein was preferable to a chaotic Iraq without him, and the administration thus adopted a hands-off policy. But as televised images of the tortured Kurds filled American living rooms, Bush was forced to establish Iraqi "no-fly" zones and provide the minorities with air cover. He followed up with punitive air strikes when the Iraqis violated the "no-fly" rules.

Neither Bush nor Scowcroft contacted Nixon during this period, leaving the former president to speculate that the overwhelming public support for the victory over Iraq was buoying their feelings of invincibility. Bush may not have been amenable to hearing Nixon's advice, but the former president prepared another memorandum anyway, hoping to set Bush on a proper course and inject some humility into a White House intoxicated with a well-deserved but short-lived victory.

As Nixon sat at his desk, dictating the memorandum, on April 18, Bush called to invite him to lunch at the White House. When Nixon told him that I would be delivering the letter the next day, Bush said that he would be at Camp David in the afternoon but that I could leave it with Scowcroft. Nixon's demeanor changed immediately. Although he felt that Bush should turn to him for advice, he knew that he did not have to and was particularly gratified when he did.

He completed the memorandum to Bush the next morning and told me that I could not read it until after he had conferred with Bush at the White House. I made my second trip to the Oval Office later that afternoon and deposited Nixon's letter at Scowcroft's office in the West Wing. Scowcroft called the next day to offer his thanks and to alert Nixon that the White House luncheon in the former president's honor would include Bush, Scowcroft, Cheney, and Gates. Guarding against Baker and his associates, he warned Scowcroft, "No State Department people."

Bush hosted Nixon at the White House on April 22. Joining them were Vice President Dan Quayle, Chief of Staff John Sununu, Cheney, Scowcroft, and Lawrence Eagleburger, deputy secretary of state and one of the few at State whom Nixon trusted. Nixon spoke with them for almost two hours, focusing primarily on the upheaval in the collapsing Soviet Union and the ramifications of the Persian Gulf War, including the survival of Hussein.

"Everyone was quiet and just listened to me," he told me the next day. Although he respected each of the participants, he was frustrated by the size of the group. "The more people you add to a discussion, the more diluted it becomes. I could have talked to each individually, and in fact I should have talked to just Bush and Scowcroft alone first. Oh well," he shrugged, "it's their White House.

"The meeting was all right, but not particularly productive. They all listened intently and shook their heads in agreement when I said that there will never be peace as long as Saddam is in there; but you know, Bush is out there thinking God knows what. Reagan was very good in that he picked some excellent advisers. I just don't see that with Bush, and by that I mean people who would stand up for him no matter what. They're smart guys, but I don't think there is any real loyalty there, and that—more than anything else—is what a president really needs."

He paused. "Cheney and Scowcroft are probably the closest to me ideologically. If anyone listened, I hope they did. I hit the Russian thing hard. I told them that not one dollar of American aid should be sent to the Soviet Union until it demonstrates a real commitment to democratic reform, and they seemed to take to that. The war is over, but the problems of dealing with Russia will always be there, and they're always going to be there, and they're far more important than Saddam Hussein. I tried to bring them to the mountaintop, to make them see the big picture, but I don't know if they got it.

"I have the feeling that Bush is inclined to agree with me but could be swayed if Baker made a different recommendation. Quayle is still learning about foreign affairs, although he has good instincts. Cheney is a solid and responsible hawk, and Scowcroft and Eagleburger have been around long enough to know what's going on. They're all decent guys and smart, but I don't know—they just don't have the vision. And since the two men at the top—Bush and Baker—don't have it, you can't expect anyone else to have it either."

At the end of the war, the administration saw a providential opportunity to renew the peace process in the Middle East. With Iraq defeated and burdened by sanctions, the régime in Kuwait restored, Israel protected, and the delicate international coalition intact, the regional dynamics had changed, offering new chances for peace. Seizing upon the momentum lent by the victory over Iraq, the administration announced a Middle East peace conference sponsored enthusiastically by Baker. Nixon had little hope for the conference, calling it "a nothing thing. It's just a forum for the same old lines. The real negotiations always go on in private." The war may have changed the prospects for peace by bringing together Israel and her neighbors against a common threat, but, he cautioned, it also may have reinforced the enmities that originally made them enemies.

The Arab-Israeli conflict survived both the cold war and the Persian Gulf War. Nixon believed that the historic handshake between Israeli prime minister Yitzhak Rabin and Palestinian Liberation Organization chairman Yasir Arafat on September 13, 1993, could have delivered the momentum needed to usher in a new era of peace between the Arabs and the Israelis. The peace agreement between Israel and Jordan, signed on July 25, 1994, seemed to bear this out, although the violence on the ground in Israel and its surrounding territories continued unabated. The Persian Gulf War stemmed, at least temporarily, the flow of rising instability in the region. The continuing Arab-Israeli peace process could do the same, perhaps more dramatically and for a longer period of time. The agreements between the PLO and Israel and between Jordan and Israel were major breakthroughs but simply first steps on the long road to a lasting and just Middle East peace.

Nixon thought that with the American success in the Persian Gulf War, the Soviet Union no longer supporting Israel's Arab enemies, Egypt not anti-

Israel since the 1979 signing of the Camp David Accords, and the correlation of forces now favoring Israel, the chances for an enduring peace were the best they had been since the creation of the state of Israel. Failure to capitalize on these advantageous factors could cost Israel in the long run and make peace even more elusive. Citing Rabin's political courage, Nixon commended his ability to make peace with Arafat while Israel was strong enough to do so.

On August 9, 1992, exactly eighteen years after his resignation, I joined Nixon in New York for his private meeting with Rabin, as an observer and note taker. I arrived at the Plaza Hotel and made my way through a small group of demonstrators protesting Rabin's decision to legalize Israeli contacts with the Palestinians. When Nixon arrived, we went together through the international press pool into Rabin's suite. The prime minister was a slight man with a soft, reassuring voice that belied his decorated military background and his reputation for tough but fair political leadership. They exchanged warm greetings, and when Nixon introduced me, the Israeli prime minister flashed me a look of cautious suspicion.

"We can trust her?" he asked Nixon.

When Nixon answered yes, Rabin extended his hand to me and offered a gracious welcome. His aides arranged us for a photo opportunity, and the press was invited in. They arrived in two chaotic waves, with reporters crashing into one another, shouting questions that the two principals left unanswered.

Once they were ushered out, Rabin began their conversation by describing the conditions in the region and giving an assessment of the Soviet collapse. Nixon followed with his own observations and warned Rabin that the current propitious conditions for peace would soon evaporate. He argued that both American and Israeli interests would be best served by a settlement based on the land-for-peace formula.

"If Israel retains the occupied territories, it will corrupt its moral cause. Although the four million Israelis and one million Jewish émigrés from the Soviet Union exceed the two million Arabs in Israel and the occupied territories, it is destabilizing and dangerous to keep the Arabs captive," he told Rabin. Israel, if it maintained its possession of these lands, would degenerate into a binational garrison state, corrupting the spirit of the Jewish nation and undermining the moral purpose behind the U.S. commitment to its survival.

Rabin, for his part, introduced some ideas on the peace process, and Nixon, appreciating Rabin's difficult political position, offered him advice for his negotiations with the hard-liners in the Knesset. They seemed to enjoy a warm rapport: the prime minister, stating repeatedly how much he cherished his association with Nixon, called him "one of Israel's best friends."

And Nixon considered Rabin a good man, a distinguished military leader, a true statesman, and a friend with whom he could discuss international politics openly and honestly and with a common understanding.

Several weeks later, on September 30, I joined him for a follow-up meeting with Israeli foreign minister Shimon Peres at the United Nations Plaza Hotel. Peres was gregarious, open, and frank as they discussed many of the same issues, including the initial overtures to the PLO. With powerful domestic constituencies with vested interests in the conflict, Rabin and Peres faced enormous political difficulties at home as well as with Arafat. Nixon told both of them, "It takes a strong leader to wage war but an even stronger leader to make peace."

When we left the meeting with Rabin, I asked Nixon if he followed a standard format during his conversations with heads of state. "Well," he replied, "what you observed today is the way I've always done it. The host opens the conversation, and the guest follows up. I think that we should be talking about the state of the world and leave the bilateral negotiations to people at the lower levels. With Khrushchev and Brezhnev, the areas between the U.S. and the Soviet Union were so vast and the bipolar situation was so stable that we talked about many different things, like China and arms control, but only in the broadest senses. We never got down to the nitty-gritty, and we shouldn't have. That's why you have a Cabinet and undersecretaries and so forth. Once we got through with what we needed to discuss, Brezhnev usually wanted to talk about sort of safe subjects, like sports."

"What?" I asked.

"It's crazy, I know," he replied. "But that was Brezhnev, always looking to see what made America tick, and there were things about this country that he just found irresistible," he laughed. "But getting back to strategy—on my 1953 trips, I gained an appreciation of the situation that small and strategically vulnerable states find themselves in, like Israel. Small states love to play a role—that's why we used [Romanian dictator Nicolae] Ceaucescu with North Vietnam. He was a good channel. And as far as Israel is concerned, they're lucky to have Rabin now. He's the strong, silent type but a hell of a fighter. Because Israel is so vulnerable, they have *had* to produce top-flight people. We are so powerful that we don't have to—and we don't—always produce the best. The Israelis always do, and they're just damn smart." Nixon hoped that his private diplomacy with the Israelis would bring them closer to the just peace they deserved and the entire region so desperately needed.

———

The war accomplished several important objectives. It temporarily rectified the regional imbalance of power favoring Iraq. It isolated Iraq in the Arab world and burdened it with debt and reparations. It reassured Israel that the United States would continue to provide for its protection. It proved that the end of the cold war did not mean the end of conflict. It justified the post–cold war American military. It inspired a remarkably resilient international coalition to roll back the invasion. It left no doubt about our willingness to defend our interests and sent a signal of deterrence to potential aggressors. It rallied America at home and restored a sense of mission lost by the end of the cold war.

It failed, however, to achieve key objectives. It did not turn the United Nations into an enduring, definitive international forum for peace. It did not solidify the highly touted new world order. It did not establish a comprehensive security framework for the region. It did not institute stable regional arms control. It did not eliminate Saddam Hussein's Iraq as a future threat. It did not diminish Iran's stature as the region's most dangerous power. It did not institute democracy in newly liberated Kuwait, and it did not redistribute wealth in the Middle East. And despite the victory for the United States and the success of the new rules governing U.S. intervention, the war failed to combat the legacy of Vietnam.

The Persian Gulf War, for its scale, diplomatic achievements, involvement of a vital interest, and military success, was supposed to have finally defeated the syndrome. It was supposed to have shown the world that the United States once again had the will, resources, and commitment to meet the challenges of aggression and restore the reliability of American power. But as early as February 25, two days before the cease-fire, Nixon knew that the war would not offset the impact of Vietnam in terms of setting a new precedent of invincibility.

"This war was well run, but I'm afraid that it will not be a watershed," he said, his eyes narrowing. "It was too short, and frankly, even though one casualty is too much, this one had too few casualties to mean anything beyond what it did: expel Iraq from Kuwait. The hangover from Vietnam is still with us, unfortunately, and will be with us until, frankly, all of these generations pass from the scene or we have another world war."

"That's a drastic remedy," I said.

"The aftermath of Vietnam left us with a drastic situation," he replied.

The resurgent patriotism at the war's end was positive for the country but represented more of an overcompensation for the end of Vietnam, which lacked the yellow ribbons and the parades, than a celebration of the relatively quick and painless Persian Gulf War. Where Vietnam disproportionately tore the country apart, this war disproportionately brought it together. As quickly as the war was waged, the outpouring of patriotism and Bush's astronomical approval ratings evaporated. For Nixon, the Persian Gulf War was an inevitable and politically useful conflict but not enough of a contest to counteract the bitter lessons of Vietnam.

—

In a region where the threats are layered with fragile opportunities for peace, the United States had to lead. This was the essence of Nixon's philosophy, which he continually and diplomatically imparted to the administration during the crisis in the Persian Gulf and which he felt guided the overall success of American policy. The United States should try to lead through the United Nations, much as it led in the cold war through NATO, but failing that, it should act unilaterally to protect its interests. Nixon firmly believed that America's leadership abroad was the strongest guarantee against corrosive cynicism at home and the best defense against tyranny where it still thrived.

"Public opinion responds to threats, not to opportunities," he wrote in *Time* magazine on March 16, 1992. "It is easy to mobilize support to meet a clear threat but difficult to rally it to seize a fleeting opportunity. If our leaders put foreign policy on the back burner until world events produce a new threat, our moment of opportunity will have vanished."

Act, he urged Bush, before events force you to act. A new world order did not diminish the need for American vigilance; it multiplied it. A new age did not mean the disappearance of old problems. The war in the Persian Gulf proved that perpetual peace had not been achieved, that democratic enlightenment had not reached every corner of the world, and that there was still no substitute for American power. Nixon's role in the crisis, as it was throughout his post-presidential years, was to influence American policy beyond the point of merely instructing current leaders on the mechanics of war. He wanted them to see "the bigger picture" and to be able to act as decisively in peace as they did in war. Above all, however, he wanted to teach them how best to balance power and ideals so the United States could be a catalyst for peace and stability, even in the shifting sands of the Middle East.

# CHAPTER 4

# THE LEGACY OF
# VIETNAM

As the sun set on a warm summer day in 1992, Nixon and I sat in the study of his residence, discussing the upcoming presidential election. The evening news flickered quietly on the television in the corner, more as background noise than as a source of information. Suddenly, the sound of an explosion came from the television, and Nixon, annoyed by the distraction, reached for the remote control to turn it off. As he aimed the remote at the television, he froze when he realized that the arresting images of violence filling his screen were from the Vietnam War. He put the remote control down slowly and watched the scenes from the war unfold before him.

"Isn't it ironic," he said softly, "that I was the president to preside over the last years of the war and then finally to end it?" He shook his head sadly. "It was a miserable goddamned thing. And to think that I was the one who had to face down those hippie hoodlums who opposed it. My God, I wasn't just from another generation from these people; it was like I was from a different planet. The differences in values and ideas and everything else were enormous. The gulf was huge. I don't think I really appreciated it at the time, but now I can see how it was so . . . ironic."

Few issues gnawed at Nixon's conscience like the legacy of Vietnam. The war defined his presidency, a generation, and an approach to war and peace that lasted through the end of the century. The divisiveness it created rumbled violently under the very foundations of the country, inspiring a minority of detractors to orchestrate loud cacophonies of protest and Nixon's Silent Majority to speak through their votes. Nixon, representing values that suddenly appeared antiquated and irrelevant, was caught in a widening cultural, social, and political chasm that he could neither control nor ignore. With war and the costs it exacted seen as increasingly obsolescent and barbaric, those who opposed action in Vietnam gathered the media attention, the political momentum, and the shifting moral high ground. To them, Nixon's prosecution of the war defined him as an unenlightened enemy of the good and just. Few of them could understand his reasons for continuing the war, and even fewer could relate to him as a president. The irony, as he said, was not lost on him.

"I am a square," he said on May 27, 1993, drawing a square in the air with his two forefingers. "My values are traditional: God, country, family. I am absolutely opposed to the destruction of those values that came about during the Vietnam era. Free love, drugs, tearing down your country, denying God, selfishness, and indulgence—everything I despise took root when I was president, and there was so little I could do to stop it. It's incredible that I got the support that I did. I represented everything they were trying to overthrow, and there I was, president."

Vietnam haunted him, not as the memory of a war he believed was an honorable attempt to stop the creeping spread of communism but as the ignition of the cultural revolution that eroded the traditional pillars of justice and decency in American life. Elements once considered radical in American society began to be accepted as mainstream. Ideas and behaviors once prohibited came out from the shadows. Thinking once considered outrageous came to be integrated into a new values system. Nixon, at the center of the social earthquake, remained unmoved by the radicalism and became even more committed to an acceptable end to the war that inspired it.

"This president," he said, pointing to himself, "was not about to be bullied by some noisy war protesters. If they disagreed with the war, fine, they had the right to voice their opinion. But I was elected to do a job, and prosecuting that war until it could come to some kind of honorable conclusion was my responsibility. The test of great leadership is to lead public opinion, not be led by it. In the case of Vietnam, that loud group of protesters was mistaken for public opinion. If they really were public opinion, I would never have been reelected in 1972 by such a large margin—if at all.

"But considering the circumstances at the time, I met that test of leadership: I made policy that served the national interest instead of the demands of a loud minority. Look, Vietnam was a war on two fronts: on the battlefield and on our set of values. The war itself was tragic enough." The tragedy for Nixon was that he could prevent neither the outcome of the war nor the assault on the traditional values that were, in fact, his own.

"Do you think, then, that the upheaval was unavoidable?" I asked.

"Unavoidable?" he repeated. "Maybe. Destructive? Absolutely. And Vietnam was the catalyst."

Nixon often remarked that he hated the Vietnam War every day of his presidency. He despised it for the tremendous costs it exacted: human, material, and moral. He despised the decisions he had to make to send soldiers into danger. He despised it when he had to meet with the courageous families of those who had lost loved ones either through death or through capture and assure them that he was pursuing an honorable end to the war. He despised it for the toll it took on his presidency and on the confidence of the American people in their government.

He believed that the U.S. goals in Indochina—preventing Hanoi's Communist régime from conquering the free countries in the region and protecting American interests there—were worthy. Peaceful means, however, had failed to achieve them. North Vietnam's direct and indirect aggression against its non-Communist neighbors presented Nixon with a stark choice: either continue to oppose the Communists militarily, or abandon those threatened. The choice, he believed, was a false one: the United States had a moral and strategic imperative to support the forces of peace and freedom against those who sought to destroy them.

"Goddamn it!" he exclaimed, shaking his head on September 14, 1992. "I cannot believe that Quayle could be so irresponsible as to say something to the effect that even Richard Nixon has admitted that the Vietnam War was wrong. Now, my God! What was he thinking? That's historically inaccurate! I wound down the war, but I never opposed it. The media took him on for that comment, not to defend me but to knock him. And you know what? I like him, but he deserved it on this one. I can't believe that he would say something so stupid. Maybe he's being influenced by some of the people around him who were anti-Vietnam. I don't know. I just wanted the damn war done right."

On November 3, 1969, he delivered what he thought was the most significant foreign policy address of his career. When he took office in January 1969, 550,000 troops were in Vietnam. During the campaign, he had pledged to end American involvement in a way that would serve our interests and protect our reputation. Despite the fact that he had begun to withdraw troops as a first step toward that goal, the antiwar movement launched massive protests around the country to demand immediate and total withdrawal, a process supported by the majority of Americans polled. His Cabinet and Republican leaders in Congress were split. Some even warned that if he continued to prosecute the war, it would quickly become known contemptuously as Nixon's war.

He had been tempted to take the most politically expedient route: blame the Democratic presidents who had originally committed the troops, Kennedy and Johnson, bring the troops home en masse, and sacrifice Saigon to the Soviet-backed North Vietnamese. That plan would have brought greater tranquillity at home and in Vietnam and would have given him a better chance of uniting the country behind his administration's other initiatives, but at the enormously high price of allowing the Communist domination of Indochina. He was unwilling to pay it.

Rather than letting the situation degenerate into "Nixon's war," he knew he had to make it "America's war," by taking the case for continued American sacrifices in Vietnam directly to the people who were being asked to make them. "And so tonight," he said on national television, "to you, the great Silent Majority of my fellow Americans, I ask for your support. Let us be united for peace. Let us also be united against defeat. Because let us understand: North Vietnam cannot defeat or humiliate the United States. Only Americans can do that."

The speech was tremendously successful. The Silent Majority to whom he directed his appeal spoke by supporting him, and he was able to continue the policies that culminated in the Paris Peace Accords of January 27, 1973. "The Silent Majority speech was probably my greatest speaking triumph, apart from the Fund speech, which saved my political career," he said on September 9, 1992. "The month before, hundreds of thousands of demonstrators marched into Washington and protested, sometimes very violently, around the White House and the Capitol. Peace-at-any-price congressmen and senators, not to mention those who had been dovish all along on Vietnam, demanded that I withdraw unilaterally. Even some of my friends and supporters began to pile on. [Vice President Spiro] Agnew and Haldeman were for it—and so was Henry [Kissinger]—but only because they had to be. Everybody else was against it, including Bush, who was soft on the whole war. I listened to everybody, but I knew all along what I needed to do. I went on the tube with very little advance warning, even to the networks. I didn't want one goddamned thing about that speech leaked. And I knew that I would have to write much of it myself, particularly the end, if it were to carry any weight. I wrote that last passage by hand at two in the morning the day of the speech. It proved to be decisive. The support was overwhelming and made my job of ending the war in an honorable way easier."

Nixon believed that in any conflict the United States has to realistically evaluate the importance of the interests at stake, the nature of the threat to those interests, and the best way to defend our position. When the interests are not vital but peripheral, we should seldom commit forces directly. But when vital interests are threatened, we have to be prepared to make a strong and direct commitment to protect them. While we should explore ways to prevail without resorting to force, we must back them up with a willingness to use it if necessary.

Nixon never wavered from this philosophy, even when our engagement in Vietnam put it to the test. The American policy in Vietnam was based on two main objectives: first, to defend critical interests in Southeast Asia by preventing the Soviet Union from gaining a foothold along the vital sea-lanes connecting the Persian Gulf and Indian Ocean to the Pacific, through which Japan ships almost all of its oil imports, and second, to maintain the credibility of our international commitments by trying to stop North Vietnam's expansionism, which threatened South Vietnam and the rest of Indochina. When Hanoi prevailed in 1975, we had failed to achieve both objectives: Moscow installed major naval bases in Cam Ranh Bay and Da Nang, and the Vietnamese Communists quickly took over Cambodia and Laos and overtly threatened Thailand.

"After the fall of Saigon in April 1975," Nixon said on January 3, 1992, "those who supported the North Vietnamese in Vietnam and elsewhere jumped for joy, but it didn't last long. Over the past sixteen years, the Communist rulers have not brought liberty and prosperity to Vietnam, but what they have brought is despair and poverty. Their people live in abysmal conditions, and yet all they do is blindly pursue policies to keep themselves in power. So Vietnam is still one of the poorest countries in the world. And we see this all the time whenever another mass exodus of boat people leaves Vietnam, looking for hope somewhere else. Those are the people everyone should be listening to: they risked their lives and gave up what little they had to escape the misery the Communists brought."

Even with our defeat, however, Nixon believed that we had attained part of our goal. We preserved the freedom of our friends and allies in the region for more than a decade. More important, by holding off the North Vietnamese until the mid-1970s, we allowed the region's developing countries, some of which gained spectacular economic success, to win valuable time to consolidate their own non-Communist régimes.

In retrospect, Nixon saw clearly that the outcome in Vietnam would have been different had a more prudent and militarily feasible strategy been adopted. Under the Kennedy and Johnson administrations, the forces lacked a well-defined military mission. Both Kennedy and Johnson treated the conflict essentially as a civil war within South Vietnam that could be resolved by suppressing the Communist guerrillas and promoting economic progress in South Vietnam, while in reality the guerrillas were simply one of North Vietnam's tactics for conquering Saigon. As a result, the United States deployed its forces to fight the insurgents in the south while leaving the enemy's source of men and supplies to the north largely unchecked. This policy put the United States on an eternal military treadmill: the north could fight such a conflict for years while the patience of the American people was certain to wear thin much sooner.

Nixon laid the blame for the mishandled approach squarely on Robert McNamara, Kennedy's and Johnson's secretary of defense and the principal architect of the war. "Bob McNamara," he said when we spoke on November 14, 1992. "I have a low opinion of him. He was smart as a whip but very arrogant and full of himself, which prevented him from seeing very clearly. He was the typical elite intellectual type—cold and mean."

"One of the best and the brightest," I said.

Nixon smirked. "Best and the brightest. That was all part of Kennedy's crap. Please. McNamara was very smart, but that didn't mean he knew a goddamned thing about running a war. On Vietnam, he designed the gradualist strategy, which, as we know, screwed up the war beyond belief and left me with a hell of a mess. But what bothered me most was that he was disloyal. He turned on Johnson, and he would have been nothing without Johnson. One of our biggest mistakes was sending him over to the World Bank, where he didn't do a damn thing. Kissinger suggested it, thinking it would quiet some of our critics, but it was a bad mistake."

When Nixon became president, his policy was aimed at reversing the McNamara strategy, limiting our involvement to interdicting the flow of troops and arms from the north into the south, and training and supplying Saigon's forces to fight the ground war. He blamed the Kennedy policy for making this impossible at the outset. When the Kennedy administration helped to destabilize South Vietnam by plotting a coup to overthrow its government, which led to the murder of President Ngo Dinh Diem, the resulting political and military chaos forced the Johnson administration to intervene massively to prevent defeat.

"Johnson, of course, had to escalate our commitment, but those who criticize me for doing that miss the point completely," he said on February 2, 1991. "We didn't escalate the war; we ran it down by matching gradual withdrawal with other strategies. Escalate was one thing we did *not* do."

When Nixon took office in 1969, he tried to redirect the U.S. approach by attacking the Communist staging bases and supply lines in Cambodia and Laos, bombing and mining the harbor through which North Vietnam received supplies from the Soviet Union, bombing North Vietnam's rail links to China, and undertaking a program to train and equip the South Vietnamese to assume the fighting from American troops. These steps enabled him to reduce and finally end our involvement in the war.

Further, Nixon argued, his critics missed the point when they claimed that his decision in April 1970 to order attacks on sanctuaries in Cambodia from which the North Vietnamese launched hit-and-run attacks on American troops was an expansion of the war. When the Joint Chiefs of Staff recommended unanimously that these sanctuaries be eliminated in order to protect the lives of the U.S. forces and those of the South Vietnamese allies, Nixon took the advice. The initial attack on two of the major sanctuaries accomplished its objective but sparked sharp public protests. Nixon ordered further attacks on the remaining sanctuaries anyway, arguing that he would be criticized just as much for eliminating six sites as he would be for eliminating two. The operation was successful, and the Communists dropped their plans for another offensive that year. For Nixon, this was not an expansion of the war but a necessary maneuver within the parameters of the current war.

"I really can't stand these sanctimonious people who say that we expanded the war. They don't know what the hell they're talking about. What we did in Cambodia was absolutely correct," he said on June 13, 1991. "The enemy cleverly had moved the conflict out of Vietnam, and so we had to pursue them or lose more lives. The idea that our bombing those supply lines into Vietnam caused the Khmer Rouge was the most blatantly ludicrous theory on Vietnam. There are so many crazies out there talking nonsense about the war that it's hard to keep the facts straight. No, we did not cause the Khmer Rouge, and we did not expand the war. The enemy carried it across the border. We didn't. And to claim that we were on the wrong side just distorts what we tried to do, which was the right thing. Period."

In Nixon's view, morality had a peculiar place in the great questions of war and peace. Before a president could justify putting soldiers on the battlefield, he had to make the case for just political ends and military means if he expected to get the kind of domestic support he needed to prosecute a war successfully. "The cause must be moral," he said on September 9, 1991. "The strategy and tactics must be to limit the suffering to civilians. And it's got to have a chance of succeeding. Otherwise, no president has any business going to war."

In the case of Vietnam, the morality of our involvement became the central issue in the public debate. Antiwar activists argued that our participation simply propped up corrupt and repressive governments in South Vietnam and Cambodia and that the people of these countries would be better off if we withdrew unconditionally. While some actively supported the Communist side, most thought that our allies were not worth defending.

Nixon rejected this view out of hand. He believed that although those whom we sought to defend in the region did not represent perfect democracy and human rights, any doubts about the justice of our cause should have been erased by what happened after we left. In Vietnam, the Communists killed tens of thousands, and six hundred thousand South Vietnamese perished in the South China Sea as they fled the country. The very crises we fought to avoid, such as the killing fields of Cambodia and the boat people and "reeducation camps" of Vietnam, erupted when we failed. "Fewer people were killed during the anti-Communist war than during the Communist peace," he said, and after seeing the horrors of the Cambodian holocaust and the Vietnamese exodus, he felt that a conclusive moral judgment could be rendered on our intervention in Vietnam: it had been, as Reagan had also said, "a noble cause."

Since the fall of Indochina, those who challenged the morality of the cause have argued that the war was unwinnable. They maintain that since the South Vietnamese were ineffective fighters, the collapse of the country in 1975 in the face of the north's disciplined invading force was inevitable. Since our policy protracted an unwinnable war, they say, it caused unnecessary suffering and left us with the dubious mantle of immoral, Machiavellian leadership.

Nixon raged against this argument. "The war was winnable," he said on September 9, raising the subject as we discussed the forthcoming publication of *Seize the Moment*. "Because an event turned out one way doesn't mean that it had to happen that way. By the time of our final withdrawal, we had put our allies in a position to survive without the presence of American combat forces. We really tried with Vietnamization to make the South Vietnamese into a pretty effective fighting force. At the time, we thought that since we had no choice but to withdraw, that we could substitute them for us. Of course, we knew that even with our equipment, they couldn't do the job we could, but since we had to get out, that was it. Besides, they had proved themselves in 1972, when their ground forces stopped a massive North Vietnamese invasion, so we didn't think a loss was inevitable."

"Arming and training the South Vietnamese seems like it was the only way for us to—"

"Get the hell out. I know," he replied. "Looking back, though, I think that the biggest flaw with the Paris Peace Accords of 1973 was that the cease-fire provisions allowed North Vietnamese forces to stay in some South Vietnamese territory captured in the '72 invasion. But at least we backed up the goddamned treaty with power. We kept up the threat of airpower in the event of a North Vietnamese invasion and continued to provide the south with economic and military assistance. We tried to do it, against all odds, until the stupid and shortsighted Congress undercut us on both counts by cutting off the money. I know they were under enormous pressure, but my God! Our deterrent was gone, and that was the end. We won the war," he said, pointing upward, "but then lost the peace," he concluded, pointing downward.

"By 1973, we had achieved our political objective: South Vietnam's independence had been secured. But by 1975, the Congress destroyed our ability to enforce the Paris agreement and left our allies vulnerable to Hanoi's invading forces. If I sound like I'm blaming the Congress, I am. Their constituents were screaming to get out, and they were in a hell of a position. But what some of them didn't understand was that we had a responsibility to see it through to an honorable conclusion, even if it meant doing the politically unpopular thing. The pressure of waging the war in Vietnam broke Johnson, but I was damned if it were going to break me."

Folding his hands in his lap, he repeated his point: "Johnson left a broken man." He paused. "No, as president, I always knew that we had a responsibility to leadership no two-bit protesters were going to destroy. I couldn't stop them from destroying our values and our culture, but I could stop them from telling us that we weren't fit to lead."

He acknowledged, however, that the war demonstrators had provided a useful service. Their protests gave him an effective counterpoint to argue against as he summoned his Silent Majority to support his efforts in the war. The us-versus-them strategy played into the existing divisions over the war and allowed a defiant Nixon to assume the political high ground.

"The networks always made their decisions about whether or not to show the demonstrations based on whether or not they served their liberal agendas," he said on December 13, 1992. "In '68, they showed the demonstrations because, of course, they didn't want me to win. In '72, they didn't show them because it didn't help them. I was fairly successful in turning those demonstrations around to my benefit because they polarized the debate and left me with more support for the war than I otherwise would have had."

I asked if the demonstrators were one of the enemies he invoked when he spoke to the Silent Majority.

"Absolutely," he said. "The Silent Majority needed to know that they weren't the only ones who were appalled by the antiwar demonstrators. Their president was too. I remember so well when [John] Connally came to the White House one day in 1971 when it was under siege by antiwar demonstrators. He had an ability to cut straight to the heart of things. He said, 'Mr. President, it may not be pleasant to have to be harassed by these unkempt, noisy, and sometimes violent mobs, but in politics it is not necessarily bad to have enemies, particularly when they are an obnoxious but small minority.' He was absolutely right, and when I told him so, he recalled a meeting at the White House many years before, when Roosevelt was giving some political advice to a group of young Democrats. He told them that if a leader didn't have enemies, he had better create them. The best way to inspire your troops is by rallying them against a visible opponent. Loyalty turns out to be fierce," he said through clenched teeth. "They didn't know it at the time, but the antiwar demonstrators actually hurt their cause. They were loud, but they weren't right. And that's what the Silent Majority saw."

He pointed at me. "You know, the biggest misconception about Vietnam was that those protests were peaceful. They were *very* violent. Remember Bobby Kennedy's line that if he lived in the inner city, he could stir up a rebellion? Violent means—that was their tactic: rocks, bombs. It was a hell of a time. In Korea, it was clear that we were fighting the Commies. In Vietnam, it was much harder to get the message across. Same basic battle but a different era, different time."

Nixon felt so strongly that the message never got across that he dedicated his sixth book, in 1985, to a comprehensive debunking of what he called "the myths of Vietnam," a full explanation of how and why we went into Vietnam and how we "won the war but lost the peace." Of his ten books, *No More Vietnams* was the only one he said he felt an obligation to write. Ten years after the fall of Saigon, he still needed to demonstrate that we were on the right side of history. In his new introduction to the book in 1990, he wrote that he had made a profound error with the title by trying to cleverly co-opt an antiwar slogan: " 'No more Vietnams' can mean we will not try again. It should mean 'We will not fail again.' "

What disturbed Nixon the most, however, was that the war was largely responsible for corroding the spirit of exceptionality that gave us a moral foundation for our powerful leadership role abroad. "We had always led abroad prior to Vietnam," he said when we discussed his last book, *Beyond Peace*, on June 16, 1993. "The question was whether or not we would continue to do it. After the war, of course, there was very little support for doing anything abroad. Many said that we lost our moral justification, although I disagree with that. We still had it, but it became much less acceptable to do anything abroad. So the war was over, but we faced a new problem: how to keep us together and united without an outside mission. It's something we never really had to face before. We had two world wars and the cold war this century to serve that purpose. Then we had Vietnam, which screwed it up. But it did force us to look at ourselves because we couldn't really look outside anymore for a purpose that could bring us together or make us fight for a common cause."

This theme found its way into *Beyond Peace*. As Nixon prepared drafts of the manuscript, he struggled to separate the message from the messenger. When I walked into his study on September 4, 1993, he stood up from behind his desk and tapped part of the manuscript. "I'll tell you, I'm worried," he said, walking around the desk and into the middle of the room. "Our critics may justifiably say, 'Who is this guy to talk about the crisis of the spirit when he contributed to it with Vietnam?' which they blame us for, although they shouldn't since we inherited the goddamned thing, and Watergate, which was, of course, a product of Vietnam. Now *we* know that the seeds of the crisis we are talking about here were planted long before the war and Watergate and the end of the cold war. The breakdown on the values side was probably inevitable, though Vietnam and Watergate accelerated it without question."

When I suggested that if he took responsibility for his role in accelerating it, he might get a fair hearing, he laughed. "Fair? I don't think I've ever seen fair in my entire political career. No, I'm not looking for fairness, but I do want to get a discussion going on the collapse of the whole values thing. The idea that America is better off since the '60s is a bunch of bull. That cultural revolution was extremely destructive." The cynicism and cultural destruction wrought by the war and Watergate were so closely related to Nixon that he knew he would be blamed, at least in part, for their development. The great irony was that while Nixon embodied traditional values, he would be forever associated with their dissolution.

The election of Bill Clinton to the presidency in 1992 represented for Nixon the final triumph of those who opposed the war in Vietnam. Clinton had protested against the war at home and abroad and had taken active measures to avoid the draft. His equivocation on the issue during the campaign made even more ignominious his behavior during the war. For Nixon, the role of commander in chief required someone with military experience or, at the very least, someone who had not condemned the military and actively avoided its call to serve. He maintained the hope that the draft-evasion issue would be enough to terminate a candidacy he considered illegitimate.

"Let's face it: almost everyone is a draft dodger if given the chance. War is horrible. No one wants to get his ass shot off, and everyone lies a little. But Clinton has been so dishonest about it all along and so dishonest about being from that spoiled-brat Vietnam era that I'm sure it will hurt him," he said on September 9, 1992. "And many of his advisers were partisan anti-Vietnam sons of bitches, no better than he was. So there you have it: he'll have a Cabinet full of people as irresponsible as he was."

As Nixon saw it, if Bill Clinton the president had to face the same type of opposition to policy that Bill Clinton orchestrated as a young adult, he would gain a more sophisticated understanding not only of the wrenching decisions presidents need to make but of the moral ambiguities that often attend them. It was, therefore, with mild amusement that he watched Clinton explode at a heckler on July 26, 1993, admonishing him that his disrespectful actions represented what was wrong with America.

"That was a good one, wasn't it?" he asked me. "His reaction was classic, considering that he was part of the bunch that showed no respect in protesting the war." For Nixon, Clinton's opposition to the war had more to do with protecting a selfish interest in his own future than with conscientious objection. That he could run for president—and win—indicated to Nixon not only that the countercultural revolution had come full circle but that it had wreaked more damage than even he had anticipated.

On November 11, 1992, Nixon called to me as I walked past his open office door. "Monica? Do you want to come in here for a minute, please?" I closed the door behind me and sat across from the former president, who twirled a pen between his fingers. "I still can't believe that Clinton won. I mean, I can believe it, but I don't want to believe it. I read in *Time* or some other place that Clinton told someone 'softly,' 'If I win, it will close the book on Vietnam.' How do you like that? Poor guys from the ghetto getting their asses shot off, and here's Clinton winning the presidency. It really is too much for me to take. People talk about justice. Well, there isn't any on the political scene today, that's for sure."

"Did you hear that Clinton delivered a Veterans Day speech that focused on getting a full accounting of the MIAs and POWs from the war?" I asked.

He shot me a sharp, suspicious look. "He *said* that?"

"He did," I said.

Nixon exploded: "The media is so hypocritical, protecting him on this draft-dodge issue! What a disgraceful thing. The guy has absolutely no scruples. His victory in the election is proving that it was all right to be against the goddamned war. Everything we stood for, everything we fought for, is going straight down the tubes."

For Nixon, Vietnam was not only a wholly destructive military and political event but a crucial cultural turning point for America in the late twentieth century. Right and wrong, good and evil, freedom and tyranny, morality and amorality, faith and distrust, and tradition and iconoclasm were on trial. Vietnam in all of its manifestations seemed to award premiums to the wrong, evil, tyrannical, amoral, distrustful, and iconoclastic elements in society. One of the greatest crimes of Vietnam, according to Nixon, was that its false hopes, false ideals, and false prophets misled the country down a path from which there was no return. If the country lost its innocence because of Vietnam, he believed that it was an innocence permanently abandoned.

And if Clinton's election "closed the door on Vietnam," a new Senate investigation of the Vietnam MIAs and POWs reopened it. The issue first gained attention on June 16, 1992, when Russian president Boris Yeltsin, in Washington for a summit with President Bush, remarked that the Soviets had held some Vietnam POWs. Nixon had mixed feelings about the announcement. "Yeltsin is usually a responsible guy, but I don't know why he'd come out with this now. It's good for Bush because he can make an issue out of it, but Yeltsin has opened up a Pandora's box. Now the Senate may not give aid to Russia. I know that he was trying to come clean so that some could have an easier time voting for aid for Russia, but it could have the opposite effect. I can't guarantee that any one of those senators will see the big picture. They're so caught up in these chickenshit issues that they can't see from the mountaintop. If Russia loses its gamble with democracy, then we can forget about the POWs."

The MIA and POW issue infuriated him. His ability to enforce the Paris peace agreement had been hampered by a profound backlash against U.S. involvement in the war, which preceded another handicap, Watergate. The backlash was evident when antiwar resolutions came perilously close to passage in 1972 and when in January 1973, three months before Watergate became a major issue, the House and Senate Democratic caucuses voted overwhelmingly in favor of withdrawing our troops in exchange for our POWs. Nixon admitted that he had been caught completely off guard by the intensity of the backlash. It was inconceivable to him that after sacrificing over fifty-five thousand lives in a twelve-year struggle to win a just peace in Vietnam, the United States would casually disregard what those soldiers died to achieve.

He knew that those who opposed American involvement in the war would not support his policies even after withdrawal. He did not anticipate, however, the tremendous difficulty in securing support even from his political allies. An unexpected combination—fierce opposition from the doves and quiescent passivity from the hawks—enabled the antiwar measures to win approval of Congress in 1973, which removed for the North Vietnamese the last threat of an American retaliation and in turn destroyed Nixon's last chance to achieve a peaceful resolution of the war in Vietnam, including an airtight accounting of those missing in action and held as prisoners of war.

In the summer of 1992, Senator John Kerry headed the Senate Select Committee on POW-MIA Affairs to explore whether and to what extent the Nixon administration willfully left POWs in Vietnam in order to secure the peace agreement. Nixon and Kissinger were outraged. Since the end of the war, they had claimed that under no circumstances had they knowingly abandoned American soldiers in Vietnam, that those Americans accounted for were brought home, and that none were sacrificed. The Kerry Committee set out to uncover evidence to prove otherwise.

On August 10, Nixon took a frantic call from his former secretary of state. "Kissinger is beside himself," he told me after the conversation. "He's worried about this Kerry Committee and thinks we should speak out. I'm not sure it's worth it. They're just on an ideological fishing expedition. And what they're really trying to do is justify Clinton's activities during Vietnam. Let him off the hook—that's all they want to do, and I don't want any part of that.

"But they're looking in the wrong place. There's nothing there. I don't know why Henry has his back up. Everything we did on that issue was aboveboard. He said he was going on the tube to say that our administration did not prolong Vietnam to use the POWs as bargaining chips. Can you imagine such an outrageous thing? I don't blame Henry for getting angry about that, but he shouldn't be worried about them finding anything because we didn't do any of the things they're suggesting. You never know what Henry's going to say, but at least he's taking them on."

In negotiating the end of the war, Kissinger had made provisions for the safe passage home of the POWs. That the Kerry Committee could impugn him and his efforts in behalf of the Americans in Vietnam was not only unfair but irresponsible, and he reacted swiftly. He gave interviews denouncing the committee's mission, vowed that the committee would never find evidence to support the idea that the Nixon administration had abandoned Americans in Southeast Asia, and sent transcripts of these interviews to anyone with influence on the matter, including Nixon. The day after he spoke to his former boss, Kissinger appeared on *Nightline* and issued an impassioned defense of the Nixon administration's policies on POWs and MIAs in Vietnam.

"We negotiated," he began, "because we did not want to turn the Vietnamese, who had relied on our promise, over to the Communists. It is an outrage to suggest that we would knowingly leave Americans in the hands of the Communists. It is a disservice to our country. It is cruel to the families concerned that it should be believed that any American official would knowingly leave Americans in Communist hands. I do not accept . . . the implications of what Senator Kerry, who was demonstrating against the war at that time, is saying."

He continued, "The record makes clear that I recommended, from March on, bombing attacks on North Vietnam for violating the agreement. We held one more round of negotiations in May, in which we had three additional provisions about the return of prisoners and accounting for missing in action. We might have been able to use that agreement in order to enforce the additional provisions. Two weeks after that agreement was signed, the Congress prohibited any military action in or near Indochina. Two months after the agreement was signed, the Congress cut out the economic aid."

Kerry, also appearing on the program, pressed him: "Did you, Dr. Kissinger, come to Congress and say to them, 'I have a list of eighty people, and indeed we have others we believe to be unaccounted for; you mustn't pass this until we have a full accounting'?"

Kissinger gave a qualified answer: "In my press conference on June 18, 1973, in presenting the new agreement, I pointed out that we were not satisfied with the accounting for the missing in action and that that was one reason we had a new negotiation on the subject. I'm sure that I expressed, on a private basis, my dissatisfaction with the carrying out of the agreement on many occasions, and I know that President Nixon sent a formal letter to the Congress. . . . I am agnostic on the issue of whether the Communists kept prisoners. It is quite possible that they did. Senator Kerry knows that when he called me, I told him he could make a great contribution if he'd put the issue to rest. I thought he would put the issue to rest of whether the Vietnamese inhumanely, maliciously, and in violation of the agreement kept prisoners. It did not occur to me that American officials would become the victims of such investigations."

On August 13, Nixon waved Kissinger's *Nightline* transcript at me. "Well, Kissinger really gave it to them, and I knew he would," he said, smiling. "He's absolutely right on this. Their insinuation that we used those poor POWs as bargaining chips is outrageous. I spoke to [attorney] Jack Miller about being subpoenaed, and he said that they *can* subpoena me, for God's sake. I don't know. They've really made a mess of a non-issue." For the first time, Nixon seemed visibly worried. "It's a simple thing—if they even stopped their crazy crusade long enough to think about it. If we went to war to protect the South Vietnamese from the terror of communism, of course we would go even further to protect Americans there."

When we met the next day at his office, he was interrupted by a brief call from Kissinger, after which he replaced the receiver and threw his hands in the air. "Henry is so worried about this," he said. "What the hell. If I have to testify, I will. I'll tell them what I know, which isn't much."

"They'll be expecting a lot from you," I said.

"Goddamn it! I don't have the answers they're looking for, and neither does Henry, because we did what we said we did. They can't get blood from a stone." If forced to discuss the highly charged issue in a televised Senate hearing, he would make it clear that he had no additional information beyond what had been part of the public record since the end of the war.

On September 19, his patience with the committee's activities began to wear thin. When I walked into his office that morning, he was standing facing the window, and he whirled around when he heard the door close behind me. "I am so angry that this goddamned POW issue is bearing down on me," he said, his sense of security about it now gone. "They're only pursuing this to vindicate Clinton and his gang from abandoning their duties to this country during Vietnam, but to drag Kissinger and me through this now is unforgivable."

He turned his frustrations on the committee's chairman, Senator Kerry. "Look at the ringleader! Kerry, my God. Here's a guy who was carrying placards in front of the White House, protesting because it was his right! And there I was, trying to fight the war and end it so that all of those people who died didn't die in vain, and I had to deal with people like Kerry—and Clinton, for that matter.

"All of these people are antiwar, anti-Nixon. And now they're trying to say we weren't strong enough in trying to get the POWs back. We *did* get all of the POWs back; it was the MIAs we never got a full accounting for. I said this in my March 29 [1973] speech. Did they want us to bomb again? We barely got the December bombing through, never mind another round. And these are the people who wanted the bombing *stopped*, and they never would have put up with more economic, political, or *military* help.

"I'll tell you, I'm relieved that Haig and Kissinger are going to testify. They'll kill the committee; they'll devastate them. But I told Henry that he cannot leave *any* space between his position and mine, and he assured me that he wouldn't. To show you how Henry protects himself, though—he was strongly for the December bombing, then he backed away when we were criticized for it, then he was for it when it worked. And he claims that he came back to the White House one day before the speech; I looked in my diary, and sure enough he came back *two* days before and had Scowcroft consult with me. Now, Scowcroft didn't even blink without telling Kissinger, and that was fine, that was the way Kissinger operated. But Kissinger *did* know what the speech said, contrary to what he has said. He knew very well that I was going to go ahead with the bombing."

Two days later, as the committee's hearings were under way, Nixon exploded in fury at the testimonies of former secretaries of defense James Schlesinger and Melvin Laird. Nixon walked into his office, slammed the door behind him, and walked in a circle before speaking. "Their testimony— to the effect that we could have done more on the POW issue, insinuating that we knew more than we did—was so weak that I can't even believe it. They're out to protect themselves when there is nothing here to protect themselves against. What was there to gain by answering the questions the way they did? Hell, only to make me look bad." He raised his voice. "Very few of our goddamned people are any good. They don't stand up for us. When Haig said that I mentioned POWs *and* MIAs in that speech, Kerry said, 'True, but Nixon didn't emphasize it.' Emphasize it? What else did they expect me to do, for God's sake? I ended the war and brought home everyone we possibly could—everyone who was accounted for. My God, can you believe it?"

He shook his head. "Well, at least Haig took them on, and Kissinger is furious. He's going to kill them tomorrow. I know I can count on him."

As Nixon predicted, Kissinger's testimony before the Senate Select Committee on POW-MIA Affairs, delivered on September 22, 1992, was devastatingly effective. He quashed the committee's suggestion that not only had the Nixon administration knowingly left behind American soldiers but it could have done more to get the full accounting and return of those either held or missing in Vietnam.

"The committee . . . owes the American people a statement of the simple truth," he intoned. "Some prisoners may—I repeat *may*—have been kept behind by our adversaries in violation of solemn commitments. No prisoners were left behind by the deliberate act or negligent omission of American officials." With these facts stated unequivocally at the outset, Kissinger then delivered a stirring defense of the administration's policies.

"For not withdrawing more unconditionally, we were harassed by protesters, attacked in the media, criticized in countless congressional resolutions, and ridiculed for our concept of national honor.

"Never once did we receive any criticism from any source of the kind now emerging from this inquiry. The pressures we experienced were in the other direction—that we were not making enough concessions, that we should withdraw unilaterally in the expectation that then prisoners would be released by an act of grace of their captors."

Kissinger turned toward the immediate concerns of the committee: "The last known POWs were released on March 28 [1973]. Those who leaked that President Nixon or his advisers, in announcing that all prisoners had been released, knew that we were keeping prisoners behind disingenuously neglected to mention President Nixon's statement that 'there are still some problem areas. The provision of the agreement requiring an accounting for all missing in action in Indochina . . . [has] not been complied with. . . .' That is *all* we knew, and nothing has been produced or can be produced to indicate the contrary."

Kissinger continued with persuasive intensity: "It is the ultimate irony that our Herculean efforts to get an accounting in 1973 should be twisted twenty years later into 'evidence' that we knew POWs had been left behind.

"There is, as well, the question of what more we could have done. During this period . . . I favored military retaliation against Hanoi's repeated violations. The president felt that on balance it was better to have one more negotiating round. Certainly there was little political support in the U.S. for stronger measures."

He concluded with a defense and a challenge: "The Paris Accords contained clear and binding commitments that all prisoners throughout Indochina would be accounted for and returned. If the Vietnamese violated these provisions, it was not because of any omission by the responsible U.S. officials but because we had been stripped of the weapons we might have used to enforce that commitment.

"I am proud of what my colleagues and I accomplished under heartbreakingly difficult circumstances. I challenge critics of the accords to say precisely how they would have achieved a better outcome under those circumstances."

Kissinger's testimony effectively ended any serious effort by the committee to pursue the issue. Its failure to produce evidence contrary to Kissinger's statements and his devastating counterattack put an anticlimactic spin on its activities. If Nixon had been called, his testimony would have been identical to Kissinger's, and the committee, wary of creating scandal where it did not exist, chose not to call him. It did, however, indicate an interest in hearing select White House tapes.

Initially, Kerry's committee wanted access to Nixon's tapes to search for evidence that Nixon and/or Kissinger had concealed from the American public information about a faster release of the POWs and a fuller accounting of all those held or missing in Vietnam. The committee threatened to subpoena the relevant tapes but met with resistance from Nixon and failed to press the issue. As the possibility lingered that new tapes might be released, however, rumors circulated that the tapes contained incriminating information on this matter.

On September 26, Nixon remarked dispiritedly, "Mrs. Nixon cannot believe that I am still fighting the ridiculous committee and that awful thing they claim I said on the tapes. They're saying that on one tape I say, 'Let's leave them [the POWs] there to put Vietnam behind us.' Now Monica, I said a lot of things on those tapes, but I'd never say such a thing. A comment like that isn't on those tapes or anyplace else. The actual quote was that we were deciding on whether to do a Vietnam speech or a Watergate speech, and I decided to do one on Vietnam and get it out of the way. But they didn't use that quote in that context. You see how they are so intent on distorting my record that they make up things as they go along?"

Unlike the Watergate tapes, these tapes could not be subpoenaed because they were not part of a criminal investigation. "There are no legal grounds here to subpoena the tapes. We would win in an instant; that's why they won't press it. And I don't want to provoke a constitutional crisis." He paused. "Again."

Three days after Kissinger's appearance in front of the committee, Nixon wrote a lengthy and obstinate memorandum to his attorneys Jack Miller and Stan Mortenson regarding the tapes. After listening to the hearings, he told them that he had made two decisions: first, he would not make any tapes available to the committee, and second, he would not meet with Kerry and the minority ranking member of the committee even though former president Ford had already offered to speak with them. He thought it would be a grave mistake not only to talk to them but to turn over even a single tape, since he predicted that the committee would not be satisfied with just one and because it would set a precedent for such actions in the future.

Shades of Watergate colored his next remarks. He wrote that he had spoken to Scowcroft about "holding the line on the tapes," and since Scowcroft had participated in the conversation in question, he suggested to Nixon that the tapes fell into the category of "executive consultation," a term used to protect the privacy of papers or materials that involve not decisions but the process of reaching those decisions. The tapes, he wrote, met that standard, and Scowcroft had told him that he shared that view. Regardless of whether the National Security Council supported that position, Nixon decided to stand firm on the issue. "I went down that slippery slope 18 years ago with [special prosecutor Leon] Jaworski when time after time he told Al Haig that he would be satisfied with this or that tape or tapes. As we all know, it didn't work out that way!"

He then turned his attention to containing the issue publicly. He suggested that if the committee demanded tapes, he would indicate that the tapes were even more strongly protected by the executive-consultation formula than were his written materials. And with regard to the committee's demand for a personal interview, he would rely strongly on the "Truman precedent" to decline such an interview and would remind Ford's and Reagan's attorneys and the appropriate people in the White House and/or the Justice Department of that precedent.

Nixon shored up his own defensive posture by citing reassuring conversations. He wrote that he had spoken to both Kissinger, who had received very positive reviews of his appearance in front of the committee from other members of the Senate, and Hank Brown, a member of the committee, who told him that "we had won."

Further, Nixon indicated that Brown had said that Dole went before the committee and demanded that the senators who voted against the Dole amendment in June of 1973 be called to testify as to why they had not supported action then for a full accounting of the POWs and MIAs. Dole, he wrote, encouraged him to hold the line against the committee, which led Nixon to believe that the committee was in a weak position. Dole, he reminded his attorneys, was a "man of principle, but in an election year, he would not be so stupid as to support what he believed was a losing position." He had told Nixon by phone that he was going to take a hard line against the committee on the Senate floor and that Kerry had "raised hell" with the committee's staff for allowing him to appear.

Nixon concluded his memorandum with a parting shot. The only thing he would consider saying, he told his lawyers, was that Kissinger had the responsibility for negotiations on the MIA-POW issue, that his March 29 statement was absolutely true, and that he had nothing further to add.

Nixon would tell the committee precisely what Kissinger had already told it and in so doing destroy any chance for a news-making appearance. The Congress in 1973, the antiwar movement, and its supporters in the media had deprived Nixon and Kissinger of the means to enforce the Paris Peace Accords, including the provisions regarding the POWs and MIAs. Congress, therefore, had to bear a large share of the responsibility both for the fate of any Americans not returned by the Vietnamese and for the slaughter of over two million people by the Communist victors in Vietnam. To those who now asked why after two decades the United States was still waiting for an accounting of American soldiers from the government in Vietnam, Nixon replied that Congress, in dealing with a régime that respected only force, had put its faith in diplomacy without the power to back it up.

As the 1992 presidential election drew closer, Nixon grew even more concerned about the effect a Clinton victory might have on the legacy of Vietnam. "We haven't heard anything else from the Kerry group," he said on October 10. "But I can't imagine that they're through with me yet. You know, the media tries to have it both ways, but with this issue they just can't. They cannot claim that Vietnam is yesterday's issue in criticizing Bush for going after Clinton's draft status—or the lack of it—and then say it's *today's* issue by building up these hearings. If Bush loses, he will have erased the '72 victory, because that was a referendum on Vietnam. A Clinton victory will reverse that by saying it was OK to have been against it." He shot me a look of utter disgust. "I simply cannot accept the fact that all that I worked for, everything that we accomplished with regard to that war . . ." He paused and swept his arms over his head in a gesture of loss. "Gone with one election."

Despite the lack of promising evidence condemning Nixon, the Kerry Committee continued to press its investigation. By the end of 1992, Kerry had suggested publicly that he still might summon Nixon to testify, and Nixon remained defiant: "What the hell. I can't believe that after all this they're still at it. I'll just say that Kissinger testified and that I have nothing to add. I *don't* have anything to add. What are they going to do? They can't force me to say things I don't know. If I sit there with nothing to say, that will put an end to their questioning of me. That whole committee, with a few exceptions, are jackasses. And I know I've said this before, but very few of our people are any good. [Senators] John McCain and Hank Brown are OK;

they're smart and tough, but I don't think they grasp what this means historically for Kissinger and me. Well, McCain probably does because he suffered through the goddamned war. And Ford is the one who is really responsible for this mess. The former presidents were going to present a united front—Reagan was not going to cooperate, and neither were the others—but Ford agreed, and now we all have to go through it. Henry doesn't want to release any of the tapes for this because it opens a Pandora's box on other issues on the tapes. And we know what kind of trouble *that* can bring."

Instead of issuing subpoenas for Nixon and his White House tapes, the Kerry Committee submitted a lengthy questionnaire that covered all aspects of the POW issue. Nixon flipped through its pages, threw it back down on his desk, irritated with the time it would require, then picked it back up and examined the questions more closely. "Well, I suppose answering these things on paper is better than having to do it down there in person." He took the small tape recorder out of his desk's top drawer and tested the battery.

"Testing, testing," he muttered into the microphone. He played it back. "OK," he said, pointing the machine at the questionnaire. "I'm going to dictate the answers to these questions, though I hate like hell to give them one minute on it." He spent a day contemplating and taping his answers, then submitted them to his attorneys for evaluation.

"My lawyers told me that my answers are too harsh and that I should tone them down," he told me on December 28. "*These* answers are too brutal. Imagine! The Kerry group is torturing those poor MIA families and suggesting that a president would knowingly withhold that type of information. My God! My answers *should* be brutal. These questions are 'When are you going to stop beating your wife?' questions. Here, take a look."

He handed a copy of the questions and answers to me, pointing at the pages as he turned them over. "They are some of the most insulting questions on Vietnam I have ever seen. I took them on, especially Kerry—that SOB threw his medal over the fence at the White House. Here I was trying to end the goddamned war so that his service wouldn't be in vain, and he's throwing his medal back at me. So my replies to the questions are tough, so what?" He paused. "Well, maybe I'll soften some of them, but not the ones that matter."

He watched me peruse his answers. "And with regard to my remarks against normalization, I don't think I should take them out. I feel so strongly that we should absolutely not normalize with Vietnam until that brutal régime is gone that I intend to keep those comments in my answers. I know those libs don't want to hear it, but too bad. They need to hear what's right no matter how unpopular it is. I want my report delivered by hand to all of the good members of the Senate, not just the chairman of the committee—

he'll use it for his own purposes. It's very important to build backfires with our own people, especially Dole."

He took the questionnaire from me and scanned one of the pages for a particular answer. "Here. I originally had written that 'the Congress and the American people would not have supported increased bombing for the release of POWs,' but I changed it to just 'the Congress' because the American people *would* have supported it." He put down the questionnaire. "Anyway, they're all a bunch of bastards. They've got their headline: NIXON ADMINISTRATION DECEIVED AMERICAN PUBLIC. It's absolutely false and misleading. But it may be a blessing in disguise, because at least I have the opportunity to get out the right facts on this and nail everyone who was against the war." He smiled. "And that's really what this is all about, isn't it?"

Two days into the new year, he decided to leak his answers to the committee's questions to make them part of the public record. He also took another worried call from Kissinger.

"Apparently, he thought he devastated that committee, which he did, but they're not satisfied, and they're coming after him again," he told me. "Henry is concerned about every little nugget of this thing. While no one will read the entire report—it's over one hundred pages—reporters will read the executive summary, and he's worried that they'll play every little negative in that. I tried to give him a lift by reminding him that this is the twentieth anniversary of his message to me of the breakthrough of the Paris peace talks, when he told me that it was my birthday present. That's in *The Memoirs*. But I think about what we were doing twenty years ago, and then they bring up this business of 'Who shot John?' I'd like to preempt them by getting out our answers without building up the story too much." He shook his head. "Well, that's just a bitch."

Nixon's answers apparently silenced the committee. He heard from a source that Kerry leaked the fact that their early draft report—written before receiving Nixon's answers—suggested that Nixon was responsible for withholding information on the MIAs and POWs but that it "was overruled" by Nixon's pointed answers. "That's the way the game is played," Nixon said with some satisfaction.

The Kerry Committee report was released on January 13, 1993, to little media attention. It offered no new evidence, no hard conclusions, no smoking gun. Nixon and Kissinger were vindicated in what had essentially been an investigation in search of a nonexistent bombshell. Nixon was relieved, though not surprised, and gratified that it had attracted so little media coverage.

"*The Washington Post* will run something, but I don't give a damn," he proclaimed. "This whole thing was for nothing. Kissinger and I did everything humanly possible to get an accounting of every soldier there and then to get them home as soon as possible, and for this nothing committee to suggest otherwise is unforgivable. It shows you how deep and pervasive the anti-Vietnam feeling is; these people never give up. And then they wonder why the country hasn't healed itself."

Answering the Kerry Committee's questions left Nixon a little bitter and very disappointed. The POW issue was symptomatic of the rifts remaining, not only from our military involvement in Vietnam but from the resulting political agendas. Nixon knew that he would always be a target for those who opposed the war. Legitimate debates over his policies were reasonable; witch-hunts with no credible basis were not. In Nixon's view, the Kerry Committee crossed the line of reason. Hoping to uncover some sinister plot by the president to endanger the lives of those being held in Vietnam, it invited speculation that Nixon had done yet another grave disservice to the country, even though the committee did not have the evidence to prove it.

In late 1992, Nixon gave me a copy of a recent poll showing that 60 percent of respondents stated that they believed that American involvement in Vietnam was wrong. Nixon grimaced. "The goddamned media did this. They never let up on the Vietnam thing. Every year you see some new story, some new twist on the 'Vietnam was wrong' theme. It's relentless, so when you consider this poll, can we realistically expect any more?"

Nixon had answered his own question. Anti-Vietnam sentiment and the attendant cultural transformation were so much a part of the American experience that a complete reversal of them was not a realistic expectation. Nixon could only hope that the passage of time would dilute the values and cynicism that Vietnam had inaugurated. The war abroad had ended, but the social and cultural vestiges at home were longer lasting and more widespread. The military war, Nixon said, took place on the battlefield; the cultural war took place in the deeper recesses of American society. Presidents could not reverse it. Another war could not reverse it. Prosperity could not reverse it. Vietnam would linger as long as the values it spawned flourished. For Nixon, this was one of the war's greatest tragedies.

As the years passed, some of the storms blowing around the Vietnam issues subsided while others grew in intensity. Until 1991, the United States remained completely closed off diplomatically from the Vietnamese régime. As the potential for limited free-market economic growth increased in Vietnam, however, the Bush administration began to reevaluate the diplomatic position. In late 1991, Nixon was notified that the administration was studying the question.

"This is not the time," he remarked. "There is no compelling reason to extend recognition until they change their system. Let communism die in Vietnam without American interference. We have a tragic war history there. We lost tens of thousands of soldiers there. Recognize the brutal régime that claimed so many of our people? What are we talking about? Morally and politically, it's just not right."

Those who argued for recognition emphasized the evolution of Vietnam from an isolated Communist enemy to a more economically open and less ideologically hostile state eager to escape the past. They contended that the reasons for American animosity had been eliminated: capitalist Southeast Asia was economically strong and confident while Communist Indochina was weak and divided; the collapse of European communism and the disintegration of the Soviet Union made the United States victorious in the cold war; Vietnam had withdrawn almost all of its occupying troops from Cambodia in 1989; and the Vietnamese had struck a deal with China that made peace a possibility in Cambodia.

Those who advocated recognition acknowledged that Vietnam's government remained Communist even as it carried out sporadic and incomplete economic reforms. Centuries of Vietnamese hostility toward its neighbors would not be forgotten easily. But, they argued, since the United States did not bar its citizens from doing business with régimes ideologically similar to Vietnam's (such as China's) and maintained diplomatic relations with more threatening régimes (such as Iraq's immediately after the invasion of Kuwait), Vietnam offered a diplomatic opportunity, particularly since it was being tempted by the freedom and prosperity enjoyed by the rest of Southeast Asia. A relationship between the United States and Vietnam promised hope since American aid, trade, culture, and science and technology could play a decisive role in supporting the Vietnamese liberals striving to lift their nation out of poverty and free it from repression. This was the time, they argued, for America to show magnanimity by recognizing Vietnam.

Nixon disagreed vehemently with this line of reasoning. Normalizing ties with Vietnam was contrary to almost twenty years of principled policy in dealing with the former enemy. When Assistant Secretary of State Richard Soloman announced in early 1992 that if Vietnam cooperated with POW and MIA investigations, the United States might agree to normalize relations within two years, Nixon was outraged. If American interests were meant to foster a more peaceful world based on a community of stable, open, democratic nations, then Vietnam presented a case in which the Asian tradition of patience would serve the United States better than a rush to normalize relations.

"I can't think of any reason to recognize Vietnam now," Nixon said on October 24, 1992, "other than to enshrine the paranoia and remorse of the Vietnam generation as official U.S. policy toward Vietnam and the war forever."

His fear that the administration would move forward with plans to recognize the former enemy was expressed in an essay he prepared for placement on one of the nation's top op-ed pages. He wrote it during the first days of January 1992 and was committed to its publication: "We have to get the damn thing in print." It did not, however, get to print. Nixon pulled the piece after considering the potential political consequences of its publication.

"The train may have left the station on this issue," he said on January 11. "I'm not sure I want to waste any political capital I may have with Bush by going after him on this. Let's sit on it awhile and see what develops."

The piece was the capstone of Nixon's views on Vietnam to that point; his decision not to publish it represented the beginning of a pragmatic evolution in his thinking. Whereas his new views on Vietnam had begun to take shape, the article was the last expression of his old opinions.

"As communism gasped its last breath in the former evil empire," he wrote in "Don't Aid Hanoi," "the West has moved toward adopting policies that will help keep it alive in Vietnam. This is an appalling development."

The most potent arguments of those who wanted recognition were that granting diplomatic recognition would foster economic and political reform in Vietnam and that the United States would lose trade and investment opportunities to Japan and Europe if we hesitated to establish new relations. Nixon immediately denounced these arguments as strategically unsound and morally flawed.

It was common practice for Western nations, particularly the United States, to withhold diplomatic recognition as a means to condemn the legitimacy of aggressive or repressive régimes, unless such a policy harmed Western strategic interests. In the case of Vietnam, he wrote, no interest of the United States or the Vietnamese people would be served by granting the appearance of legitimacy to the "international outlaws" in Hanoi, who had imposed a brutal reign of terror on South Vietnam after their conquest in 1975.

Since Vietnamese officials acknowledged that they had no intention of liberalizing the political system, refugee traffic was still "all one-way: None wants to go back, and thousands are willing to risk death to get out."

He then hit upon the hot-button political issue in the United States. The Vietnamese, he said, had been "cynically obstructionist" in resolving the cases of the 2,273 Americans listed as missing in action in the Vietnam War. Western intelligence services knew that Hanoi had more information about many MIAs who died than it revealed to American officials. Instead of releasing all of the information, Hanoi engaged in a "cruel and macabre exercise" of telling what it knew about the remains of our servicemen bit by bit every few years.

Hanoi's régime did not deserve recognition as a member in good standing of the community of nations. If we recognized and provided economic aid to the Communist hard-liners in Hanoi, we would "break faith" not only with the South Vietnamese who fought against them but with the millions of Americans who had served loyally in Vietnam.

He drew the popular parallel to China and then destroyed the analogy: those who argued that it was inconsistent to maintain relations with China after Tiananmen Square while isolating Vietnam were wrong. China was a major power whose actions affected American interests around the world, but Vietnam was not. China was a nuclear power, but Vietnam was not. China's Communist Party had a major faction, led in the past by Hu Yaobang and Zhao Ziyang, that supported political liberalization, but Vietnam's did not. Only in China was continued engagement the best strategy for fostering reform through peaceful change.

He closed the piece with a powerful argument rooted in national interest. Since our greatest leverage in dealing with Vietnam was a normalization of relations and the economic benefits that would flow from it, we should make our conditions for it clear. If we did not get something for it up front—such as free elections in Laos, the demilitarization of Vietnam's economy, the end to the persecution of former South Vietnamese officials, and a start to political reform in Vietnam—we would never get such concessions out of Hanoi in the future. And if the Vietnamese refused to compromise, it would not be in our interest to "throw a life-line to the flotsam of the wreck of the Soviet empire."

Nixon wanted to pursue a policy of enlightened patience: rather than provide aid that would refurbish Vietnam's creaking legacy of Ho Chi Minh, the West would better serve the people of Vietnam by waiting until communism collapsed there under its own weight. A decision to normalize relations prematurely with a fundamentally unreformed Communist Hanoi would postpone the day when political liberty and economic freedom did return to Vietnam. The point of recognition now was not to protect American foreign policy interests, as many of its supporters claimed. Instead, it was to gratify a segment of U.S. opinion by formalizing acceptance of the American failure in Vietnam. This meant indirect endorsement of the actions of Vietnam dissenters and nonservers who claimed that the war was wrong and futile. For Nixon, waiting for a non-Communist Vietnam to emerge was the most prudent and moral of all strategies.

This passionate defense of the status quo policy toward Vietnam never went to press because Nixon began to replace his visceral opposition to recognition with a qualified acceptance of it. If the train had "already left the station" on recognizing Vietnam, Nixon intended to be on board.

When Patrick Buchanan announced his candidacy for president several weeks later, Nixon considered using him as a mouthpiece on the issue.

"Buchanan is a bulldog; he'll go after them. But when you get the word to him," he instructed me on February 22, "be sure that he goes after Baker and not Bush. Let Buchanan smoke the issue out." Like the op-ed before it, however, the plan to use Buchanan did not come about. Nixon realized that he could not rely on others to spread his message, particularly on Vietnam. If he opposed recognition, he would have to be the one to voice that opposition, which he was not prepared to do.

By December of that year, Nixon believed that Bush intended to recognize Vietnam in order to prevent the new president from capturing the issue for himself. Both Nixon and Bush were convinced that Clinton wanted to bring closure to the Vietnam issue—and his own activities during the war—by being the first president to go to Hanoi under normalized diplomatic conditions.

"Scandalous," Nixon spit out on December 16. "I almost lost my breakfast when I saw that Bush is allowing business contacts with Vietnam instead of letting Clinton handle it. He has totally lost me on this. I know he doesn't want Clinton to get the credit, but come *on*. Clinton is a disgrace on the whole Vietnam thing. Let him take the heat and talk to the Vietnam veterans groups who oppose it. What about the fact that they suppress half of their people—the South Vietnamese—and treat them like second-class citizens? No, Bush is making a huge mistake."

Nixon's frustration with Bush's decision to move toward recognizing Vietnam spilled over into complete disgust when Clinton made clear his similar intentions. On February 1, Nixon had lunch in Washington with Dole and a small group of freshman senators, after which he told me that he "hit against normalization with Vietnam hard; there is no way we should even consider such a thing until they quit abusing human rights and reform their government. Clinton is for it. He's just panting to go to Hanoi and walk through the streets, where he'll be welcomed by millions of Vietnamese." He grimaced. "Imagine! The ultimate Vietnam War draft dodger recognizing Vietnam. Unbelievable." And several months later, still obsessed with Clinton's intentions, he proclaimed, "Maybe we're wrong not to say anything. Maybe we should go public and lay down a marker not to recognize. Regardless of what these other clowns say, Vietnam has *not* come clean on the POWs, and now all of a sudden it wants to? They're only doing now what they should have done twenty years ago. We might consider putting something out on this issue, but on the other hand maybe it's best to let Clinton go ahead and then hit him with it."

Nixon's vacillation was revealing. Despite his long-standing resistance to recognizing a repressive régime in Vietnam, he had already begun to be persuaded by elements of the China analogy. For years, he had argued that although the best way for the United States to encourage political and economic reform in China was through direct contact between peoples and governments, the best way to stir reform in Vietnam was to ignore it and allow communism to perish on its own. For Nixon, the dichotomy was pragmatic. China could not be ignored despite ideological differences; Vietnam had to be for those same differences. By late 1993, however, Nixon had completely reversed his thinking.

His new book, *Beyond Peace,* was nearing completion, and he was relatively satisfied with the manuscript. He felt, however, that it did not contain the kind of groundbreaking, unexpected arguments that had distinguished his previous books, and he intended to include at least one. After careful consideration, he settled on his bombshell for *Beyond Peace:* support for the eventual normalization of relations with Vietnam. "It was frankly difficult for me to do," he said on January 15, 1994, as he worked on drafts of the passage, "but it must be done. It will be a surprise to all those who know me, but it's a brilliant formulation."

The formulation that appeared in the book drew parallels to and distinctions between Vietnam, Cuba, and North Korea. Nixon used the three cases to make his "surprise" point about Vietnam:

> Of the three remaining communist states (apart from China), North Korea remains a serious, active threat, not only to South Korea but to the peace and security of the entire Pacific Rim. . . . Until it ceases to be a threat, we should continue to treat it as the pariah nation that its leaders still persist in making it.
>
> Vietnam and Cuba are like North Korea in that both are still run by repressive communist regimes. Between the two there are dramatic differences. But neither presents an active threat to the peace internationally.

In the cases of Cuba and Vietnam, the question of how best to serve the national interest, the interests of the people of those countries, and the interest of the world community had been reduced to a simple decision: keep them isolated, or invite them to rejoin the world.

Nixon used the China example to advocate resuming relations with both. "Of the two," he wrote,

> Vietnam presents the easier choice. . . . Increasing economic integration with the world brings greater economic freedoms, and economic freedoms build powerful internal pressure for political freedoms.
>
> We should start by separating the question of our political relationship with Vietnam from that of our economic relationship, letting each develop at its own pace. Even if we are totally satisfied that the Vietnamese

government has done all it can to account for Americans missing in action in the Vietnam war, we should keep the political relationship in a deep freeze as long as Hanoi continues to treat as second-class citizens the millions of South Vietnamese who were our allies in the war.

This was the hard-line basis for the next advice:

> We should follow the administration's decision to lift the trade embargo with vigorous efforts to encourage investment in Vietnam and draw it further into the global economy, not to help the present Vietnamese regime but to strengthen the forces of change.

Dropping the embargo and opening the way to trade, investment, and economic interaction while ensuring that ideas and information flowed as freely as the goods was the best way to promote political change in Vietnam and, similarly, Cuba. Rather than reflect a permanent change in his view, Nixon's advocacy of the open door was about setting the tone of the upcoming policy decisions on Vietnam. Lifting the embargo was still anathema to him, but the time had come to show that he was willing to put the war behind him. He did it not to vindicate Clinton and others who opposed the war but to offer a line of reasoning that would dilute the impact of the inevitable.

The irony of Nixon as the president who prosecuted the final years of the Vietnam War extended to the irony of Nixon as the former president who grudgingly supported normalizing relations with the old enemy. The struggles between principle and pragmatism, ideology and policy, and idealism and politics were found not only in the debate over America's evolving policy with Vietnam but in Nixon's own approach to the Communist adversaries he had built his career trying to bring down. When it became apparent that the Bush and Clinton administrations intended to recognize Vietnam, Nixon decided that since he could not beat them, he would join them, even if the idea were repellent to him. The polarizing effects of Vietnam had done enough damage.

"Everything that was wrong with the Vietnam generation can be summed up in the Katherine Anne Power case," he said on October 7, 1993, referring to the woman who, as part of a small cabal of antiwar thugs, had robbed a bank and shot and killed a police officer, a father of nine, in 1970. Following the murder, she became a fugitive and avoided trial for twenty years by assuming a false identity. In late 1993, however, Power came forward and offered herself up for justice, leading many sympathetic commentators to reflect on the psychological trauma the former flower child suffered. Nixon was revolted.

"This was one of the most disgusting events of that whole era," he said. "This woman was not some little misguided thing running around one afternoon with a bunch of rabble-rousers who spontaneously decided to rob a bank. She had a goddamned arsenal in her apartment—rifles, pistols, shotguns." He jabbed at the air with his forefinger. "She knew *exactly* what she was doing; any suggestion to the contrary is a lie. She firebombed a national guard armory and had a history of lawbreaking that would condemn anybody else. She set out to stir things up—and violently. She didn't care whom she hurt or killed or what she did to help rip apart this country. 'Everybody was doing it' doesn't cut it as an excuse, particularly in the Vietnam era. She epitomizes selfishness. There she was," he continued emotionally, "claiming a moral high road against the government during the war as she shot and killed a man who tried to stop her from wreaking more havoc. And only now, after twenty years of living with herself, she has a crisis of conscience? Please."

When I mentioned that, like the main character in Dostoyevsky's *Crime and Punishment,* her conscience had become her prison, he replied bitterly, "Good. I hope she hates herself."

For Nixon, blaming society rather than the criminal was one of the most insidious consequences of the '60s. The sympathy for Power expressed by many in the media rivaled that for her victim, prompting Nixon to include a scathing passage about the case in *Beyond Peace.* "Our understanding of those who demonstrated against the war should not lead us to excuse those who resorted to violence," he wrote. "In opposing war against an enemy abroad, these people waged war against innocent people at home." Enough excuses had been made for the Vietnam generation. Nixon wanted fair play, even twenty years later.

His search for justice on the Vietnam issue grew out of a need to turn back the effects of the cultural revolution it had spawned. The war was over, but the effects roared forth. In his books, speeches, interviews, and essays, he railed against the immoral behaviors and attitudes, the self-righteousness and selfishness, the greed and indulgence, of the Vietnam era. He argued for the wholesale restoration of modesty, self-reliance, self-denial, magnanimity, and obedience to law and God. Whatever credibility he maintained after his presidency he applied to achieving that objective. Repairing America's damaged cultural fabric was as much a part of his post-presidential mission as was contributing to the foreign policy debates of his time.

In the end, however, Nixon hoped that the war might yet be seen as just a chapter in the story of Southeast Asia's adoption of a free-market philosophy and political liberties. A free Vietnam would finish the post-Vietnam debate in the United States by vindicating the military engagement and those who stood for the traditional values assaulted by the protest movements.

Nixon could only work toward restoring some of the cultural principles lost in Vietnam. It was ironic, as he said, that the president who presided over the last years of the war also tried to recover some of the values destroyed by it. That Nixon, the self-described square and the only president to resign, would continue to rage against the cultural, social, and political effects of Vietnam struck his supporters as noble and his detractors as laughable. *He* considered his efforts obligatory. He saw his mission as a sincere attempt to stop the moral hemorrhaging brought on by both Vietnam and Watergate. "Vietnam and Watergate are with me forever," he said on September 14, 1993. "I can't erase them, but I can try to turn back what they brought on."

His post-presidential years were devoted to trying to correct the effects of those two events. On Watergate he could only defend himself. On Vietnam, however, he waged an aggressive and active battle against the values the war had inaugurated. The survival and proliferation of those values depended on the silence of those who disagreed with them. The United States had to accept the victory of the north in Vietnam. It did not have to accept the victory of the countercultural values at home. For Nixon, any success in reversing that revolution would be one of the more positive legacies of Vietnam.

# PART III

SCANDAL

# CHAPTER 1

# WATERGATE

In the early-morning hours of June 17, 1972, President Richard Nixon slept soundly on Grand Cay, a small island in the Bahamas owned by his good friend Robert Abplanalp. One thousand miles away, in Washington D.C., five men were arrested for burglarizing the Democratic National Committee headquarters at the Watergate complex, and one of them, James McCord, identified himself as the chief of security for Nixon's reelection committee.

The president awoke on that Saturday morning oblivious to the criminal machinations in Washington. After talking with Chief of Staff H. R. Haldeman by telephone for several minutes about supporting federal aid to parochial schools and finding a way to contact the traveling Treasury Secretary John Connally, he spent the day boating with Abplanalp and another close friend, Bebe Rebozo.

On Sunday morning, June 18, Nixon picked up a copy of *The Miami Herald* that lay on the kitchen counter of his house in Key Biscayne, Florida. Under the main headline, about troop withdrawals from Vietnam, he saw a small story in the middle of the page about the arrests at the Watergate complex. He scanned the opening paragraphs, dismissed the escapade as "preposterous," left the paper on the counter, and went for a swim.

That evening, he picked up a copy of the last volume of Winston Churchill's World War II series. Though Nixon did not know it at the time, he held in his hands a book whose title would become the bittersweet theme of his political career: *Triumph and Tragedy*. The events of June 17 and those of the next two years put a devastating twist on a uniquely American story,

begun in the poverty-stricken citrus groves in California and seemingly finished on the South Lawn of the White House on a hot day in August 1974.
   With one eye on the future and another on history, Nixon infused his
presidency with visionary realism, and he used that realism to launch far-
reaching domestic and foreign policy initiatives. As he discovered, however,
triumphs are often scarred by unfortunate events and unintended consequences. When those who achieve great things fall, their lives take on another dimension. The drama of accomplishment is matched by the drama of
defeat; the potential for greatness is dashed by the reality of self-destruction;
and the promise of historical acclaim is drowned out by the inescapable
drumbeat of historical condemnation.
   Nixon prided himself on being a fighter, an unapologetic believer in personal and political resurrection, and a master of the isolating climb back to
respectability. After news of Watergate first became public, Clare Boothe
Luce handed Nixon a copy of Saint Barton's ode: "I am hurt but I am not
slain! I will lie me down and bleed awhile—then I'll rise and fight again." It
became his mantra until his role in covering up the nation's most infamous
"third-rate burglary" forced him to resign the presidency. He knew then that
he was slain politically and that the triumphs of his career might never be
viewed in their own right but only as part of the tragedy of a flawed presidency. Victory became inseparable from defeat, and Nixon, once a towering
symbol of personal pride and political talent, would be forever seen as a man
broken by his own misguided ambition.
   As he reached for the mantle of greatness, he slipped and fell as fast and
as hard as any legendary tragic figure. Despite his formidable post-
presidential accomplishments, Watergate defined him in a way that nothing
else could; it disappointed his supporters, heartened his adversaries, and
painted him as a fundamentally illegitimate force in American politics. That
Nixon himself gave his enemies the ammunition with which to destroy him
made the entire episode even more unbearable—for Nixon and for a country weary of self-defeating engagements abroad and divided by a counterculture offensive at home. A self-made political force, Nixon was ravaged by
an epic tragedy, partly of his own making and partly the result of a national
upheaval so sweeping and powerful that it toppled the institutions and people that stood in its way.
   Ultimately, however, Nixon emerged battered but not slain. After leaving
office, he retreated to California to write his memoirs, then began the slow,
deliberate process of rehabilitating himself. He delivered a major address to
the Oxford Union in 1978 and wrote the best-selling book *The Real War* in
1980. Step by step, book by book, speech by speech, he began the comeback.
It was a miraculous achievement considering the depths to which he had

fallen and even more triumphant in its scope and effect than he ever anticipated. He could not control what others said or did regarding Watergate, but
he could control how he handled it. Instead of "wallowing in Watergate," as
he said, he turned his attention to the issues of the day; instead of dwelling
on the past, he focused on the future. He knew, however, that it was the way
in which he handled the future that would determine how others would
view his past.

Although he had tried to set aside the effects of Watergate, by the end of
his life he realized that they would be part of his political character forever.
Rather than bury the scandal completely in his own mind, he wrestled with
it, tried to understand it and come to terms with its inevitable historical impact. For Nixon, Watergate was both an external demon of others' judgments and an internal one of torment and anguish, regret and defiance, the
experience of triumph and tragedy. Just as his political career had been a
complex web of brilliance and folly, his final thoughts on Watergate wavered
between insightful understanding and defensive dismissal of the affair. Perhaps he was protecting himself from its brutal verdict, or perhaps he was
simply trying to convince himself that the spectacle was finally over.

When I began working for Nixon in 1990, I did not expect to discuss Watergate with him. I was hired as a foreign policy and research assistant and
intended to keep my discussions with him limited to foreign and domestic
policy. I discovered quickly, however, that while he was not comfortable talking about Watergate, he felt a need to discuss it, to explain his side of the
story, to recite it before a member of a generation that did not hold Watergate as an active memory, and to get his first indication of how the next generations would perceive him and his presidency. Surprisingly neither bitter
nor forgiving, Nixon shared with me many thoughts about the scandals he
had either endured or observed.

Unlike our discussions of other subjects, which were often scattered over
many days, our discussions of Watergate were few but lengthy. His resistance to the topic was overcome by his need to review it one more time, as if
he could will it to a happy ending. Watergate did not lend itself to stray
comments; when he chose to discuss it, it got his full and serious attention.
Nixon did not recoil from the opportunity to talk candidly about Watergate
but was curious to hear how the next generation of historians might view it.
It was an unusual position for Nixon: typically, he issued judgments of
others' mistakes and accomplishments, but when discussing Watergate, he
could not escape his own judgment, the prison of his own regret, or the
ghosts of his past.

"You read *In the Arena*," he said to me on September 14, 1990. "Do you
think I spent too much time in it talking about Watergate?" The question

hung in the air, weighted down by its significance as his first comment to me about the scandal. He continued, "I didn't want to spend any time in that book talking about it, but because it was billed as my most personal memoir, I had to say something. Once I started on it, though, I had to go full speed ahead and just say everything that needed to be said. The reason I asked you if I spent too much time on it was because that's all the press focused on. None of the other stuff in there, like on the Russians or the other personal stuff, made it into the news or even the reviews. Watergate—that's all anyone wants. Almost twenty years of Watergate is enough. I shouldn't have fed into it with this book, but I guess I had no choice."

Watergate had created another trap for him: if he had written a memoir that did not address it adequately, he would have been criticized for denying the scandal, his role in it, or its effects on the country; if he had written one that confronted those issues directly, he would have been criticized for offering inevitably self-justifying explanations. He was torn between wanting to tell his story and wanting to avoid revisiting the entire episode. Ultimately, he devoted a large segment of *In the Arena* to Watergate, because he decided that it was better to tell the story himself than to leave it for others to re-tread. Again, he went on the record as the last best witness for the defense.

A good scandal deserves a good villain, and Nixon believed that he could strip Watergate of a chief executive possessed by dark furies and deprive the scandal itself of some of its historical significance if he addressed the issue as objectively as he could.

"I wrote *In the Arena* because I thought it would do some good," he said on January 3, 1991. We were sitting in his office talking about the situation in the Persian Gulf when he turned the conversation to Watergate. Propping his feet up on the ottoman, he continued, "You know, I thought it would be good to get my side out. But if I were doing it again, I would not include the Watergate crap because it's all the reviewers concentrated on, and they neglected everything else. You agree?"

This time he let me answer. "They did focus almost exclusively on it, although you understand why they did it," I said, and he shrugged in agreement and asked if I thought the book should have focused so intently on the scandal.

When I told him that he needed to relate his side of the Watergate story, he sighed. "I know, which is why I did it, but I'll tell you something: I hate like hell to keep talking about the goddamned mess. It was a mistake. I took responsibility for it, I apologized for it, and I'll always pay the price. Of course, the press has an interest in not letting anyone—particularly themselves—forget about it because it was their story, their creation."

He paused and looked right at me. "No, that's not right. It was partly their creation, but mostly my own. It took me a long time to accept the fact that what happened was my fault; I could blame the press and [White House counsel John] Dean and [special prosecutor Archibald] Cox and whomever, but the bottom line is that I brought it on myself." He swallowed. "I knew that I was a target. I had been a target ever since Alger Hiss, because during that case I did the worst thing that you can do to the press: prove that they were wrong. They were wrong to stand up for Hiss, this smooth establishment guy who also happened to be a Communist spy. I proved the case against him, and there he went, off to jail. But he was one of their own, and they never forgave me.

"So look, I knew that they were out there ready to pounce. And my mistake was giving them the reason to come after me."

"Do you mean you should have been more careful?" I asked.

"Right," he replied. "I should have been more careful."

"Careful in terms of not getting caught," I said, "or in terms of not doing anything wrong in the first place?"

He stared at me for a few long moments. "No, I mean that I should have been more careful about not doing anything wrong or even give the appearance of anything wrong. Look, I never wanted to accept the fact that there is a double standard out there: Democrats survive by it, Republicans get killed by it. Kennedy could be as dirty as they come—and my God! He did some outrageous things in there! But he was protected. Johnson—same thing, although to a lesser degree because he wasn't Kennedy. Somehow I made the mistake of thinking or maybe not even thinking—maybe it was an unconscious thing—that I could act like them."

When I said that he had assumed that "politics was politics," he replied, "Well, that's what I thought, but it wasn't that way. There are standards for Democrats, standards for Republicans; then there were standards for me. I was in a totally different category. The press didn't trust me after Hiss, and they were just out there circling and waiting. I should have known that I was somebody who couldn't even sneeze in the goddamned White House without having somebody order an investigation. So to that extent, I was stupid."

When I asked if he made a mistake by taping his conversations, he replied, "Yes and no. No, since almost every president since FDR taped at least some, and Kennedy and Johnson were the worst, but yes since they didn't turn out to be what I wanted them to be."

"Which was?"

"My own record of my presidency, like the others' [tapes], and not what they turned out to be," he replied.

I asked him if he ever forgot that the tapes were running, and he looked at me, rolling his pen between his fingers. "Well, you know, I'd go in there and start talking with Haldeman or Ehrlichman or Kissinger or whomever, and we'd be talking about something, and the tapes were the furthest thing from my mind. Johnson told me to save every scrap of paper related to the presidency, and when he showed me the recorders, why, I thought they'd be useful for historical purposes." He smiled. "And I guess they were!"

That early conversation revealed several important points. Nixon acknowledged his own culpability in the affair and his own hand in the destruction of his presidency. He recognized that he had been a special case, not subject to the same rules that had been applied to his predecessors but held to a different standard by a distrusting press and an army of enemies. Instead of accepting the double standard and holding himself to a higher standard, he took for granted that he would be given the same protection as those who had come before him. Rather than serving as personal recollections, his taped conversations were turned against him, his own words becoming the source of his undoing. Therein was the tragedy and the sad irony: the defendant became his own executioner.

The tapes haunted him for the rest of his life. He spent the twenty years from his resignation to his death fighting the public release of the thousands of remaining hours of his taped conversations. Many of the discussions related to Watergate had been made public as part of the criminal investigation, but Nixon believed that, like other presidents, he had a right to maintain the privacy of his other material. Again, he was misled by his belief that he would be protected as his predecessors had been. Despite his efforts to keep the rest of the conversations private, the National Archives continued to make public additional hours of the tapes, leading to a chronic revisiting of Watergate in the headlines.

"I guess some additional Watergate tapes come out tomorrow," he said on June 3, 1991. "I think it's tomorrow, anyway. I don't know if people are interested in that anymore. Maybe they are. No, the press still is, so they force the public to be. But you know, for every remark that I probably shouldn't have made, there are hundreds that are good and positive and show what we were up against and what we were trying to do. But does the press show those? No. Do they even put the questionable remarks in context? No. Or do they even show that a few sentences later I take it all back? No." He paused. "Watch and see what the coverage is."

Four days later, when he returned from a brief trip to Florida, he summoned me to his office. As I sat down, he smiled and asked, "So what's your view on the release of the tapes?"

I told him that I was relieved that the piece he wrote for *The Washington Post* on Russia had been published that week rather than the next week, since it preempted the news of the release.

"If they want to wallow in Watergate, let them! I know. Not much we can do. Don't get discouraged. Don't lose your enthusiasm," he said, as if to convince himself. "Every once in a while, there'll be a new orgy over the tapes, when they release more."

"Just because it happens occasionally doesn't mean it's any easier for you," I said. "Or for any of us around you."

He pursed his lips. "You are really bothered by this?"

When I offered to write some letters to various newspapers in his defense, he shook his head and appeared to blink away some tears. "I admire your guts and your youthful enthusiasm," he said, "but the damage has been done. The words are there, and that's it. We can defend it to a certain degree, but you know what I mean. Some of it just can't be defended, other than to hear the entire conversations in context.

"I'll tell you, and this may seem like a minor thing compared to some of the other things on the tapes, but the criticism about my coarse language bothers me, and it bothers Mrs. Nixon. If you could have spent five minutes with Johnson or Kennedy, your ears would've curled. All presidents swear, and everyone acted like I was the first one."

"That's because we can hear you doing it, but we can't hear the others," I said.

"I know," he replied. "But it bothers Mrs. Nixon because I don't use that kind of language with her. I don't use it with you . . ." He stopped. "Well, maybe sometimes. But the point is that the pressures of that time were unbearable. I don't know how Mrs. Nixon took it. It was so hard on the family."

When I asked him how he survived that period, he answered, "It was because of them you know—Mrs. Nixon, Julie, Tricia, and David [Eisenhower] and Ed [Cox]. They were so strong, even when everything was coming apart. They stood by me, and never once did they complain about how it was affecting them, and it devastated them. Not once did they let me see them shaken, because they knew that if they let me see that, then I'd break down. They were so unselfish. And to not fight back! I could see that they wanted to get out there and defend me, to turn back the lies and distortions, to let the bastards have it. But they couldn't, of course, and so they just took it. Day in and day out, they took it. I don't know how, but they did."

He straightened himself in his chair. "Not taking anything away from the others, but I don't think any of them could have taken what I did. For two years, every news story and broadcast began with Watergate. Every day, day in, day out. I didn't read them—I knew what was going on—I only read the summaries. But wasn't that something?"

I told him that the contributions he had made to American foreign and domestic policy since leaving office ensured that his career would be judged beyond the trauma of Watergate.

He cleared his throat. "I hope you're right. You can't just lay down and die when this kind of thing happens. I pledged to fight back long ago, when anybody else would have packed it in. But I was never a quitter. As I said in my resignation speech, quitting before my time was up went against everything I believed in and everything I was taught. So I had to quit then, but I resolved after that that it would be the last time. It may have seemed fatal, but I wasn't going to allow it to be. I couldn't control what people said about me or about what happened, but I could control what I did with the rest of my life. Whenever these things come up, like more tapes or whatever, those who are anti-Nixon are going to stay that way. Those who are pro will stay that way. It's those in between who get swayed.

"Those who were after me during Watergate were after me for a long time. They weren't interested in Watergate as much as they were interested in getting me on Hiss and on Vietnam. I gave them what they needed, but believe me, Watergate was just the excuse."

"Are you saying that if it weren't Watergate it would have been something else?" I asked.

He shrugged. "That's my theory."

His theory was that since he had been surrounded by enemies on his right and on his left—those who opposed his anti-communism, his exposure of Alger Hiss, his policies for a "peace with honor" in Vietnam, détente with the Soviet Union, and rapprochement with China, and his very rise to national power—his destruction was almost inevitable. Those who considered him a toxic force in American politics sought to prosecute him as aggressively as he had prosecuted Hiss. For Nixon, Watergate surrendered the hidden consequence of the Hiss case: that as a force immune to the intellectual viruses of the left, he had to be brought down.

On July 1, as we sat in his office at his residence, I told him that I intended to read the newly published book *Silent Coup* by investigator Len Colodny and journalist Robert Gettlin. In their explosive new history of the Watergate affair, they argued that the true target of the break-in was not Lawrence O'Brien, the chairman of the Democratic National Committee, but a high-priced prostitution service being run by the Democrats for out-of-town male visitors. They contended that the break-in at the Watergate complex was ordered by White House counsel John Dean not for political purposes but in an attempt to locate information about any connection his wife, Maureen, may have had to the call-girl ring.

The credibility of the authors lent power to their arguments. Both came out of the political left, and neither had an interest in exonerating Nixon. They claimed that they began the project not to clear Nixon but to get to previously unknown or uninvestigated truths about the origins of the break-in, the cover-up, and the circumstances surrounding his decision to resign. After an exhaustive examination of the case, they concluded that Nixon unwittingly became a player in a scheme that escaped the control of the original mastermind. His destruction, they maintained, was an unintended consequence of his own foolish impatience and almost pathological need for control. Rather than excuse Watergate, Colodny and Gettlin set it in perspective by showing that it was the result of a convergence of many forces—forces much larger than any of the principals involved.

This idea supported some of Nixon's own theories about Watergate. During the early 1970s, Washington was a place of great tumult; the streets were filled with intrigue, emotion, fear, and hundreds of thousands of anti-Vietnam protesters. A master of formal, old-time politics, Nixon was an anachronism in an era in which political guerrilla warfare was being waged against him. He was the first president since Lincoln to face a sustained, organized, and relentless opposition to a war. And by the time Nixon inherited the disastrous situation in Vietnam from his predecessor, veterans were throwing their medals back at the White House and confidential secrets were being spirited out of the Pentagon. It was a national convulsion, and Nixon, ill-equipped to manage it, turned to methods such as wiretapping and IRS audits that, although routinely used by other presidents for over thirty years, suddenly became objectionable.

Spiraling out of control with political and social hysteria, the country was primed for a purge, and Nixon, with his own help, was overthrown in a frenzy of collective madness.

"Despite what most people think," he said, "I still don't know everything about the case. Never did. People seem to think that I was plotting everything. I tell you, when I first heard about the break-in, I thought, 'My God! Who would do such a stupid, idiotic thing?' But I really didn't think anything of it in terms of its affecting *me*, not right away anyway. I didn't order the goddamned thing. I didn't know anybody involved. And I didn't know that any of my people knew the people involved. I didn't know a goddamned thing until people started telling me things.

"Not only did I have very limited information about the break-in after it occurred, I had limited information the entire time, and I was working from all kinds of misleading information from everybody else. Dean would come in and tell me one thing, Haldeman another, Ehrlichman another, and Haig something else. I'd make decisions based on what they were telling me, but they all had their own agendas and their own asses to protect. So imagine— I was in the middle of it, not knowing half the things that were going on. I knew what they told me, and I could deduce some things from that, but it was just a mess."

Waving his hand in the air, he continued. "Well, despite the fact that they were all running around in the midst of Watergate, we had quite a gang then. Most of them meant well, anyway. We all did. Made some mistakes, tried to defuse something that should never have happened in the first place." He stopped. "Rose [Mary Woods, Nixon's longtime secretary] wasn't interviewed for this book, was she? She never liked Haig and didn't particularly like Henry either. They were so involved with their own power that they really didn't take the time to be nice. But say whatever you want about my people—and they did make mistakes—but they were pros. Kissinger and Haig—top of the line in their fields. Haldeman—the best goddamned chief of staff I have ever seen. Ehrlichman—tough as nails. [Charles] Colson—loyal to the gut.

"Every president needs people who can say no, who can fight the battles but who can also tell the president the truth, as hard as that may be. These guys were so loyal that maybe they didn't want to tell me everything they knew. I don't know. But one of the hardest decisions I ever had to make—apart from the decision to resign, which was the hardest—was to fire Haldeman and Ehrlichman. They were the toughest, most loyal guys around. They worked their asses off for us. They took the slings and kept fighting. Sacrificing them was a bad, bad mistake," he said, shaking his head, "because then the press smelled blood—that I was vulnerable, you know—and they pounced, and then it was all over. I don't think, in retrospect, that I could have made any other decision, but if I had to do it all over again, I wouldn't have fired them. I would have held on to them and given those bastards out there *nothing.*"

"Is that one of your biggest regrets related to Watergate?" I asked.

He shook his head again. "There are so many regrets related to Watergate. First of all was the way I handled the entire goddamned thing from the beginning. Instead of trying to keep it quiet, since I didn't have anything to do with it, I should have gone straight to the American people and told them what the hell happened and how everyone involved was going to pay the price. Going directly to the people is a tactic that should be used sparingly, only for very important things, but I had a pretty good track record on that score."

When I mentioned the 1952 Fund speech, he pointed at me. "I had the truth on my side then. I should have used that approach on Watergate, while I still didn't know anything. That would have nipped the thing in the bud. If people hear the explanation directly from the president—well, generally they listen and understand. I didn't do that. I should have. The whole goddamned thing could have been averted."

I asked if he thought that the American people are forgiving, and he replied, "Yes, they are, but only if you level with them from the beginning. If you keep things from them or otherwise conceal the truth or stonewall, as they said about Watergate, then there's no way in hell they are going to let you get away with it. No way. And they shouldn't, because there's been wrongdoing. Now, don't get me wrong—I've been around politics for a long time, and it's a dirty and cynical business, always has been and always will be. Scandal has been around forever. But to express shock over one situation and not another is just not right. That's where the double standard comes in."

"Anything else?" I asked.

He blinked. "I'll tell you right now—the way I treated [Secretary of State William] Rogers was terrible. I had Kissinger, and he and I kept so many things from Rogers, and that was inexcusable. I used Kissinger when I should have been using my secretary of state, and we had our reasons, but it wasn't right. I didn't even tell Rogers about the China thing until it was a done deal. I regret that because Rogers was smart and a good man."

He paused. "And Dole. I replaced him, as you know, at the Republican National Committee, with Bush. Dole was loyal, tough, and out there defending me all the time, even when it wasn't popular, which was most of the time, and even when what was happening couldn't easily be defended. He took a lot of slings, and I just didn't treat him very well. It was a terrible thing. I appreciated everything he did for me, but I was so wrapped up in my own problems that I just never thanked him the right way."

He shrugged. "Replacing him with Bush? Well, I don't know. Bush had a hell of a time because it was Watergate, and any head of the RNC was going to get killed. He told everyone how much he hated being there and came to me and said, 'Send me to China.' Maybe I did Dole a favor by getting him the hell out of there. But I owed him more of an explanation than I gave him at the time. And poor Ford. The pardon was the kiss of death politically, and he still did it. You've got to admire his guts on that score." He looked down and back up at me. "Watergate destroyed a lot of people, but I'll tell you—I regret treating them the way I did probably more than anyone else, apart from the family, of course."

He paused. "I've said this before, and I'll say it again: I should have created an atmosphere in the White House where acts like a cover-up were unthinkable," he said. "I didn't, and that was my mistake."

People fell around him because of that mistake, and his grief was not just reserved for himself and his family but for them as well. He carried the twin burdens of being the only president to resign and having damaged people whose fortunes had the unhappy coincidence of being wrapped up with his own.

In an attempt to prompt a more favorable historical judgment and to reverse some of the harm done to those involved, Nixon spent his final years writing books, speaking out on global and domestic politics, and repairing his relationships with such people as Dole and Colson. Restoring the personal relationships took place privately; restoring the public image occurred in the newspapers and in front of the television cameras.

"Whenever I go out to talk about some new project, book, or whatever," he said to me on January 7, 1992, "I expect to get some questions related to Watergate. Very few reporters are going to let me sit in front of them and let me talk about what I want to talk about. They want their piece of the Watergate pie. OK, so we deal with that. But what [ABC's Ted] Koppel did to me today was inexcusable."

In Washington to promote *Seize the Moment*, Nixon taped Koppel's program *Nightline* and immediately after ruled it a mistake. Koppel had used the opening moments of the interview to ask questions that Nixon deemed unnecessarily antagonistic, such as why the country should listen to a man who had deliberately abused his presidential power. Watching the taping from the control room, I saw Nixon's expression slacken and his face grow pale. Despite his anticipation of such questions, they always came as a mild shock.

"Did you see Koppel's face when he asked those questions? Anti-Nixon all the way," he said to me when we returned to the hotel. "Do you see what we're up against? I've given up on the media. With very few exceptions, they are bad. There is no chance in hell that they will ever give me a fair shake. I could understand it during the Watergate period—but now? They just can't—or won't—separate what that was about from what I'm doing now."

He stopped and clenched his fist. "I have spoken out my entire life for what I've thought to be important to the country and to the world, and I'll never let Watergate stop me from doing that. The haters are still out there, and they won't listen to me anyway. But I'm not going to quit speaking out. They can stick it where that's concerned. But the more important point is this: if you are a conservative, then the press is your enemy. They may pretend to cover you fairly, but they never do. The press will try to ruin you, or at least discredit you, as often as they can. My mistake was that I gave them what they wanted."

Nixon did indeed give them what they wanted. He gave them a series of domestic crimes. He gave them the tapes to prove in his own words that he was involved in attempts to conceal the criminal activity. He gave them half-truths. He gave them stonewalling. He gave them defiance, and they pressed harder. He gave them the sword, and they used it.

On Saint Patrick's Day 1992, I went to the residence to talk with Nixon about the speech he had delivered six days before, at the Nixon Library–sponsored conference in Washington. He had decided to edit the written version and distribute it to those who had not attended the conference, in order to spread his message about the need to aid the democratic forces in Russia. When I arrived, I saw that he was wearing a tie designed with shamrocks.

"See this tie?" he said to me. "It comes out of the closet once a year. Have a seat." We spoke about the mailing list for the speech, and when Colson's name came up, I mentioned that I was nearing the end of *Silent Coup.* Nixon shot me a concerned look. "You are? When will you be done with it?"

"Probably in a few days," I said.

"Good," he replied. "I want you to tell me what you think of it. I haven't read it, of course, and won't, but I'd like to get your read." He paused. "You know, I heard that CBS is doing a one-hour special in June for the twentieth anniversary of the break-in. I wish they'd stop hitting this thing over and over again, but that'll never happen. So here we go again."

In an effort to keep the subject from slipping away, I asked him bluntly, "In retrospect, and apart from not going to the country right after the break-in, what would you have done differently?"

He bit one end of his pen. "Everything. Or almost everything. Going right to the people was number one. I should've done that. I should have fired anybody involved or implicated in the break-in, whoever they were and whatever they knew. Covering up for my associates or friends—that's what they called it, and it was a mistake. And I never should have even considered having the CIA intervene to stop the FBI from investigating."

"The smoking gun," I said.

"June 23, 1972," he said. "I really thought at the time that since some former CIA guys had been involved in the break-in, the CIA would have an interest in putting a stop to it. That was a major mistake. Thank God [Director of Central Intelligence Richard] Helms and [CIA deputy director Vernon] Walters ignored it, because it wasn't only illegal but stupid, and when [FBI director Pat] Gray called me later, I told him straight out to do whatever he needed to do with regard to the investigation, and Haldeman and Ehrlichman were to cooperate until the thing was over. There wasn't any obstruction of justice there because no one followed up, but my mistake—which is what led to the resignation—was in even considering the goddamned thing to begin with."

When I asked if he could attribute it to poor judgment, he shook his head. "More than that. Let me tell you something about crises. When you are president and in the middle of one—one that isn't international or even domestic, because you can separate yourself from those and think rationally, but I mean personal crises that can blow up into political ones, like Watergate—you can get so wound up that you can feel your better judgment go out the window."

He blinked hard. "I shouldn't have even thought about it, never mind talked about it. Same thing with the hush money for [Watergate burglar E. Howard] Hunt. Dean, Haldeman, and I talked about it, which is what everyone focuses on, but they pay no attention to the fact that later in the conversation I told them it was wrong and not to do it. No money was ever paid. In fact, this is the one thing about Watergate that separates it from other situations: no one ever profited from the goddamned thing. Not one red cent was made by anybody."

I reminded him that people were concerned with the abuse of power, and he replied impatiently, "Yes, yes, I know. That's why they play up the fact that I talked about these things and ignore the fact that I dismissed them as wrong a few sentences later. And that's why they played up the fact that I wanted the IRS to audit [Lawrence] O'Brien." He clenched both fists. "I will never apologize for that. It wasn't illegal. Kennedy and Johnson had me audited all of the time. And the IRS is loaded with Democrats anyway; what smart conservative would want to work there? They constantly subjected my family, friends, and political supporters to audits, including, incidentally, Billy Graham." He threw up his hands. "Billy Graham, for God's sake! What I did was political practice at the time and totally legal. And I'd do it again."

He was equally unapologetic when I raised the issue of destroying the tapes.

"Thinking back to the time, I really believed that there was enough on those tapes to clear me. I said some stupid things on them, but then I always took them back. I thought that everyone would hear what I heard: frank conversation but nothing illegal. I hadn't actually done anything or even ordered anything. But the tapes became like a noose, and finally I just had to resign."

"Knowing what you do now, would you have destroyed the tapes?" I asked again.

He lowered his eyes and simply nodded his head yes.

Again, Nixon's rather remarkable but misplaced faith was evident. Just as he believed mistakenly that his taped conversations and political tactics would be as protected and accepted as those of other presidents had been, he also thought that the tapes contained material that would vindicate him. When he lost the battle over their release during the Watergate period, he turned them over, confident that incriminating remarks would be neutralized because they were subsequently disregarded or because they were never acted upon. What he failed to realize was that the unethical and illegal suggestions he made, even if never carried out, were incriminating in their own right. He could not escape the sound of his own voice considering questionable courses of action with subordinates, talking through the situation, receiving information piecemeal, reacting furiously. The tapes seemed to shock even him, as if the voice being played back belonged to someone else. Twenty years later, he wanted to shut the voice off completely.

In retrospect, he wished he had destroyed the tapes so that Watergate investigators would have had to prove their case without his help. Without the tapes, they would have been forced to present a circumstantial case built on hearsay. Without the tapes, obstruction of justice would have been hinted at but probably left unproved. Without the tapes, Nixon would have had better control of the case. And without the tapes, neither he nor anyone else would have had to ever hear those words again. For Nixon, the fact that the destruction of the tapes would have itself constituted obstruction of justice was irrelevant. The investigators accused him of obstruction of justice, and if he had destroyed the tapes, at least he would have done something in his own behalf to deserve the charge.

On March 20, as I sat with him in his office, discussing Bush's endorsement of Nixon's idea to increase dramatically the aid given to the Russian democratic forces, he turned to me abruptly and with a horrified expression said, "The [Nixon] Library wants to hold its own panel discussion about Watergate for the twentieth anniversary on June 17 with [G. Gordon] Liddy and [Len] Colodny."

I told him that I was firmly opposed to the idea for two reasons: first, other presidential libraries did not hold forums on débâcles that occurred under their presidents, and second, it would never be considered a full and fair discussion of Watergate.

He pointed at me. "It'll just be more headlines. And it will never be just limited to who ordered the break-in, which wasn't us. No, I'm going to kill the idea." He picked up the telephone receiver.

"By the way, I've finished *Silent Coup,*" I said, and he promptly hung up the telephone.

"What's your view?" he asked.

I told him that Colodny and Gettlin launched a full investigation into all of the evidence, including material that had never before been made public, and made a compelling case for the way Nixon was silently and inadvertently removed from the presidency by actions that at first had nothing to do with him. The president, by getting involved in something he did not fully understand, was misled by those like Dean who lost control of what they had set in motion.

"It's right on Dean," he said. "He was a traitor and a liar and out for himself from the beginning. He was the one who was feeding me lies about what was going on. And there I was acting based on what he told me. He had a personal stake in covering up the facts, and I didn't know that at the time."

"They do say that Al Haig was Deep Throat," I said, referring to the secret source of *The Washington Post*'s investigative reporters Bob Woodward and Carl Bernstein. "They have him coming and going from the White House at all hours, unexplained disappearances, giving convoluted explanations . . ."

Nixon closed his eyes and shook his head. "No, they are wrong about that," he said. "Haig was not the source. He was damn loyal. He did know Woodward, I think, but that doesn't mean that he was running around with him in parking garages in the middle of the night, although anything is possible. But no, it wasn't him."

"Then who?" I asked.

Nixon smiled. "I don't know. I really don't. Not Haig. I have some ideas about who it is."

I pressed him, and he laughed. "Look, whoever it was was close to the inside."

"Or at least had access to someone on the inside," I said.

"That may be, but I don't think so. I don't think it was anybody who was getting information from someone else and then passing it on. It was someone on the inside doing it himself. Haig was close, but I don't think he did it. There are other candidates, which if you think about hard enough may make sense."

I brought up the idea that Deep Throat was a composite figure or a fictional creation.

"No," he said with a sharp nod. "The source was one person, a real person. It was one person who thought he had a lot to gain by spilling his guts to those two guys. So let's consider motives. It could have been someone who wanted to be president, but that doesn't really work because anyone coming out of my White House after Watergate was not going to win an election. So it must have been someone who thought he could win with the media, someone who was proving his liberal credentials by talking secretly to the *Post*, someone," he said, pointing a finger in the air, "who wanted a journalism career or media career. And it wasn't Diane [Sawyer]. Whoever it was was just trying to save his own ass, bail himself out from a sinking ship. Dean was a traitor, but the source—well, he went even beyond that." He stopped and shifted his attention back to *Silent Coup.* "You can see why the press killed the book. They didn't cover it. Any other theories about Watergate just don't make it."

I wrote to Colodny and Gettlin to tell them that I appreciated their even-handed approach in exploring new theories about Watergate. On April 13, Colodny called me to say that he and Gettlin appreciated my letter, that Dean had filed a libel suit against them, that the Democrats knew about the call-girl operation and were conducting a cover-up of their own at the time, and that *The Washington Post* had assigned three reporters to investigate their assertions but could produce no evidence contrary to what they had put forth. When I told Nixon of the call later that day, he was surprisingly uninterested and said simply, "No matter what anyone comes up with, the Watergate story is over."

As the twentieth anniversary of the break-in approached, Nixon grew apprehensive and annoyed. When CBS invited Julie and David Eisenhower to participate in its Watergate special, he exploded in anger. "It has been a relentless onslaught for eighteen years since the resignation!" he said on May 8, pacing slowly in his office, stopping only briefly to point his pen at me. "That's what people remember—every day for one and a half years, Watergate was the headline. Our friends mean well, but they're naïve. They go on these programs to get our side out, but they just add credibility to the program's claims of fairness—[former health, education, and welfare secretary] Bob Finch goes out there fighting; Colson and Ehrlichman are bright, but I don't know what kind of impact they have; and poor [director of communications] Herb Klein. [Former press secretary Ronald] Ziegler was good with the press but wanted good relations with them. To hell with that! They shouldn't do it. And the nerve of CBS to ask Julie! My God! Where were they on the anniversary of the China opening, or détente—the forward-looking events instead of the past?"

I mentioned Stephen Ambrose's biography of him, which I considered rather favorable, "though for the wrong reasons."

"I know," he said. "Ambrose thinks I was a closet liberal and that had I survived, we never would have had the rise of Reagan. He may be right on that score, but that's like damning me with faint praise. Or the wrong kind of praise. And Tom Wicker's book [*One of Us*] is the same kind of thing."

"What about *Silent Coup?*" I asked.

He shook his head. "Didn't get enough play. And even though those guys are Democrats and should have gotten far more attention, they didn't." He paused. "I haven't written enough. Look at Churchill. He wrote volumes. Maybe I should write more."

Nixon believed that he had to look to himself to effect his rehabilitation. Ambrose, Wicker, and others might write relatively positive biographies and contribute to different thinking on Nixon's presidency, but the Herculean effort needed to resurrect his political image was his responsibility alone. In a desperate reaction to every new Watergate-related anniversary—the break-in, the resignation—he grew more committed to advancing his own renewal. Nixon was left alone again to fight his last battle.

The numerous and continual Watergate anniversaries led Nixon to calculate how his every move on those dates would be perceived. He wanted to avoid being available to the press for comment, and he wanted to avoid the appearance of trying too hard to offset whatever negative publicity the anniversaries might generate. In late May, he decided to postpone a planned trip to Russia "until after the orgy over the Watergate crap. I'll be coming back on the ninth or tenth [of June], right in the middle of it. You give them credibility on their story if you're too visible," he said to me as we sat in his office on May 26.

I asked if his trip might offset the impact of the stories.

He shrugged. "A little, but they'll use it to get out their own stories. If I wait to go to Russia, *I'll* have the last word." He stopped and reconsidered. "No, I guess I can't scrub the trip. Yeltsin is expecting me, and he's far more important than any of these little media bastards. But I'm going to lay low that week. If I get caught by the press, I'll say, 'If we're talking about twentieth anniversaries, where were you on twenty years of SALT, détente, China, ABM, et cetera?' Right? But I don't want to be contentious. Just let it rest. It's not worth it."

Nixon then folded his hands in his lap, leveled his gaze at me, and asked a completely unexpected and pointed question. "Why," he said slowly, "do you think people hate me?"

I looked at him, and he just smiled, waiting for an answer. I told him that he was a target of a hostility fueled by long-standing partisan differences dating back to the Hiss case, policy differences that could be traced to anticommunism, unforgivingness for his extraconstitutional activity during the Watergate crisis, frustration over his defiant refusal to give in to defeat, and anger over the threat he represented as a conservative continually able to command the headlines.

Nixon bit his lip, then smiled. "Well, that's a tall order. The problem with Bush is that no one hates him. An effective leader needs enemies because then you know you're doing something right. But those same enemies will come back and get you, and if you let them destroy you, why then they've really won."

Shades of his 1974 farewell speech to the White House staff colored his comments, though those views had become such an integral part of his philosophy by the end of his life that he spoke them with a sense of serenity instead of dramatic urgency. In order to survive, he had to believe that philosophy wholeheartedly and allow it to motivate his need to fight back. Confounding his enemies became less a matter of revenge and more a matter of his own unwillingness to accept the sentence they had imposed on him. Instead of retreating into exile and isolation, he was as visible and controversial as ever.

Five days before the twentieth anniversary of the break-in, Nixon called me into his office. He was already sitting in his usual corner chair, and he asked me to sit down.

"Get ready for Watergate week," he said. "Doesn't bother me. Does it bother you?" Before I could answer, he issued a flurry of remarks that indicated that it did indeed bother him. "The *Today* show is doing a week-long story. That's going too far. I can see one day, but a week? Please. It's not going to change a single mind. And [CBS's Mike] Wallace is going to do a hatchet job—after all we've done for them. They are just wallowing in it."

He paused and raised an eyebrow. "It's going to be a painful week, but nothing like we went through for a year and a half until August 9, 1974. Day in and day out. I couldn't pay attention to it, or it would have killed me, and it almost did. Well, let's see what they do with it, still making it a story after twenty years."

The next Monday, June 15, Nixon opened his copy of *The New York Times* to find two pages dedicated to the anniversary. He called me in immediately, placed the front section of the newspaper on my chair, and pointed to it as I walked toward him.

"I see the *Times* gave it two pages," he said. "Take it with you. It's a bore. But don't let it depress you. And I see that *Time* didn't have anything on it. I can't believe that that was intentional, but good for them! Remember what they did to Khrushchev? Made him a nonperson? That's what I'll do to CBS and the *Post* and maybe even the *Times* after this. Just ignore them. They're nothing to me. CBS's special was originally two hours, but they cut it back to one because, I think, they couldn't hold the audience." Suddenly, he got up and jabbed my arm with his finger. "I don't want you to get depressed about this," he said, as if to convince himself. "It doesn't mean anything. You understand?"

I understood that it meant a lot more to Nixon than he was willing to admit. Each Watergate-related headline was a blinding experience for him, a new bruise on an old wound that he thought had healed long ago. He refused to read the stories or watch the programs, but he knew that their cumulative effect was to try to silence him with a cacophony of negative reminders of the past. Interestingly, on June 17, the actual anniversary of the break-in, Nixon said nothing about Watergate and focused instead on another scandal: Iran-contra.

The day before, former secretary of defense Caspar Weinberger had been indicted for the role he played in secretly diverting profits from arms sold to Iran to the Nicaraguan contras, leading Nixon to condemn the development as an outrageous act of prosecutorial politicking.

"Bush said he didn't know anything about it," Nixon said to me in his office on June 17. "That's bullshit. He was vice president, for God's sake. Reagan told him everything, but let's face it—Reagan wasn't really running the show on Iran-contra. It was Weinberger and [Lieutenant Colonel Oliver]

North and the others. But what the hell did they do? Not tell Congress about the money being diverted? What the hell! Most presidents don't tell Congress what they have in mind—including Kennedy. He was the worst at that. Do you think he ran the Bay of Pigs plan past the Congress? Or his plans to knock off Castro? Money changed hands on that score; don't fool yourself. But of course, he was never held accountable.

"So here we've got poor Weinberger as the fall guy for what every administration does. And they were going to go after Weinberger anyway, because he's a smart son of a bitch. The smarter you are, the bigger threat you are, which means they're going to come at you with everything they've got. And the reason they keep hitting it is not because it was an extraconstitutional thing but because it was anti-Communist." He pounded his armrest with his fist. "That's what that was all about. North and Weinberger got to the heart of it, like I did with Hiss. They were against the goddamned Commies! It wasn't about arms to Iran; it was about aiding the contras. The contras were anti-Communist, and these libs wanted them to fail, and here was Weinberger and the rest of them trying to help them bring democracy to Nicaragua. They couldn't stand it.

"I called him this morning to console him on the goddamned thing. This is similar to Watergate. Of all our people, not one stands up to take the bastards on. What's wrong with them? They don't have any guts."

He left me with a warning: "Don't watch the show [the CBS special] tonight."

I did, however, watch it and reported to Nixon the next morning. He stood facing me as we spoke.

"You saw it?" he asked, surprised. "Did you survive it? I didn't see it, of course, but—well, it wasn't that bad, was it?"

I had to tell him that it was fairly destructive. He took a step back and looked shaken. "Oh," he said. "Well, what can we expect from CBS? [Dan] Rather and [Walter] Cronkite?"

When I told him that they ran some excerpts from previously undisclosed tapes, he exploded. "Where the hell did they get those? Goddamn it, we are supposed to know when tapes are coming out." He paused. "No one from our side went on the damn thing, did they?"

I told him that they did not.

"Good," he replied. "I don't want any of our people to do these things ever again. They think they're helping, but they're not. They can say what they want about Haldeman and Ehrlichman, but they were damn good. Professionals—nothing like the clowns running around the White House today." He paused again. "They didn't have Dean on, did they?"

I assured him that they did not, but they did suggest that FBI director Pat Gray was Deep Throat.

Nixon shot me a look. "I can't believe that they would suggest Gray. No, it wasn't him. He didn't know enough."

I asked him how he could be sure, and his eyes darkened. "Well I guess I don't know for sure, but I can't believe that he would be the one. Did they go at the Haig angle?"

"They did but sort of dismissed him as the source in favor of Gray," I replied.

"No, I don't think it was either one, although they can't put a rest to these rumors, can they? Well, CBS didn't suggest I ordered the cover-up—" He caught himself. "I mean the break-in?"

"No, they didn't go that far, because there's no evidence of that," I said.

"Never was," he replied. "Because I didn't order it."

"No, and they can't be that irresponsible to suggest it without evidence," I said. "But they did imply that you began the cover-up the next day."

Nixon dismissed that with a sharp wave of his hand. "They've had their fun and games. Take this down," he said, pointing to my writing pad. "I will not do anything again for *The Washington Post, Newsweek,* CBS, Koppel, and even [Bryant] Gumbel, because although I like him, he gave a whole week to this crap, and he had the power to stop it."

When I asked if he were creating a new enemies list, he laughed and replied, "Let me tell you something. All politicians, if they are effective and serious, have some kind of enemies list. Somebody in my administration did it, but you should never be so stupid as to write it down when you are president. The others may not write it down, but it's there. Kennedy and Johnson were notorious for them, and I was on both of them. Kennedy had my IRS returns audited, and Johnson had me bugged! You cannot go into politics and not have made some enemies over something." He leaned in and lowered his voice. "And if you give these people anything more than a polite smile, then you are a fool."

The fact that Nixon saw himself surrounded by enemies caused many of them to deride him as paranoid. But the adversaries were real and actively bent on his destruction, and Nixon vowed not to endure their assaults without resistance. His enemies were political and ideological; rarely were they quiet. Most prided themselves on being his adversaries. Nixon recognized that though their opposition was primarily ideological and not personal, their hatred was expressed in relentless vitriol that made it personal. Nixon ascribed the hostility to his positions on the two definitive issues of his political career prior to Watergate: the prosecution of Hiss, which involved the explosive question of Communist influence in the government, and the Vietnam War, which divided the nation over the need to stop the spread of communism in Southeast Asia. Despite being correct about Hiss and having ended the war, Nixon had earned the permanent animosity of those who opposed his policies. They sought his removal from the political scene as aggressively as he sought the removal of his own political enemies in a harrowing dance of mutual destruction.

August 9, 1992, the eighteenth anniversary of his resignation, passed without comment, but four days later he made a remark that indicated that he had been thinking about it. I had been ill, and Nixon traveled to my house to bring me some materials that he wanted me to review and to discuss the poor state of the Bush campaign. When I mentioned that the president had too many inexperienced aides around him, Nixon sat straight up, changed the subject, and said, "In other countries, like England, leaders and others resign when the time comes—Lord Carrington when the Falkland Islands dispute became a disaster—and Margaret Thatcher. Resignation is considered a point of honor, the respectable thing to do. In America, it's the opposite, and that's why people hang on longer than they should. Resignation is considered an admission of guilt, a failure."

I asked if he regretted resigning, and he looked down. "No, no, it was the right thing to do at the time. I wasn't going to, you know. I wasn't going to let the bastards win. The family, of course, wanted me to fight on. But I finally decided that the country deserved better in terms of a full-time president."

When I mentioned that he had made that argument after the 1960 election, when he decided against ordering a recount, he said, "I didn't want the country to come to a grinding halt, although my suspicions were correct on the fraud issue. But in '60, I always knew I could come back and have a second chance. In '74, there would be no second chances."

There would be no second chances and no relief from the relentless barrage of reminders about Watergate. If Nixon had continued the battle in 1974 rather than resign, not only would the country have been paralyzed by impeachment proceedings, but it would have been left with a president who was a defendant, not a leader. Ending his presidency prematurely may have been abhorrent to everything he believed, but he did it, and twenty years later he still believed the choice was the correct one.

Like Watergate, the Hiss case—one of the episodes he thought was responsible for inspiring his initial enemies—continued to haunt him. On October 29, Hiss claimed that he felt "vindicated" by a report from a Russian military officer, General Dmitri Volkogonov, that said Soviet archives failed to show that Hiss had been a Communist Party member and a spy for Moscow. Nixon exploded: "Five other Russians before him claimed that he was and that [Whittaker] Chambers and I were right. And these five had access to the KGB archives, where the records are. You don't study the *party* archives! They've been sanitized. Spies don't carry a party card; if they do, they're not spies. You've got to look at the KGB files, which, of course, have been destroyed." He shook his head. "It's depressing. The media called today, and I told them 'no comment.' Hiss was a goddamned spy, and they still don't want to admit that I was right. With that case, I had enormous credentials as an anti-Communist, which kept the far right with me. So they stayed with me even though I was for civil rights and some other things they were not. But as far as Hiss goes, the press was wrong, and now they're trying to prove that they were right so they can say my entire career was built on a fraud."

He was still furious several weeks later when the Russian general recanted, saying that he had not made a thorough search of all of the intelligence archives and that he could not give any assurance of Hiss's innocence. Volkogonov's retraction was not reported by ABC, CBS, NBC, CNN, *The Washington Post*, or *USA Today*, all of which had reported the original story. Only *The New York Times* acknowledged the general's admission, leading Nixon to despair that "they put the lies in headlines, but the truth they bury back with the corset ads." Although he claimed to have disregarded the press long ago, he still became frustrated with what he perceived to be unfair coverage.

He did, however, enjoy a rare and significant legal victory on November 17, when the U.S. Court of Appeals ruled that he could receive compensation for the confiscation of his presidential materials. Upon reviewing the history of the use, control, and disposition of presidential papers, the court had found that Nixon had a "well-grounded expectation of ownership." It held that Nixon, like every other president before him, had a "compensable property interest" in his presidential materials, and that since the 1974 Presidential Recording and Materials Preservation Act severely restricted Nixon's rights to his papers, it constituted a "taking of that property" requiring the "constitutionally mandated remedy of just compensation."

Nixon was elated: "My lawyers usually call me with bad news—'Well, we've lost another one.' But today they called with this good news. Mortenson wrote a hell of a brief, saying that all the presidents' papers from Washington on belonged to them. They had a liberal judge there who they thought would rule that the papers belong to all the people, but he didn't. They upheld it, so I'm delighted. I've been paying every year—since the Watergate years—legal fees of one hundred twenty thousand dollars, at least. I still have a few million to go. I can't get the money from this decision because I'm not going to be in the position of profiting from it; it will go to the library. But isn't it something?"

He had finally won a Watergate battle. After almost two decades of legal wrangling, he had been given a decision that resisted the trend established by previous decisions related to the case. After having paid Watergate-related dues for eighteen years, he was finally getting some of them back. The decision seemed to hearten him, as if waiting years for a favorable verdict on this one matter made the painful and expensive fight worthwhile. If he had had no choice but to quit the presidency, then he would also have no choice but to fight back at every turn. When he lost battles, as he often did, disappointment was expected but profound; when he won the rare battle, it was a momentous vindication, not of his actions during Watergate but of his vow to continue the fight.

"I don't regret for one minute pursuing these legal battles," he said on November 21, pointing to me, "because I had to give in on the presidency, but that's it. One of the greatest tragedies of Watergate, apart from the horrible personal tragedies, was that I couldn't build the new conservative majority, and I was going to start with newspaper reporters. Those giving Clinton a free ride won't knock down his ideals because they're theirs too. I was going to get conservatives in there to take these people on. That's why in '72 they had to bring me down. They knew I was after them and that I'd succeed."

Again, Nixon advanced a theory about his downfall that subtracted him from the equation. His adversaries may have been actively seeking his destruction because they feared his ability to build his "new majority," but his own culpability was secondary. It was a blind spot or a defense mechanism, and though it protected him from fully recognizing his offense, it allowed him to come to terms with the course of events. His theories about Watergate, regardless of their legitimacy, were more about creating a psychological shelter than about advancing a new truth.

On Christmas Eve 1992, lame duck president George Bush issued pardons to Iran-contra figures Weinberger, Robert "Bud" McFarlane, and four others, delighting Nixon and enraging Bush's political opponents. "I have never been so glad to read a *Times* editorial," Nixon said when we spoke by telephone on Christmas Day. "They went crazy over the pardons! Isn't that great? I called McFarlane yesterday to congratulate him. I'm so glad that Bush stepped up to this; he should have done it sooner—it would have helped him with the election—but at least he did it. McFarlane said that I always stood by my people although that wasn't the best thing to do, and Reagan didn't. Bud served Reagan so well; he's a loyalist. And, poor guy, he said that I was the only one who called him. I never felt so good making a call.

"Now, of course, [special prosecutor Lawrence] Walsh is going after Bush, saying that he didn't disclose some notes. It won't mean a damn thing. Bush's notes won't show anything; he's so cautious. I'm sure he didn't write anything down. I hope not! Imagine—all this after six years of Iran-contra! But it still doesn't beat the almost nineteen years of Watergate.

"I saw some footage on ABC of past presidential pardons, and they showed my farewell wave, but the wrong one. Remember that was a single hand, a solemn wave. They always show a campaign wave with the victory sign, to make me look defiant and smug. I did do that at the end, but only after I was ready to board the copter. It's a subtle thing, but important."

He may not have been smug, but he remained defiant. The image of strength was crucial to projecting survival and implying future recovery. The victory sign he displayed as he prepared to fly away from the tumultuous past and into the uncertain future signaled an intention to come back, an unwillingness to accept his sentence, and a rejection of the conventional wisdom that he was finished. He had come back from political death before, but this time it would require a stronger will, greater patience, and less control of his own fate. On that last walk from the White House, he tossed the victory sign into the air not as an act of smug self-righteousness but to convince himself that he could indeed recover.

On August 9, 1993, after spending exactly nineteen years fighting Watergate battles, he won another one.

"Monica!" Nixon bellowed to me over the phone that day. "Well, we've got some good news. The court ruled in our favor on the tapes. They ruled that the archives cannot release any more tapes until all the private conversations are returned to me. This is a very significant victory. [Lawyers Jack] Miller and [Stanley] Mortenson were mobbed by the press and couldn't believe how biased they are. Only Brokaw ran something, a picture of me waving good-bye and the story, and today is the anniversary of the resignation, of all things! None of the other bastards ran a goddamned thing. But believe me, if the decision had gone the other way, they would have! You know, those lawyers work so hard; it's such a battle. But they won first the compensation suit and now this. It's very significant. I tell you I am thrilled."

He remained delighted the next day, when he arrived at my home, where I was editing *Beyond Peace.* He bounded through the door and walked straight into the kitchen. "Do you mind if I use the phone? I want to call Mortenson and congratulate him."

He picked up the receiver, dialed the number carefully, then whirled around to face me. "Stay here. I want you to hear this. Stan? Hi! Well, you won a big one yesterday. It's a hell of a battle. I see the *Times* ran a story and quoted someone from the civil liberties group saying it won't hold up. It will, right?" He paused and listened. "Well, I'll be goddamned. OK. Thanks again, Stan. You've done a hell of a job." He replaced the receiver. "He thinks it's going to hold up. Can you believe that after nineteen years we're still fighting this goddamned thing?"

When I mentioned that the dispute over the materials was no longer a matter of full disclosure but was a political battle, he shook his head.

"They're always looking for more profanity or conspiracy or some damn thing. This is a temporary injunction; they're deciding whether to go for a summary judgment, which is final. But if they do, they lose this. It's always a battle." He clenched his fist. "The press *hate* this, the fact I won. They're always looking to put the final nail in the coffin. That's why we may be ignored on this book. Do you think the interest in me is down?"

I reassured him that that would never be the case.

"We know that there are fewer out there who remember Watergate or who care, anyway. We'll see. Well, today is not a day to dwell on Watergate. We won a big one." He paused. "You have a piano in the other room, right?" I nodded. "Come here." I followed him into the family room and watched as he pulled out the piano stool, sat down, and played a chord. He turned to me, "You sing, right?"

"A little," I said.

"OK, you must know this one," he said, and he started to play "Happy Days Are Here Again." I sang a verse with him, which he wanted to repeat, then he sang the second verse alone. When he finished the tune, he turned to me and said, "There. That was our celebration. Two Watergate victories under our belts, which is two more than I ever expected."

The poignancy of the moment was in Nixon's desire to share his unbridled joy over a legal battle won nineteen years after the original war. It was a vindication of his position since Watergate that the remaining conversations and materials belonged to him and not to the government. Finally, he would be treated as his predecessors and successors had been, which had been his fatal assumption when he began his presidency.

As he slowly made his way back to political respectability, he was both outraged and amused by the scandals that involved his successors. Iran-contra sullied Reagan's reputation, at least to the extent that he was ridiculed for claiming not to remember what had transpired, and Whitewater engulfed Clinton. Just as the term "Watergate" covered a complex series of crimes, cover-ups, and other charges, both proved and false, so the label "Whitewater" related to an intricate web of possible acts of misconduct by the Clintons in an Arkansas real estate venture and its connection to a now-defunct savings and loan institution, Madison Guaranty. As the investigation of the Clintons' involvement in the financial dealings of the Whitewater Development Corporation and the bankrupt Madison Guaranty unfolded, an array of politically damaging questions arose. These included the possibility that funds from Madison had been improperly diverted through Whitewater to pay off debts from Clinton's 1984 gubernatorial campaign, the possibility that the Clintons received income tax benefits from the failure of Whitewater to which they were not entitled, the suspicious circumstances of the suicide of White House deputy counsel Vincent Foster, and the possibility that federal regulators had improperly shared information with White House staffers regarding the ongoing civil and criminal investigations. The president and Mrs. Clinton continually denied any illegal or unethical conduct, and the intricate tangle of allegations, players, and interests made the scandal almost incomprehensible to the public.

Nixon's antennae for political scandal and culpability at the highest levels were very sensitive, however, and he immediately took an interest in the case and in the potential for politically devastating developments. Two weeks before Nixon got news of the favorable court decision on the tapes, Foster committed suicide, beginning a cycle of speculation for Nixon about Whitewater that almost always included references and comparisons to Watergate.

"I think that what we have here is a major political problem," he said to me several days after the suicide, on July 29. "This death must cut right to something else, like that land deal, or their taxes, or something. There's a reason why they are being so secretive and maybe even—well—obstructing the investigation."

Obstructing an investigation, as Nixon knew, could not only create a major scandal from a minor one but could bring down a presidency. Having endured Watergate, Nixon knew the sense of panic Clinton had to be experiencing, but having been destroyed by it, he believed the circumstances were ripe for political justice. He wanted Whitewater pursued as vigorously by the Republicans as Watergate had been by the Democrats, Clinton held as accountable for misdeeds as he had been, and all presidents held to the same high standard. Again, Nixon made the mistake of believing that other presidents would be held as accountable as he had been.

On December 15, Nixon's frustrations over Republicans' inability to exploit Whitewater exploded. "This is a mess. There is so much corruption involved here that they are all up to their eyeballs in it, particularly Hillary, since she handled all of their finances. The Foster suicide smells to high heaven, but they probably won't reopen that investigation. The taking of the files [from Foster's office] was definitely obstructing justice. Look at what they did to us! My attorneys—Miller and Mortenson—have been fighting Watergate-related crap for twenty years now. I've spent over two million dollars in legal fees. None of it was worth it. Do you think that in twenty years the Clintons will still be fighting Whitewater?" He pointed a finger down at his desk and shook his head. "Anything the Clintons turn over now will have been totally sanitized. If our people don't step up to this, so help me—" He clenched his fist. "Of course I can't say anything, for obvious reasons, but they had better go after them on this."

Contrary to his realist tendencies, Nixon was strangely hopeful that the Republicans might match the Democrats' hunger for investigating scandal on the other side of the political aisle. If the Republicans failed to pursue the investigation, they would reinforce the double standard that they perceived as injurious to them and protective of the Democrats. Whitewater was a serious issue with potentially devastating political consequences. If the Republicans were to establish themselves as legitimate forces for oversight, as the Democrats had long been, they would need to press the investigation aggressively and responsibly. For Nixon, anything less would be tantamount to political surrender.

His concern about Whitewater began to gather momentum as public interest in the scandal started to swell. Early in the new year, 1994, he remarked on the maneuvering related to the case and its parallels to Watergate. "The big news is that there is a follow-up on that Clinton savings and loan scandal and the Arkansas connection. The *Times* called for a special prosecutor—so did *USA Today*—can you believe it? There must really be something to it if *they* are calling for a prosecutor, not that anything will come of it. [Attorney General] Janet Reno said no; she gets high marks, but she's a partisan witch. She's about as political as Bobby Kennedy was in that job. But I must say that the media so far has been pretty fair on this. They smell a scandal, and that's better for them than writing the good stuff. But with a Republican, they would be all over this, and I mean *all* over this. To think that Hillary came after me! They are making the same goddamned mistakes we did."

Lowering his voice, he continued. "It isn't that they are stonewalling—although they may be—it's the appearance of stonewalling or having done something wrong. That was our mistake: giving the *impression* of wrongdoing. It's really between the two of them. She's telling him he can't have the special prosecutor, and he knows he has to. She's up to her ass in it, and they are both guilty as hell."

The appearance of stonewalling, the obstruction of investigations, the acquiescence to the appointment of a special prosecutor, and the repeated denials of wrongdoing coming from the White House were too familiar to Nixon for them to escape his scrutiny. Not only had the Clintons equivocated on the matter, but they had refused to offer immediate and full cooperation to the investigators, indicating a lack of judgment and implying guilt. Flabbergasted by their inept handling of the entire affair, Nixon was prompted to ask a rhetorical but earnest question: "Didn't anyone learn anything from Watergate?"

That no one in the Clinton administration had apparently absorbed any of the lessons from his ordeal bewildered and fascinated him. It was another disaster of a president's own making, but Nixon could not understand why those, such as Mrs. Clinton, who had worked so passionately to remove him from office would act in ways similar to those involved in the Watergate affair. It was inconceivable to him that the same mistakes, the same bungling, the same ethical lapses, could be made by the people who had so self-righteously condemned those of Nixon and his administration. If the Republicans capitalized on this scandal as enthusiastically as the Democrats had with Watergate, then Nixon's mistakes might finally be judged more fairly.

Despite his hope that the Republicans would press the investigation, he remained skeptical that a débâcle of the magnitude of Watergate would develop. On January 21, he said, "I see that Bob Fiske is going to be the special prosecutor on Whitewater. I don't know much about him, but if he turns out to be a Baker type, we're doomed. We don't need a softy or an elite intellectual type on this; we need a tough son of a bitch. But I still don't think anything will come of it. His friends in the press will protect him no matter what. We didn't have that advantage."

Clinton, like Nixon before him, ignored the scandal and hoped that it would disappear into the haze of its own complexity. Unlike Nixon, however, Clinton did not simplify it for his adversaries by offering incriminating evidence recorded in his own voice. Regardless of whether Clinton were protected by the press, he assisted his own cause by appearing undistracted and removed from the scandal, not, like Nixon, at the center of it.

A telephone conversation with former president Bush on February 10 reinforced Nixon's frustration with the ways in which Republican and Democratic scandals were handled. "He didn't mention the Whitewater thing, but you know he's got to be secretly jumping for joy," he said to me. "Unless, of course, our people flush the thing down the tubes. They did it with [Commerce Secretary] Ron Brown and [Illinois congressman Dan] Rostenkowski. Those guys are guilty as hell and corrupt up to their eyeballs, and they're all still at the trough. It's our own people's fault; they are just not up for the big play. My critics used to say that Watergate was a gift to them; here we have a gift from the Clintons, and no one is up to using it.

"The point has to be made that unlike this situation, no one ever profited in Watergate. Here you have financial gain *and* abuse of power. I remember when they went after [Commerce Secretary] Maury Stans for one thousand dollars; meanwhile, Ron Brown takes millions, and nothing is done.

"And here was Hillary, on the impeachment committee, screaming about the eighteen and a half minutes, and now she's in Little Rock, shredding."

That last remark was a biting criticism of the hypocrisy of those who pointed to Watergate as a classic example of abuse of presidential power, then hid behind denials and excuses to dismiss their own wrongdoing. Republican and Democratic presidents had engaged in unethical behavior, yet only the Republicans seemed to suffer the severest of consequences. And the public, meanwhile, had become largely inured to the effects of scandal, having witnessed Watergate and subsequent examples of disgrace. They were desensitized to its effects and demanded not the removal of their president, as they had with Nixon, but a reprimand and a resumption of the nation's business. If the American people were so cynical about corruption in government that unethical and possibly illegal behavior at the highest levels no longer concerned them, then selective prosecution of certain individuals and not others did not improve the situation. Nixon believed that rather than contribute to escalating cynicism, Republican efforts to apply an equal standard of justice to the Democrats might induce both sides to act more ethically, by chipping away at the double standard.

To Nixon's great surprise, the press continued to follow the story. "The double standard is still at work, but at least they are following it up," he said on April 4. "They can't like doing it; Clinton is their man. But when they smell a story, they will climb over anyone and anything to get it. Tony Lewis's column gave away their bias: he said that the media blew it out of proportion. Can you believe it? They said it's nothing like Watergate. I say, 'It's worse. In Watergate, we didn't have profiteering, and we didn't have a body.'

"I remember the night before the resignation Eddie Cox said, 'These people hate you,' and he was referring to Hillary and [Clinton White House counsel and former Watergate attorney Bernard] Nussbaum and their crowd. Our people today don't have the passion to go after him or her. You know, in the early months of 1973, Watergate didn't affect the polls, but when the Ervin Committee got started and it got on the tube, that's when it took off. When these hearings begin, it will get more attention. At least let's *hope* that it gets more attention.

"I'm going to call Dole and tell him to put someone good on the select committee. We can't have a bunch of dumbos asking the questions."

Nixon took the unusual step of advising Dole on whom to place on the congressional committee investigating Whitewater, because he wanted the Republicans to maximize the public impact of the hearings. If they did not produce damaging evidence or dramatic testimony, their explosive potential would fizzle, and public sentiment would swing back to Clinton. The hearings, then, had to be executed carefully and responsibly, not by those looking for short-term political gain but by those interested in exposing wrongdoing and holding the Clintons accountable. The justice for Nixon was in the idea that finally another president would be held to the standard to which he had been held.

"Clinton and Hillary are guilty of obstruction of justice, maybe more. Period," he said on April 13, after watching the evening news. "Our people must not be afraid to grab this thing and shake all of the evidence loose. Watergate was wrong; Whitewater is wrong. I paid the price; Clinton should pay the price. Our people shouldn't let this issue go down. They mustn't let it sink."

It was a desperate plea for fairness not only in the prosecution of presidents guilty of wrongdoing but in the historical analyses that would follow. If Nixon were to be held to the highest ethical standard—as he should—then his successors should be held to that standard as well. Investigative reporters should ferret out unethical behavior as aggressively with other presidents as they had with Nixon. And presidents should conduct themselves with the greatest integrity because the office deserves it, not because the law threatens them with prosecution if they do not.

This, however, describes a perfect political system, not a real one. And Nixon believed that the American political process, replete with its double standards, ideological battles, and media influence, would never correct itself as long as human beings held the offices and did the reporting. He did, however, hold out a slim hope that his mistakes would be put in context with his accomplishments once there was enough time and distance between his presidency and the ultimate history that would be written and once his presidency was compared with those who had come before and after him.

Our final conversation about Watergate took place on April 8, just five days before those last remarks about Whitewater and nine days before Nixon succumbed to a devastating stroke. As I walked up the front path to the residence, where he wanted to meet because he felt "under the weather," I heard him tap on the window from the third floor. When I looked up, he waved to me from his study.

"Oh, hi," he said as I cleared the top of the stairs. "Come in and sit down. The news last night didn't have on a thing. It was so dull that I couldn't believe it. You know, I have to watch it because I need to know what the hell is happening, but I actually look forward to not seeing it, like when I'm on vacation or when [Nixon grandson] Christopher is here, because he watches *The Rockford Files*, and I can't get to the news then."

He straightened his tie, retrieved a sheet of paper from his desk, and walked toward me. "Here," he said, handing it to me. "Read this. No, not the whole thing, just what I've underlined."

The page was ripped from the March 19, 1994 issue of *The Economist*, and the article was a review of James Cannon's biography of Gerald Ford, *Time and Chance*. Nixon had highlighted a paragraph that commended Cannon for recounting the "whopping lies" told by Nixon, "that sinister man." Nixon had placed a horrified exclamation point next to the passage.

"Well, what do you think?" he asked. "I've been called evil, but I think 'sinister' is a new one. This is what we are up against, and it will never stop regardless of how much good I do and how many times I apologize and how many dues I pay. This is it," he said, pointing to the paper. "This is the way it's going to be."

When I said that he had made a choice to remain visible after leaving office, he replied, "If I had retreated into a cave, then they would have won. They would have bullied me into submission, and that's exactly what they wanted. So of course I wasn't going to let that happen." He flashed a knowing grin. "They were afraid of a comeback because of my record on that score. *The Memoirs* was the first step toward making myself realize what had happened and how I could start to fix it. Once I stepped back from the scene and spent a few years thinking back on that time, I understood a few important things," he said, tapping the air with his fingers.

"First of all, not only was Watergate a third-rate burglary, but it turned out to be a very damaging thing to the country. Now look, politics is a dirty business regardless of how many ethics laws are passed and how many politicians lose their careers because of scandals. Nobody really learns from politics; nobody really learns from others' mistakes once they get power of their own. So even though I had been victimized by all kinds of dirty tricks—everything from being wiretapped by Bobby Kennedy and Johnson and having my tax returns audited by Kennedy—I understood that that's how the game was played.

"Now, that doesn't excuse Watergate. In fact, it probably makes it worse, because I should have known that while the press was not willing to cover the Kennedy or Johnson crimes in this area, they would be all over anything I did. Instead of setting a higher standard for myself and my staff—well, I just played according to the rules that had been there since Roosevelt and which were fine-tuned by Kennedy and Johnson. And that, as we know, was a mistake."

He blinked hard. "I always knew there was a double standard out there; I just didn't realize that when it came to me, there'd be a triple standard! When I said that Watergate was part political vendetta, this is what I meant: my enemies were out to get me no matter what. When I gave them Watergate, they went crazy with false accusations, which they didn't even have to make since Watergate had enough about it that was wrong, not to mention the party-line votes and totally partisan power plays on their part.

"Watergate started out as a minor crime, which blew up into a major one when I got involved and then just became a national problem when the press and the rest of them got a hold of it. Sure, I can say that I should have fired everyone involved and sought out the truth right away and gone to the

American people right away. But I don't think that if I had done even that, it would have turned out much differently."

"Do you think that your critics would have found any way to bring you down?" I asked.

He shook his head. "I think that Watergate went far beyond anything they even dreamed of."

When I asked how he handled the fact that he gave them the ammunition with which to destroy him, he answered, "Well, you know, it's hard to accept that you caused a great deal of damage to a career you have spent your whole life building and hurt the people around you," he said. "It's a *very* difficult thing. I finally faced up to the fact, though, that if I were going to survive this thing and make it up to my family and the country, then I was going to have to accept it for what it was: a major defeat in a lifetime of ups and downs, peaks and valleys."

"It was a big defeat, though," I said.

"Yes, but if I were going to recover at all, it was going to have to be that way. I thought for a long time that Watergate was my last political campaign, but after seeing things like that," he said, pointing to *The Economist* piece still in my hands, "I realize that it was only my second-to-last political campaign."

Whenever Nixon looked back to that time, he was struck by the incomprehensible sadness of his own downfall and suffering. In order to survive, as he put it, he had to at once be the central character of the Watergate story and an observer of it. He had to separate his own activities in the scandal from his analysis of it. This kind of detached observation allowed him not only to understand the impact of Watergate and his role in it but to distinguish the man he was then from the man he was at the end of his life.

Whatever control he retained over his political life he used to restore his position close to the center of power. Influencing people and events now required the subtle patience of a man making a comeback, not the brash tactics of a man in power. Determined not to let his enemies have the final word, Nixon constantly tested his courage, forcing himself to tackle the very issues or experiences that he most dreaded. He often said that nothing matched the "mountaintop experience" of victory earned through hard work and dedication, but seldom did he allow that euphoria to last. When he played "Happy Days Are Here Again" on my piano, it was a rare and uninhibited example of the joy he so often denied himself.

His reflections on the drama of Watergate illuminated the legendary paradoxes and contradictions of his character. He issued quiet and emotional explanations, fierce defiance, defensive justifications, bitter criticism, earnest apologies, and determined lack of remorse. Alternating between unforgiving anger and reflective contrition, he made a tormented journey through regret and understanding.

That process was personal, but his journey back to political respectability was very public. He made a virtue of the fact that he was not just another former president; he had reached great heights and fallen greater distances. Just as a premature death enhances the memory of those it claims, Watergate had endowed him with a mystique that he would not have had if he had completed his second term in office. With this in mind, he strove to preserve his unique position and protect his slow and self-directed rehabilitation.

As president, Nixon thought that he could manage both the vision required to be an effective president and the details of management. He was wrong. The visionary accomplishments suffered when he became immersed in the petty and treacherous aspects of a minor break-in. That he was able to revive himself from a trauma that would have left most politicians terminally defeated inspired awe even in his most vicious opponents. By his own will, Nixon had destroyed himself, and by his own will he brought himself back.

Inevitably, however, the mistakes of Watergate haunted his every move. The scandal cast a large and menacing shadow over American politics, entrenching an existing culture of political mistrust. Although scandal in American politics did not originate with Watergate, that episode accelerated the politics of destruction and what Oliver North called "the criminalization of policy differences." Nixon, aware of his role in this annihilative process, attempted not to reverse it but to moderate its effects. By contributing positively after a devastating downfall, he paid reparations and provided a cautionary tale to those inclined to wrongdoing. With a few bad decisions, Nixon had muted an extraordinary career and spent the rest of his life grappling with the consequences.

As he thought about writing his last book, *Beyond Peace*, Nixon desperately wanted to address the political, social, and cultural decay threatening to undermine the moral example America had long provided. With increasing mistrust of government and pervasive immorality, the United States was experiencing a collapse not unlike the one Nixon had endured. He wanted to address this decline but stopped himself with a self-conscious evaluation of his status on the American political scene.

"I really feel that there is a need to talk about the fact that we are falling apart at the seams morally," he said on December 16, 1993. "And I think we've done an adequate job talking about it as well as we could here in this book. But I would've gone a lot further if I didn't have the problem. I should be the one talking about moral decline, but Watergate took away any chance I have of talking about that kind of stuff credibly. Our critics will say,

'Who is Nixon to talk about this? He contributed to it! He's the Watergate guy, the Vietnam guy, resigned in disgrace.' War and scandal. That's it. Every day I go out there slugging away. And every time I do, I pay the price. You see the articles—'disgraced former president,' 'evil.' You know what I mean. So getting my point of view across is always compromised by that— the fact that what happened, happened—and by the fact that I'm perceived that way. So even though I know my concerns about the American decline or about certain people's political characters—like Clinton's—are right, I cannot state them publicly because I will be crucified for it. And it's a sad thing because it's just not worth it."

Though it was a pained admission, he knew that Watergate had destroyed forever his ability to address publicly the moral state of the nation. He would never be a credible witness on the matter, and instead of addressing it, as he did with almost every other challenge he faced, he simply set it aside.

If personal integrity—rather than the sordid business of secrecy, compromise, and trading favors—produced politically good results, politicians would be saints and democracy would be unnecessary. In our resistance to the reality of politics, particularly after Watergate, laws designed to defeat human nature and politics itself were passed. Not only did the new ethics laws fail, but they destroyed many politicians and others whose wrongdoing was either exiguous or nonexistent. The result has been a permanent contempt for politics and those who practice it and a system that generates public outrage over even the appearance of impropriety but ignores the underlying corruption until a political actor gives it a face.

Nixon personalized modern American scandal to the point where even his rehabilitation was premised on the comparison with scandals subsequent to Watergate. Though willing to accept his role in accelerating the epidemic of mistrust, Nixon refused to allow it to be the final word. He built a remarkable post-presidential career, and he used those years to address the issues and causes that concerned him, mindful of his past but hopeful for his future. In the end, triumph and tragedy came together for him in a final lesson in repentance, humility, defiance, and ultimately, recovery.

# CHAPTER 2

# KENNEDY, CLINTON, THOMAS, AND PACKWOOD

W̶e all have our weaknesses," said Nixon on February 7, 1992. "Human nature being what it is, we all succumb to something: maybe power, maybe money, maybe booze or drugs, maybe cheating around. In Clinton's and Kennedy's cases—all of the above. But whatever it is, it's there. And as long as governments are run by people—well, we're always going to have some kind of scandal cropping up."

Political scandals have the explosive power to ruin careers and destroy personal lives; personal scandals, if endured by those in public office, can do the same. Watergate was a political scandal that became a personal crisis; President Clinton, Supreme Court Justice Clarence Thomas, Senator Robert Packwood, and after his death, President Kennedy, endured personal scandals that became political ones. As those cases demonstrated, however, both types of scandals usually become one and the same.

Although political character is generally an extension of personal character, reconciling the two is often an arduous and damaging process for those holding public office. Their political values—those for which they are willing to fight on the floor of the House or Senate or in the Oval Office—may not be reflected in their personal behavior once the cameras and reporters are gone. They may speak out in support of women's issues, then subject the women around them to sexual harassment. They may offer the public an image of marital bliss, then engage in clandestine extramarital activity. They may talk about family values, then disrespect and dishonor their own families. When the balancing act between the public persona and the private personality requires so many deceptions and self-created illusions, the double lives often come crashing down, bringing with them public outrage and private tragedy.

Unlike political scandals, which can be subject to investigations by independent counsels and congressional committees, personal scandals of public officials are usually immune to formal censure unless there is a crime involved. If, however, the personal crisis renders the politician unable to do his job or brings upon him great ignominy, the public may offer a reprimand of its own by demanding a resignation or failing to reelect him.

The personal lives of candidates and officials, once protected by recognized rights to privacy, have become legitimate campaign issues regardless of whether the public attaches any importance to them. The "character issue," once so vital as a supplementary guide for voters on the fitness of a candidate for office, means that discipline, caution, moderation, and morality in a personal life indicate that those virtues will likely be exercised in public life.

Those moral standards, however, are constantly changing, leaving public servants scrambling to reassess what might destroy them and what might be forgiven. The alleged extramarital affair of presidential candidate Gary Hart disqualified him from the Democratic nomination in 1988, but the charges of infidelity against Bill Clinton failed to derail his candidacy four years later. As the values and mores of the country changed, so did the standards by which we measured our politicians. Nixon struggled to keep up with the changing code of conduct as he gauged the destructive power of the personal scandals he observed.

"The Kennedys set the pace for this whole thing," he continued on February 7 as we discussed the allegations of infidelity against Clinton and their effect on his candidacy. "Joe Kennedy used to encourage the boys to go out and get into as much trouble as they could. He'd set them up with women and told them to have fun, even if they were married. Maybe *because* they were married! There was no respect there for the wives. None," he said, shooting me a disgusted look. "They had to prove that they were men, you see, and get their father's approval, never mind their poor wives. Those women—Jackie, Ethel, Joan—went through hell, especially poor Joan. Can you imagine having your husband [Senator Edward Kennedy] get drunk at a party, get into a car with a young girl, and then drive off a bridge, killing her?" He shook his head. "My God! No wonder she hit the bottle. And she had to stand by him through the entire goddamned thing, including the cover-up."

He lowered his voice. "You know, the police didn't even investigate Chappaquiddick for three days. A cover-up! Everyone was involved in that cover-up. And there the guy sits, still in the Senate, a hero to the women's groups.

And they love him because he's a lib; never mind that he has destroyed more women's lives than can be counted."

For Nixon, the indiscretions of the Kennedy men began the examination of personal corruption as a test of political suitability. The moralism that had long animated American politics began to unravel, but in a distinctly one-sided way. Personal character was deemed less important to the responsible execution of public duties while political character was still expected to be unimpeachable. It was an ultimately untenable arrangement, and the victims were seemingly random: Gary Hart for sexual misbehavior in 1988 but not Clinton in 1992; Nixon for Watergate in 1974 but not Reagan for Iran-contra in 1987; Clarence Thomas for alleged sexual harassment in 1991 but not Clinton in 1994. When Nixon examined these anomalies, he believed that the selective prosecution had more to do with political ideology than personal improprieties. But the ultimate casualty of scandal was the optimistic system that put its faith in the idea that human nature was essentially good.

When the charges of infidelity were leveled at Clinton in January 1992, Nixon became fascinated with the candidate's response and the country's reaction. Gennifer Flowers, a cabaret singer from Arkansas, claimed that she had had a twelve-year affair with the then governor and had taped conversations between them to prove it. Clinton was faced with two options: he could ignore her allegations, or he could address them directly. In a move reminiscent of Nixon's 1952 Fund speech, Clinton chose to take his case straight to the American people.

On January 26, with Mrs. Clinton sitting dutifully by his side, the Democratic contender gave an exclusive interview to *60 Minutes,* in which he defended himself against the charges and admitted only to past marital problems. The strategy worked in terms of convincing voters that since it was a non-issue for the couple in question, then it should be a non-issue for them. More significantly, by diffusing the matter as a personal problem, he diffused it as a political one as well.

"He knows that the charges are true, or he would have easily lied rather than go on the tube and wiggle his way out of it," Nixon said on January 28. "The problem with the womanizing charges against him is that voting for him becomes the voters' choice. It's now their *choice* to vote for an adulterer. In the Kennedy case, nobody knew anything. Those who did kept it quiet or were in cahoots with him. But here voters have a problem. Do they really want to vote for a guy who has cheated on his wife?" He paused. "Maybe it doesn't even matter anymore, you know. Look around—sex, drugs, violence everywhere. It's a sad thing because that kind of stuff means a decline of a great power. Greece went through this. So did Rome. All of the great civilizations collapsed because the people turned into selfish, amoral things.

"Remember when this whole thing got started, in the '60s and '70s? Counterculture, they called it. It was counterculture all right, but a bad, bad thing. Morals went out the window. Nobody cared about other people, just themselves. 'If it feels good, do it'—that was the saying. And they sure did! And what did we end up with? A serious drug problem, free love without responsibility, more violence. A goddamned mess." He leaned in. "I'll tell you something: the reason that it may not matter to people that Clinton is guilty of cheating is because many of them are guilty of it themselves."

The presidency had evolved into an office to be occupied no longer by someone holding himself out as a moral example for the rest of the country but a man like any other, vulnerable to human weaknesses and willing to admit it. Though Nixon acknowledged that he had damaged the political ideal of a president, the weakening of the personal ideal distressed him. If the purpose of the government, and the presidency particularly, were to elevate, educate, and enlighten the people, then ideally those entrusted with public office should represent the finest moral examples. When they designed the presidency, the Founders intended it to be held not by someone who was "one of us" but by someone who was, essentially, better than we are: a personification of moral virtue to which we could all aspire. It was a tall order, but as the only person elected by all of the people, the president had a responsibility to symbolize their potential as individuals and as a nation. Through political scandal, Nixon had let them down; through personal scandal, those who followed him into public life lowered the standard for acceptable conduct even further.

Clinton's election in 1992 verified for Nixon that the country had adopted a more permissive view of personal morality. For many, expectations of virtue in presidential candidates were lowered dramatically. No longer was it considered scandalous to have a president who had evaded the draft in wartime or admitted to past drug use or to causing "pain" in his marriage, as Clinton had. No longer was betrayal in personal life a disqualifier from public office. No longer was personal character considered a significant indicator of political character. No longer did a lack of judgment in personal life presage a lack of judgment in a political life.

"I can't say anything for obvious reasons," Nixon said on November 8, 1992, five days after the election. "But I think that the country's willingness to elect someone like Clinton, who is so bad on the personal side, shows that we are on our way down. I'm realistic, and I've seen all kinds in there. Roosevelt, Kennedy, and Johnson had their affairs, but no one knew it, and so the country was spared then. Now everyone just lets it all hang out. The president is a womanizer? So what?" he said, throwing his hands in the air. "This is the attitude we have because of that '60s attitude that everyone is doing it. Well, no. Not everyone did drugs then. My girls didn't do them. And not everyone was into free love or running around. But we are left with a culture that condones it because we have become so used to it. It's everywhere. My God, the other day I left the TV on after the evening news, which I never do because it's so bad, and I couldn't believe what they had on: stories about actors overdosing and a movie star's third marriage and a drama with loads of violence. Can you believe it? And it all seemed normal, even to me, until I started thinking about what I was being offered on the tube during that half hour."

He pointed his pen at me. "So you see, the people elected Clinton because they're surrounded by immorality on all sides. It gets to the point where it doesn't affect them anymore. So they sit and listen to what he has to say about health care and saving the spotted owl and changing government as we know it and are tone-deaf when it comes to his personal character.

"The press, who do this crap too, feed us the line 'The personal side doesn't matter. The people just want him to get things done.' So there you have it. The people hear it, they believe it, and that's it. We get a president who is a nothing morally, but since he's a liberal, it doesn't matter."

Nixon's concern was that since Clinton's personal scandals had been muted during the campaign, potential political scandals in his White House might be diffused as well. The precedent for lower moral expectations was in place and, with it, the reduced capacity for outrage over behaviors that would have been condemned less than a generation ago. It was a profoundly disturbing development, though Nixon acknowledged that he could not talk about it publicly because Watergate had contributed to the escalating cynicism that served as its foundation.

When Congress passed the Ethics in Government Act in 1978, in the flush of the new puritanism after Watergate, it tried to rid politics of its impurities and corruption without recognizing that ethics standards designed to fight political corruption were as irrelevant and ineffectual as any others made to fight human nature.

Despite those ethics laws, the seismic cultural change evident in the country's unconcerned responses to the personal scandals of Kennedy and Clinton indicated to Nixon that the political game now had a different set of rules. By using the powerful political tools of charisma and charm to excuse their personal weaknesses, Kennedy and Clinton mined a political advantage: people could more easily relate to personal flaws than to political ones. Perhaps only the forty-one men to hold the presidency could relate to charges of abuse of presidential power, but almost everyone could understand charges of personal betrayal or deception.

Forgiveness on the personal level, then, was more easily dispensed. Kennedy's and Clinton's transgressions were excused as basic weaknesses of human nature; Nixon's transgressions, because they were political, became sins inflicted upon a nation. As he grappled with the differences between personal and political integrity, Nixon tried to reconcile them and determine the impact of their apparent separation in the minds of the voters.

Nothing, however, prepared him for the events of the week of October 6, 1991. On that day, *New York Newsday* published allegations of sexual harassment against Supreme Court nominee Clarence Thomas by an Oklahoma law professor, Anita Hill. She claimed that in late 1981 and through much of 1982, Thomas had sexually harassed her as she worked with him at the Equal Employment Opportunity Commission. Her descriptions of the harassment were graphic, shocking, and politically explosive. The fourteen male senators on the Judiciary Committee, charged with conducting the hearings for Thomas's confirmation, were forced to extend the hearings to include a public discussion of the allegations, for which they were not prepared. They had expected an easy confirmation of Thomas, who as the preeminent black neoconservative in the Reagan administration had been investigated previously by the FBI and confirmed by the Senate four times.

Even after the committee members had spent eight days on the original hearing and were set to send the vote to the full Senate but then decided that they needed more time to look into Hill's charges, they anticipated an uneventful vote to confirm. They did not expect to be part of the bizarre drama that unfolded around them during that second week in October. They also did not expect, since Thomas's public life had been examined exhaustively and found to be spotless, that his opponents would level charges against the only area they had at their disposal: his private life.

The inquiry into Hill's charges involved the highest political stakes and an imposing mix of volatile social issues. With their riveting and unanticipated turn of events, the hearings ranked among other historic televised dramas: the Hiss case of 1947, the Army-McCarthy hearings of 1954, the Watergate hearings of 1973, and the Iran-contra hearings of 1987. Just as those hearings defined their eras, the Thomas confirmation hearings escalated into a defining moment, for the Senate institutionally, for women's issues culturally, and for the abortion issue politically.

On October 8, the allegations captured Nixon's attention. We met in his office to read through galley proofs of *Seize the Moment*, and when we finished incorporating his changes, he threw the manuscript on the floor, took his eyeglasses off, and pointed them at me.

"What do you think about this sexual-harassment business against Clarence Thomas?" he asked.

"Well, I don't know enough details about this case in particular . . ." I began.

"Then tell me what you think of the issue generally," he said.

I told him that while many such claims are legitimate, they are often not given serious attention because sensationalized cases like this one chipped away at the credibility of the issue. And since the events do not often occur before other witnesses, the victims are afraid to come forth, and the charges are difficult to prove.

He pointed the eyeglasses at me again. "OK, but where is the line drawn between regular conversation and harassment? When does, say, a compliment become abuse?"

I replied that when it is used as a weapon by someone in authority to intimidate another, it could create a hostile environment.

"I see what you're saying. OK. So men—mostly—use it to get what they want, so to speak, from the women who work with them."

When I explained that no one should have to contend with unwelcome advances, he considered his next question. "How do they prove it? It seems to me that it's got to be one person's word against the other's. Right?"

"That's true," I replied. "Without a witness, it's hard to prove. And how many men are going to allow a witness to that kind of behavior?"

"I know of a few," he laughed. "Sexist bastards!"

His curiosity on the subject was surprising. As a product of a generation wholly unfamiliar with the term *sexual harassment* and its effects, he seemed determined to understand its development as a social issue and the potential force it brought to the political arena. With prosecutorial precision, he asked what constituted harassment, how it could be proved, and how those ideas could be applied to the specifics of this case.

"I've been thinking about what you said with regard to the sexual-harassment issue," he said the next morning when we met for a discussion. "It's interesting to me that in this day and age, men feel like they can puff themselves up by putting women down. Any guy who does this type of thing—and I mean make inappropriate comments or withhold opportunities from women, like you said—seems to be awfully unsure about what he himself can do. I don't know if they're trying to get a date or are afraid of losing their jobs or what, but I see what you mean about making it uncomfortable for the woman."

He picked up a newspaper from the floor. "The details of this case are pretty sordid, I think. But you've got to wonder why she waited ten years to move on the damn thing. That casts her whole case in doubt. She sounds like a woman scorned, but what she is doing is going to deprive everyone else out there suffering from this sort of thing of a fair shake."

I said that it was important to separate the general notions about sexual harassment from the specifics of this case, and Nixon agreed.

"The fact that the Judiciary Committee postponed the vote until they could examine it means they need political cover on the thing. The women's groups would have gone *crazy* if those men on the committee didn't take this on. There would have been an uproar! They probably realize that Hill's charges are a nothing thing, but they've got to go through the motions, or they'll be killed. It's all politics, on her side and on the committee's."

The subject continued to fascinate him on October 10, the day before the hearings began. Immediately, he recognized their potential as a politically charged tug-of-war between parties, genders, and races. Like the Hiss hearings, which riveted the nation with charges of espionage, and the Army-McCarthy hearings, which spellbound observers with tales of Communist subversion, these hearings captivated the nation because of the contentious nature of the two social issues at their center: sexual harassment and abortion.

"I heard on the news or someplace that a woman claimed that she was offended because a man told her she was so pretty he'd like to chase her around the desk," he said as he sat across from me in the office. "Now, I can see where the compliment got screwed up. Instead of telling her she looked nice, he went too far. Am I right?"

I told him that depending on the context of their working relationship, even a relatively innocuous compliment could constitute harassment.

He looked shocked. "Really? My God! Well, I agree it was inappropriate, but harassment? I don't know," he said, raising an eyebrow. "Maybe these women are too sensitive."

I asked if he were playing devil's advocate on the issue, and he smiled broadly. "I'm provoking you. So go ahead."

I explained that women wanted to be able to work in a secure environment and have their work judged on its merits. Inappropriate behavior and comments degraded and humiliated the target and disgraced the offender.

"I understand it," he responded, crossing his arms, "but I see how it can be abused. Say someone doesn't get a raise—why, she can charge sexual harassment! A relationship doesn't work out? Sexual harassment! This is the problem: the legitimate cases out there can't get a fair hearing because there are too many fake cases—like this one, I think—to screw it up. So the whole issue goes down the tubes."

When I mentioned that those who opposed Thomas leveled charges at him that could not be proved or disproved, he replied, "Right on! By going after him on sexual harassment, they could go after what he believes in."

"I think," I said, "that these hearings have little to do with sexual harassment and everything to do with—"

"Abortion. I know it," he said. "If I were Bush, and Thomas is defeated, and I needed to choose another nominee, I'd stick it to all of them and go for a white woman reactionary card-carrying right-to-lifer! That would drive them crazy! But you see what they have done? They are out to destroy him because he's pro-life. And since he doesn't have any political problems, they have created a personal problem." He paused. "These hearings are going to be bigger than Watergate.

"But look, those senators had better mow down her credibility right away, or they're going to lose a guy who'd be a very good justice. Ask her why she waited so long before coming forward. Ask her if she has any witnesses or proof. Ask her if she has ever talked to NOW [the National Organization for Women] or that group—what is it? The national abortion rights group [the National Abortion Rights Action League] or any of those people. Because if she has and they can prove it, then that's it. She will be shown for what she is."

"A weapon in the abortion battle," I said, and Nixon nodded in agreement.

"So you don't believe her?" I asked.

"My instinct is to say no, I don't believe her," he said. "But I'll answer that question again after the hearings."

On Friday, October 11, the Senate Judiciary Committee opened the hearings to investigate Hill's charges against Thomas. In front of the television cameras, she recounted her story of harassment and verbal abuse by Thomas. Sexually explicit and emotionally unsettling, her testimony described humiliation and psychological entrapment. It was a classic case, she implied, of sexual harassment, of a man reacting to a woman who had declined his advances and of a woman who now dared to fight back.

Nixon was aghast. "Can you believe the words we heard coming out of the United States Senate today?" he asked when he called me that night. "My God! I thought I was watching a movie—and a filthy one!—never mind a confirmation hearing. I must say that she was unshakable. She was lying through her teeth, or at least making some of it up, but she was as cool as a cucumber. And talking the way she did about the sex stuff! I'll bet [Senator Orrin] Hatch wanted to die, sitting up there listening to her and having to ask her questions! He's such a straight arrow. Mormon, you know. God, he must have wanted to crawl under the chair. And the rest of them!" He laughed. "Did you see them? [Senator Howell] Heflin, for God's sake? [Senator Howard] Metzenbaum? Please. And [Senator Edward] *Kennedy?* My God! That guy has absolutely no credibility on any issue relating to women whatever. He looked like he was on the sauce. Probably had to be to sit there at all. And [Senators Arlen] Specter and [Alan] Simpson are smart as whips; it was probably all they could do to sit there with straight faces. I'm telling you they had to take this on for political reasons, but it's being done on an ad hoc basis. Harassment OK, but the hearings themselves have become a scandal!"

When I expressed my concern that the Senate was moving ahead on the hearings without substantiating any of Hill's claims, Nixon agreed. "That's it right there," he said. "It's the women's groups and the abortion issue."

"What they don't seem to grasp is that abortion will never be illegalized in this country," I said, "because although the issue is still controversial, there is no way that *Roe v. Wade* is going to be overturned."

"No way," he repeated. "I was in there when the decision came down [in 1973]. It was the right decision. A woman should have a right to a legal abortion, but the government should not be in a position to subsidize it. I'm not going to say I agree with abortion, but I'm also not going to say it should be illegal. If any president were going to try to make it illegal, it would have been Reagan, and he didn't."

I told him that the strategy against Thomas could backfire on the Democrats, and Nixon replied, "I told you what I'd do if he goes down—nominate Phyllis Schlafly and drive them crazy!" He laughed. "But I'm afraid they're going to win this time. I don't think Thomas is going to make it. You agree?"

I told him that although I thought he would survive the confirmation process, the trauma of the hearings might deter other outstanding candidates from accepting nominations or seeking office themselves.

"Who the hell would want to go through this?" he asked.

Over the weekend, on October 12 and 13, the hearings proceeded, producing a parade of witnesses who attested to Hill's credibility or lack of it without offering any real evidence. What emerged was an unflattering portrait of the accuser: a woman of uneven temperament, with political biases, a history of cavalierly charging sexual harassment, and a reputation for dishonesty and dissembling. The hearings degenerated into a chaotic forum for the mutual destruction of Thomas and Hill; the accused, his accuser, and their sponsors were all left wounded in front of the nation. Even when Thomas himself, the best witness for his own defense, claimed that the hearings were "a high-tech lynching for uppity blacks," he became a party to the mass hysteria. Everyone involved, including the senators charged with running the hearing, lost control of the situation. It became less a matter of sexual harassment than a matter of ideology and less a matter of the immediate personalities involved than a matter of the wider agendas of politically active groups. As Nixon recognized, Thomas and Hill were pawns in a great struggle over political philosophy, a fact that all parties understood at the time but were defenseless to combat.

On Monday, October 14, when the hearings were over and the vote to confirm was scheduled for the next day, Judiciary Committee chairman Joseph Biden stopped two of Thomas's witnesses outside the hearing room and told them that he believed Thomas, not Hill. Nixon, unaware of Biden's comments, came to the same conclusion.

"Well, you asked me to ask you if you believed her after the hearings," I said as we sat in his office on October 15, several hours before the vote.

He put his feet up on the ottoman. "No, my opinion hasn't changed. I believe him. She was either lying or making a lot of it up just to get back at him," he said. "Look, it could have been that he did ask her for a date and she turned him down, and he was hurt and said something inappropriate to her maybe once or twice. I don't buy all this other stuff she said about the porno movies and other things. I'm sure she embellished a lot of her story, if not the whole thing. Or maybe she asked him out and he said no, and she was angry and used this chance to get back at him. She could have liked him, you know. I don't know what happened there, and it doesn't matter. The point is that the American people support him two to one. How do you explain that?"

I suggested two reasons: one, Hill did not provide evidence to support her charges, and two, the public separated the facts of this case from sexual harassment as a general issue.

"I know that there are a lot of legitimate cases that shouldn't be thrown out just because this one wasn't legitimate," he said. "Anita Hill may have done what she was sent out there to do—namely, destroy Clarence Thomas—but she may have ruined it for a lot of women who have real claims. The women's groups are so hypocritical. They didn't care about that. They just cared about getting him!"

He recrossed his legs. "Well, the vote is today, and I predict that they will go fifty-two to forty-eight to confirm. That will be the vote. Those who were for him are going to stay for him, and those who opposed him are going to vote against him. I doubt these hearings changed a single mind down there."

Nixon's prediction was correct, and I called him after the vote to commend his prescience.

"Well, I've been around this loop before, so I'm pretty good about predicting things like this," he said.

I told him that when Senator Kennedy said that the vote brought "shame to a victim," Specter replied that we should not have to hear about shame from Kennedy.

Nixon erupted in laughter. "I love it! Kennedy has a credibility gap on the woman thing a mile wide, so he shouldn't be out there talking like that. He looked ridiculous up there. No wonder they restricted the questions he could ask. Jack [Kennedy] was the original sexual harasser, and Ted wasn't much better. And [Lyndon] Johnson—why, he was almost as bad. And if we're talking about sexual harassment as a disqualifier from high office, then half those guys in the Senate would have to leave!"

Nixon had felt a true affinity with Thomas. Both of them, he believed, were damaged by forces larger than they were. Both were caught up in an upheaval of issues and ideologies that swept them away in a mad rush to judgment against the principles for which they stood. It was unjust and unfair, but it was the reality of American politics of the late twentieth century: agendas were the higher good, and people and institutions were to be sacrificed in their name.

"I have some poll numbers I'd like to run by you," he said to me the day after the vote. "Listen to this." He put his eyeglasses on and raised a paper in front of his face. "Over fifty percent of women polled say that they have been harassed." He took the eyeglasses off and lowered the paper. "Can this be true? That sounds like an awfully high number."

When I told him that harassment was fairly widespread, he paused. "Well, then, that's pretty bad. But I think that there's going to be a backlash against women because men just won't hire them. They can yell discrimination, but then they'll have to prove that. But look, why should a man hire a woman if she can hang the sexual harassment threat over his head? Why risk it? I know it's wrong because there are real cases out there, but think about it. By the way, I got a kick out of Hatch and Specter putting Teddy in his place! That was worth the price of admission right there!"

He switched gears. "You know in the Hiss case we took on the entire liberal establishment and won," he said.

"But in this case, the interest groups fought the battle against him," I said.

"And they still managed to hurt him. Thank God he survived," he said, "which is more than we can say about us or some of our friends."

Two weeks after the vote to confirm Thomas, the case still lingered as part of a national discussion on sexual harassment and the subtexts of abortion rights and partisan gamesmanship. Nixon decided to travel to Washington on October 29 to meet with Senators Simpson, Specter, and Hatch, the three members of the Judiciary Committee whom he admired most during the course of the hearing. I waited in an adjoining suite while they spoke with him at the hotel, and upon their departure, Nixon summoned me.

"They're formidable guys," he said. "All smart as whips. Specter is a tough son of a bitch and very serious. Exactly what we need up there. Simpson is a wonderful fellow and never lets a thing get by him. And Hatch is just about the straightest arrow you'll ever meet. I'm glad they're on our side!"

He straightened his tie and sat opposite me. "They told me some very interesting things about Hill. Very damaging evidence."

"Can they use it in the public debate?" I asked.

"No. It's FBI stuff," he replied. "I told them that as I found with the Hiss case, it's the small things, the evidence you don't think is important, that devastates a witness. You've got to nail the little lies.

"But Hill was aggressive, cold, and not very smart. Some of the evidence on her character wasn't admissible. But in the end she devastated herself."

In the end, after the lights went out in the hearing room and Hill retreated to Oklahoma, the partisan trenches were a little deeper. Neither the Democratic nor the Republican interpretations of the hearings were easy to accept fully. They were not the product of a disinterested search for the truth, since it was obvious that the hearings would never have taken place if the committee had not panicked over the publication of charges of which it was already aware and had rightly concluded could not be substantiated. But the hearings were also not an exercise in racial discrimination, since the scandal followed closely the pattern of others in which there was no racial component.

Both sides were guilty of cloaking their agendas on abortion in self-righteous indignation over the harassment charges and, consequently, damaged their credibility on both issues and hurt the political processes designed to manage the debate. The Thomas confirmation hearings triggered a national discussion about sexual harassment when they should have also alerted the American people to the extent to which people and institutions were being laid waste by deceptively silent philosophical wars.

The case of Senator Robert Packwood, also accused of sexual harassment, provided another vivid example. As the Oregon Republican prepared to run for a fifth term in the fall of 1992, he was considered a source of progressive leadership within the party, with a strong reputation for supporting women's and civil rights and a chance for the party's presidential nomination. The dynamic Senate career and the hopeful future, however, came crashing down in late October 1992, when two reporters from *The Washington Post* presented Packwood with allegations of unwelcome sexual advances by women who had worked with him. He denied them and provided statements aimed at discrediting the women, thereby stalling the publication of the allegations until after his reelection on November 3.

Three weeks later, however, the *Post* reported that ten women had charged sexual misconduct by Packwood, who replied that he was sorry for causing "any individual discomfort or embarrassment." Like Hill's allegations, these charges were graphic and shocking; unlike Hill's story, these stories could be substantiated. It was another personal scandal that had erupted into a political one and another private tragedy that turned into national drama.

When I called Nixon after the evening news on November 23, the day after the story broke, his first reaction reflected disappointment and disgust. "Hi Monica! How are you? Nothing on the news except I wrote to Packwood about a speech of his I saw, and now I see he's in this sex mess."

"And it seems to be quite a mess," I said.

"Goddamn it! What's wrong with these guys?" he asked. "Packwood was very smart and had a great future in front of him. He could be mean—I mean in terms of not being a nice person—but he was one hell of a senator. And now he's gotten himself involved in this crap. How could he be so stupid? It's the sexual-harassment thing."

"And after the Thomas hearings, he must have been panic-stricken," I said.

"Unless he just really didn't realize what the hell he was doing," Nixon said. "That's possible too."

Four days later, Packwood's desperate situation escalated when he checked into an alcoholism diagnostic and treatment program, leading Nixon and others to speculate that it was a move aimed to generate sympathy in the week before the Senate Ethics Committee was to take up his case.

"Packwood has big problems," I said to Nixon on November 28 when we spoke by telephone in the evening.

Nixon let out an audible sigh. "I know. It's sad. But he shouldn't resign. These charges are twenty-three years old. Like Hill—where was she before this? Ah, well, times were different . . ."

I asked him if he were certain that Packwood should not resign.

"Not yet, anyway," he responded. "Let's take a look at these charges, have the hearings, and then see. It may be nothing, it may be big. I don't know. But now he's got the booze thing. I think he may have done that to offset the harassment charges. I'm not sure about the wisdom of doing that sort of thing."

"You mean using one scandal to offset another?" I asked.

"It rarely works," he replied. "Of course, we tried to offset Watergate with the good stuff—summits with the Russians, things like that. Didn't work. And those were times we used *good* things to offset the bad. You can't use one bad thing to offset another bad thing. It just adds up to more bad news."

When I said that I did not think that Packwood would survive the assault, Nixon agreed: "They're after him now, and there will be no letup. With booze and sex scandals, I don't see how he can survive it. But I'll tell you something: if they force him to resign, they should force Kennedy and everyone else with a problem to resign, which means we'll have almost no Senate left! I know these people!"

On the first day of December, the Senate Ethics Committee began its inquiry into the allegations against Packwood, and nine days later, in a move toward damage control, the senator proclaimed, "My actions were just plain wrong. I just didn't get it. I do now."

Nixon shook his head. "I admire Packwood's guts," he said to me on December 10 after he returned from a meeting with Dole in Washington. "But I'm afraid it's too late. There's no way that they're going to let him get away with this, particularly since Thomas was confirmed. I told Dole that he should not allow Packwood to resign until all the evidence is out. But you know, Packwood *was* notorious for chasing women around desks. Oh, boy. He must have caught some of them because now they're letting him have it!"

"Don't you think they should," I said, "if what they're saying is true?"

Nixon looked at me. "If what they're saying is true, then yes, he should be held accountable. The problem is the goddamned double standard. How many women has Ted [Kennedy] chased around desks? And Clinton? Oh, my God, more than you know! And what about the other Democrats guilty of the same thing? There are so many of them down there that do this sort of thing—and have for years—that you wouldn't believe it. And I know what you told me about harassment when the Thomas thing happened. So yes, go ahead on Packwood, but go ahead on the other clowns too." He paused. "But they won't. It's an excuse to get a Republican, that's all."

For Nixon, the Packwood case represented another example of the war over ideology taking on another form. If Packwood were guilty of the allegations of misconduct, he should have to pay the price. But continually sacrificing Republicans and not Democrats for the same crimes was discriminatory, unjust, and damaging to the system. This is why Nixon urged Dole to tell Packwood not to resign immediately. If he had given in to partisan pressures, his opponents would have won their battle earlier than they expected. Nixon's advice was to force them into a prolonged and bruising fight for the political advantage. Though sexual harassment was a serious issue that warranted attention, in this case Nixon thought it might have also been used as an excuse, as in Thomas's case, to carry an ideological conflict into another arena.

Like Nixon before him, Packwood then made a major blunder. On October 6, 1993, in a deposition before the committee staff, he referred to his personal diaries, which began a lengthy legal fight over access to them. After the committee voted unanimously to seek the diaries, ostensibly for the reason of investigating potential criminal conduct regarding jobs lobbyists offered to Packwood's ex-wife, the full Senate voted 94–6 on November 2, 1993, to allow the Ethics Committee to enforce a subpoena calling for Packwood to submit the diaries. The day before the vote, Nixon was concerned about the precedent he had set on these matters during the Watergate period.

"First of all, this battle over the diaries—they asked for it!" he said, referring to Packwood's opponents. "And he gave them what they were looking for by mentioning the goddamned diaries to begin with. It was like our situation with the taping system. [Assistant to Chief of Staff H. R. Haldeman Alexander] Butterfield said it, and I was stuck having to admit that I had the system. Here, Packwood opened his goddamned mouth about the diaries, and they found another reason to go after him and those diaries."

When I mentioned that, like Nixon's tapes, his diaries were still private property, he shot back, "They won't be private for long. He's going to have to turn them over, you know. There's no way around it. He must be scared shitless. But he should do what I did: fight the bastards all the way to the top until they're exhausted. Now, maybe he will destroy them, although that will mean jail for obstruction of justice. But what the hell. They're going to make him suffer anyway."

He paused. "This isn't about harassment. I'm sure he did a lot of what these women are saying, and that was wrong. But let's look at the real reason they're coming after him: it's about getting his Senate seat. Just like with Thomas—it was about getting the Supreme Court seat. Politics. Pure and simple."

Nixon's prediction about Packwood's having to turn over the diaries was proved correct. On December 16, 1993, U.S. District Judge Thomas Penfield Jackson ordered the senator to give all diaries, tapes, and transcripts to the Ethics Committee so that it could pursue a thorough investigation. The contents of the diaries proved to be highly embarrassing to Packwood, who wrote rhapsodically about passionate affairs and vivid fantasies. His private thoughts and actions suddenly became very public, and Nixon, though uneasy that "the sex issue" had entered the political forum again, issued a final set of thoughts about the case on February 6, 1994.

When I went to the residence that Sunday afternoon to continue editing *Beyond Peace* with him, he handed me part of the manuscript and sat across from me in his study.

"I think we should have this done pretty soon," he said. "The quicker we get it out of our hands, the better. I just hope that this book adequately addresses what is happening in this country. Everything changes so fast that the book may even be overtaken before we're published. And I don't just mean on the foreign policy side. We can't control that. I mean in terms of the values stuff.

"The country is far more accepting of things it wasn't just a few years ago. Look, Gary Hart was destroyed by the womanizing crap, and Clinton survives. Thomas survived the harassment charges—barely—and now we've got Packwood hanging on by his teeth. This kind of behavior isn't just morally wrong; it's stupid for a man in power. But do you see what I mean about the changing views of the country?"

I told him that voters were less inclined to predict a candidate's political performance based on the way he conducted his personal life.

"But that's always driven by a view to what they believe in," he said. "If they're a lib, why, they're given more rope to swing around on. If they're a conservative, they get enough rope to hang themselves. Hart was the exception; most libs don't get destroyed by this kind of thing because the women's groups are all for them. Packwood stood up for women in the Senate, but once he got behind closed doors, he was chasing them around desks, for God's sake. How do you make sense of that?"

Nixon had touched upon a significant distinction between political and personal characters. If the two were greatly disparate, the tension could produce a public meltdown of the kind Packwood experienced. The most successful politicians were those who could easily reconcile who they were personally with who they were and what they stood for politically. Even the slightest discrepancy, as in the cases of Clinton and Packwood, could provoke disaster.

Nixon believed that Clinton's election in 1992 had marked a fundamental shift away from a judgment of political candidates on the basis of both political and personal characters. The fact that a candidate seemed like a good person meant less in terms of his potential as a good leader. Instead, political and personal characters became increasingly separate measures by which to assess the candidate. Political positions mattered more than stellar records of personal conduct, and rather than evaluate candidates on the basis of what kinds of people they were, voters were increasingly judging them based on what they said they would do once elected.

In Nixon's view, this marked an unfortunate development. What appeared superficially to be intense manifestations of political moralism—such as the Clarence Thomas hearings or the need to hear Clinton's explanation of charges of infidelity—were actually reactions to struggles between partisan enemies. Socially volatile issues were used as weapons in the political wars to provide cover for wider agendas. Sexual harassment was on trial in the Thomas and Packwood cases as a decoy for the more profound battle over political control and the control of ideas.

Partisan scandal, like sexual misconduct, is a constant in political life and will continue to take whatever forms the law does not allow. If personal corruption, however, no longer pointed to the potential for political corruption in the voters' minds, then Nixon believed that the reverse must also hold true. Political corruption did not necessarily point to personal corruption.

Nixon had been an honorable family man. He did not betray his wife. He did not chase women around desks. The abuse of power of which he was accused came in a different form.

Nixon saw clearly what modern scandal really involved: it was less about the scandals themselves than about the political agenda of the opponents launching the allegations. Watergate was about Nixon's stands on Hiss and Vietnam; Iran-contra was about the validity of anti-communism; the Clarence Thomas hearings were about a woman's right to an abortion; the Packwood harassment case was about gaining a Democratic seat in the Senate; and Whitewater was about the hypocrisy of liberal Democrats who condemned the greed of the 1980s and then indulged in it themselves and tried to conceal it. Each scandal was a unique situation, but all were motivated by a deep and powerful political force. Enemies had to be removed; pretexts had to be found.

The result is a society inured to scandal, distrustful of its leaders, and impatient with political wars of annihilation. But as long as the system remains dominated by ideological opposites, the temptation to bring the other side down through political or personal scandal will be unavoidable. The unwritten code of party loyalty and individual honor kept the system from unraveling until Watergate, when those apparent virtues began to appear to be merely smoke screens for corruption.

Abuse of power, whether committed against people or institutions, in acts of political deception or personal betrayal, represents a serious breach of trust, which can result in a removal from office. It becomes a coup, of sorts, when those seeking to destroy an opponent get the unanticipated benefit of having the opponent help to destroy himself.

That was the essence of modern scandal, and Nixon, having been a primary architect of it, knew that its devastating effects would be reigned in only when human nature was perfected or when scandal ceased to be politically profitable. And since neither was imminent, the players in scandal would continue to waltz across our political landscape, taking pieces of our faith in the system with them.

# PART IV

## REFLECTIONS

# CHAPTER 1

# ON PHILOSOPHY, RELIGION, AND HUMAN NATURE

God, of course, is the greatest philosopher of all," Nixon said.

The remark came shortly after my arrival at his residence on August 26, 1992, for an afternoon meeting. Nixon stood at the window and turned toward me as I got to the top of the stairs to his study. On the ottoman in front of my chair lay his well-worn King James Version of the Bible, open to Matthew 5:9.

"Read this," he said, handing it to me and pointing to the verse: "Blessed are the peacemakers: for they shall be called the sons of God."

"You see," he said, taking the Bible from me, "those who establish peace are those of virtue. But peace alone is not enough. It must be joined to a higher purpose."

He sat down, laid the Bible in his lap, propped his feet up, took a sip of diet cola, and continued. "Peace should never be an end in itself. It's a great goal, but it's not a panacea. The search for peace must be part of a greater goal—you know, *something* that will give it meaning."

I asked if he considered himself a peacemaker, and he turned the question over in his mind before answering. "Well, I tried. We ended Vietnam; we had China and détente with the Russians. I think we made a significant contribution to peace in the world. But the point is that we did not simply seek the absence of war. We sought a peace with justice. That's what I told Mao the last time I saw him, when he was very frail but still sharp as a tack, and I meant it. But what I meant then is different from what I mean by peace now. Back then, it was to end the struggle of East and West in a way that would eventually defeat communism. Now, we need a mission, as we say, beyond just peace."

He narrowed his eyes. "Do you see what I mean about searching for a peace that has a greater meaning to it? Without that, peace is just a flimsy holding pattern to the next war."

His musings on the meaning of peace formed the basis of much of his own political philosophy. Two of his books, *Real Peace* and *Beyond Peace*, dealt specifically with how to define and achieve a meaningful peace in an international realm dominated by conflict. He wanted to be remembered as a peacemaker even as he prosecuted a war. He wanted to build a lasting peace even though he knew it was an elusive goal. He wanted to be the president who replaced confrontation with cooperation, adversarial relationships with partnerships, and war with real peace. Yet as a realist, he knew that it could only be achieved through a hardheaded appreciation of the realities of power. War and peace, the two great issues for the statesman, formed the basis of his thoughts about leadership and his approach to classical political philosophy.

Nixon was a voracious reader. Even as president, he allocated time for the reading he wanted to do despite having to get through all of the reading he was required to do. During his post-presidential years, Nixon spent hours of each day reading. In addition to reading *The New York Times* and *The Wall Street Journal* daily, he read *The Economist, Time, Newsweek,* and *U.S. News & World Report* weekly, as well as selections from *National Review* and *The New Republic.* In order to have more time for his books, he usually read these publications quickly.

"I need to read the papers and magazines to know what's going on and what people are saying about it. But I hate like hell to spend more time on them than I have to," he said that day. "And why bullshit with people? It takes time away from the great books." He lifted a copy of one of Aristotle's works and pointed it at me. "This is heavy stuff but worth it. There are so many books left to read, and my time is running out. You have a lot of time left. I don't. I'd like to read so many more, and others I've read I need to read again, but there is just so little time."

Nixon did, however, find the time and usually turned to philosophy. The bookshelves in his study were laden with the complete works of the ancient Greeks, the Romans, Saints Thomas Aquinas and Augustine, Niccolò Machiavelli and other Renaissance thinkers, Martin Luther and John Calvin, Thomas Hobbes, John Locke, Alexis de Tocqueville, David Hume, Edmund Burke, Jean-Jacques Rousseau, Jeremy Bentham and John Stuart Mill, G. W. F. Hegel, and Karl Marx. He read and reread these works, usually by sectioning them according to theme and by underlining important phrases that he could compare with his own political thinking.

Primarily, however, Nixon thrived on active discussions of classical political philosophy. He delved into layers of meaning and the practical significance and historical ramifications of what had been written. He always tried to link the great minds with his own; for Nixon, philosophy was a way to connect with the thinkers who had advanced the intellectual bases of all human action. Good and evil, right and wrong, good and bad government, and peace and war were issues that intrigued him on a core level. Human nature and what it means for government and international affairs were an endless source of inquiry for him. What the great philosophers thought of the human character had a profound effect on what he thought of his own. Many of his contemporaries had passed judgment on his nature, but the philosophers whom he read could not, and that allowed him to reflect objectively on the good and bad sides of his own—and mankind's—character.

"I believe that man is both good *and* bad, both light and dark. The evil, though, overrides the good in certain situations because although he has the potential to be good, his inherent evil tends to overwhelm him at times. Hobbes was right when he said that the life of man is solitary, poor, nasty, brutish, and short. It's a constant struggle, not that the struggle is a bad thing. On the contrary, I think it's a good thing," he said to me as we sat in his study during the late afternoon of September 24, 1993.

He turned to me in his chair and added, "As you know, I could never discuss this kind of thing in public because of the Watergate silliness. People will say, 'Who is he to talk about good and evil? He's just evil.' " He picked some imaginary lint off of his sleeve and then spoke more slowly. "It's too bad, because I've given this human nature stuff a lot of thought—particularly during and after the presidency. It was inevitable for me."

Nixon was not an optimist. His belief that man's inherent bad side often overwhelms his good one pointed to a basic mistrust of others. Though he was criticized throughout his public life for this fundamental skepticism, he made no apologies for it. Instead, he looked for the answers about human nature in the Bible and in the great works of philosophy. "Philosophy—" he said on January 29, 1993. "I don't always understand it, but it's worth reading for the great questions: What is the best form of government? What is the state of nature for man?" He sought the answers from antiquity in order to separate himself from the modern world, with its unjust judgments and skewed realities. Current issues were important but transient; the most enduring philosophical questions carried the possibility of transforming him, and he pursued them.

Despite his appreciation for their works, Nixon held most intellectuals in utter contempt. His disdain grew out of a belief that their intellectual brilliance bore a coldly arrogant condescension toward less sophisticated minds. "Intellectuals are generally not nice people," he said on May 2, 1991. "Their great minds do not make them good people. The modern intellectuals are particularly bad; they're intellectual snobs and hypocrites. The conservatives are cold—they say they don't care, and they don't. The liberals say they care, and they don't. I have more respect for a true-believing Communist than for an American liberal."

Most intellectuals, he believed, are not only arrogant and self-righteous but lack a broad respect and appreciation for other people and allow themselves to be seduced by the power of their own ideas, which often contemptuously disregard the human aspect of humanity.

"I know I repeat this often," he said on October 22, 1991, "but it's one of the truest things I've ever known: to succeed in almost anything, but especially in politics, you need three things: brains, heart, and guts. Unfortunately, most intellectuals only have the smarts. Most completely lack courage and have absolutely no heart whatever," he continued, handing me his dog-eared copy of Paul Johnson's book *Intellectuals*. "Intellectuals hate to admit that they're wrong. And most have led decadent lives; most are moral disasters. Read this, and you'll see what I mean."

*Intellectuals* is a collection of biographical vignettes of some of the world's most influential thinkers, including Jean-Jacques Rousseau and Karl Marx. The theme that links their lives is that though they professed to embrace humanity in the abstract, they abused and neglected those closest to them. They dedicated their lives to commenting on humanity as a concept yet mistreated their intimates. "Rousseau fathered all kinds of kids out of wedlock and refused to acknowledge them while abusing his mistresses," Nixon said. "Marx was an alcoholic and lived like a sloth. These are not admirable people. Their ideas have made them great, but they were not good."

He knew that his own public tragedy precluded any discussion of his views about human nature, but he could have them verified privately by reading that other great minds had experienced epic failings.

His antipathy toward intellectuals and what he perceived as their "tyranny" over thought ultimately boiled over when, shortly after her husband's inauguration, First Lady Hillary Rodham Clinton embarked on a much heralded "search for meaning." On May 23, 1993, *The New York Times Magazine* published a cover story on Mrs. Clinton, accompanied by ethereal photographs and a political cartoon likening her to Joan of Arc.

"Scandalous," he remarked when I met with him the next day. "They have canonized her." But of the numerous subjects covered in the piece, Nixon focused on Mrs. Clinton's philosophical musings. "Hillary is the prototype intellectual. She's out to solve the world's problems, but personally she's as cold as ice. The intellectuals are all bad. I don't want them running anything, do you? It's what we fought [in Nixon's administration], and it's what Clinton *is*. And Hillary is their spitting image," he said, pointing to the magazine. "Her remarks here do not seem thought through and appear disjointed and—I don't know—blathering. She and Michael Lerner float out there on this stuff, but there is something to it," he said. Revealing that she had been speaking with Lerner about man's search for meaning and how it related to policy making, Mrs. Clinton argued that the vague "crisis of the spirit" and "sleeping sickness of the soul" plaguing us individually and as a nation required immediate spiritual attention and remedy.

"I have battled with these questions for years, and so have most philosophers. Hillary makes it sound like a new phenomenon. I'd like to talk about these things, but how can I avoid the way-out sappy sentimentalism of Hillary?" he asked on June 16 while exploring themes for *Beyond Peace*. "I want to avoid the gushy shit of the Hillary and Lerner crowds. The moral relativism—which is what they're wallowing in—is a legacy of the '60s. It's the Rousseau bullshit: man is *not* naturally good but evil, as we know. Government didn't make people bad. People aren't born equal or perfect." He shook his head. "Hillary and her crowd advocate government solutions. They're so wrong. Got a problem? Let government fix it, spend more on it, debate it to death! No. The question and answer are more profound: What are we here for, beyond acquiring things and establishing peace? I don't know, but I do know that we are really talking about a religious answer, but can we provide it? It's easy to say what is wrong, but we want to be able to say what is right." He spoke impatiently, and his thoughts, like Mrs. Clinton's, were a jumble of ageless questions without definitive answers.

"Hillary should be given credit for thinking about this crisis of the spirit, but the search for higher meaning in life cannot be answered by any of us," he continued. "I think we have to wait until we die to know the answers. I really do. Peace comes with death, but I think it's only after we have passed from this life that we can know the answers to the questions that philosophers have been tossing around for centuries."

When I asked if he thought that God reveals the answers to us when we die, he leveled his gaze at me. "Well, if that's how you want to look at it. I believe that when we pass from the scene, we will know why we were here and what our higher purpose was," he said, pointing to the ceiling. "And although we can try to analyze it here, I don't think that they are questions that we can totally appreciate or answer."

Nixon's search for the answers led him through most of the great works of philosophy. He became focused on individual philosophers and read their works for days at a time. By submerging himself in their themes and issues, he tried to comprehend their broader interpretations and more subtle intentions. He sought escape through their words, enlightenment through their arguments, and intellectual validation through their wisdom.

"The works of the ancient Greeks were assumed to be the absolute truth, until they were confronted by challengers," Nixon said on the morning of August 31, 1992, during one of the many discussions we had about philosophy that were wide-ranging, interpretative, and often inspired by global, domestic, or personal events.

The presidential campaign was quickly approaching the election-day endgame, and Nixon searched Plato and Aristotle for insight he could apply to the contemporary American political process. He picked up his copy of Plato's *Republic,* opened it, and put on his eyeglasses. "The *Republic* is supposedly about justice. He's interested in challenging the conventional wisdom that justice is the advantage of the stronger, and by that he means basically that the force of speech is the best weapon in terms of domination and control. This is what he says: those who are strongest use rhetoric to reduce others to their will by appealing to views they *already have,*" Nixon said, emphasizing the last two words through clenched teeth. "This is the problem most politicians have today. Plato was interested in the power of challenging and provoking people into changing themselves, which is, of course, the mark of a great and effective leader. Rhetoric seduces its subjects; dialectic, as it's known, changes them. It *changes* them."

He put the book on the table and removed his eyeglasses. "I think that the bottom line for Plato was to put reason into politics. We could certainly use more reason in politics today. But the point is that appealing to people's base emotions does nothing meaningful. This is why Plato expelled the poets from the ideal city; they ruled by emotion and denied individual responsibility in favor of the group. Plato wanted to replace the emotion of the poets with rationality. Not a bad point. Everyone has feelings, but you shouldn't lead by them."

Two days later he had dispensed with Plato and turned his attention to Aristotle. When I walked into his study, he had Aristotle's *Politics* marked and open in his hands. "Plato is good stuff, but I find Aristotle much more accessible and interesting, don't you? He gets into the state-of-the-soul stuff, but what I think is most interesting are his views on the different types of rule. He says—and this is what is relevant today—that political rule must be regulated by *laws* in order to be constitutional. Laws! And that it must rest on consent. Plato, of course, was more of an elitist. He believed that rule by the upper crust was the best form of government. But Aristotle pointed out that the best form is some kind of mixture of democracy and elite leadership. He seems to think that having each of these groups represented will produce the most stable and legitimate government. In other words, no one wants to trade it in because they're all getting something out of it. Sound familiar?"

He laughed and closed the book. "No wonder the Greeks are timeless. They were asking the timeless questions! What is the best form of government? We mustn't lose sight of the fact that it's the corrupt goddamned leadership class that's the problem," he exclaimed, pointing at me. "Now you can see why I can't vent these thoughts in public, but it's true. Aristotle believed that the corruption of a government comes from a deficiency of education; the corruption of ours comes from too much education! These intellectual elitists are the most corrupt goddamned people in the world."

He shifted in his chair and continued. "Democracy by itself answers nothing. It's only as good as its people, so we must change people, but that's not possible. So where do we turn? Mobocracy? That's the worst form of government. This is what I mean about the Perot majoritarian bullshit, with the electronic town halls. Mob rule? No meaningful representation? Is that how you are going to govern the goddamned country? No! The Greeks were right: replace emotion with rationality, tyranny with consent, and mob rule with some kind of representation."

A guarded idealist, Nixon believed that the purpose of good government is to enlighten and improve the lives of those governed. But as a hardheaded realist, Nixon knew, like Edmund Burke, whom he often quoted, that the search for perfection must not be allowed to become an enemy of the good. "Perfection in man and in government is impossible, but we have to continue searching for it because we become better for it," he said on July 22, 1993, after giving another cursory reading to Immanuel Kant's *On History*, a work he considered crucial for its groundbreaking thesis of perpetual peace. Kant argued that history moves through a progressive series of stages until all or most governments become liberal states. And since liberal governments are less inclined to initiate war, particularly against one another, peace would expand as those régimes spread, until a lasting, comprehensive "perpetual peace" was achieved.

"German philosophy is so dense!" he continued. "Kant's ethical writings are almost incomprehensible. But the 'perpetual peace' stuff is interesting even if it is wrong. There is no such thing as perpetual peace; I don't care how many democracies you have. There will always be vital interests which states will go to war over. There will always be some kind of strategic problem or ethnic explosion or religious hatred to start the ball rolling. Conflict is, and always will be, a fact of life. Period. And there's nothing we can do to change that. Kant was hopelessly idealistic on this score. [Woodrow] Wilson believed that too—you know, the crap about 'Well, if we all got together and talked about our differences, the world would be at peace.' That's nonsense. We can try to manage those differences, but there's no way to prevent them."

Several days later he called me, quoting Joseph Schumpeter, who developed Kant's ideas on the progression of liberal government. "The libs hate him because he was for free markets before anyone else was."

Although Nixon did not agree with Kant's liberal idealism, he understood that with the collapse of the Soviet Union and the end of communism
in Eastern Europe, democracy appeared to be on the march, endowing
Kant's arguments with some contemporary relevance. "Democracy may be
spreading, but it doesn't amount to much unless people know how to run
it," he said, leading into a pointed analysis of the work of the great Renaissance thinker Niccolò Machiavelli.

"I decided to reread some of Machiavelli's stuff because he is by far one of
the more interesting philosophers." As we sat in his office on January 14,
1993, Nixon picked up his briefcase and removed a small volume. *"The
Prince,"* he said, waving it in the air. " 'The ends justify the means'—that's
all most people see in Machiavelli. I'll bet that's pretty much all most people
are taught about him. That line is, of course, central to his arguments, but
his stuff is far more complex than that one thing. Critics have used that
phrase to criticize our foreign policy, but those who did clearly have no understanding of how the real world works. The reality is that trade-offs are
necessary; you do not have the benefit of working with perfectly good states
and opposing perfectly evil ones. There is a lot of gray in foreign policy.
Sometimes what is desirable is so far away from what's possible that you've
just got to settle for what you've got. And sometimes this leads to policies
that may be not the best in some way, but the reality of the situation requires it."

He insisted on reading not just *The Prince* but Machiavelli's longer, more
complex *Discourses* as well. He viewed *The Prince* both as a handbook for
statesmen and as an analytic work relevant to the modern world. Its lessons
clearly resonated with Nixon, who defended even its most morally ambiguous assertions. "The critics who go after Machiavelli obviously have never
held a goddamned office or tried to run a country. Machiavelli was a diplomat, and he had the experience to write about what he knew. International
politics hasn't changed one iota since he wrote in the early sixteenth century. Not one iota. Sure, the players have changed, but the rules of the game
are exactly the same. So, considering that, what the hell is wrong with what
he argued?" Nixon asked, counting his next points on his fingers.

"He says that leaders should act decisively as soon as they detect a threat;
he says that they should be capable of using cruel and inhumane methods
to maintain the state, which we disagree with now, but back then that was
necessary to hold the goddamned places together; and he says that appearances are what's most important. Machiavelli must have foreseen the importance of television! He would have been the first to call [political and
media strategist Roger] Ailes!"

He opened his copy of *The Prince* and turned to a heavily underlined page.
"A good state needs a foundation of—what does he say?" His eyes scanned

the page and settled on the phrase. " 'Good laws and good arms.' You see, for him war was an art, not even a necessary evil." He closed the book and continued. "There is a deeper dimension to all of this. All those years ago, he said that leaders must be able to use force but that it's difficult for them to match the method to the situation. And this, of course, was well before we had the range of weapons we have today. This is the problem: a leader must appear virtuous and also *be* virtuous, but he must at the same time be crafty when the circumstances require it."

He shot me a quick look. "That was Machiavelli's meaning. But he was getting at what effective leadership is all about, and anyone who argues that leaders must be totally pure are arguing the impossible—that we aren't human, which, of course, we are. And for those who rise to the top, good and evil, side by side, are there. Integrity makes a good leader, but so does cunning, as Machiavelli calls it."

He opened the book again and searched for another quote. " 'Men judge more by the eyes and not the hands.' What do you think about that? Boy, there's the truth! We judge reality by appearances, even if those appearances have nothing to do with reality. But what I find most significant, not in here but in the other [*The Discourses*], is his emphasis on political action. He says it so clearly: political action is the best way of life because it's the only way to achieve greatness. And isn't that what we are all searching for?"

"Greatness?" I asked.

"Well, yes," he replied, "and to have our lives *mean* something."

Nixon's search for the meaning of his own life led him to examine the philosophical sources of the country that had shaped him. Locke, Montesquieu, and Rousseau fascinated him insofar as their ideas resonated with or challenged his own thinking on government. His remarks on Rousseau came as we continued our conversation on June 16, 1993, and as the Clintons' plans to expand the role of government and rectify some of the economic imbalances created by capitalism began to crystallize. Nixon rejected outright Rousseau's premise that forms the basis of such liberal thinking: that man, by nature pure, has been corrupted by decadent civilization and therefore needs to achieve total equality in order to reassert his fundamental goodness.

"Nonsense," he said. "We were never what Rousseau calls the noble savage, running around in blissful ignorance. No! We knew we had both good and evil from the beginning. We were never indifferent toward one another; there was always competition. My God, we are competitive by nature! And as far as his social contract goes, his idea of everyone submitting to the so-called general will is just a smoke screen for forced equality. It's leveling, goddamn it!" he said in disgust, clapping his hands together. "It was a bad idea when Rousseau had it, and it was a bad idea when Marx had it."

Nixon's distaste for government-directed social equality stemmed from his belief that all men are *not* equal, that we are endowed with different talents and abilities, blessed with different opportunities, and cursed with different burdens. Government can arrange for equality of opportunity as well as it can, but it cannot reengineer the human character or condition.

"Reread Locke," he instructed me on June 1, 1993, as he began writing an early draft of *Beyond Peace*. He read extensively in preparation for writing his books and turned to John Locke when the time came to write his chapters about America. Many of Locke's ideas formed the foundation upon which the leaders of the Revolution and the framers of the Constitution built the uniquely American philosophy of the proper relationship between the individual, society, and the state.

Locke argued that in the state of nature before the formation of society or the beginnings of government, man lived a self-sufficient, solitary, and relatively happy existence. In nature, he had the right to life, liberty, and property. He had the right to self-preservation, to refuse to submit to any ruler without his consent, and to possess those things in nature with which he had mixed his labor. For Nixon, these themes formed the basis for the political, religious, intellectual, and personal freedom that give the American experiment its remarkable character.

"Locke, unlike Rousseau, never gave in to the idea of forcing equality. He knew better. He knew that that was a battle against nature," he said that day. "Instead, Locke's idea of the social contract meant that when we joined the state, we transferred our power to the government or, really, to the whole community. So even though we weren't equal in nature, we became equal in the eyes of the government. That's a crucial distinction.

"Now, Rousseau of course argued that the need for society and government came out of force, that we just got tired of beating the hell out of each other to survive. But Locke, I think, comes closer to the mark. He says that it actually grew out of the inconveniences we faced because we didn't have the organization we needed to secure the rights we had in nature. We found that our lives ran a little easier with a little organization, meaning, of course, civilization."

"Which led to government," I added.

"But he was careful to point out that no society or government could legitimately overturn the natural rights. They cannot be taken away. And as you know, we see these ideas over and over again in the Declaration of Independence and in the Constitution. Government is necessary, but so is limiting government. Its purpose is not to create a perfect society, as the libs believe, but to secure the rights that man had before society even existed. It's good stuff and absolutely right. This is what I want to work into our American chapter in *Beyond Peace*. Limiting government is nothing new, and when we come out with our ideas, I want to use Locke to back me up.

"And by the way," he continued, "just because Locke was right about natural rights doesn't mean that democracy is for everyone. We have to face up to the fact that many states just don't have the traditions and institutions to make democracy work. I know that it may not be the acceptable thing to say, but it's true. Some nations simply cannot do it; most countries in the third world have had a hell of a time. But we must keep in mind that democracy does not guarantee good government or economic prosperity. We can endorse freedom and human rights around the world, but we should never be in the position of imposing our values on others. It's not right, and it doesn't work."

Among the English philosophers to whom Nixon turned for enlightenment on governance, Locke was important, but Edmund Burke was a favorite. On March 14, 1993, when we met at the residence, he told me that he had begun two books on Burke, one by Russell Kirk and another by Conor Cruise O'Brien. "Burke was not noted until he wrote against the French Revolution, and then the shit hit the fan. The libs can't *stand* him because he was against the socialism of the revolution—all that Jacobin leveling crap. Burke was for representative government, and God forbid if that meant republican democracy!" he laughed.

As he did with Alexis de Tocqueville, Nixon considered carefully Burke's writings and speeches on representative government, giving particular attention to Burke's advice on balancing constituents' opinions with a representative's own judgment. "This is one of the toughest things anyone in office has to deal with," he said as he read from a speech Burke gave to his constituents in Bristol in 1774. "Listen to this: 'Your representative owes you, not his industry only but his judgment; and he betrays instead of serving you if he sacrifices it to your opinion.' " He closed the book. "He was right on. In some cases, when your district is overwhelmingly for or against something, it's foolish to vote the other way unless you can really make your case.

"I remember so well the vote for the Marshall Plan. I took a mail poll in my district and found that seventy-five percent of my constituents were against any and all foreign aid. But when I came back from Europe after seeing the major devastation from the war, I was convinced that only a massive infusion of American aid could prevent them from sliding the way of Eastern Europe. It was an enormously hard sell, but I made speech after speech arguing for aid, and eventually the voters came around to my position. I voted yes for the Marshall Plan without risking my seat. Politicians need to understand the power of persuasion. Public opinion is one thing; *leading* public opinion is another."

Burke's thoughts on representative government were rooted in his broader ideas on human nature and man's ability to do good. Nixon quoted Burke from 1791: " 'Men are qualified for civil liberty in exact proportion to their disposition to put moral chains upon their own appetites,' " to which Nixon replied, "Unfortunately, if people can't control themselves, the government will. This is the liberal philosophy that government should provide all the solutions, including the moral ones. It's wrong, and it's bad. The American people must look mainly to religion, the family, and to what they themselves believe in for meaning, *not* the government—the government least of all! Conservatives have got to make the case for traditional values and individual responsibility in ways that go beyond the mushy moral relativism of the libs and the radical instincts of the religious crazies. If we do it the right way, these kinds of spiritual themes can bring people together instead of ripping them apart."

He stood up, shuffled over to his bookcases, and searched the titles until he found Alexis de Tocqueville's *Democracy in America*. "This," he said, wielding the book in the air, "is a masterpiece. As you know, I like to make predictions, but Tocqueville was the master of getting it right on. Over one hundred and fifty years ago, he recognized the importance of religion in American life, morals, and stability. He considered religion even more important for democracies because it instills habits, like moral responsibility and conscience. *That* is what is missing today—a sense of conscience."

He sat down and flipped through the pages until he came upon the quote he wanted. " 'The idea of the infinite perfectibility of man'—this is the ridiculous idea that human nature can be perfected. Well, it can't, and Tocqueville knew it. Let me make this clear: we should strive for perfection, but all the while knowing that it can't be achieved. I know it sounds crazy, but it's the only way to go about understanding what we're here for. Tocqueville knew that democracies were particularly prone to believing that man *could* be perfected. That's why we—well, the liberals, really—try the Rousseau type of social engineering. That bullshit will never work," he said, revealing the essence of his own philosophy: although government can elevate the human condition through good laws and a good example, it can never alter human nature.

His concern that the Christian Coalition was gaining disproportionate influence in the Republican Party led him to seek out another aspect of Tocqueville's philosophy. "Listen to this," he said, turning to another page. " 'Religions should be more careful to confine themselves to a proper sphere, for if they wish to extend themselves beyond spiritual matters, they run the risk of not being believed at all.' You see, this is exactly why I counseled Billy Graham not to endorse me in 1960. He wanted to; I said no. I told him that he would undermine his own ability to change people spiritually if he got involved in politics, which is designed to change nations politically. A clergyman's job is to change people, not governments. Church and state—two different things. Those on the religious right and left have their place—*out of politics,*" he growled, curling his right hand into a fist. "They have important things to say, but they should not try to take over the government. They know very little about running a government or dealing in the real world, and what they do know is wrong."

Nixon's antipathy to those seeking to infuse politics with a particular spiritual agenda ran parallel to his view condemning moral nihilism. He read with curious interest the writings of Friedrich Nietzsche, who considered amorality a universal state already achieved. Nixon asked to borrow my copy of *Beyond Good and Evil,* a title that inspired the title of his final book, *Beyond Peace.*

"I can't find my copy," he said, accepting the book from me on January 24, 1992. "I must have lent it out to someone. I can't believe I'm missing my Nietzsche! I always try to look at his stuff during a presidential campaign to remind me of why I went through the damn fire."

He had the volume read by the time we met the next day. "Most consider Nietzsche a madman," he said. "I think that's debatable."

He read a few passages to himself and then looked up. "Nietzsche is considered crazy because of the *Übermensch* stuff—you know, the super-ideal of man. Nietzsche got blamed for what Hitler twisted into unspeakable crimes against humanity. But that shouldn't stop us from looking at the rest of what he says. Listen, Nietzsche has this phrase—'the unbent bow'—with regard to the soul. He's talking about the tension in the soul that moves individuals and history." In a theory that resonated particularly strongly with Nixon, Nietzsche argued that conflict is the engine that drives human progress and that without struggle, man grows soft and life becomes meaningless.

"This is the finest phrase in the book, which is probably why it's the most famous: 'What does not destroy me makes me stronger.' Life without struggle isn't worth a tinker's damn. People always try to make life more comfortable, easier. But that doesn't mean we're adding anything to the experience. In fact, we're taking away from it. Growth only happens when there is struggle, when there is failure. Struggle *makes* life. I'm for it."

He paused. "On the subject of war, he says that it's necessary to keep the tension in the soul and to force human progress. It brings people up and gives them a duty, a higher calling. It's not possible now, not these days, not with nukes. But he was on to something in the sense that people *need* a mission; they need a calling greater than themselves. War served that purpose;

it kept people sharp, united, tough. That option doesn't exist for the United States anymore."

I asked if he meant that we needed a new mission for the country beyond meeting material needs, and he responded, "Yes. Remember when I saw Mao for the last time and he asked me if peace were our only goal? I replied that we sought a peace with justice. I always mention that because it's such a perfect example. But now we're looking for something beyond even peace. It's in the struggle, isn't it?"

Nixon believed that although brutal struggle and reckless risks should not be glorified as Nietzsche recommended, the most important achievements in life involve at least some risk, struggle, and adversity.

"The most difficult things to achieve in life are valuable because they involve hard work and a fight. Getting to the presidency, for example, is something that's worth something because very few are willing to endure the hardship involved in getting there. Keeping the soul tense—bent, as Nietzsche says—is the key."

At the end of his life, when his influence was real but his power was no longer formal, Nixon spent much of his time exploring what it means for the United States to be the only remaining superpower of the twentieth century. If the country were going to renew itself, it not only had to reassess its emphasis on material wealth and other earthly trappings of power, but it had to recommit itself to the idea of struggle. It would not be an easy task, particularly since achieving a higher common good depended on individuals' pursuing their own enlightened self-interest, the unintended consequence of which was a kind of selfish contentment that unbent the bow.

Nixon was most concerned about this collective weakening. The open system insulates American politics from the storms of religious or ideological battles, but it also creates the danger of an obsession with materialism. Foreseeing a day when secular values will triumph, Nietzsche warned against what he termed "the last man," a creature completely obsessed with material security and comfort and incapable of giving himself to a higher cause.

"Not only is the last man selfish," said Nixon, "but he is pathetic. Imagine not being able to achieve anything great because you have grown so soft and lax that you simply don't have the energy or courage to do it? Material things make life more comfortable while you are here, but they are just *things*, for God's sake! What defines you, what makes you who you are, is what you accomplish, and everything worth accomplishing requires a struggle. Of course, no one wants to hear that, but it's true.

"Only if you have experienced pain, been through the fire, been *tested*, have you lived. Greatness comes through the tough decisions with a risk involved, the risk to lose it all, like with the Fund speech or the decision to mine Haiphong. At that Cabinet meeting, I asked for their opinions—"

"But didn't you *tell* them your decision?" I asked.

"Well, like [William] Rogers said, 'I'm for it if it will work!' Everyone is for something when the final decision doesn't rest with them." And then, with a revealing and hopeful comment about his own status, he added, "Those who take on the risk become eligible to be great."

His thinking on Nietzsche's philosophy naturally led him to Hegel's *Philosophy of Right*. A highly complex and intricate work, *Philosophy of Right* deals with the self-development of the idea, the unity of thought and being, and dialectic, the form of rethinking the process itself. Like Rousseau, Hegel was initially enthusiastic about the egalitarian rhetoric of the French Revolution but ultimately rejected it. He wanted the individual to realize that the world is good and rational, that it is a reflection of God, that man is a part of it, and that he should see his place in it.

"I find Hegel almost impenetrable," Nixon sighed on May 10, 1993. "It's so complex, so German! But it's worth trying to slug through it. The good thing about Hegel is that he can be quoted to support almost any proposition."

He shook his head. "Most of the time I can't make out a goddamned thing in this stuff, but once in a while I come across something that makes sense. He argues very effectively against the stagnation of bureaucracy and man's need to be a bigger cog in the wheel, as if the wheel means anything in the first place. We tend to get lost in the endless petty, meaningless parts of life. We never really look at the bigger picture. Hegel feels it's pretty hopeless, and I really don't know. He talks about morality and the ethical life as the right paths, but I don't think most people are up to it. Most people don't have it in them anymore to take on the grueling self-examination he's talking about."

"People don't want to do it because they may not like what they see," I added.

"I know," he replied. "It's easier to bury everything. I mean, Hegel even says that differences in wealth create an underclass that gives up on the ethical life, but I don't think it's just limited to the underclass; I think that it's more far-reaching than that. What we are looking for is something to lift people out of the mundane—the peace equivalent of war. I don't know if we can answer it. I don't even know if it exists."

When those questions vexed Nixon, he turned to a subject to which he could more easily relate: war. Like Nietzsche, Hegel believed that war is necessary, because only with the mobilization and sacrifice of war do people see the meaning of transcendent duty. War creates disorder, which in turn creates a new order that will eventually spawn another war. The pattern is cyclical and universal.

"Hegel says that since every state is going up against the others all the time, war is the inevitable result," Nixon continued. "He's pretty much on target here, although he doesn't leave much room for negotiation and cooperation. Conflict cannot be avoided, but sometimes war can be averted."

It was, however, Hegel's ideas about economic development that fascinated Nixon the most, since they had given rise to a philosophy he spent most of his political career trying to defeat—communism.

Although Hegel did not completely dismiss the market as a way to allocate resources, his ideas paved the philosophical way for Karl Marx. Hegel argued that since the occupation defines the individual and since work requires knowledge, the person becomes an entity. His concern was that this kind of objectification will lead inevitably to great imbalances in wealth, which in turn will create envy in the poor man and a self-perpetuating cycle of poverty. If operated properly, the market can be a universal, ethical structure, but Hegel saw that it was not, and Marx jumped into the theoretical breach.

Nixon was alternately fascinated and repelled by Marx's writings. Marx, he believed, crafted brilliant ideas with impeccable logic but was completely misguided on the subjects of governance, economics, and human nature. The collapse of communism in the Soviet Union and Eastern Europe bore this out, though the continuing political and economic struggles of the new "democracies" there forced Nixon to reflect on Marx with a new perspective.

"Marx's ideas were powerful on paper," Nixon said to me on April 28, 1993, "but once they were interpreted and put into practice, they wrought more destruction on the human race than probably those of any other philosophy."

For Marx, increased human productivity leads to a division of labor, which in turn rivets people in positions from which they cannot escape. This kind of enslavement means that power remains in the hands of the few and the privileged, resulting in the degradation of humanity and the end of natural development. In order to prevent this cataclysm, Marx argued that we have to plan social goals collectively, liberate the exploited class, and thus begin, not end, history. He spun the idea of social revolution, claiming that the true liberation of humanity requires not just simply understanding the world as Hegel thought, but *changing* it. The state must be destroyed.

"Marx thought of the workers' revolution as a triumph of democracy, but he was very suspicious of democracy," Nixon said. "He opposed the Jacobin movements of the French Revolution that said 'Just seize political power and force equality.' Of course, Marx thought that this was a big mistake; he thought that it would lead to terrorism and coups unless the social forces were ripe. Marx was big on timing. That's where Lenin screwed it up: he was too impatient."

I mentioned that he was a revolutionary who wanted to see the results right away, and Nixon added, "But ideas don't always show their true colors in practice right away. Marx was far more patient, although I think he was more of a thinker than a practitioner. And also, once democracy, or some form of it, was achieved, Marx was skeptical that the proletariat would be able to use democracy to come to power and achieve socialism. His idea that there would be no central army and no bureaucracy and that the state would eventually wither away was hopelessly idealistic. Socialism can only be maintained by force, as we have found out. But despite these enormous problems with the theory, it led to unimaginable suffering and evil because people like Lenin brought it to life—brutally, I might add."

As he wrote *Beyond Peace*, Nixon reread *The Communist Manifesto* and parts of *Das Kapital,* searching the failed theories for insights that could be applied to the new age. On June 15, 1993, he sat in front of me with the two volumes in his lap. "Marx's stuff contains a lot of good lines without good solutions. Communism was deadly dull. People trapped under communism saw beyond their borders richer democratic societies that had color and light, and they wanted it. Freedom was a part of it, but materialism was most of it. The Marxists produced Olympic winners, but they didn't produce much else." And on July 7, he added, "The materialist right, like some of our friends over at *The Wall Street Journal,* says it's hunky-dory if we only had completely free market capitalism. But capitalism without compassion isn't enough. The materialist left says the answer is the Great Society. But even if we could satisfy all material needs, there would still be one hell of a void. The meaning of life, of what the hell we are doing here, will never be found in material things. If we're looking there, we're looking in the wrong place."

Nixon then turned to the meaning of the end of communism and its pioneer state, the Soviet Union: "Look at what happened there. Godless communism. My God! Imagine people telling other people that they can't believe! And the only thing that they were allowed to believe in was the state! If it weren't for the intimidation factor with the use of force, communism wouldn't have survived five minutes, never mind seventy years. I think that when we talk about the reasons for the collapse of communism, we give short shrift to the spiritual angle. People *need* to believe.

"It's the same thing with socialism. What we're seeing now is not just the collapse of communism but also of socialism. I remember [Secretary of State John] Foster Dulles saying in '54 or '55—which was heresy then—that there is no doubt that those who could understand the intricacies of the atom will see the contradictions of communism. He saw it then, but while we helped to bring about the end of the cold war, we did not *do* it. Dulles said that no idea but communism has expanded so successfully with so little. And, of course, he was right. But the idea simply could not survive when it came down to applying it to real people."

Nixon tossed his copies of *The Communist Manifesto* and *Das Kapital* to the floor. "Communism could not succeed because it was based on the fundamental errors of denying self-interest as a motivating force and by banning God. Any system that tries to deny or even punish people for spiritual beliefs or tries to replace them with secular ones is doomed to failure.

"Now, look at our own system: it isn't perfect, but it allows diversity and spiritual beliefs. Of *course* military power contributed to the end of communism and the Soviet Union, but so did the people's need to worship as they wished. Communism made the state the all-powerful authority; capitalism allows for material wealth but *also* for spiritual fulfillment," he said, pointing a finger in the air. "Capitalism has its down sides, but it's worth the price. It always outproduces a command economy, and it lets people achieve for themselves. Government should bring people up, but it should also get the hell out of the way. I'm not a libertarian, but I do think that there is far too much government where government has no business being. One of the biggest mistakes we can make is to let the failures of socialism creep into our system."

He paused as he picked up *The Communist Manifesto*. "If you were to read all of this, and Lenin too, you will never find the two ideas vital to a real democratic order: one, the worth of all people is the foundation of society and government, and two, the need for limitations on the powers of the state. So it was fatally flawed from the beginning: it was an unworkable idea; it rejected the ideas of individual rights and limited government; and it used force. And it was because of those things that communism led to every type of crime against humanity," he said, shaking his head. "And unfortunately, it took generations down with it."

Having built his political career on anti-communism and having led the country through a period of the cold war, Nixon was disturbed by Marx's ideas in practice and fascinated by them in theory. Ideas are power; good ideas have the ability to improve the human condition, and bad ones have the ability to destroy it. Nixon's interest was in whether, to what extent, and under what conditions the ideas of the great thinkers were applied, either to the world of thought or the real world of human interaction. He was intrigued by their origins and ideological or practical consequences. The fundamental questions of human nature and war and peace compelled him to explore his own deeply held beliefs and inspired his final search for meaning.

During that search, he always returned to the theme of peace. Although he believed that the basis for real peace among nations is the acknowledgment that conflict is inevitable, he struggled to gain a similar understanding of personal peace. For Nixon, the search for peace in this life was as frustrating as it was necessary. He perceived a universal struggle to understand that peace alone, personal or international, is not enough. It has to be combined with some meaning, whether it is justice, goodness, spiritual contentment, or devotion to God.

In mid-August 1993, Nixon found another reason to examine the issues of spiritual understanding when Pope John Paul II began a visit to Denver. Surrounded by great crowds, the pope spoke of faith, repentance, and redemption, inspiring his listeners—including Nixon—with messages of hope and possibility. News coverage of the visit was extensive, particularly when the president and first lady greeted him on August 12.

"Well how do you like this?" Nixon asked when we met in his study late in the afternoon. "The pope and Clinton together! The saint and the sinner! What a pair!"

"What an image," I said, sitting across from him.

"I thought so!" he replied, laughing. "And Hillary standing there. Oh, boy. I'd love to know what the pope was thinking at that moment. But I'll tell you," he said, propping his feet up on his ottoman, "it's an interesting thing. The pope is going to talk about hypocrisy, and he's got Clinton standing next to him. OK, but let's look at the broader issues here.

"People may disagree with the Church's teachings, but I feel it must not waver at all. It must not compromise. The second it does, that's it. It loses its power to teach right and wrong. And there must be a standard of right out there. The religious right is all about sloganeering. They don't know why they believe what they do, unless it's to gain political power. Catholicism is doctrinal. It's been thought through and examined for centuries. It's the enduring thing that people relate to and the mystery. I think that the Church lost a lot when it changed from the traditional Latin for the Mass to English. I know why they did it: so people could understand what was going on, so they could understand the message. But the mystery and the tradition were all part of it."

I asked if he believed that the ceremony is just as important as what is being said, and he replied, "Oh, absolutely. And that's true in politics or in anything else, but particularly in religion. It's the ritual that people hold on to, because it's consistent over the years, and it has the power to sweep them up even if they're a little weak on the message.

"But getting back to the pope, he will have an enormously successful visit here, as he does everywhere, because there is a spiritual vacuum out there, not just in the United States but around the world. There is a craving," he said, clenching his fist, "for something to believe in, but not just anything— something meaningful, something real."

When I mentioned that God has always been there, he shrugged. "I know. But somewhere along the way, people got lost. You don't have to look far to see that. My God, just turn on the evening news or MTV! So even though God has always been there, people haven't."

He paused. "The search is almost as philosophical as it is spiritual. We want to know why we're here and what else is there. I know I'm gassing around here, but you know what I'm getting at," he said.

I asked if he thought there were a spiritual revival taking place.

"Well, I'm not sure I'd go that far. Everybody goes about God in a different way. As you know, I'm a Quaker, and I believe in God, and I believe in turning to Him.

"But it was never in the sort of gross way depicted by those Watergate writers, of Kissinger and me falling on our knees. I asked him to pray with me, and we did, in a private, meaningful way during a dark moment. No, I'm private when it comes to that sort of thing. I read the Bible, but I don't go out there preaching about what I know or think about it. That is mine to hold on to."

When I asked him if his faith ever faltered, he replied, "Well, I must say, during the darkest days, when I really felt like I had nothing left, it did. But it didn't last long before I realized that that was ridiculous. What happened was my fault."

He paused. "You know, when you are president or a senator or congressman or whatever, you start to think that you know best. Not true. And when you are chosen as a leader, you think that you can save a lot of people from themselves. You can try, but it's a tough, tough thing. The bottom line is that the only one you are going to save is you."

I asked him to explain why younger people seemed to understand that premise.

"Well, that's just it. Wherever the pope goes, he seems to reach, to really *reach*, the young people. They do respond when they hear a message like that. Now, the Vietnam generation has a lot of work to do on this score, but the younger people—why, it's a hopeful sign."

He got up and walked over to his bookcase. "Do you know that book by— hmm, I think his name is [M. Scott] Peck? I think it's *The Road Less Traveled?* Been on the best-seller list for years?" He walked back toward me. "I can't find it. But anyway, I never really got into it, but the first line is great: 'Life is difficult.' Whammo!" He thrust a fist in the air. "It *is* difficult. And if you think you can get through it without God's help, well then, you're a fool. We talk about philosophy and finding the answers to the great questions. But the only question that is eternal, no matter what your religion is, is, Do you believe?"

Apparently, Nixon did not have to pose the question to himself. He seemed to find a contentment not only in his relationship with his God, but in his dependence on Him. For a man who had avoided relying on anyone or anything, this was significant. Nixon realized that his life was not his alone, that it was designed by a higher power, and that free will offered as many opportunities to fall away from faith as to embrace it. His faith may have faltered, but he found his way back; when circumstances were desperate and his days dark, his faith remained. Just as he thought that our ability to engage ourselves in a higher enterprise defines our secular lives, he thought that our ability to believe in something greater than ourselves defines our spiritual lives. And ironically for a man who had spent his life trying to gain political control, he believed that giving oneself up—both to a worldly cause and to the divinity of a higher power—is the only way to truly be fulfilled.

"As I look back," he said when we spoke in his study on November 30, 1993, "although it has been a rough ride, it has been worthwhile. I might not want to do it again, but I wouldn't have missed it. There are always some regrets. But none connected to the decision to go into politics or to persevere with what I set out to do. The reason is that I know that I have lived for a purpose and for the most part achieved it. I didn't do it perfectly, as the critics keep reminding me, but I tried. I did what I thought was best knowing what I knew at the time, and that's all we can really expect from ourselves, isn't it?" He paused. "You must live your life for something more important than your life alone. You will miss the meaning of life if you don't get lost in a cause bigger than you are. That's the only way you can find yourself."

Nixon's insistence that we cultivate an appreciation of the spiritual dimension of life stemmed from his own belief that it is the key to inner strength. He was able to survive tragedies and come to terms with what he had done and failed to do by conceding that his life's path was not completely under his control. That God had guided him gave him reassurance, which is why he read the Bible not simply for its spiritual nourishment but for its philosophical answers. Philosophy allowed both a separation from the modern world and an examination of the ideas that have shaped it. For Nixon, the interplay of theory and practice, spiritual and secular, ancient and modern, was where the public and the private converged. With every great work, he entered into a spirited interaction with the author, engaging in his ideas and comparing them with his own.

Perhaps above all, Nixon wanted to be remembered as a thinking man. Philosophy served this end: the issues and ideas that marked the centuries served as a basis for his own thinking. And by his life's end, he believed that he had gained a penetrating perspective into human nature and the meaning of our experience as citizens of a state and as individuals on earth. Where politics was transient, philosophy was ageless; where politics was mired in the mundane and immediate, philosophy transcended the modern world; where politics defined his life, philosophy had the power to transform him.

He considered himself a man of thought and action, an uncommon statesman who combined the virtues of the ancient philosopher-kings. Wisdom and moderation, courage and dedication, spirituality and decency, were his gauges of success. In the pages of the works of those who came before, Nixon found a path to greater enlightenment that, unlike almost everything else in his life, was not subject to public scrutiny. It belonged to him alone. His tireless examination of the eternal questions did not yield any conclusive answers, but the answers themselves were not as important to him as the need to know that he had tried to find them.

# CHAPTER 2

# ON FAMILY

Richard Nixon was so much a part of the national consciousness as a public figure that it is often difficult to comprehend that he was also a son, a brother, a husband, and a father. It was, however, these relationships that defined his private life, just as his tenure in the House, Senate, vice presidency, and presidency defined his public life. In a lifetime of spectacular political successes and failures, his private relationships offered a sanctuary of limitless understanding, comfort, and above all, love.

Nixon was able to persevere in his public life because of the private web of support, patience, and dignity his family spun around him. His source of certainty and stability in an uncertain and tumultuous world, they provided strength when he lacked it, humility when he grew self-important, humor when he became too serious, and an escape from the public world when it became oppressive. He put his faith in them, and they in turn gave him unconditional support. They grounded him, reminding him that despite the often lonely political battles he fought, he was not alone.

Nixon never took for granted the tremendous sacrifices and contributions of his family. It was because of their unwavering commitment to him that he was able to accomplish what he did, both in and out of office. His triumphs, defeats, and recoveries were as much theirs as they were his. Because he chose a public life, they did as well. Through the great trials of his career, they exhibited a quiet bravery, fighting back tears of pain and disappointment, holding their heads high with pride and defiance. Their devotion and commitment could not have been manufactured: they grew out of genuine devotion and empathy and had a strength that few outside their immediate circle could comprehend.

He often referred to his parents, Hannah and Frank Nixon, as the inspirations behind every choice he ever made. They instilled in him the sober sense of duty and a legacy of determination that carried him to the presidency and sustained him through his numerous comebacks. Their fidelity to family, faith in God, and respect for the opportunities created by hard work became the foundations on which their son built his life. Armed with their legacy of resolve, he battled back, just as they had always taught him. In his farewell remarks to the White House staff on August 9, 1974, he resurrected the memory of his mother, whom he called a saint. And after he left the presidency, he wrote his memoirs, the first line of which was "I was born in a house my father built." They were simple references but profound in their meaning: his parents endowed him with the drive to succeed, the refusal to accept defeat, and the need to always remember humble beginnings even while achieving great things.

"I'll never forget my mother," he said to me on November 9, 1992. As he discussed a new book that would address the issues of national and individual purpose, he thought of the most philosophically grounded person he had known: his mother. "She was a thinking woman. Finding meaning in life for her was never beyond finding meaning in God. When I said that she was a saint in my farewell speech, critics said I went overboard. They didn't get it: it was a very emotional time. I was resigning the presidency, for God's sake, and I couldn't refer to my mother? What are we talking about?"

He shook his head. "My mother taught me about hard work, endurance, and patience, although patience was never my strong suit—but my God, she was patient! She had one of the strongest hearts I have ever seen, a lot like Mrs. Nixon that way. She sacrificed everything for us. She worked like a dog, through pain and tears and you name it. She watched her sons die." He blinked hard. "Incidentally, I'm not one to bare my emotions in public, but when my mother died, I let it all out, right there on Billy Graham's shoulder. It was just one of those overwhelming moments. I missed her terribly, but I'm just so glad that she didn't live to see Watergate. That would have destroyed her."

"Because of the charges against you," I said, "or because of the end result?"

He looked right at me. "Both. She had a great sense of what was right. I never would have wanted to have disappointed her. I remember so well when she told me, 'A gentleman has never heard a joke.' Politeness and honor were the most important things to her, next to her faith. Every time it seemed like the world was coming down on us, she was so strong because she put it all in God's hands. She never gave up."

When I mentioned that Mrs. Nixon had a similar strength, he laughed and said, "I always knew that women were the stronger sex. Now, my father was a totally different person but strong, just like my mother. Good God, did he work hard. He did everything from sheep shearing to carpentry—anything to support the family. I remember one morning we had all gotten up and he was swearing over a bowl of something. Back then, the only breakfast food we had was cornflakes, oatmeal, and Grape-Nuts. And my old man was saying that breakfast food wasn't worth a damn. 'Put sugar and cream on sawdust and eat it, why don't we?' he said. It was funny at the time, but I think about it now. We had nothing, and my father always tried to make something out of nothing."

I asked him if he believed that traits such as ambition are inherited.

"Absolutely," he replied. "Of course, there are other factors, but the genes are there. My father was so driven, and we were the same. Try, work, succeed," he said, pointing a finger in the air. "If you fail, get the hell up and try again. Failure was never accepted. He valued education because he never had it. He *made* us want to learn. And he was a fighter. Both of my parents were fighters. They didn't believe in giving up. Quitting was for the weak. Quitting meant that there was something that you couldn't do, and they always taught us that there was nothing out there we couldn't do."

For eighty-one years, he carried with him his parents' principles: the need to accomplish, to blaze a trail, and to lead and not be led. They taught him that success means never retreating, even in the face of great adversity, and they showed him that strength does not derive from haughty self-righteousness but from faith.

It is not surprising, then, that he chose a spouse who held similar ideals. Mrs. Nixon possessed great inner strength, faith, courage, and a quiet fortitude that sustained him when he faltered. Every time I watched them interact, I saw a special bond of love, warmth, and respect. They treated each other kindly and often surprised each other with small gestures of affection that meant far more to them than ostentatious displays. He fluffed her pillows when he knew she was preparing to rest; she chilled his favorite drink, white grape juice. He brought her cold water when she was sick and chocolate when she was well; she dressed for the dinner they shared every night. And after those dinners, they sat together quietly and watched the evening news, sharing their joy or disappointment over the day's events. Like many couples, a silent language seemed to pass between them: they exchanged glances of recognition when words were burdensome, and they understood. Their turbulent life together in the public arena had finally come to a close, and now they seemed to find the privacy they had long deferred.

"I want you to come meet Mrs. Nixon," he said on July 12, 1990, shortly after I began working for him. "She's in the office today to do some things, and she knows you have joined the team, and she'd like to meet you too." He walked with me from my office to the conference room, where the former first lady was seated, signing autographs for a charity event.

"Pat?" he said. "This is Monica."

She looked up, smiled warmly, and took my hand with both of hers. "Well, hello. I've heard so much about you. Dick tells me that you're right out of college. What a wonderful opportunity for you to be here."

I thanked her, and she squeezed my hand. "Don't let Dick give you a hard time, now," she said, smiling at him. "If he does—well, just report to me."

He turned to me. "Are you going to squeal on me?"

"Only if you give her a reason to," she said, winking at me, and Nixon leaned forward and gave her arm an affectionate squeeze.

Her gentle teasing about his demanding nature and his playful response showed that they had found a balance: after years of supporting his ambitions, she could finally enjoy the private life she had long wanted. She was no longer required to traipse across the political stage or suppress her feelings about his decisions or judgment. Liberated from the demanding role of active political spouse, she turned her energies inward, to their home and family.

On October 31, 1990, Nixon met with me at the office and extended an unusual invitation. "As you might have heard, Halloween is very big at our house," he said. "It turns out to be quite a day. We open up the yard, and all the town's children and their parents are invited in, and I go out and pass out candy. It's quite a show. I think you'd like to see it, wouldn't you?"

The sight of the thirty-seventh president of the United States greeting trick-or-treating children by his front door intrigued me.

"OK, good," he said. "Come by around four, and just wade through the crowd and find me."

At the appointed time, I drove to Nixon's house and found it surrounded by parked cars, state troopers, and hundreds of children and their parents. The children, decked out in festive costumes, frolicked around the yard while their parents, unnerved by the prospect of meeting the former president, hoisted video cameras anxiously as they awaited Nixon's emergence. It was a crisp autumn day, and as I walked up the driveway past the children playing in the leaves, I smelled the scent of burning wood coming from the fireplace in Nixon's study.

I walked past the crowd assembled at the front door and entered the house, which was lit brightly in every room. Hearing the door close behind me, Nixon called to me from the study. "I'm glad you came! You've got to see this," he said, coming out of the foyer and toward the front door.

"Should I get your coat from the closet?" I offered.

"No," he said. "Don't want to bulk up. Go ahead of me, and stand to the side."

I opened the door, and the spectators, anticipating seeing the former president, gasped hopefully and then, upon seeing me, let out a disappointed sigh. As I moved to the side of the house, I heard them gasp again as Nixon finally stepped through the door. Camera lights flashed, and children excitedly lifted their baskets of candy toward him. Their parents leaned toward him, extending nervous hands and lingering by his side. Nixon, meanwhile, basked in the glow of their attention. He spoke to each child as if he or she were the only one standing in front of him, and greeted the parents as if he were still running for office.

As I scanned the crowd, I saw a man struggling to make his way toward the former president. Like many of the other guests, he was in costume, but unlike the others he was wearing a Nixon mask. Instead of expressing shocked surprise or dismay, Nixon jovially extended his hand to the alter ego and without missing a beat said, "Well, Mr. President, it's a pleasure to meet you!" The man laughed, lifted the mask, and introduced his son. A few other visitors in the crowd sported Reagan and Bush masks, leading Nixon to remark that he had seen more American presidents that day than he had in his entire life.

About a half an hour later, I joined Nixon as he went back into the house to wait for the next group of Halloween revelers to assemble. As I followed him into the study, Mrs. Nixon beckoned to me from the kitchen.

"Hi, Monica," she said. "I see Dick's got you observing the annual Halloween ritual." She leaned close to me and lowered her voice. "Look, Dick won't tell you this, but I will. Halloween is his favorite holiday. He just *loves* it. You see him out there. He's like a child. It's as if he's the one trick-or-treating." She laughed and held my hand. "It's good for him, though. He needs a pick-me-up like this once in a while. And I know he's glad that you're here to see it."

The door to the kitchen swung open, and Nixon looked at both of us. "Are you two plotting against me?"

"Maybe," she said.

"I didn't realize that you had come in here," he said to me. "It was the strangest thing. I was talking to you, and when I turned around, you were gone. Well, what did you think of what we just did?"

I looked quickly at Mrs. Nixon, who tried to conceal a smile by turning away, then told him that opening his home had been a generous gesture.

"Well, they enjoy it," he replied.

Mrs. Nixon laughed. "And so do you, dear. So do you."

Nixon smiled. "It's just a nice thing to do. Besides, it's important for you to see the other side of politics. It can't always be about important discussions of foreign policy. You have to get out there and meet the people, talk to them . . ."

"Win them over," I said.

"Yes, but not for the purely cynical reason of getting their vote, but to really listen to them, hear what they're thinking, and get a feel for who they are and what they need. People call it kissing babies, but that's all part of it," he said. "And now you've seen it."

"It's getting cold out there, Dick," Mrs. Nixon said. "I know you don't want to wear your heavy coat, but you should put on something; maybe that Ultrasuede coat I got you last Christmas?"

He looked at her, then at me. "You must see this jacket," he said, leaving us to fetch it.

Mrs. Nixon turned to me again. "Dick can be quite romantic, you know," she said. "I think that fact would surprise a lot of people."

Nixon returned holding the jacket, which he swung around so I could see it from all angles. "Isn't it lustrous?" he exclaimed, to which Mrs. Nixon replied, "Dick, it's meant to be worn, not admired. Put it on. Your crowds await you."

He lifted her right hand, squeezed it, then turned toward me and motioned for me to follow him outside. As we opened the front door, his daughter Tricia and grandson Christopher walked in, and Christopher announced immediately that he was heading off to the bushes to explode some "stink bombs" he had gotten in the city.

"Stink bombs?" Nixon asked, flashing a concerned look at his daughter. "OK," he called after his grandson, "just don't scare any of the guests."

It was a remarkable afternoon. As he stepped out of the house, I heard Mrs. Nixon laughing with her daughter in the kitchen and a few visitors outside whispering about seeing "living history." Not only did I see Nixon engage in the kind of populist politics that inspired more people to vote for him than for any other politician in American history, but I witnessed the part of his life that was separate from politics and insulated from its unforgiving and brutal nature. The warm displays of affection and gentle banter among the family revealed a profound connection established by years of shared experiences, both public and private. Nixon's restless spirit may have needed the constant action of the tumultuous political world, but it also needed the safe shelter only his family could provide.

"Dick is out walking the dog with a flashlight," Mrs. Nixon said when I went to the residence at six o'clock on January 4, 1991. "I know he was waiting for you, but Brownie couldn't wait," she laughed. "Please come in. I was just making myself some dinner, but I find that food has no interest. Terrible, isn't it, not to want to eat? Oh well, I force myself." She put her hand over her heart and laughed. "If you want to see an atrocious cook, just watch Dick try to make something. Oh! I think he's coming in now. You may have your chance!"

"Pat?" he called from the hallway, and when he heard us in the kitchen, the door flew open, and the dog bounded in ahead of him. "Hi! Well, it's cold out there. I'm going to make some coffee."

Mrs. Nixon tried to stop him. "Dick, why don't you let me do it?" she said.

"Nonsense," he replied, walking to the cabinet. Mrs. Nixon watched silently as he struggled to open a can of coffee, spilling many of the grounds on the counter. "Damn it! I'll get it," he said angrily as he tried to clean up the mess, only to create a bigger one. Exasperated, he turned to Mrs. Nixon for help. "Pat, do you mind?"

His reliance on her was absolute. Not only did he fare better when he listened to her advice, but he grew stronger and more patient just by being around her. When she cautioned him against a certain course of action, he almost always heeded her suggestion. When she offered to help him, he almost always let her, and when he did not, he suffered the consequences. And when she offered a sympathetic ear, he unburdened himself and walked away fortified simply because she listened.

He also found great solace in the support and pride of his daughters. Accomplished in their own right, they championed the causes of both of their parents with unparalleled devotion and loyalty. They were their parents' fiercest defenders, strongest advocates, and closest confidantes, just as their parents were their faithful protectors and most enthusiastic sponsors. The pride flowed both ways.

On December 13, 1991, the Nixons invited the small staff to their new residence for their annual Christmas party. The former president, sporting a burgundy smoking jacket, and Mrs. Nixon, wearing an ivory ensemble, greeted me together at the front door. She took my hand and gave it a long squeeze.

As they entertained us with amusing stories from the past, they exchanged silent glances and occasionally reached their hands out to each other as they made their points.

"I remember the '53 and '58 trips so well," Mrs. Nixon said. "Sukarno in Indonesia was such a womanizer! He always had the most glamorous gals around him."

"And remember the awful conditions we endured, Pat?" he asked. "My God, there was no indoor plumbing there at the time. Outside was also known as the bathroom."

"And we had to sleep with all kinds of mosquito netting around us because it was so humid, and the insect problem was terrible!"

"Those were quite some times," he said. "Eisenhower just let us go, and we spent months traveling from place to place, seeing things for the first time, which is always the best time." He looked at me. "Monica, you're the youngest here. You'll see all of these places."

Mrs. Nixon agreed and added a good-natured warning: "Just remember to bring your mosquito netting with you!" She stood slowly. "I'd like to show all of you my favorite room."

We followed her downstairs to a sun room decorated in her favorite colors, yellow and green. "We decided to put the Christmas tree in here, since I spend most of my time in here," she said. "We have been collecting decorations for over fifty years, from all over the country and the world. Some of them are really spectacular." She reached underneath the tree and distributed gifts to us, including a book about the White House art collections.

As they bid us good night, I saw the former president slip his arm through hers so she could lean on him. When I got to the end of the front walk, I turned to wave good-bye and was struck by the image of them standing arm in arm in the doorway. They cared about each other, and it showed. No longer bound by the demands of public office and free from the relentless scrutiny that accompanied it, they spent more time simply appreciating each other. Standing together, their arms linked, they were one, not just in marriage but in experience.

On Saturday, February 29, 1992, Nixon shared the day with his two grandsons, Alex Eisenhower and Christopher Cox. They attended a New York Knicks basketball game at Madison Square Garden and got an unexpected surprise.

"I took Alex and Christopher to the game this afternoon," he told me by telephone that evening, "and the game was fine, except when the cheerleaders put on their half-time show, they noticed me in the audience, and they sang and danced for me. That was fine too, except they came into the crowd to get closer, and in the middle of their dance routine one of them landed in my lap! I felt like Gary Hart on the *Monkey Business*! They might mistake me for Ted Kennedy! Oh, my God!"

We laughed together. "I told Mrs. Nixon about it," he continued, "and she thought the whole thing was very funny. She's such a good sport."

"Imagine what this will do for your reputation!"

"Nothing good," he laughed. "Oh, boy. It was one of those things. But you know, I'd rather watch sports on TV, in my own chair, because I ended up signing about one hundred and fifty autographs, and that was fine too, but I didn't see much of the game.

"But getting back to Mrs. Nixon, she's always been a trooper. She's made the *Good Housekeeping* list of most admired women for years, even when she was out of the public eye. And whenever we went abroad, she always kept her own schedule, and many times she went by herself. They called her a goodwill ambassador, but she *was* goodwill. My God, when I think about what she went through, I can't believe she did it. She packed up the entire

White House in forty-eight hours when we left and didn't sleep at all. The entire thing was such an ordeal for her and for the girls. But they were so strong, and they took it upon themselves to be strong for me even though they were devastated."

He paused. "I wouldn't have made it without them," he said, pausing again to collect a memory. "I remember many years ago, I was carrying Tricia, and I slipped on some ice and fell. I went to Bethesda—they served Congress—and saw a navy doctor who didn't set my arm right. Ever since, I've needed to have one sleeve shortened! But I don't regret carrying her. She was such a little girl then. And now I look at my own grandchildren, and they remind me so much of Tricia and Julie. [Julie's daughters] Jennie and Melanie put on shows for Mrs. Nixon and me, just like Julie used to. They are something!

"Julie was always taking the lead, and Tricia was always so creative. The credit belongs to Mrs. Nixon. She's a great, great mother. She always believed that people matter, regardless of who they are. She's just as compassionate to people on the street as to kings and presidents. We believe the same things in that regard. Her concern is real. She feels for people. And she was one of the brightest first ladies to have ever served. Edith Wilson was aggressive but not very bright. Eleanor [Roosevelt] was very smart, and she did her own thing. Mrs. Truman was pleasant, just not very bright. Mamie [Eisenhower] wasn't interested in policy; she just liked to play cards and parlor games. Jackie [Kennedy] was Jackie. Lady Bird [Johnson] is a tough cookie. Poor Betty Ford and Rosalynn Carter—they just had a tough time in there. Nancy [Reagan] is smart and tough. Barbara [Bush] is tough too. But Mrs. Nixon was really something special," he said, "and I'm not just saying that because she's my wife."

Nixon saw much of himself in her: wisdom, drive, strength, defiance, compassion, and forgiveness. She inspired him to be a better leader, husband, father, grandfather, and person, and he died believing that his strength had become hers and vice versa. When he wavered, she was there by his side, encouraging him with comforting words and supporting him by telling him the truth, even when it was not what he wanted to hear. Their relationship had survived primarily because she had been his best friend.

After Mrs. Nixon died, on June 22, 1993, he turned to his daughters for reassurance that the family would maintain its sense of unity. On Julie's birthday, July 5, 1993, Nixon brought them together for a family discussion.

"We had some very good talks about where we go from here," he told me later that day. "All for one and one for all. That's the way it's always been with us, and that's the way it's always going to be. Mrs. Nixon would not have wanted it any other way. I think it was a good birthday for Julie. Heidi took the kids to see the dinosaur movie [*Jurassic Park*], and we had a turkey dinner and a cake for her [Julie]." He paused. "It was good that we were all together. By the way, do you remember how you used to get Mrs. Nixon's absentee ballots ready for her?"

I did.

"And do you remember during the primaries a few months ago, you gave me her ballot, and I gave it back to you because I thought she was too sick to deal with it?"

"Right," I said.

"Well, she asked for it," he said. "She said, 'Where's my ballot?' I thought she was so sick that voting would be the last thing on her mind, but I was wrong. She missed it. I felt terrible that I kept it from her." He cleared his throat. "Well, this year will certainly be different without her. But Julie and Tricia will be coming up pretty regularly, although I told them that wasn't necessary, but they want to do it. And of course, they give me a great lift."

As Thanksgiving approached, Nixon's spirit seemed to improve. Apart from Halloween, which he enjoyed for its playful and whimsical masquerade, Thanksgiving was his favorite holiday because it is uniquely American, lacks the material expectations associated with Christmas, and focuses instead on the bonds of family.

"I'm really looking forward to Thanksgiving this year," he said on November 23, 1993. When I entered the residence, he called to me, and I followed his voice into the kitchen. "It's the only holiday we're all together. The girls like to have their own trees and things at Christmas, so Thanksgiving is a big day for me. Usually, I just ask Heidi to make me a toasted cheese, but of course on Thanksgiving we'll have all of the traditional foods which make every year so great.

"Here," he said, handing me a glass of white grape juice, "we have a ton of it for the holiday, and I thought you'd like some. By the way, every Sunday in the fall like this, I make myself some hot dogs and watch football. And I always toast the rolls so I think I'm actually at the game!" He laughed. "After doing five or six hours of grinding work on the book, it's really a great escape. Watching all that rough and tumble, I'm just glad it isn't me out there getting beat up."

He took a sip of his juice and pointed the glass at me. "And after Thanksgiving, you know what time of year it is, don't you? Why, it's Radio City time."

Every year, Nixon eagerly anticipated the Christmas show at New York's Radio City Music Hall, and every year he saw the show at least twice: once with his grandchildren and once with the Rebozos and the Abplanalps. With its splendid musical numbers, dazzling dance routines, and breathtaking sets, the show was one of the few indulgences he allowed himself.

"When was the last time you were at Radio City to see the show?" he asked me on December 12, 1993.

"Years ago," I replied.

"Well, you must go. It's really something to see. It just gets better every year. The Rockettes are terrific, and the ending—the birth of Christ—is very moving. It's just great, and if I can swing it, I'd like to take the staff this week.

"By the way, did you hear what happened to us last night? I was taking the Rebozos into the city for dinner and Radio City, but we never made it because the roads were so icy. It took us three hours to get there, and we missed the whole show, so if we can get tickets for Friday, we'll go. You must see it. I don't know if I can deliver it, but there's the promise.

"We did go to dinner at '21,' and I hadn't been there in years! It was really great, but I'm just not going to go out like that all the time—you know, the social stuff. I don't mean to be serious all the time, but I want to have useful conversations, one-on-one, not bullshit around with strangers or acquaintances, not at this time in my life. Going out with the Rebozos or Abplanalps is one thing; going out to just be seen is another and not my bag." He plastered a faux smile on his face. " 'Oh, hello, how are you? It's been *years!* " He grimaced. "God, I hate that crap.

"But if we go to Radio City, we'll have a ball. I promise."

On the warm winter day of December 17, Nixon's limousine pulled up to his office to pick up the staff, and as we piled into the back, he slid to the side so that he could be next to the window.

"It's so warm for this time of year, isn't it?" he said, taking off his coat. "I'm glad we got tickets to the matinée show." He looked at his watch. "I just hope we don't hit any traffic."

Once in the city, we did indeed hit the gridlock traffic that paralyzes midtown Manhattan every Christmas season, and Nixon, still warm and needing fresh air, opened his window. As we sat at a standstill, a small crowd began to gather on the sidewalk, many of those in the group peering into the limousine and smiling with recognition. Nixon, oblivious to the fact that the window was down, continued talking to us until he glanced outside and saw the assembled group.

"I wonder what's happening," he said. "There's a crowd out there looking at something."

"Sir," I said. "They're looking at you."

He glanced at me, startled. "Oh. Well, then," he murmured, turning toward the crowd. "Hello, nice to see you," he said, waving gingerly as he slowly put the window up. "I had forgotten that the window was down and that people could see in. Oh well. That's nothing. They all seemed nice."

We finally came to a stop by the side entrance of Radio City Music Hall. As soon as Nixon stepped out of the limousine, he was mobbed by hundreds of people wanting autographs, handshakes, or merely a glimpse of him. He did his best to accommodate them before escorting us through the crowd into the theater. Once inside, a line formed quickly behind him, and the ushers tried to move the audience members back to their seats so the show could begin.

Nixon was mesmerized as soon as the lights went down and the curtain went up. I watched him watch the show, and I could see an innocence renewed in him, as if the Christmas stories of his childhood were just as fresh then as when he had first heard them over seventy years before. When the melodies swept over him, he smiled to himself, and again I was struck by the image: the man who had dominated American politics for over a half century was totally captivated by the simple beauty of a Christmas pageant.

It was the final scene of the show, however, that truly gripped him. As the birth of Christ was reenacted, the narrator told the audience of a man born to a peasant woman in an obscure village, who worked as a simple carpenter and never "wrote a book or held an office" or did any of the things that accompany greatness. And in the end, He died at the hands of His enemies. But, as the narrator reminded us, every person who has lived since has been affected by that "one solitary life."

When the scene was over, I looked at Nixon, who was clutching a handkerchief. The message had shaken him. Writing books and holding offices had been his life's work, but suddenly they seemed a bit less important.

The final scene at Radio City granted him what he sought: perspective. Greatness did not come only out of grand pronouncements or epic achievements; it could come from a simple truthfulness to oneself. And although Nixon did not turn his back on the human drives of ambition and determination, his priorities never excluded faith and family. They endured, as few other things had.

On Easter Sunday, April 3, 1994, three weeks before he died, he spent the day in New York with Tricia, strolling down Fifth Avenue. As they made their way slowly down the street, an ever growing crowd embraced them. It would be the last crowd he would ever encounter, and even as he told me later that day how "gratifying" it was to sign "over six hundred autographs for people from all over the world," it meant more to him to have his daughter by his side.

"The recognition from all those people was extraordinary," he said, "and they were all very respectful. But it was just nice to talk to them knowing that Tricia was right there to see it all and . . ."

"Share it with you," I said, finishing his sentence.

"That meant a lot," he said.

The spectacular victories and defeats of Nixon's public life distinguished him as one of the most controversial presidents to have ever served the American people. The quiet serenity he found in his private family life is less well known, even though it was the key to his political and personal survival.

When others were interested in his politics, his family was interested in his well-being. When others were interested in what he had to say, they were interested in what he felt. And when they were criticized for the life he chose, he defended and protected them, even when he failed occasionally to defend and protect himself. His choice made them public people, but their compassion not only kept him grounded but gave him the fortitude to persist, particularly during the darkest days.

"The saying goes that behind every great man is a great woman," Nixon said to me once, "but I'm even luckier than most. I have three." Their courage steadied him, their strength emboldened him, and their love fulfilled him. And in the end, he saw clearly what truly mattered: of all the people he had known and served and of all the power and things he had acquired, only God and family did not fall away.

# CHAPTER 3

# ON AGE, MORTALITY, AND PURPOSE

On the morning of January 9, 1994, I woke and reached for the phone, fully prepared for the ritual that marked Richard Nixon's birthdays. I dialed the number of his study, where I knew he would be brooding over the official addition of another year to his life. Though forced to concede that "no one lives forever," he intended to fight the inevitable every step of the way.

The phone rang several times before Nixon answered. I heard him clear his throat, still clogged with early-morning fatigue, and grumble a cautious "Hello."

"Good morning, Mr. President," I said. "I wanted to be one of the first to wish you a happy birthday."

"Well, isn't that nice," he said, without much enthusiasm. "I know you always remember these damn things, and I don't celebrate them anymore, but that greeting was so nice that I think I'll celebrate this year!"

Every January 9, I wished him a happy birthday, and every year he cursed the day. He was politely appreciative of the good wishes but despised what they represented: another reminder that his life was one year closer to its end.

"Aren't you the one who always tells me that age is just a number?" I asked, repeating the cliché he often told himself.

He laughed. "Well, it's easy to say when it's not your birthday. The girls offered to come up for a visit today, but I said no. I didn't want anything—no fanfare, no fuss, nothing. It's Sunday, and no one is really around anyway. I even told Heidi that all I want for lunch is a good tuna salad and for dinner she could leave me hot dogs, which I can heat myself."

I asked him if he wanted me to bring him anything, aware that he was balancing a subtle plea for sympathy with an assertion of self-sufficiency.

"No, thank you," he replied. "I'm going to watch the [New York] Giants play and, hopefully, win, and do some reading. That's it. How does that sound to you?"

It sounded a bit sad and lonely. The former president of the United States was alone on his eighty-first, and last, birthday. Mrs. Nixon had passed away six months earlier, leaving him alone to wander the halls of the house and obsess on his own mortality.

I pictured him sitting in his chair in the study, feet propped on the ottoman, a glass of grapefruit juice at his side, a pen in his hand, and a book in his lap. Instead of reading, he would be gazing out the picture window, watching winter continue to stifle the life around him and wondering when its forces would come to claim him.

Of the many subjects we discussed during the four years I worked with him, he was most uncomfortable talking about aging and mortality. He had spent his entire adult life running for office, leading the country, struggling to come back, and facing his own mortality only insofar as it meant how he would be portrayed in the history books.

As the years passed, however, mild denial replaced the detached attitude he had long held about death. Self-effacing remarks betrayed his real concern about his advancing age. Humor concealed his fear. Others' deaths were excuses for him not to have to think about his own. Occasionally, however, the fear gripped him and surfaced in a paralyzing torrent of doubt and panic.

"I saw Billy Graham the other day. He looked good, but he was complaining about growing old," he told me on January 31, 1992. Nixon was tired and distracted, having just returned from New York City after a live interview on *Good Morning America* to promote *Seize the Moment*. The conversation with Graham seemed to affect him on a profound level: considering himself ageless was difficult when his contemporaries kept reminding him that he was not.

"You know, as I sat in that dressing room this morning, looking in that three-way mirror—and, by the way, I'm not one to really look at myself, except when I shave—I realized that I look damn *old*." He looked at me and then quickly looked away. "I see how young you are and how young almost everyone else around me is, and I—well . . ."

He cleared his throat. "I see some of my contemporaries, and they look so bad. I see the younger set, and I feel their age intellectually, but physically I have to face the fact that I am old."

The former president turned in his chair toward me, held up his right hand to preempt any comment from me, and flashed a weak smile. "I don't mean to be depressing or fish for compliments. I didn't even mean to dump all of this on you. But looking at myself in those hard lights of the studio, it occurred to me that you should be thinking of yourself. As Deng said, 'Don't attach yourself to one chariot.' You should hook up with a rising star, not a falling one."

Before I could protest, he smiled and continued. "How can you stand to be around such an old person?"

"I don't know any old people," I replied.

He let out a hearty laugh. "Ah, so that's how it is going to be."

Nixon never came to appreciate the aging process as anything other than a slow physical decline. He considered it not an enriching final passage but a highly pressured, compressed time in which everything had to be accomplished immediately because "who knows how much time is left." With death coming ever closer, Nixon felt he had to make his intellectual contributions at breakneck speed: books were written every two years, fact-finding trips abroad were taken every year, speeches were delivered every few months, op-eds were published in the country's top newspapers just as often. It was an unconscious strategy: by accelerating his schedule, he hoped to decelerate the inevitable end of life, or at least fill it with activity so he did not notice its arrival.

A comic event on October 7, 1992, brought some levity to his attitude toward aging but also underscored his insecurities. Nixon called me in the evening to talk about President Bush's latest poll numbers and to inform me of a misguided practical joke.

"Hello, Monica. I thought I'd save you the cost of the call tonight. It's still a nickel, right?" he laughed. "If this isn't a good time to talk, why, I'll just call back," he said.

When I told him that I could take the call, he continued. "Do you want to hear the joke of the day? It's really unbelievable. Last night at about eleven o'clock, Mrs. Nixon, Julie, and I were watching the news, and John Taylor [director of the Richard Nixon Library and Birthplace] called. I thought, 'Oh, my God. Who died?' And he says, 'I'm so glad to hear your voice, Mr. President. All day, I've gotten inquiries from the Associated Press and the *Los Angeles Times* to the effect that President Nixon has died.'

"*Died!* Can you believe it? So I told him, 'My God! No! I am very much alive!' Where do they get these things?" He laughed loudly. "Monica, they thought I had *died*, for God's sake! The next time they ask, I have instructed him to tell the press that we have no comment!"

The episode, humorous on its surface, also pointed to Nixon's preoccupation with dismissing the fact that someday he would, indeed, die. He often referred to a bottle of 1913 Lafite Rothschild kept in his wine cellar as his "motivation to live to one hundred."

"I know my doctor has prohibited alcohol for the rest of my life," he said on October 31, 1992, referring to a heart condition for which he was on medication, "and you know, Bebe always says that I should get a second opinion! But if I live to be one hundred years old, I am drinking that Bordeaux, goddamn it! In the year 2013, both of us will be one hundred, and that's how I'll celebrate. And if I drop dead after drinking it—well, then, at least I will have died enjoying myself!"

Nixon believed that he would live well into his nineties, even as he entered his eighties. In mid-December 1992, as his eightieth birthday approached, he pleaded with me not to discuss it: "Please don't bring it up. I really don't want to think about my age. The Rebozos wanted to come up from Florida, but I said no. I don't want to hear about it. I mean it."

He did mean it. His rationale was that if he did not celebrate time's passage, age could not have an effect on him. If he did not talk about aging, he was immune to its effects. If he did not acknowledge his birthdays as formal reminders of the fragility, brevity, and temporary nature of life, he did not have to suffer the devastating consequences.

This inner struggle was apparent when he called Ronald Reagan for his eightieth birthday, on February 6, 1991. I entered his office that morning and found him sitting in his corner chair, frowning behind a copy of *The New York Times.*

"Today is Reagan's birthday. It's a big one, you know. Eighty." He stopped. "Eighty! My God! And I'm right behind him."

He picked up the telephone receiver and asked to place a call to Reagan in California.

"Ron? Well, I wanted to wish you a happy birthday. I hope it's not too early for you out there."

Nixon laughed and continued: "The forty-first anniversary of your thirty-ninth birthday? Well, that's a great line! I'll have to remember that one."

When Nixon hung up the receiver, he folded his hands in his lap and sighed. "Time waits for no one."

I smiled. "Not even presidents?"

"*Especially* not presidents!" he laughed.

Suddenly, he sat straight up in his chair, leaned forward, and said, "Have I ever told you what I think of the death thing?"

"What do you mean by 'the death thing?' " I said, stunned by the question.

"Well, my thinking on death goes like this: I know the goddamned thing is inevitable, but there's no reason why we should all brood over it. Look, I go to all of my doctors at least once a year, more often if something is bothering me. I do *not* understand why people—older people mostly—don't go. I know they're scared, but they should know what the hell is going on. I always get clean bills of health, and the doctors tell me that I'm in great shape, and I know I'll live at least another year, or so they say.

"But my view on the death thing is this: I really don't want a big fuss made at my funeral. I hate going to those goddamned things, and everyone is so sad and crying—or pretending to, like this: 'boohoo'—and it's just an awful scene. No. I really don't want all of that. When I go," he said, his voice quivering, "it will be fast and painless, I hope, and without all of that sentimental, wrenching bullshit."

He blinked hard and continued: "I don't mean to be morbid, but I have to write, think, and so forth while I still have it all together. When I pass from the scene, it will be quick, not some long drawn-out thing. But I have to contribute while I still can."

On August 17, 1993, I went to the residence in the afternoon to work with him on a draft of *Beyond Peace.* He sat across from me in the study, sipping white grape juice and wielding his pen like a weapon. "As you know," he said, "this book will be my most philosophical in terms of what I see for the country. I'm not one to write a lot of introspective crap about myself—even *The Memoirs* and *In the Arena* were limited in that regard, though *In the Arena* was a bit more revealing. So in this book, I'm not going to dwell on how I feel about getting old, although there may be a forum for that later. Maybe an article for *Reader's Digest* or something, to let others know that life is what it is—full of the highest highs and the lowest lows. Look at my life: it's been a hell of a ride."

When I asked if he would have traded it for a quieter life out of the public eye, he replied without hesitation, "No way. Although sometimes I wonder if anyone is ever really ready for a public life. Being president is not something you're ever really ready for even though you spend your entire life getting ready for it. You can't escape controversy, and although we expect it, it makes living a normal life pretty hard." He looked directly at me. "You have your whole life ahead of you. Mine is all past, behind me."

He picked up a recent copy of *The Economist* that had a photograph of Clinton on the cover. "This guy is young. He looks good—energetic, vigorous—"

I stopped him. "How can you set yourself up for a comparison with Clinton?"

He threw the magazine to the floor. "I know it's silly, but I just think—well, if I were forty years younger, I could do so much more. I know everyone tries to buy more time, particularly when they get to be my age, but it's always different when it's *you.*"

He continued through clenched teeth: "Monica, you *need* something to live for. Everyone does: countries do, people do. And everyone should maintain a youthful spirit. Sometimes it's hard to do, but you *must*, otherwise aging will just get you down and defeat you."

Nixon's resilience was his primary source of strength. By constantly coming back against great odds—against political opponents and critics—and by dismissing those who discounted and disparaged him, Nixon was able to rise above defeat and prove to himself and to others that he was virtually indestructible. Though death was the only force that he acknowledged could defeat him, he did not allow it to dominate his thoughts when they could be put toward more constructive purposes.

"Discipline," he said to me on October 1, 1993. "Discipline is the key to living life well." With winter fast approaching, Nixon could no longer take the long outdoor walks during which he said he did his best thinking, and he would be consigned to indoor exercise on a stationary bicycle.

"You see, I could say to myself, 'It's cold outside. I can't take my walk, so I'll sit and mope.' But I don't. I say, 'OK, I can't be outside, but I need exercise anyway,' and I do it. Without discipline, so much of life is lost. I've always followed a fairly strict routine of exercise because without that you're just going to become mush. Reading and giving speeches and writing keeps the brain from becoming mush, but you've got to keep the body up to par, or the brain won't really matter if you can't get out and talk about things. So today I swam, and I'm going to miss it when it gets really cold. I'm in pretty good shape. I don't drink, I don't smoke, I don't play cards! What do I do?"

"Nothing fun," I said.

He laughed. "I know it. But at my age, even a little fun could be deadly! You can't stop the passage of time. My doctors always tell me that I'm going to live another year, so I must be doing something right."

Whenever he did something wrong, however, he paid a heavy price, physically and psychologically. Usually careful about maintaining a healthful diet and exercise regimen, Nixon occasionally overextended himself and became sick or was injured. Recuperation, with its lack of interaction and activity, was a miserable time, trapping him alone with feelings of vulnerability and weakness.

On April 25, 1992, Nixon was in Florida, visiting his good friend Bebe Rebozo, when he fell and sprained his ankle. He called me in the afternoon to give me the news.

"Monica? Oh, hi," he said. "Well, we ran into a little problem and spent the morning at Miami Hospital."

"What happened?" I asked.

"Well, coming down the stairs at Bebe's, there was an unexpected drop, and I twisted my ankle," he said. "I'm in a goddamned wheelchair. I always said I'd never end up in one of these. The doctor said the bone didn't break, so I must have strong ones. I guess I'll be around for a while. He says I should be ambulatory in two weeks."

I asked if he were experiencing a lot of pain.

"Well, you know how this is," he said. "I didn't want to take the painkillers, but I really had to. I'm coming home tomorrow, and I'll see you on Monday, although I really look like hell, so don't be shocked."

I went to the residence early Monday morning with some materials for his review and a card on which I had written a quote from Hippocrates: "Healing is a matter of time, but it is also sometimes a matter of opportunity." When I got to the top of the stairs to his study, I found him sitting on the windowsill, obviously racked with pain. As he stood, he reached for a bookshelf for support and leaned too heavily upon it, bringing the shelf and its contents crashing to the floor.

"Goddamn it!"

I rushed to his side, helped him to his chair, replaced the bookshelf, and asked if he were feeling better.

His face was flushed with pain, anger, and frustration. "Not really," he said and pointed to his shoeless feet. "I tried to put my shoes on, but I'm too swollen. I hate to have you see me like this: no shoes, in pain, can't do anything . . ."

I suggested that he see another doctor, and he grimaced. "I wasn't going to, but the pain is just too bad. You know how I feel about going to the doctor, and that's when I'm *well!* It's awful, with the doctors poking at you, strangers all taking a pinch and a pull. But I have no choice."

The next day, the doctor put his foot into a soft cast and gave him some assurance that the pain would eventually subside. I went to the residence later that afternoon.

"As you can see," he said, waving a hand toward his foot, "I went to the doctor, per your request, and I'm glad I did. It's still painful, but at least I'm on the healing track." He winced. "The pain comes and goes, and I can't really walk, which means I'll be doing a lot of reading in this chair over the next few days, so send over any interesting material."

He folded his hands in his lap and smiled. "I don't mean to be morbid, but this kind of thing gets me thinking about how much time I really have left. I don't know how you can stand to be around such an old person!" he laughed. "But I've got to wonder if I look like hell on the tube. You know, I really don't want to be out there looking like an old, withered thing. It's just something to think about. We have to face the fact that time is going along. Nothing we can do about it."

His face brightened. "I'm in surprisingly good health for someone of my advanced age, but I'd rather not mention my age! It's important to always look ahead, never back, because someone may be gaining on you! When you get to my age, though, it's hard to look ahead because you never know how much time is there. But I still always say, 'Look to the future, because if you do, you'll live to see it.' "

Though he tried desperately to avoid thinking about the aging process and death, the subjects haunted him. Throughout his life, he worked to project strength, vitality, invincibility, and resilience. But every time he became ill or was injured, he was reminded of his physical fragility. He did not fear the process of dying as much as what it represented: the end of his chance to contribute, the final loss of control, the end of his comeback. Death was the one opponent he could not vanquish and one that did not offer any second chances.

He had lost people close to him in the past, but three deaths in 1993 affected him particularly profoundly. Within five months, former Texas governor John Connally, Mrs. Nixon, and his former chief of staff H. R. Haldeman died, leaving Nixon stunned by fear and loneliness. Death had come for those around him, and soon it would come for him.

"Mrs. Nixon is very sick," he said on December 22, 1992. "And I mean very sick. She's in bad shape, worse even than when we went to the opening of the Reagan Library and she collapsed. She's down to under one hundred pounds, and she's five foot seven. But she has a cough, and we're all on her to see a doctor. She won't go. I don't know how she does it. She's so brave, and she never complains, even when she's in excruciating pain. She's so strong and fragile at the same time."

During the four years I worked with the former president, Mrs. Nixon was alternately healthy and gravely ill. Emphysema made her breathing difficult and strenuous activity impossible, but her physical frailty was matched by an indomitable spirit and strength of will. Every time she became sick, she fought back until she recovered. And every time she recovered, she appeared to be stronger than she had been before the illness. In early 1993, however, she finally succumbed to the power of death's slow march.

I talked with Nixon by telephone in the early afternoon of March 2, 1993. He sounded upset, and when I expressed concern, he replied, "Well, it's Mrs. Nixon. She caught a touch of the cold I had, and on top of the emphysema she could hardly breathe, so we had her brought to New York Hospital."

"Is she all right?" I asked.

He did not answer.

"Are you all right? Sir?" I asked.

His voice was trembling. "Well, I can't really talk right now, but I want you to call me later," he said quietly, "so I can cry on your shoulder."

His comments startled me. Never before had I heard Nixon admit such vulnerability or show such raw emotional distress. A master of concealing his personal concerns, Nixon rarely allowed anyone to know his most intimate feelings; it usually took a crisis, such as Mrs. Nixon's dramatically deteriorating health, for him to express real and uninhibited sorrow.

When I called him later, he said, "I'm better, but what the hell. I'm supposed to be indestructible. So much for that. I'll be going to see her at the hospital every day she's in the place, so I may not be in the office that much." He sighed. "Well, that's that, I guess."

She regained some strength and returned home, but on April 25, Mrs. Nixon was brought once again to New York Hospital with severe respiratory problems.

"They brought her blood pressure down," he told me the next day, "which was a bit of a crisis for her, and she has two private nurses. We decided to do that after my prostate operation. Bebe came up and was waiting with me beforehand when this strange nurse came in and asked my name and said, 'What are you in for?' Can you believe it? So since then, we wanted to avoid that incompetence and hired our own. She's having a really rough time. She's kept up her spirits, which is remarkable since she's pretty bedridden. And there are other complications, which we won't discuss now. But when the news stories say it's serious, I'd agree with that."

Three days later, with Mrs. Nixon still in the hospital, the former president called me to say that he had begun to think about her funeral arrangements. "I don't mean to depress you, but I went to the hospital to see Mrs. Nixon today, and though her spirits are high and the doctors say she has a strong heart, it doesn't look good. If something happens, we'll do it at the library, not Washington and not New York. I think it's only right that we have a plan ready to go."

Nixon made no attempt to conceal his despair. Sadness crept into everything he did and every word he spoke. He often left sentences unfinished and walked aimlessly down the hallways of his office and home. He neither ate nor slept well. He stared out of windows, and he paced. Never before had he had to confront what his life would be like without his life's partner, the woman who had supported him in triumph and tragedy, through his well-known peaks and valleys and, indeed, through sickness and health. The end of her life was upon him, and he found her quiet suffering and the prospect of going through the rest of his own life alone unbearable.

"Please come in," he said when I entered his study during the late afternoon of May 3. The house was dark and, with the exception of the sound of the news coming from his television, quiet. "I was just reading and doing some other things . . ." He turned off the television, moved to his chair, and asked me to sit down. Several long moments passed.

"Well, Mrs. Nixon is feeling a little better, but it's only temporary. She doesn't know how serious it is—you know, the big *c*," he said. "In older people, cancer moves much more slowly, so it's a long process. It's a very difficult time for us, as you know. She has two or three months, maybe more, maybe less. But her spirits are high," he said with a weak smile. "She came downstairs today and said, 'I'm going to make it.' And our job is to keep our spirits up so her spirit doesn't fall. We must do that," he said, clenching his fist. "It's so hard when she thinks she's getting better but she isn't. It's most difficult on the girls—Julie and Tricia. They're having a hell of a time."

"And how are you doing?" I asked.

"Well, you know, I'm realistic," he replied. "You've got to face the facts as they are. Don't you worry about me. We'll all get through this thing."

By the middle of May, Mrs. Nixon was in very grave condition. Breathing had become almost impossible, her weight was dangerously low, and the pain had become oppressive. As her family surrounded her each day, she grew more ill, but her attitude remained remarkably positive. Just as they were determined to keep her spirit up, she was determined to keep hers up for their benefit.

On May 17, I met with Nixon at the office. He had decided to title his last book *Beyond Peace*, and we spoke about its meaning.

"I'm intrigued by our title," he began. "*Beyond Peace*. It's interesting, catchy. As you know, what we mean by it on the surface is that peace is not enough, not anymore. What is our goal, our mission, beyond peace? That's the question. But there is a more profound meaning here that most people won't catch. It goes to the meaning of why we live our lives, because peace is not going to come in this life. No way. People are born restless, some more than others. Peace is in the grave, not here. As you get older, you realize this more and more.

"Incidentally, I saw Cronkite on the Bob Hope special, and he looked so damned old. He's about as old as I am. Jiminy crickets! This latest crisis has shown me that life is limited and you must live every day as if it's your last. I want to make the most of every moment.

"But let me say this: if something happens to Mrs. Nixon, and it's just a matter of time at this point, I want you to be out in California. And I don't believe in funerals, so it will be a simple service. But you can come—that would be fine—you can help with the press. Besides, you should be there anyway."

He shifted in his chair. "And one more thing: I want you to watch the news stories on her, and if there is *any* negative remark anywhere, I want you to blister them. We *will not* tolerate that," he said, pointing at me furiously. "I chose a public life; she didn't. They'd better leave her the hell alone. And if they don't, go after the bastards. All right?"

I agreed.

"Good," he said. "The last thing we want to have to deal with is that bull-shit. Julie and Tricia are hysterical, and I am fatigued. I don't want them to have to see anything negative. One of our friends sensed what's going on through intuition and told us, 'I think she's dying.' I mean, we all have to die, but . . ." He swallowed hard. "Well, she'll have peace soon while all of us run around trying to find peace around here."

A week later, he was so anguished when I met with him that he resorted to pacing. "I'm not one to confide easily in people," he began. "But I don't want to burden Tricia and Julie with this. I had to find out about California state law, because I thought that burials had to be in cemeteries, and we, of course, want to bury her at the library. The reason I bring this up is because this weekend Bebe mentioned Jean Paul Getty's desire to be buried at his library, and he couldn't be until the legislature passed a law."

I mentioned that I thought that the Reagans had arranged the previous year to be buried at his library.

"Good point," he said. "We have to make sure so we aren't screwing around at the last minute. I remember de Gaulle saying that he didn't want a monument when he died. Neither do I. The library is a monument. I want a simple stone. And if there's a screwup with this burial thing, we'll just be buried somewhere else.

"The hardest part about this is that we know what's at the end, but we don't know when it's going to happen. It's very grueling."

On June 4, Nixon received more bad news: his good friend John Connally was seriously ill and close to death. After calling Connally's family, he summoned me.

"I called the family because he's just very sick," he said. "Fibrosis—whatever that is. He's going to die. He has pneumonia, and it looks like the end." He shook his head. "I have enormous respect for him. He and Bush never got along down there because, frankly, Bush was elite and Connally was not. Do you know that he never, ever mentioned being in the car with Kennedy when he was shot? Not with me, not when he campaigned, never. Now that's character!"

He looked down. "You know, it's a depressing thing. Connally's dying, and he's much younger—seventy-five, I think. And I think about myself and how old I am—all wrinkled—and I think, 'My God! I'm seeing people like this?' I'm one of the last ones standing. I remember when [Herbert] Hoover was asked how he would handle his critics, he said that he planned to outlive them all. Well, I've outlived many of them, though certainly not all, and I'll just bet they are dying for me to kick the bucket. That's why I don't plan on dying!" he said, laughing for the first time in a long time.

Mrs. Nixon's health continued to deteriorate, though on the days she felt relatively well, the former president sat with her outside, hoping that the beauty of late spring would bring her some relief. He talked to her, read to her, watched television with her, and cared for her. By making her as comfortable as possible, he was trying to prepare himself for the idea of losing her. He moved around her quietly, efficiently, deliberately, concealing his own fear and desire for both of their pain to end. In our discussions, however, he was openly sad, distracted, and troubled by hearing words of comfort when Mrs. Nixon needed to hear them more than he did.

"As you know," he said on June 15, "Mrs. Nixon went to the hospital yesterday. She walked to the car, but she's very weak. With these diseases, you just get weaker and weaker. They had a wheelchair for her . . ." He paused. "This morning, I had Heidi cut up some fresh papaya for her because that's her favorite, and it's all we can do to get her to eat anything. She needs strength because she's losing it every day. She comes down for dinner but has a hell of a time getting back up to her room. And there's not a goddamned thing you can do about it."

For a man who had built his career on projecting strength and control, the feelings of helplessness were overwhelming. All of the formal power in the world could not save his wife's life or that of his friend and confidant John Connally.

"Sir?" I asked, when I called him at home later that day. "I just heard that Connally has died, and I wanted to extend my sympathy to you."

"Oh," he said, followed by a long silence. "He did? I didn't know. Well, I talked to his wife this morning, and he wasn't doing well at all. I'll go to the funeral, of course."

He was clearly distressed. Death surrounded him, bringing its unpleasant reality ever closer, intruding upon his well-ordered life, looming with its mortal guarantee. He could not escape it now, regardless of how hard he tried.

On June 17, he flew to Austin to attend Connally's funeral, and early the next day, when I saw him in the office, he ordered me to travel with him into New York City for a doctor's appointment so we could talk about the service and his concerns about Mrs. Nixon.

"I'm sorry to have abducted you like this," he said in the limousine on the way into the city, "but I have to go to the doctor, and I need to talk to you about some things related to the book and tell you about yesterday. I guess the stress of all of this has finally caught up with me. My back and neck are very sore, so I'm going in for a treatment.

"Anyway, Connally's service was very well done. The family was sobbing, and when I spoke to them, I told them that his children are his best memorial, which I often say about Mrs. Nixon, and it's true in both cases. And I told them that he was big in every way: big intellectually, bighearted. I told them that when he never once mentioned being in the car with Kennedy when he was shot, it showed a lot of class and great character. I traveled eight hours back and forth just to say that, but it meant a lot to them. I'm glad I went."

"Why wasn't Senator [Phil] Gramm there?" I asked.

He slammed his briefcase closed. "You know, you're right. That is inexcusable. Of course he should have been there; it's his goddamned state. We will not forget it; we won't do anything for him again. Ann Richards, by the way, was terrific with me. She's so good; I wonder why we don't have any like her on our side. Lady Bird [Johnson] was there with eleven Secret Service agents. Now, we gave that up to save the taxpayers the millions it costs every year, and we're not worth anywhere near what she's worth. Pay for it, already!"

He paused. "Bush wasn't there either, but that I understand. They were blood enemies. But the Fords and, frankly, the Reagans should have been there. Well, we remember our friends."

When I asked him about his relationship with Connally, he smiled. "He had principle. He was the only one who advocated mining Haiphong Harbor. He said, 'Do it, and don't worry about the summit.' He was right, and he said that the Cabinet should have been fired for not supporting it. He was strong, smart, good with people. Becoming a Republican killed his political life, and he was a damn good one, which is why I can't believe our bastards weren't there," he fumed.

When New York came into view, he tapped me on the shoulder and said, "There it is, Sin City! I hate like hell to have to make this trip every time I have an ache or pain, but this is where my doctors are, so what the hell. The drive isn't bad, particularly because I'm not driving!

"You know, yesterday, when I was in the airport on the way home from the funeral, an old black man recognized me and asked how I was and how Mrs. Nixon was; he remembered. He told me he was in 'Mr. Truman's war'— Korea. And he said that he supported me in Vietnam. I signed autographs for him and his grandchildren. That was something. When I got home, I told Mrs. Nixon, to give her a lift. She was really struggling, but she seemed to understand and gave me a little smile," he said, smiling a little himself.

Connally's death affected Nixon profoundly since it came when he was already grieving over Mrs. Nixon's failing health. The death was a shock and a tragic distraction from the slow end he was observing at home. When he spoke to Connally's family about his legacy, he was preparing to speak to his own family. When he offered words of comfort to Connally's family, he was rehearsing those of his own. And when he complained about the attendance at Connally's funeral, he was expressing a latent fear that Mrs. Nixon's funeral, and perhaps even his own, might be dismissed. Connally's death did not just rob Nixon of a friend and confidant but prepared him for the ordeal that he would face just several days later.

I walked into Nixon's office on June 21 to find him bent over his desk, with one hand on his back.

"Are you all right?" I asked.

"Oh, yes, yes, I'm OK," he said, trying to stand upright. "It's just my back. It must be the stress. It hurts like hell. But that's not really the priority here." He moved slowly to his chair and sat down, his face flushed with pain. "Mrs. Nixon is in very bad shape. It looks like this is it."

He waved a hand in the air. "I'll be fine. It's the girls, you know," he said, trying to turn attention away from his own agony. "Julie and Tricia have been through so much in their lives. This is just very difficult. There was a little debate among us because Mrs. Nixon didn't want a service, but I said that she doesn't just belong to us but to the country and to the world."

Looking away, he continued: "Today is our fifty-third anniversary. And her mind is still there; she remembered it. That was . . ." He stopped.

"I still can't believe Connally's funeral. I'm sick of the entire Republican establishment. They're a sad bunch. No one is up to the fight, and no one has any loyalty. That funeral was a disgrace.

"Well, I don't want to mope around, so once we get through this crisis, I'm going to go headlong into this book [*Beyond Peace*]. We need to get the thing done anyway."

"We can probably get an extension on the deadline," I said.

"No," he shot back. "I will do it every hour of every day if I have to. I'll be up to it. I need to think of other things anyway."

About an hour after our conversation, I heard his voice come across my intercom. "Monica? Drive me home, please."

I hesitated. Taking Nixon on the three-mile trip from the office to his residence was a harrowing experience. It occurred only rarely, when the limousine was being repaired or had been sent to fetch his daughters or grandchildren, but it always inspired the fear that every imaginable auto-related catastrophe might occur with the former president in the car. I agreed to take him home primarily because I had no choice.

"Well, the limousine is in the city, I think, picking up Tricia, who is coming out for what looks like will be Mrs. Nixon's last night. Julie is already at the house," he said as we walked to my car. I opened the passenger side and moved the seat back to give him more room for his legs. Once he was safely seated with his briefcase on his lap, I closed the door. When I got into the car on the driver's side, I asked him to put on his seat belt.

He looked at me blankly. "I rarely use one in the limo, though I should," he said. "How does it work in this car?"

I got back out of the car, opened his door, swung the seat belt across him, and asked him to hold on to the end so I could secure it when I got back in the driver's seat.

"Well! That was a project!" he said, and as I went to put the key into the ignition, he grabbed my arm tightly. His face was paralyzed with fear. "I can't go home."

"What?" I asked.

"I can't go home," he repeated. "Not yet."

I looked at him again. The former president of the United States, seated in my small car, was telling me that he was not ready to go home to his dying wife and mourning children. "OK," I said slowly. "What would you like to do?"

"I just need a few more minutes," he said. "Can you maybe drive around a bit?"

"I can do that," I said. "Anywhere in particular?"

"Why don't you go by the old house in Saddle River and drive around there."

I started the car and drove cautiously through his old neighborhood. He asked me to stop the car in front of their previous home, where Mrs. Nixon had enjoyed better health and happier times with her family and where death had not loomed as immediately as it now did.

"I used to walk all around here," he said. "Past these houses, including that one, which we considered buying at one time. Mrs. Nixon could never walk that far, so she couldn't come with me, but I used to take the dog and my flashlight and go up and down these streets. I can walk where we are now, but it's not as private."

A few moments of silence passed. "In this book, which I am going to devote my entire attention to after this is over, I want to state unequivocally that there is nothing wrong with making money. Liberals have this way of making people who work hard for their money feel guilty, and I want to blast the hell out of that. They talk about humanitarian projects, but how are you going to pay for them? I remember so well going to Burma in '53. They were such good people. I asked the prime minister, who was a socialist, how he was going to pay for the roads and schools he had planned. 'The government,' he said. But he knew private enterprise was the key.

"And I also want to hit hard the idea that being a housewife is not honorable. My mother worked harder than anyone else, and she was a wonderful person. Mrs. Nixon had so many responsibilities, but she raised the girls so well and took care of the family singlehandedly because I was not available, really."

The rambling thoughts came to an end. "OK," he said, drawing a deep breath. "I'm ready. You can take me home now."

When I stopped the car in front of the residence and released Nixon's seat belt, he looked quickly up at the house and then back at me. "Here we go," he said. I opened the car door on his side and extended my hand, which he took for support. "I hate to rely like this on anyone," he said, "but my back is in very bad shape. OK. I'm OK." He straightened his back as much as he could, then moved slowly up the front walk and into the house, closing the door quietly behind him.

Those moments in the car with the former president were tender, revealing, and powerfully poignant. Nixon, who prided himself on strength, invincibility, control, and the ability to do the most difficult and distasteful tasks without dread, had sat desperately in my car, unable to confront the final hours of his wife's life. He was powerless, lost, vulnerable, fearful, and grief stricken, confronting the very emotions he had battled against successfully for most of his life. During those moments in my car, he was no longer the indestructible former president, the man thrusting the defiant victory signs in the air, the iron-willed master of the comeback. He was now simply another husband about to lose his life's partner.

My telephone rang at six-fifteen in the morning on June 22. "Monica? Well, it happened about a half an hour ago."

"Mr. President, I am so very sorry," I began.

"OK, thank you," he said. "I need you to come up here as soon as possible because the press will descend pretty soon, and I want you to call some VIPs and tell them yourself before they hear it on the news."

I asked if he were all right.

"I'll survive it," he said, his voice sad but steady. The story made its way around the world as he stayed ensconced in his study. As I spoke to him by telephone throughout the day, he seemed composed, eager to hear how the funeral plans were developing and how others were handling the news. His world may have been crashing down around him, but he was remarkably calm, determined to keep emotional collapse at bay.

The next morning, Nixon came into the office and summoned me immediately. Agitated and short-tempered, he issued a flurry of ideas about *Beyond Peace*, gave orders about how he wanted the press handled, and expressed frustration with the way the Clintons were managing the debate over the role of government. "Because of your interest in Tocqueville, I thought you'd like to see this review of the new book by Henry Steele Commager. I know he was a favorite of the universities, but I don't know if he's still up to it. This old fart—writing a one-hundred-and-thirty-page book and selling it for twenty-four dollars! Good God! What would he say?" He put his eyeglasses on. " 'Presidents Nixon and Johnson escalated the war.' Typical bullshit." In the middle of this caustic tirade, he picked up the telephone and placed a call to his daughter Julie.

"Hello? Is Julie there?" he asked. "This is President Nixon, her father."

He asked Julie several questions about the funeral planning and then turned to me. "I can't believe that the Bushes aren't coming. Something about Mrs. Bush's brother having died. But no funerals are on Saturdays unless it's something like this. They could have made it. And Clinton, *that* son of a gun! I can't believe he had nothing to say when they asked him about Mrs. Nixon. And yesterday was the perfect time for him to offer Hillary's condolences, but he didn't. They'd better send someone of Cabinet level. Why not Gore? It had better be someone of rank."

I asked how he was feeling.

"I'm OK," he replied. "I'm not going to take my walks for a week; I want to avoid seeing people. Tricia and Christopher are coming today." He fixed his gaze on me. "I didn't sleep last night. Do I look bad? I know I look like hell. I've been working on my remarks for the funeral. It should be . . ." He stopped. "I see that *The New York Times* did a fine job on the obituary. The picture on the front page was a terrific one," he said, picking up a copy from the floor next to his chair. The photograph, taken during his vice presidency, was a touching image of Mrs. Nixon walking with her two young daughters on the beach in Mantoloking, New Jersey. Interestingly, the *Times* chose a photograph of her that excluded her husband and any suggestion of the political world in which she so reluctantly lived. Instead, the newspaper chose to publish a final image that she would have chosen herself because it reflected her most treasured role: that of mother.

"The photos on the inside were very nice," he continued. "But they should have put the obit on the front page. They put every liberal asshole on the front page. It shows what we're up against, but overall they did do a good job."

Early the next morning, he asked in a somber but steady voice that I come into his office. "I'd like for you to put together a list of everyone who has expressed sympathy and what they said. I'd like to know, when all of this is done. Did you see Safire's piece?"

"It was superb," I said.

He pointed at me. "Top of the line. That's what we're talking about. I think, on balance, the coverage has been good. Julie was upset over an *L.A. Times* piece; that's the last time I do something for them. But I thought *The New York Times* piece was all right."

I asked him if he had been able to sleep.

"Last night," he replied, "for the first time in a while, but I was up at five. I heard, incidentally, that [adviser to the president David] Gergen called, and they were going to send Hillary, but there was a scheduling conflict or something. That's not right. They'd better send someone from the Cabinet, or they'll be put back in the rafters and out of the line of the television cameras."

He stood up, grasped at his back, and lurched forward. I reached out and steadied him.

"It's my back, maybe because I haven't really slept." He smiled weakly. "OK. I'll see you in California tomorrow."

On June 25, I awaited Nixon's arrival at the hotel in Fullerton. When he finally called for me in the late afternoon, I found him in his pajamas, robe, and slippers, standing bent over by a curtained window. He turned slowly toward me.

"Well, my back has now completely given out," he said. "My osteopath volunteered to come out here and straighten it out, but that wasn't necessary."

"But you're in a lot of pain," I said, moving to help him to sit down.

"I'll survive," he said, positioning himself carefully in the chair. "As you know, this has been a very difficult time for all of us, ever since we found out in late April how sick she really was. And right to the end she kept saying 'I will get better,' and we knew she wouldn't. Oh well, at the end, at least the pain was gone. Maybe the morphine hastened it . . ." His voice trailed off as he looked around the room. He wanted to talk, but conversation was labored; he wanted silence but could not bear it; he wanted to be alone but needed company. Racked with physical and emotional anguish, he was torn between wanting to share the pain and wanting to isolate himself.

"I'd like to know how many visitors have been to the library to pay their respects," he continued. "I think there have been several thousand so far, which is good, don't you think? I guess it is." He paused. "How bad do I look? I'm getting myself deliberately tired so I'll be able to sleep tonight. I can't get through tomorrow without sleep.

"You know, Billy Graham has been terrific. He's so good at the comforting stuff. But it was hard, seeing the coffin for the first time . . ." He stopped and looked at his hands.

"We were on the plane, the old Air Force One I went to China and the Soviet Union in, which was nice of the administration to provide." He stopped again. "What color is your dress for tomorrow?"

"Black."

"Of course," he said, shaking his head. "Of course. I'll receive everyone tomorrow after the funeral."

I asked if he would be able to handle it.

"Yes. I cannot have Bob [Abplanalp] and Bebe [Rebozo] and the others fly across the country and then not see them. Incidentally, Julie suggested a heating pad for my back, so you may want to ask her about that. It may help.

And I may take Julie and Tricia on a vacation after this, to get their minds on other things. OK. You can go now."

When I asked if he needed anything else, he simply shook his head and waved to me as I turned toward the door. With an exhausted body and a distraught mind, the former president prepared to give a final farewell to his wife, whose courage, devotion, and resilience had matched his own. Their lives grew around each other like vines on a trellis, reaching upward together and battling against adversity. For the first time, he had to deliver a speech without her waiting eagerly to applaud it. He had to stand alone now and speak about her as a memory.

I did not see him again until he arrived at the library for the service. The small crowd stood as Mrs. Nixon's coffin was brought in and the former first family filed in behind it. Haldeman, who was seated directly in front of me, whispered suddenly, "The president's lost it." I looked at Nixon. At the sight of the casket and the guests, he had broken down and sobbed uncontrollably, shoulders hunched forward, frame trembling, tears pouring from weary eyes. The collapse in pain and sorrow became one of the day's most searing images and shocked even Nixon when he saw a film of it later.

After the formal service, Nixon retreated to a private holding area, where he greeted the Reagans, the Fords, and the eulogists—Governor Pete Wilson, Senator Dole, General James Hughes, and family friend Cynthia Milligan—whom he escorted to the main lobby to join the others assembled for a special reception. He was remarkably unself-conscious and spoke in calm, steady tones.

"Everyone in this room is special because you all knew Pat," he began. As the woman he "lived with and loved for over a half century," she brought "sunshine" into his life and into the lives of everyone she touched. The warm memories he shared of their life together revealed an intimate personal history that complemented the formal political history they had made and through which they had lived.

His remarks showed a side to him few knew existed. Pat Nixon was adored and admired by legions worldwide for her generosity, warmth, intelligence, and courage—the same qualities that had attracted her husband over a half century before. While Nixon spent his political life fighting ideological battles, his wife was more concerned with serving those less fortunate. Mrs. Nixon understood that her power did not come from a vote but from within. She bore a quiet strength through the triumphant victories and devastating humiliations of her husband's career and protected her daughters from the cruel world of politics. His accomplishments and defeats defined her as much as her own did, and his life became hers. The only reward she sought for such selflessness was the joy of having a loving and devoted family, which is why it was so appropriate that her life came to a quiet close surrounded by those she cared about most.

Nixon and his family returned to New Jersey later that night, and early the next morning he placed a call to me in California before my own flight back to the East Coast. "Hi! I'm glad I got a hold of you," he said, sounding more optimistic than he had in weeks. "It all caught up to me yesterday, as you could see. It all came out. I must say that when I went down to greet the Reagans and the Fords, I broke down a bit on Nancy's shoulder, and Ron put his arm around me. Poor Julie and Tricia; they tried to keep everyone else's attention away from me. I don't know what happened; I just fell apart. But it was good that I let it all out then because after that I was ready to come upstairs and deliver those remarks. What did you think of them?"

I told him that they had been a very moving tribute to his late wife.

"That's what I wanted," he replied. "What did you like about them—that they were so personal?"

"Yes, and that they drew people in. They were emotional and warm without being mawkish."

"Good," he said, pausing. "Well, we'll have more days like this. It's a very difficult time. There have been some bad obituaries, so I want you to assemble all of the good quotes on her so I can see them. And watch *Time* and *Newsweek*; I'm sure they'll be bad. I want you to, as I said, blister them and send copies to Hugh Sidey. We won't ever let them get away with it. I think the coverage so far has been very positive, don't you think?"

He then exploded in a fit of frustration over the administration's failure to send someone of Cabinet rank to the service. "Vernon Jordan? The Clintons sent Vernon Jordan? He's a fine man, but come *on.* Hillary should have been there. That was inexcusable. He comes to me to save his ass, and he can't even send a Cabinet member to Mrs. Nixon's funeral? What the hell was he thinking? Are his polls still in the toilet?"

His disappointment with Clinton, however, faded quickly when his attention turned to Mrs. Nixon's last moments. "You know, before she slipped into the coma, she was sitting in her chair with her eyes closed, and the girls said that her eyes perked up when she heard my voice. So I kept talking to her, and I told her, 'Your family loves you, the country loves you, and people all over the world love you.' And she smiled. Then I kissed her on the forehead and that was it."

There was a long pause. "What do you think?"

Stunned by his very personal disclosure, I did not answer. "Well, it was a nice goodbye, don't you think?" he pressed.

I reassured him that it was and told him that I would call him again after I returned to New Jersey later that day.

At ten that evening, I placed the call I promised.

"Can I call you back because I'm downstairs, turning off all the lights?" he said. When he returned the call five minutes later, his voice was full of sadness. "I know you had to come all the way up here, back to the office, to pick up your car after your flight. You should have stopped in. I'm all by myself."

He paused. "I'm one who has always controlled my emotions publicly, but I couldn't help it. Oh well, there's nothing wrong with that. Fifty-three years is a long time . . ." He cleared his throat. "Well, how is your morale? Are you tired? You must be, but you're young. Well, I'll see you tomorrow. Come here, to the house. I'm not in the mood to go over to the office. Oh, and Monica?"

"Yes?"

"Thank you for listening."

Nixon's pain began to turn into loneliness. Mrs. Nixon's death was emotionally jarring, but the immediate pain would eventually subside. The void created by her absence, however, would be permanent. He missed her.

"There's no one here," he said as he let me into the house the next morning, June 28. "Can you hear how quiet it is?" Halfway up the stairs to the study, he stopped and turned toward me. "Listen to that silence. My God!" He continued walking up the stairs. "I think that we need to focus more on the philosophical side in this book. Wouldn't peace be wonderful? Not necessarily. Peace isn't the end; it's the beginning. There is peace in the grave. Peace stops destruction, but it does not build anew. Remember the war protesters? 'Peace now!' And then what? Peace without honor is worse." He looked lost. "Isn't that what we are after? I mean, Mrs. Nixon has peace, but looking for it in this world is useless."

As he sat, he straightened his tie and continued: "I went into New York this morning, as you know, to see my doctors, and about a dozen people stopped me on Wall Street and said they were sorry about Mrs. Nixon. It was fine, but I just don't want to talk to anyone. And I just want to be sure that the remaining coverage on her is good."

It was not all positive. Some articles described her as a throwback to less enlightened times, when women sacrificed their own professional aspirations so that their husbands could pursue theirs. Those who argued this, however, failed to see that that was the real Pat Nixon. Never fond of the political world, she derived satisfaction and contentment from caring for her family, domestic responsibilities, and rejoicing with her husband in his victories and consoling him after his defeats. Out of a very public life, she carved out the private life she had always wanted.

Early the next morning, I found Nixon in his office, quaking with anger. He threw the obituary from *U.S. News & World Report* on the floor as I walked toward him. "I can't believe this. This goes too far. Read it now," he commanded.

The piece claimed that Mrs. Nixon had "no adoring public," no professional identity, that she was used as a political prop; it derided her wish to support her husband as woefully traditionalist and foolish.

"Do you see?" he continued. "Nobody ever made her case except for Julie. Some of our people are just incompetent, and our enemies are not. The whole thing is a damn joke. The sick-ass press!" He tore the magazine from my hands and shook it at me. "This is a distressing, shocking thing. [*U.S. News & World Report*'s editor in chief Morton] Zuckerman and Gergen must be called on this. What was the reason for this? It was just malicious. When I leave the scene, we expect that because of the politics. But to go after *her*? We will not accept it.

"Now, *Time* had a great piece. I couldn't believe it, but they were fair and decent. I want you to call Julie and Tricia and let them know that *Time* did a superb job so they're not devastated by the *U.S. News* one. How was *Newsweek*'s?" he asked.

I had to tell him that it was fairly negative, and he looked stricken. "These people are haters—of me—but to take it out on her, well . . ." His face, flushed with rage, turned a bright crimson, and I suggested that he try to relax.

"My blood pressure's fine," he said. "But the doctor wants me to go for a nuclear stress test. I don't know what for . . ."

He looked at me. "The doctor is insisting on it, and once I'm there, he'll insist on more. But even though my back is better, I'm also going to try to get in to see my osteopath." He grimaced. "The whole day tomorrow in doctors' offices. Getting old is a goddamned shame."

He spent much of the next day, June 30, visiting his doctors in Manhattan, and when he returned home, he asked me to meet with him at the residence. He tossed a pen in the air, and it fell to the floor before he could catch it. "Even though I've been under a lot of stress, the doctors say I'm going to live!" he laughed, picking up the pen. "I have no coronary problems, and they said I'm in remarkable shape. So much for that." He seemed relieved that he could stall the inevitable, at least for a while.

"I've decided to go down to Walker's [Cay, in the Bahamas] with Bob and Bebe for a few days, maybe longer. No one will know me there. It'll be nice to get away for a while.

"I see we got a nice note from Helen Thomas. She didn't love me, but she loved Mrs. Nixon. I still can't believe that the *Newsweek* piece was so bad. If they ever call, just say 'Wrong number' and hang up. That piece just shows where they're coming from on us. I can only imagine what the coverage will be when I pass from the scene. At least I won't be here to see it!"

And then, in his first comment about politics since Mrs. Nixon's death, he said, "That bombing against Iraq was nothing. If the economy doesn't improve, Clinton is finished." It was less a commentary on the president's retaliatory military action in Iraq than an indication that Nixon's fighting spirit was returning. Gradually, he began to move out of the narrow, private world of grief and back into the public realm.

On July 2, the recovery continued. He called me at the office from the residence and asked me to bring over a sampling of condolence letters from "regular Americans," so that he, Julie, and Tricia could read them together that afternoon. At two o'clock, as I carried a box of letters up his front path, the door swung open, and Nixon stood in front of me, smiling.

"My God! What a huge box! Here, put it down right away," he said. "Are there more boxes like that?"

"About twenty more," I replied.

"That's wonderful," he said. "You see, the people out there knew what Mrs. Nixon was all about, and they don't believe things like that vicious *Newsweek* piece." As I turned to leave, he asked me to call him later that night, after I had seen the news.

"I hope it's not too late to call," I said when I rang him at ten o'clock.

"Hell no," he said. "I don't sleep anyway. Oh, hold on." He put the receiver down, walked away, and returned several minutes later. "Sorry. Christopher was out with the dog, and I had to let them in. Julie and I walked earlier tonight with the flashlight and played a little game with the kids. They hide, and we try to find them. They love it. And I must say it was good for me, too. All the stress has been very wearing.

"I see that the news was pretty boring, except the unemployment figure went up, and Clinton tried to say it didn't matter. But it mattered last month when it went down! And the other interesting thing was the report about how the Clintons fired everyone in the travel office. I thought that was very interesting! Hillary's fingerprints are all over this—and that Harry Thomason! They talk about Bebe, who was closer than this Harry guy. We entertained him in the residence, but he never had an office, like this guy, or asked for any special favors. And if this had been a Republican president, they would have put us through hell. If it had been Reagan or me, they would have had us impeached! What are we talking about? They said it involves the improper use of the FBI. The FBI! We didn't use them like this! Talked about it maybe, but never did it. Oh, boy."

Nixon was back. Despair had given way to a sense of renewed mission. Politics crept back into his life, motivating him to work and think about something other than his own pain. With each new day and each new scandal coming out of the Clinton White House, Nixon became more determined to fight the political battles.

He focused almost exclusively on writing *Beyond Peace* and on articulating his philosophy about both international and individual peace. Once again, he picked up his pen and wrote about the issues that most concerned him, and he increasingly turned his energies from emotional introspection to political and philosophical debate.

"These things run deep, as you know," he said when we met at the residence on August 26. "I'm all alone in the house and—well, some days are better than others. Tricia bought me a book by an Indian guru, a doctor, I think, on aging. And the message is that you always need *something* to keep you going. I feel a little better every day, and immersing myself in our book has been good. But I must face the fact that my life is all past—behind me."

When I protested, he held up his right hand. "Come here, I want to show you something." We walked down the stairs and into Mrs. Nixon's suite, which was left decorated as it had been when she was alive. "This is now the guest room," he said, gesturing expansively. He walked slowly around the room, picking up small items from the dresser and desk and replacing them. "This is where Julie will stay. Isn't it beautifully done? Of course, the fireplace is here, which I intend to use when the weather cools down. I just thought you'd like to see it," he said, pausing before we left the room and returned to the study.

During those few awkward minutes in Mrs. Nixon's suite, he never once mentioned her name. It was no longer her room but was the "guest room," in which even he was now a guest. The brief tour of the room was a safe emotional excursion, a trip into the past without lingering long enough to feel pain, as if he could desensitize himself to the memories of the room by inviting outsiders in.

"My mother, as you know, aged very gracefully. She was full of energy and vitality until the end. It was a stroke that killed her. And my good friend [former congressman] Joe Waggoner has had a few strokes, though he's hanging in there, but I realize how lucky I've been, particularly mentally. Much of it is due to just hard mental work: reading, writing, memorizing— the grind," he said, clenching his teeth. "But some of it is also just blind luck and genetics. Work helps to divert your attention away from what happens to other people and what could happen to you. Too many older people just give up. They let their minds go soft, and that's too bad. You've got to do it or else."

Nixon worked regardless of occasional physical exhaustion, mental fatigue, and emotional pain. He feared that if he relaxed his mind at all, he would lose its formidable powers, and if he stopped contributing to the debates defining the new era, he would be marginalized and relegated to the history books too soon. He pushed himself to remain relevant not just to the American public but to himself.

As he finished writing *Beyond Peace*, in November 1993, he was plagued by doubts about its relevance and quality. He thought that the crisis surrounding Mrs. Nixon's death had diluted his thinking, particularly on the issues in the book related to the meaning of peace and national purpose. If, as he believed, the book would truly be his last, it needed to be his most profound, even if that meant postponing its publication. Perhaps in search of a source of comfort, Nixon created a familiar condition for himself: a challenge.

The contentment of the drive, however, evaporated when he received the unexpected news on November 12 that his former chief of staff H. R. Haldeman had died. The phone on my desk rang in the midafternoon.

"Monica?" he asked. "Did you hear about Bob Haldeman?"

I extended my sympathy, and Nixon continued: "He was loyal, a hell of a guy. And to think about some of the boobs running around today! They couldn't even shine his shoes. Well, to get my mind on other things, I'd like you to bring over section three of the manuscript so I can go through it tonight."

When I arrived at the residence at six o'clock to bring him the text, I found the house lit only in the dining room, where Nixon was eating spaghetti. He looked startled as I passed through the door and into the room.

"Oh, I'm sorry," I said. "I didn't mean to just barge in."

"No, no. It's just that I didn't expect you now," he said. "Please come in. Can I get you some spaghetti? Heidi's made a ton of it."

"No thank you," I said. "I just wanted to drop off the manuscript. I know you're looking forward to reading it."

He stood up and took it from me. "This ought to get my mind off of—well, some unpleasant things."

"I was very sorry to hear about Haldeman," I said. "I know how much his service meant to you."

Nixon took a step back, looked down at the manuscript, and spoke softly but firmly. "He didn't do a goddamned thing, but they got him anyway. He was so loyal and strong, exactly the type a president needs in there." He looked back up. "So far, the press has covered it all right—you know, that he had gone to jail and so forth. But Gergen said he was authoritarian. I've had it with him, too! Julie did say that CNN did a good job, and Haig was excellent on Haldeman. Incidentally, I understand that there will be only a private family service, so I won't be going to another funeral, thank God . . ."

He looked distracted and depressed, as if this death had allowed his fears about his own mortality to creep slowly back, uninvited and unwanted. It left him drained of some of his legendary inner strength and vulnerable to punishing thoughts about the end that awaited him. The three deaths of

1993—Connally's, Mrs. Nixon's, and Haldeman's—surrounded him with the dark reality he had tried so hard to ignore.

On December 29, he found himself at yet another funeral: that of positive-thinking pioneer Norman Vincent Peale. The next day, *The New York Times* ran a photograph of Nixon and Tricia at Peale's funeral, and he showed it to me when we spoke in the morning.

"Do you know how that picture happened?" he asked. "It was funny. No one stood, but Mrs. Peale's eulogy was so moving that I stood and applauded, then Tricia did, then everyone did. It was something. She's ninety, you know. The funeral was very nice. All of his children gave eulogies." He stopped. "Well, that was the funeral for this week. No more! I hope no one else dies. I'm not going to any more."

Eight days later, on January 6, 1994, when news of the deaths of Clinton's mother, Virginia Kelley, and former Speaker of the House Thomas "Tip" O'Neill reached Nixon, he could only lament, "Well, everyone's dying. Mrs. Clinton—I mean, Mrs. Kelley—they said she had cancer, but she looked damned good; she had a real love of life. I dropped Clinton a note even though I didn't know her. And Tip O'Neill! I knew him back in the days in the House and Senate. He was a hard-boiled politician—no more, no less."

When I mentioned that even Democrats had to die, Nixon laughed. "Hard to believe, huh? They'd get out of that too if they could."

As those around him continued to succumb, Nixon became increasingly aware of his limited time. He did not, however, expect to have to confront his own end as soon as he did.

On February 22, he called me at home to say that he had gone to see his cardiologist. "I don't want you to worry, but I felt an artery or some damn thing throbbing in my forehead, and the doctor said it wasn't serious, but it could turn into a stroke if I'm not careful. So I had an MRI done. I don't mean to bore you with the details . . ."

I asked how he felt, and he replied, "Well, I'm OK now. I guess it was a good thing I caught it. I haven't been sleeping much, so that on top of the other stress—well, I guess these things happen. I've had terrible insomnia, and at my age I can't afford not to be at the top of my game."

The results of the MRI came back the next day, and Nixon reported to me that he was "fine. No problems. I can go to Russia next week, put it that way. He's altering my medication a bit, and I know I'd been at the dentist, which could have pushed my blood pressure up. In any event, I'm feeling better."

He may have been feeling better, but when I saw him a day later, I wrote in my journal that "he looked bad: tired, drawn, and—highly unusual for him—mentally cloudy." His thoughts were disjointed, his sentences incomplete, and his expression vacant. His remarks about the importance of a nonaggressive Russian foreign policy lacked their usual passion, and he often just stared silently out the window for moments at a time. When I asked if he were all right, he responded immediately. "I'll be fine. I think I'm just very tired."

He seemed to improve physically over the next few days, before he left for Russia on March 4. Exhausted even before he departed, he became ill while traveling and had to make the uncharacteristic move of reducing his schedule to accommodate rest and recuperation. He despised being sick, resented the restrictions it placed on his routine, and hated relying on others for assistance.

"I saw a picture of me in Moscow that I think the AP ran, where I'm being helped down some stairs. Even though it was icy and I had a touch of vertigo, I looked old, being helped that way. This is it," he said on March 22. "I will never allow myself to be photographed that way again, all hobbled and weak. No. It will not happen again. Either I'm going to go out there healthy, or I'm not going out there."

During the last month of his life, Nixon's personality seemed to take on a different dynamic. Less impatient and inclined to bouts of frustration, he often grew quietly introspective and distracted from issues that otherwise would have commanded his attention. On particularly warm days during that April, he wanted to have our discussions outside, on his deck, where he could feel the warmth of the sun and the coolness of the breezes. Much of the intensity that had always animated him seemed to be replaced by a sense of detachment, of control slipping away, and of life perhaps drawing to a close.

I saw him for the last time on April 15. In a marked change from his appearance of the preceding weeks, he looked fit, rested, and healthy. As we sat outside, he craned his neck toward the sun and closed his eyes often in an unusual display of serene contentment.

"Beautiful day, isn't it?" he asked. "I often wonder if it wouldn't have been wiser to move to a warm place like Florida. You could have this year round. Ah well, life is short, and I've probably lived too long as it is!

"I think that when I go on this book tour, I'll get a lot of questions on the Russian thing, which is fine. That's one of the main reasons we wrote the book. And we'll get a few Watergate questions; we always do. But I'm hoping that we get questions about the more profound stuff, like a country's mission beyond peace and a person's mission beyond just happiness. I'm not sure if any of these reviewers or interviewers will pick up on it, but I'm going to try to talk about it because it's just very important. I don't care if the scholars or others say it's superficial. It's crucial, not just for countries but for people. We can't answer why we're here, but we can tackle it and hope to get people thinking." He pointed to me. "That's what we're going to do for our country over the next few weeks."

Nixon never had the chance to create that debate. On Sunday evening, April 17, he called me at home for what would be our final conversation. The talk itself was rather unremarkable in that it covered some routine topics, such as his reconsideration of his refusal to speak at universities and his decision to appear on the *Today* show to support the book. It did, however, reflect the grounded spirituality that guided him at the end.

"As you know, I went to Marie Abplanalp's wedding yesterday," he said, referring to Bob Abplanalp's daughter. "It was very nicely done. I took a lot of pictures with the guests, which was grueling, but it was great to see everyone so happy." He paused. "The only time I'm in church these days is for weddings and funerals! If there were a good preacher or minister, I'd go. But everyone goes about God differently. Besides, when I go, it's like a show. Everyone is watching me rather than listening to the important things being said from the pulpit. I don't want to take away anything from anyone else's experience, including my own."

The next morning, he had to draw upon his private relationship with God when a stroke devastated him, first claiming his sight and speech, the two senses upon which he had relied as he climbed to the height of American power: the vision to lead and the voice to persuade, negotiate, and compromise. Two days later, it put him into a coma, robbing his brain of the power to reason. And two days after that, death finally came, taking from him the very force of life.

After the death of Mrs. Nixon, he had begun to consider eternity not as an abstract issue for theologians and philosophers but as an inescapable spiritual aspect of his own life. With an honest and human blend of fear and acceptance, he faced it. What he had done during the course of his life on earth would be judged by others in eras he would not live to see. But when he considered his life, he judged it both by the terms historians would use and by his own. It was the life he had chosen, and overall he believed that it had been good.

In death, he finally found rest for his restless mind and relief from his unrelenting drive to produce, achieve, and overcome. Despite all of his formidable political gifts—his shrewd intelligence, his sense of public service, his mastery of political strategy—he needed to tempt self-destruction. He climbed great mountains of ambition just because they were there, only to tumble back down and tackle the challenge of climbing another. He courted success and failure equally, content with neither.

He faced his own history with an unbending, determined sense of purpose, believing that the mark of individual greatness comes with displaying intelligence, courage, faith, and endurance not just in times of great crisis but in everyday life.

Death ended his journey forever, but it did not diminish the legacy of stunning determination, defiance, and strength of will that he left behind. His epic history seemed to suggest, however irrationally, that he was beyond the weakness and fragility of human life and that he would somehow escape the fate that awaits us all. Giving in, even to death, was so contrary to his character that on his final day, April 22, 1994, it seemed almost impossible to accept that he had finally been defeated.

# PART V

## THE LAST
## NIXON

When Richard Nixon was three years old, he sat on a neighbor's lap in a horse-drawn buggy being driven by his mother. The buggy took a sharp turn around a corner at high speed, hurling the boy violently to the ground. As his mother struggled to stop the horse, her young child summoned his courage, picked himself up, and ran after the buggy.

He later recalled the episode as his first conscious memory, seared in his mind by its brutal shock. After he fell, his first instinct was not to withdraw in pain but to get back up, to run, and to challenge the fate that had befallen him. Decades later, the image provides a vividly poignant metaphor for a life spent running and falling and running again.

That raw instinct for survival existed at his very core, even as it evolved into the more sophisticated impulses of defiance and determination. Imperfections could be accepted, but not the failures that inevitably went along with them. Losing his balance and tumbling to great depths meant only a chance to gather himself up and run toward another challenge. Even after devastating defeats, the drive was always there, beating within him, forcing him to continue, to move forward and not look back, to build from ruin. And so he spent his life always struggling toward some kind of seemingly impossible goal and, ironically, finding a measure of contentment in that tireless journey.

He courted controversy intentionally as a way of testing that part of his character so consumed with survival. With each wrenching decision, he rolled the dice; sometimes the outcome was favorable, sometimes it was not. But for Nixon, the thrill was in those few breathtaking moments when the dice were in the air, turning in all directions before rolling to a stop. And just as the gambler becomes intoxicated by the cycle of winning and losing and by the seductive possibility that the next roll may produce an even bigger prize, Nixon was captivated by the unpredictability of the political game of chance. With each decision—to run for office, to bomb a new enemy, to talk to an old one, to initiate a debate, to cover up a crime—he rolled the dice and hoped for the best.

When the inevitable losses came, however, Nixon used them to launch his next project, not to recoil in defeat but to rise back up and try again. The resulting cycle of politically spectacular victories and crushing defeats gave him an air of indestructibility that not only inspired his controversial legend but ended any chance for a conclusive historical judgment. That invincibility was not, as some have argued, a manufactured political tool; it was really just Nixon, coming back as he always had and knowing no other way.

Nixon saw leadership as high drama, to be played out on a grand scale and without fear or hesitation. His own political career, which he directed with almost epic intensity, dealt triumphs and tragedies in rapid succession: election to Congress in 1946; exposure of top-ranking State Department official Alger Hiss as a spy for the Soviet Union, launching him into the national political spotlight; selection as Eisenhower's running mate in 1952; a well-orchestrated self-defense against false charges with the Fund speech, saving his place on the ticket; the loss to Kennedy in the closest race in American history; the loss in the California gubernatorial race in 1962; the survival of the next six years in the political wilderness; victory in 1968; the opening of American relations with China, détente with the Soviet Union, and the end of the war in Vietnam; Watergate and the resignation; and the slow, deliberate climb back to respectability.

Any one of those achievements might have satisfied most other politicians, just as any one of the defeats might have devastated them. But Nixon *needed* the struggle and needed to have the challenge in hand, particularly when prospects for its success seemed grim. He needed the risk endemic to the game because he thrived not only on its uncertainty but on the task of making the impossible possible. As we watched from the sidelines, Nixon ran, fell, and ran again, each time stronger and faster than before. And with every victory or stumble, he seemed even more invincible, as if his very survival depended on a mastery of defying ever greater odds.

At the center of American politics for almost fifty years, Nixon commanded a significance that went beyond political influence. Whether championing anti-communism or the need to help a post–cold war Russia, civil rights or ending the draft, a "peace with honor" in Vietnam or a rapprochement with China, responsible arms control, environmental protection, welfare or health-care reform or educational opportunity, Nixon was there, talking about how to keep America great. And whether making the decisions in office himself or whispering advice to his successors, Nixon was there, shaping the second half of the American century. For good or ill, he defined us.

Perhaps this is why he continues to fascinate, even in death. A son of the Depression, he built his career on relating to the wildest hopes and fears of middle Americans, who responded to his uncanny ability to relate to them by rewarding him with their votes and their loyalty. Nixon called them the great Silent Majority, and though he mined a political advantage by defending the values they cherished, they were his values as well.

What Nixon's critics saw as flaws those Americans saw as virtues: his solitude was not warped isolation; his reserve was not arrogance; his propriety was not aloofness; and his sentimentality was not hopeless traditionalism. They were part of the real Nixon, a part they understood because it was also part of them.

Nixon came to the presidency at a time when the brewing cultural storm finally struck, trampling in a great wave of countercultural fervor the conventional values for which he stood. The tools and beliefs he used to battle against its effects proved ineffective; the new era set forth to define him and would not allow him to define it. And so he chose to run again, into the eye of the storm, without stopping to consider that its ferocity might destroy him too.

Even after the immediate storm died down, the prosecution of Nixon continued. Once he became a symbol for impurity of motive and dereliction of duty, it was acceptable to pin every other wrong, every crime, every manifestation of evil on him. He became the personification of national deficiency, which in turn made his expulsion from power that much easier to execute—and live with.

In order to justify both his removal from office in view of our failure to hold others to the same high ethical standards and our provision of excuses for them where we would allow none for Nixon, we have told ourselves repeatedly that we did the right thing to him. History will judge whether or not we did. But the relentless attack on him, even as others commit crimes as egregious and are allowed to survive, has evolved into a national psychological exercise aimed at convincing ourselves that our recent history is not as damaged as it seems—and that it was solely Nixon's fault. And although he helped with his own hanging, we claimed his political scalp as a prize to show that those wrenching years produced at least one ostensibly righteous result. In him, we found a receptacle for all of our self-hatred and misguided upheaval. In his wrongdoing, we found shelter from our own.

It did not help his cause that there were few who truly understood him. There was a duality to his character that made him an enigma, even to those who knew him well. He seemed to be two men: one of thought, intellect, and the realm of ideas and idealism, the other of action, pragmatism, opportunism, and realism; one a humanist, the other a detached operator; one a driven loner, the other a political extrovert; one living in a self-centered world, the other exceedingly generous; one serious, the other frivolous; one impatient and tempestuous, the other pensive and serene; one decisive, the other vacillating. These seemingly irreconcilable paradoxes produced a man destined never to be content with a passive existence but driven by his own internal, complex motives to achieve, self-destruct, and renew himself.

Some have argued that the only reason Nixon was so active during his post-presidential years was to achieve a measure of redemption. This is only partially true. The real question is whether he would have written eight best-sellers, traveled extensively abroad, given countless speeches, and advised world leaders had he finished his second term successfully. The answer lies in the pattern of political and intellectual activity he showed *before* Watergate occurred. Built into his character was a voice that uttered ambition at every turn: politics, higher offices, comebacks. He could not silence it, even during the darkest days of his most devastating defeats, when ignoring it was most tempting. It was the part of him that forced him to run after that buggy and, later, to run after the loftiest goals and away from any conclusive sentence of failure.

He would have made those post-presidential contributions had Watergate not prematurely ended his presidency, and he would have made them just as zealously. Instead of destroying him, the disgrace forced the ambition to burn even brighter. His accomplishments after 1974 *were* part of a deliberate effort, but only insofar as *all* of his previous political endeavors—from campaigns to diplomatic breakthroughs—were deliberate efforts. With no office to seek, no government to run, no summits with which to make history, Nixon made certain that his post-presidential activities and achievements were part of a final campaign. But that campaign had less to do with personal restoration than it did with his unrelenting need to be, as he said, "in the arena."

Lining the walls of his office were enlarged photographs that trumpeted his greatest triumphs and catapulted the observer back in time: Nixon with Brezhnev, Nixon with Sadat, Nixon in China, Nixon speaking to vast crowds, Nixon in a motorcade with Pat by his side, arms extended in his famous victory sign. He set out to reshape the world, and he succeeded. No post-presidential exile could halt the momentous destiny that he saw so clearly for himself. His career was a testament to sin, grace, the promise of redemption, and the virtues of courage, faithfulness, and loyalty. He knew that nobility rested with his ability to accept his own history, to embrace the leader and the culprit, the survivor and the casualty, the good and the bad, to take the whole history of his turbulent political career and accept the complete story it told.

For most of his life, Nixon had been the ultimate underdog. His life as a child was marked by hard work, poverty, and family illness, and yet he was told, as most children were, that if he continued to work hard, he could grow up to be president. The American dream was never that far out of reach, even for the son of a poor citrus farmer in southern California.

It was that sense of immense, wondrous possibility that inspired his long journey across the American political landscape, but it was its underlying message of self-reliance that made much of that journey lonely. Despite the support of millions of Americans and his own family and friends, Nixon always believed that he was alone.

And although he preferred that private solitude, he could not resist reaching out, particularly when the public battles became too intense or when his own strength faltered. During those moments, he realized that the human experience was meant to be shared, that he needed others, and that they needed him. Though he feared that leaning on others would be perceived as an expression of weakness, he accepted it as a quiet demonstration of vulnerability that had the surprising effect of strengthening him. It was in those moments that he allowed himself to be real, ordinary, and nothing more than just a man.

In the program for Nixon's funeral services on April 27, 1994, three quotes from him appeared, each meant to remind the reader of a particular aspect of his character.

From July 28, 1960, there was a remark of striking prescience: "When Mr. Khrushchev says our grandchildren will live under communism, let us say his grandchildren will live in freedom." Thirty years later, with the end of the cold war and the collapse of Khrushchev's nation, Nixon was proved correct.

From August 9, 1974, there was a subtle cry of defiance: "We think that when someone dear to us dies, we think that when we lose an election, we think that when we suffer a defeat, that all is ended. Not true. It is only a beginning, always." Even on the last day of his presidency, he spoke not of the fall but of getting back up again, combating defeat, and finding a new beginning.

If premature death enhances the memory of a life, then a long and full life should guarantee a fair assessment of it. Nixon used his many years building a career that became a hallmark of the twentieth century by embodying what it was to be an American: raw ambition, a commitment to hard work, endurance, successes, and failures. Just as the country itself enjoyed a meteoric rise to international power and economic wealth, Nixon catapulted from poverty-stricken obscurity to the highest office in the land. Our great traditions and our misguided courses, our brightest and darkest moments, our goodness and our baseness—all seemed to reflect in his singular experience. It was a burden of symbolism too great for any one man to bear, and yet he did it, sometimes nobly, sometimes ignobly, but always with the optimistic belief that like the country, he could overcome anything.

The final quote on the program was from his first inaugural address, on January 20, 1969, and it revealed what guided his sense of duty: "The greatest title history can bestow is the title of peacemaker." His highest aspiration was not the acquisition of power for its own sake but for what he could accomplish with it: peace at home and abroad, a better country, and a better world. They were shockingly idealistic goals for a man who had always claimed to be a hardheaded realist. But he believed that the purpose of leadership was to elevate, educate, and enlighten people and that it was his job to try to improve the condition of their lives. His greatest sorrow came when his own mistakes inhibited his ability to carry out that duty. And so there was another struggle: to regain his balance and to take on the task once again, only this time without formal power.

His unceasing process of building and rebuilding gave us not only the dark monument of Watergate but also sparkling monuments of light: a warming of a cold war, an end to a hot war, an opening to an old adversary. But perhaps the most compelling legacy he left behind was the one of steely determination, strength, and endurance. If history is judged both by outcomes and by the courses leading to those outcomes, then Nixon's history is particularly complex. The final farewell of 1974 was not really final after all, because wherever there was a defeat, there was a comeback not far behind. In Nixon's life, outcomes were fluid things, to be altered, if not reversed, by his own force of will.

Deng Xiaoping once said, "Leaders are men, not gods." Most of them also are not demons. Nixon's history was neither a story of unmitigated greatness nor a litany of crimes. He was a controversial president, a renowned elder statesman, and a complicated American figure, but he was also just a man, with the same strengths and flaws that affect us all, even if they burned perhaps a little more intensely in him. As we watched him negotiate between his great strengths and his obvious, inevitable weaknesses, we saw flashes of dynamic brilliance and tragic episodes of human failing. He wanted to be remembered as a man who brokered peace between nations, but he should also be remembered as the man who ran, fell, picked himself up, and ran again, through a half century of our history, in a relentless drive to make peace with his country and, ultimately, with himself.

# INDEX

ABOUT THE AUTHOR

MONICA CROWLEY was foreign policy assistant to former president Richard Nixon in Woodcliff Lake, New Jersey, from June 1990 to April 1994. She served as an editorial adviser and research consultant for *Seize the Moment* in 1991 and *Beyond Peace* in 1994, and traveled abroad extensively with him in 1993. She is now working toward her Ph.D. in International Affairs at Columbia University. She lives in New Jersey.

ABOUT THE TYPE

This book was set in Photina, a typeface designed by
José Mendoza in 1971. It is a very elegant design
with high legibility.